Linguistic Relativities

There are thousands of human languages, each one unique. For the last five hundred years, people have argued about how important language differences are. This book traces that history. It shows how the same arguments have come up again and again, with language diversity being seen either as of no importance or as all-important, depending on broader views of human life and knowledge. A more adequate attempt to engage with language specificities emerged in the twentieth century, in the work of Franz Boas and his students. Since the 1950s, this work has been largely dismissed as yet another claim that language differences are all-important, particularly by cognitive scientists and philosophers who see such differences as peripheral. This book seeks to correct this misrepresentation and point to the new directions taken by the Boasians, directions being rediscovered in the most recent work in psychology, linguistics, and anthropology.

JOHN LEAVITT is a professor in the Department of Anthropology at the Université de Montréal.

Linguistic Relativities

Language diversity and modern thought

John Leavitt

Université de Montréal

CAMBRIDGE
UNIVERSITY PRESS

University Printing House, Cambridge CB2 8BS, United Kingdom

Cambridge University Press is part of the University of Cambridge.

It furthers the University's mission by disseminating knowledge in the pursuit of education, learning and research at the highest international levels of excellence.

www.cambridge.org
Information on this title: www.cambridge.org/9781107558632

First published 2011
First paperback edition 2015

A catalogue record for this publication is available from the British Library

Library of Congress Cataloguing in Publication data
Leavitt, John Harold, 1952–
    Linguistic relativities : language diversity and modern thought / John Leavitt.
        p.   cm.
    Includes bibliographical references and index.
    ISBN 978-0-521-76782-8 (hardback)
    1. Language and languages–Origin.   2. Linguistic change.   3. Anthropological
linguistics.   I. Title.
    P116.L43 2010
    401–dc22
    2010037103

ISBN 978-0-521-76782-8 Hardback
ISBN 978-1-107-55863-2 Paperback

For my father

Contents

Preface   *page* ix

Introduction   1

1 A passage to modernity   16

2 One reason, one world, many monads   30

3 The world at war with reason: Britain and France in the
   eighteenth century   54

4 Multiplicity and the Romantic explosion   72

5 Essences and universals through the nineteenth century   96

6 Boas and the linguistic multiverse   113

7 Linguistic relativity: Sapir, Lee, and Whorf   133

8 The other side of the mirror: a twentieth-century essentialism 154

9 The rise of cognition and the repression of languages   165

10 The return of the repressed   189

   Conclusion   212

   Notes   217
   References   222
   Index   241

Preface

I read some essays on linguistic relativity while I was in high school in the late 1960s. I took the fundamental idea to be that people in different societies could receive and operate within somewhat different construals of the world while still being human, intelligent, and competent, and that these received construals could be related to the specifics of their diverse languages. These ideas seemed worthy of pursuit, and I was surprised over the next twenty years to find linguistic relativity almost uniformly disrespected by linguists and psychologists, and often by anthropologists. This book is an attempt to understand both the ideas behind linguistic relativity and the scorn the concept provokes in so many quarters.

"The tale grew in the telling," wrote J. R. R. Tolkien at the beginning of *The Lord of the Rings*, and while my ambition as a teller has been much more modest than his, this tale, too, has been many years a-growing. I particularly want to thank Paul Friedrich for years of inspiration and support, and Claude Faucheux, Mark Mancall, and Kevin Tuite for their encouragement and good ideas. The book is dedicated to my father, Harold J. Leavitt; I like to think that he would have gotten a kick out of it. It has benefitted from the specific comments of Bernard Bate, Gilles Bibeau, Pietro Boglioni, Bernard Chapais, Robert Crépeau, Regna Darnell, Jean DeBernardi, David Dinwoodie, Johannes Fabian, Michel de Fornel, Kellie O'Connor Gutman, Douglas Hofstadter, Dell Hymes, Maggie Kilgour, Friederike Knabe, Konrad Koerner, Guy Lanoue, David Leavitt, Penny Lee, Gérard Lenclud, Jean Lipman-Blumen, John Lucy, Bruce Mannheim, Margaret Paxson, Emily Schultz, Mary Scoggin, Sonia Sikka, Michael Silverstein, Pierrette Thibault, Jürgen Trabant, and Francis Zimmermann. Many others have offered guidance, instruction, and excellent tips for this project. I cannot name them all, but want to thank Fred Adler, Pierre Beaucage, A. L. Becker, Nicole Belmont, Susan Barbatbun, Bernard Bernier, Michelle Drapeau, Jean Comaroff, Ellen Corin, Johanna Crooijmans, Surjit Das, Vibha Puri Das, Philippe Descola, Florence Dupont, Alexandre Enkerli, John Galaty, Marie-Françoise Guédon, Charlie Haas, Roberte Hamayon, William Hanks, Frank Harreman, Nicole Harreman, Lynn M. Hart, Michael Houseman, Michel Izard, Christine Jourdan, Tineke Kuijper, George Lakoff,

Michael Lambek, Emily Leavitt, Gloria Leavitt, Jacques Leroux, Chiara Letizia, Margaret Lock, Richard Lock, Anwyl McDonald, James Macguire, Charles Malamoud, Colin Masica, Gregory Maskarinec, Marie Mauzé, Marika Moisseeff, Jean-Claude Muller, Indar Singh Negi, Ralph Nicholas, Andie Palmer, Girija Pande, Mariella Pandolfi, Jorge Pantaleón, Louise-Iseult Paradis, Shekhar Pathak, Jean Pouillon, Nicole Revel, Michelle Rosaldo, Lynne Rosenthal, Mason Rosenthal, Alice Shepherd, Eric Sigman, Rajendra Singh, Pauline Turner Strong, Margaret Trawick, Meredith Tromble, Paula Varsano, Michel Verdon, Bob White, András Zempléni, and several cohorts of graduate students at the Université de Montréal. Research on which this book is based was funded by the Social Sciences and Humanities Research Council of Canada, the Fonds Québécois de Recherche sur la Société et la Culture, and the Université de Montréal.

Special thanks to my family: Lori Harreman, who read and improved much of the manuscript, Elizabeth Leavitt, Madalena Harreman-Fernandes, and Miguel Harreman-Fernandes, who have graciously put up with much distraction on my part.

In a book that is about evaluating language differences and that talks at length about translation, the reader has a right to know the author's translation tactics. The texts drawn on for this book are mostly in English, French, and German, with some passages from Italian and Latin. English is my native tongue; my French is good, my German and Italian laborious, and my Latin limps. Given that one of the central arguments is that national linguistic and stylistic differences matter, I take as given that the specific wording and style of a text are as important for my purposes as is its referential content. This means that the standard methods of translation, which seek to convey the referential content from the source text in as "normal" and unobtrusive a style as possible in the target language, and which therefore allow, for instance, changes in wording to avoid repetition, will not do in most cases here. I cannot claim to have been absolutely consistent, but this is what I have sought to do: in cases where there is no English translation of a text, I translate it myself, trying in particular to respect repetition and resonant vocabulary. Where the reference is to a work in a language other than English, assume that it is my own translation. In some cases I have used an English translation, but have sometimes modified it to conform more closely to the original. The fact that such modification has taken place is always indicated. I am grateful to Isabel Heck for very kindly going over most of the German translations and modifications.

There will be errors in this book, and most readers, if not all, will find glaring omissions. All such infelicities are, of course, entirely the responsibility of the author. To distort Mallarmé, "La chair est faible, hélas, et je n'ai pas lu tous les livres."

Introduction

Many languages

Human beings form a single species but speak thousands of different languages. Each differs from the others in its sounds, in the words it offers and what they stand for, in how words are built and how they are put together to make sentences. Speaking any language requires mastery of complex practices that take place simultaneously on many levels: a sophisticated choreography of mouth and throat to produce a distinctive set of sounds; an ear that has learned to recognize these particular distinctions; control of some tens of thousands of signs and their meanings, meanings that will be different in their boundaries and often in their centers from those of the signs of any other language; constant manipulation of pervasive grammatical categories that foreground some aspects of experience rather than others. Every one of these practices is carried out either unconsciously or with only the most limited conscious involvement. And every one of them is performed hundreds or thousands of times a day by every speaker and hearer of a given language in a way that is unique to that language.

How much does all of this matter? Does the language spoken affect other aspects of life? Does it affect one's way of thinking, of feeling, of perceiving or constructing the world? These questions have arisen in some form in most periods of history, in most civilizations. But they have been debated in particularly acute and symptomatic ways in what is usually called the modern period in the West, since about the sixteenth century. Western modernity, after all, begins with three more or less simultaneous occurrences, all of which bring many languages into confrontation: the rise of modern nation-states, each with its own national standard to be asserted over a hitherto multilinguistic territory; the rediscovery of the languages and learning of antiquity; and the expansion of European economic and political power over much of the globe.

In spite of its centrality to Western thinking for some five hundred years, the question of linguistic diversity was marginalized in the decades after 1960. This is largely due to the success of unitary theories of human thought: for most cognitive scientists and philosophers of mind, and many linguists, the possibility of significant linguistic variation constitutes at best a surface distraction, at worst a relativist threat to the very knowability of the human mind. Until quite recently cognitive-philosophical books with titles such as *Language and Thought* (Carruthers and Boucher 1998) have given virtually no space to the specifics of actual human languages, since what is of interest are "language" and "thought" in general.

Since the mid-1990s, however, language diversity has begun to re-emerge as a central issue in many disciplines. For every claim that we have identified *The Language Instinct* (Pinker 1994: just one instinct, the same for every language) and now know *How the Mind Works* (Pinker 1997: it works the same way everywhere at all times) there is a new presentation of *Evidence for Linguistic Relativity* (Niemeier and Dirven 2000) arguing the importance of the relationship between *Language Diversity and Thought* (Lucy 1992a). These debates have an important intellectual-historical dimension and usually refer back to the American linguists Edward Sapir and Benjamin Lee Whorf and their work in the 1920s and 1930s on what they called a principle of linguistic relativity. As originally developed, this is the observation that the characteristics of one's language can affect other aspects of life and must be taken into account. This is often expressed by saying that the specifics of the language orient the speaker in certain ways, representing a distinct point of view. Since the deaths of the main proponents of the idea (Sapir died in 1939, Whorf in 1941, their mentor Franz Boas in 1942), debates around the subject have tended to reduce this very broad issue to the narrower one of possible influences of language on cognition. The "hypothesis of linguistic relativity," "linguistic relativism," or "linguistic determinism," often dubbed the "Sapir–Whorf hypothesis," would in this view be the argument that language determines or influences thought, and that since languages are different, people who speak different languages must think in different ways. Often it is not clear what is meant by thought, nor what aspects of language are being used to represent "language." But the main problem with current discussions, in my view, is a lack of historical perspective.

Such a perspective reveals, it seems to me, some persistent patterns. It shows that the debate over linguistic multiplicity has been at the heart of modern Western thinking about self and other, the nature of human society and indeed of humanity, and has always represented an aspect of larger conceptions of the human mind and of the universe as a whole. The central arguments of this book will be (1) that in the modern West, the main tendency has been simply to reject or to adopt the idea that language differences are important, depending on one's philosophical preference for universalistic explanatory models that seek causes or pluralist models that seek understanding of hidden essences; (2) that in spite of usually being identified with the latter position, the work of Boas and his students represents an effort to rethink problems of language difference in a more complex way, one that is, to use terms that remain to be explained, pluralist but not essentialist, an effort that has yet to yield its full theoretical effects; and (3) that much of the work in this area since the 1960s reproduces the oppositions that the Boasians struggled to get beyond.

While the implications of language difference have been debated for hundreds of years, sometimes with the same examples, even the same terminology, being used again and again, very little of this history is recognized in what is being written now about linguistic relativity.[1]

Here is an example. The editors of the volume *Language Acquisition and Conceptual Development* (Bowerman and Levinson 2001) present two opposed positions on the relationship between language and thought. On one side is the view that

language is a mere ... input/output device to a central area of thinking. As Pinker (1994: 82) has put it, "knowing a language ... is knowing how to translate mentalese into a string of words and vice versa ...". (11–12)

On the other side they cite George Miller from 1956: "the process of recoding is a very important one in human psychology ... In particular, the kind of linguistic recoding that people do seems to me to be the very lifeblood of the thought processes" (cited in Bowerman and Levinson 2001: 12). While the authors do point out that questions of this kind go back to Aristotle, they do not note that the two opposed positions presented here – that thinking is an autonomous activity, always the same in human beings, and language is merely a way of externalizing it; or that language, on the contrary, is an integral part of the thinking process – were formulated in almost exactly the same terms by Descartes and Locke on the one hand, and Leibniz on the other, in the seventeenth century. There is a history to be traced here.

The book will concentrate on the writings of the protagonists themselves, their assumptions and strategies, their favorite examples, their surprisingly stereotypical tones of voice. While the book insists on the importance of history and is organized in a (loosely) chronological fashion, my overall perspective is not that of the historian or the intellectual historian, but of the anthropologist. I take it that observed commonalities, broad perduring themes, in modern Western culture, as in any culture, are related to the nature of daily life in modern Western societies; and that these themes, lived and presupposed by most participants in these societies, are formalized and articulated by those whose job it is to formalize and articulate: philosophers, scholars, theorists of various stripes. I take theorists, then, not as tellers of truth or lies, but as key informants, Ogotemmêlis of the modern West (Griaule 1948 [1965]).

Universals and diversity

Some things that are universal about human language are more specific than what one would imagine are requirements for any system of communication.

Some of these universals can be identified by considering any language, others not. Among observable, "evident" universals are the facts that any language allows the speaker to say anything he or she wants to say, with the proviso that some languages may have to invent or borrow words to talk about some topics; that spoken human language is linear, that is, one-dimensional in time, something that distinguishes it from, say, the bidimensionality of a painting; that human languages operate primarily using conventional signs; that every human language has a distinctive multi-levelled architecture in which some tens of non-signifying elements (phonemes) combine to produce some thousands of signs (morphemes), which combine in turn to generate a potentially infinite number of phrases and sentences.[2]

Such universals are available through simple reflection on how we speak, or how anyone speaks. And they can be misleading: recent research on sign languages (e.g., Emmorey 2002) shows that while they are fully functioning multi-levelled human languages, they use more motivated, that is, non-conventional signs than do spoken languages, and can operate in several dimensions at once, thus calling the universality of linearity into question.

Other kinds of universals can be discovered only through historical and comparative examination, and often only statistically. These include, for instance, the identification of strong tendencies in historical shifts in the pronunciation of sounds, one of the great scientific discoveries of the nineteenth century; and the discovery of implicational hierarchies of word order (Comrie 1981). Much of the most important work in cognitive psychology in the last half century has involved the identification of what appear to be innate, universal patterns in human language and thought (for a recent overview, see Carruthers, Laurence, and Stitch 2005–7).

Attempts to explain language universals have generally proposed a shared biological substratum or have looked to universal aspects of human experience in the world. Such explanations are, for the most part, perfectly reasonable and may well be true. In spite of them or on top of them, there remains the fact of linguistic difference. Language as a human faculty manifests itself in the form, and solely in the form, of specific systems, distinct langua*ges*, each different from all the others and existing in quite staggering multiplicity. So much diversity may be seen, in fact, as a corollary of the universal fact that any language is largely systematic at many levels. Given the complexity of the basic architecture of any language (a universal), each system is bound to be unique. Coherent and complex systematicity, that is to say, implies diversity. And we simply do not know how far the implications of this diversity go for human cognition, for perception and memory, for aesthetic experience, or for cultural constructions of the world.

One of the most striking universals of language, then, is its diversity – not an unlimited diversity, but a tremendous diversity nonetheless. This contrasts with the much more limited physical variation of the species. If we try to sub-classify human beings in terms of physical criteria such as blood type, general body form, or skin coloration, we end up with something like half a dozen varieties – not, of course, the same ones in each case. As against this very limited diversity of the species, we have in languages six to ten thousand extraordinarily complex systems, each operating at several levels at once, each with its own way of organizing sounds, naming things, defining, hierarchizing, and ordering its units, each with its own inherent poetics and aesthetics (in the singular or, more often, in the plural), its own jargons, jokes, puns, and idioms. Given that the usual criterion for differentiating one language from another is mutual unintelligibility, each of the thousands of such systems is complete gibberish to speakers of any other – while it's hard to say at what point a learner really knows a language, it's easy to recognize when you don't know one at all.

Not half a dozen, then, but thousands of languages. It's a scandal, and has been felt as one since the Tower of Babel.

The parable of the Martian

The contrast between the opposed takes on linguistic diversity comes out in opposed conclusions to the same parable. At least three authors have proposed the conceit of a linguistically challenged visiting space alien and the degree of diversity he – it's a boy alien every time – would find or expect to find in human languages. Two of these, George Steiner (1975: 50–1) and Claude Hagège (1986: 54–5), see the diversity of human language as a central and important reality. "A deaf, non-literate observer approaching the planet from outside and reporting on crucial aspects of human appearance and physiological behaviour, would conclude with some confidence that men speak a small number of different, though probably related, tongues. He would guess at a figure of the order of half a dozen" (Steiner 1975: 50). For Hagège, beyond six or so main types, the visitor could "deduce the existence of a dozen derived systems, corresponding to what we call dialects, which would be close enough to each other and to the principal languages that their human users would be clearly aware of the relationship" (1986: 55). Instead, of course, there are thousands of languages, and that's the point.

Noam Chomsky, the arch-linguistic universalist of our time, uses the same parable to opposite effect. For Chomsky, what languages share, especially in the way they are structured, is far more important and interesting than the ways in which they differ. This common structuring emerges particularly clearly in studies of language acquisition in children. Chomsky (e.g., 1988: 41–52) has a visiting Martian scientist have a look at human speech behavior as it is mastered by children. His conclusion is that humans speak a single language with many dialects! In the words of the psycholinguist Steven Pinker, "aside from their mutually unintelligible vocabularies, Earthlings speak a single language" (1994: 232); the single language of Earthspeak has "thousands of mutually unintelligible dialects" (240).

We should note that in standard usage dialects are by definition mutually intelligible forms of speech; the term "mutually unintelligible dialects" is either an oxymoron or a tendentious, which is to say sneaky, way of renaming what linguists have always called "languages." The two opposed morals of the parable show, it seems to me, just how divided we are today on the issue of language diversity. One of the points of this book is to show that this division, with many of its characteristic examples and discursive tricks, goes back (at least) a good four hundred years.

Universalism and essentialism

An overview of arguments on language differences shows the dominance of two opposed overall positions since the seventeenth century: for the most part, Western scholars have either declared such differences to be of little importance, or they have asserted their importance as integral parts of distinctive national or cultural wholes. In the first view, human perception and reason are everywhere and always the same; languages are either merely different ways of externalizing already-formed ideas or variations on deep structures that are universal. In these views, the apparent differences among languages are a matter of surface formulation of something that is universally human. This has been the majority position in the West at least since Aristotle (*On Interpretation*; cf. Trabant 2000b: 29–30). The historically most powerful opposed view has been that language differences signal or determine differences among radically different ways of thinking and conceiving reality, and that in any given case, language, culture, and thinking all express the same unique essence. There are therefore as many different lived worlds as there are distinct languages. Both of these are relatively (if I may use that word) straightforward and simple positions; both are what we might call easy to think. The distinction between them has been recognized repeatedly, although not always in the same terms. For Steiner, for instance, there have been "two radically opposed points of view":

The one declares that the underlying structure of language is universal and common to all men. Dissimilarities between human tongues are essentially on the surface ... [this is] the universalist position.

 The contrary view can be termed "monadist." It holds that ... the actual workings of human speech ... are so diverse, they manifest so bewilderingly complex a history of centrifugal development ... that universalist models are at best irrelevant and at worst misleading. (1975: 77)

These opposed positions on the matter of language represent local versions of broader ones marking modern Western thought (on such linguistic ideologies, see Schieffelin *et al.* 1998). As we will see through this book, models of the nature of language and models of the nature of the world have suggested and reinforced each other throughout the modern period.

The philosopher Louis Althusser (Althusser and Balibar 1965 [1970]: 186–9) has made the breathtaking claim that all of modern philosophy has recognized only two modes of causality: transitive causality, which operates through chains of events; and expressive causality, by which an essence reveals itself in manifold expressions. Althusser attributes the articulation of the two types of causality respectively to Descartes' mechanism and to Leibniz's monadism, both in the seventeenth century. One's first reaction to this is to ask how it could be anything but a gross oversimplification of four hundred years of subtle and, God knows, complicated philosophizing. Yet it resonates with other dichotomies that keep coming up in Western thought: that between the natural sciences and the humanities; between explanation and interpretation; between approaches that apply general laws to isolated facts and those that seek to reconstruct systems within which contextualized facts come to make sense. The very perennity of this kind of opposition should give us pause.

While this deeper division in Western thinking goes far beyond questions of language, it remains very much about the evaluation of difference. To oversimplify, but surprisingly little: one side seeks universal laws and uniform explanations of particular phenomena. Among the grand philosophies it is associated with the rationalism and mechanism of Descartes, the empiricism of Bacon and Locke, and their unification by Newton. It has dominated the natural sciences and the human sciences that emulate them, including in particular the cognitive sciences. Here, requiring a label, I am calling this set of approaches to the world universalism. The other side has explored multiple distinctive wholes or configurations, multiple worlds if you like, seeking to interpret each case through a unique key or essence. In its stronger expressions it sees each such world as unique to the point of being closed off from all others, what we might call hermeneutically sealed. I see this second view foreshadowed in the Renaissance fascination with diversity, then realized, as Althusser suggested, in the multiple universe posited by Leibniz in the seventeenth century, and I argue that it reached its full articulation with its application to human societies, cultures, periods of history, even the natural world, by Herder and the Romantics in the latter half of the eighteenth and beginning of the nineteenth centuries. Since then it has dominated the humanities and some of the human sciences and has represented the "humanistic" alternative to "hard" science. Here, again for lack of a better label, I am calling this approach essentialism. While details of the discussion keep changing, these universalist and essentialist positions – and they are positions in all the senses of the term, almost bodily stances, attitudes, implying distinct tones of voice and styles of argument – can be recognized from the seventeenth century to today: cognitive scientists want to be Newtons of the mind, Chomsky identifies with "Cartesian linguistics" (Chomsky 1966), symbolic anthropologists and hermeneuts talk of cultures and traditions as distinctive "webs of meaning" in metaphors worthy of Herder (cf. Hymes 1974: 120).

An important aspect of this division, one that we will see coming up repeatedly across the centuries, is a difference in defining what constitutes language. For universalist positions from the Enlightenment to Chomsky, since language is a mere way of expressing thought or the world, the kind of language to be studied is above all the declarative sentence bearing referential content. For pluralist and essentialist positions, on the contrary, since each language has a density of its own, attention must be paid to the uses of language, especially poetic and aesthetic uses.

Seeking to bring the same "view from afar" to modern Western society that anthropologists traditionally bring to very different ones, I have argued (Leavitt 1991a, 1996, 2006a) that this universalist/essentialist split might be understood as a central element of modern Western culture. This is, of course, to presuppose that the modern West *has* a culture amenable to anthropological study.

The choice of the terms universalism and essentialism is problematic, and for a number of reasons. Either term can mean many things, and essentialism, in particular, sometimes (as, for instance, in Foley 2005) labels approaches that posit a universal human essence or essence of thought – and so means the reverse of my usage here. And as I am using them, universalism and essentialism are not really opposites. The opposite of universalism would be particularism, and a particularism can abjure general laws and look to the uniqueness of each situation without seeking to interpret it in terms of expressive wholes. The opposite of essentialism, for its part, would be phenomenalism, a claim that all that matters are surfaces and appearances. One point I want to make in choosing such ill-sorted terms is that we are not dealing here with logical opposites, but with concepts that are merely opposed culturally. They do not need to be on the same plane or at opposed poles on a single axis: like natural languages, they are historical constructs, the result of a clustering of ideas around a fairly small number of salient metaphors or thought-forms, in a process of elaboration out of images that was delineated by Althusser's most direct precursor, the philosopher of science Gaston Bachelard. This is what is implied in Althusser's claim: that the modern West has been fascinated either by the image and analogy of chains of cause and effect forming networks of mechanical interaction; or by the image of individual uniqueness and self-expression, suggesting analogies of mirrors and polished globes, or of that circle whose center is everywhere and whose circumference is nowhere.[3]

The power of these thought-forms comes at least in part from the fact that they make almost irresistible sense to us given the kinds of lives we lead in Modernity.[4] The two that we have just posited are centered respectively on the chain of mechanical cause and effect, which is at the heart of universalist conceptualizations, and on an image of mirroring or echoing that makes perceptible a hidden source, which is at the heart of essentialist ones. The image of the causal chain guides our daily practical, effective interactions with most of the world; that of the reflecting source guides our daily impractical, affectively charged interactions with each other, but also to a degree with our settings, our landscapes, our homes, our arts and music, our cooking and eating, our games, our passions. These sides of our everyday lives – trying to fix the machinery of the world, interpreting the expressive surfaces of unique personalities – offer hard-to-resist analogies that anchor opposed, but not necessarily opposite, clusters of representations, arguments, and examples. The fascinating and compelling character of such images, their ability to hold thinking captive and block the generation of more adequate paradigms, is what led Bachelard to label them epistemological obstacles or epistemological blocks (see Chapter 10 below).

Notwithstanding the topic under discussion, and whatever its complexity, it is, then, easy and comfortable for modern Western thinkers to slip either into a typically universalist or a typically essentialist mode of presentation and argument: these are the modes we are offered and that are reinforced by our lived experience in a particular kind of society. In this book I will be maintaining that for questions of language and language differences, the work of Franz Boas and his students at the end of the nineteenth and during the first four decades of the twentieth century represents a third option, constructed through the refusal to adopt either of the available thought-forms and through a search for different metaphors. Particularly with its development of the notion of linguistic relativity, Boasian linguistics constitutes a radical reposing of the question of language differences. This theoretical revolution remains virtually unrecognized today. As we will see, most participants on both sides of the current language debates identify Boasian linguistics and anthropology as one more expression of what I am calling essentialism, while Boas's own approach has been presented as totally atomistic, culturally holistic, or as a weird hybrid of the two. There is some historical truth to all of these characterizations: the fact that such apparently mutually exclusive readings could all have some validity should alert us that there is something more complicated going on here than essentialism, atomism, or mere hybridity.

Beyond the great divide?

Within the debates about language diversity, both sides can muster some strong evidence. Much human thinking appears to be non-linguistic, involving various sensory modes; many people without the ability to speak can still think just fine. It is clear from experimental evidence that small children function at very sophisticated levels before they learn language, drawing on non- or prelinguistic perceptual and cognitive capacities. The universalist position is also bolstered by the facts that translation across languages is a general practice, that *something* is being translated, and that, as I have said, all human languages share important and sometimes surprising traits.

On the other side are the sheer facts of linguistic diversity: the fact that the speaker of a given language is constantly producing and receiving distinctive sound patterns, deploying distinctive signs and senses, creating syntactic structures based on unique architectures. Since no system can have a different sign for every discriminable element of experience, any language requires the grouping of such elements into categories of "the same thing," and so presupposes the forging of analogies that may be quite different from one system to another. Similarly, organizing signs into sentences requires the use of grammatical categories, which can differ among languages, meaning that speakers of different languages may *by this very fact* be turning their respective attention many times a day to quite different aspects of experience. The fact that an English speaker is locating herself in a constantly re-evoked temporal frame through the tenses that are a required part of her verbs, that a Kwak'wala speaker is locating himself in a constantly re-evoked spatial frame through locative particles that are a necessary part of his sentences, that a speaker of Wintu is required to tell how she knows every single thing she says through data-source markers that are a required part of *her* verbs – the fact that I have had to choose between two genders in composing these lines – that this is happening, between speaking and listening, many times (has anyone ever counted?) every day of one's speaking life, surely cannot be discounted.

Indeed, for many people it seems intuitively right that speaking a different language means "thinking" differently or inhabiting a different "world"; for some, this is lived as a personal experience. "I feel," writes the linguist and anthropologist Paul Friedrich, "that American as against British English, and English of any major dialect as against Russian, and both languages as against the Tarascan language of Mexico constitute different worlds. I note that it is persons with experience of foreign languages and poetry who feel most acutely that a natural language is a different way not only of talking but of thinking and imagining and of emotional life" (1986: 16). In a 2002 interview, the psycholinguist Lera Boroditsky put it:

[T]hese questions of whether or not languages shape thought tend to be very obvious to people out in the world who speak more than one language. You ask any bilingual and they say "Of course language shapes thought; I think completely differently in my two languages." (Boroditsky 2002)

If this is an illusion, it is one that has yet to be explained in a satisfactory way.

The examples of lexical categorization and obligatory grammatical categories that I gave above come straight out of Boas. The Boasians, while often adopting pluralist-essentialist language to argue against the institutionally more powerful universalist position, did not, in fact, promote any kind of integral essentialism: while defending the importance of language specificity, they maintained that there was *no* necessary link between a people's language, their culture, and their cognitive processes. At the same time, however, in what at first looks like a blatant contradiction, they did hold that the language you speak is more than a mere means of conveying thoughts and perceptions that are everywhere the same; that the "cut" of the language itself has implications for the speaker/hearer's point of view. Historians of the field have wondered over this apparent inconsistency; but it can equally be read as a sign of the complexity of what the Boasians were trying to conceptualize. The analogy that Sapir came to in the 1920s and which Whorf later adopted was to Einstein's principle of relativity: differences in the position and state of movement of an observer imply differences in his or her observations. Einstein himself had proposed that an alternative name for his theory might be *Standpunktlehre*, the theory of point of view (Balibar 1984: 119).

The Boasian view has often been presented as a form of linguistic determinism or relativism.[5] Real linguistic determinism would claim that one's language determines what one can and cannot conceive, which would, presumably, mean that speakers of different languages live in entirely different universes; translation would be impossible, and people who knew more than one language would be at constant risk of going mad. Real relativism would have to presume that there is nothing general or shared in human experience. Since neither of these positions seems to fit reality, linguistic relativity, identified with determinism and relativism, has often been dismissed (Chapter 9). But Einstein's relativity was neither a determinism nor a generalized relativism, but a principle recognizing the reality of diverse positions and looking for ways to calibrate among them. Correspondingly, the Boasians did not claim that there is no world outside our experience of the world, nor that there are no commonalities of human thought or experience, nor that there is no way to move in thought among different states or situations, and certainly not that "everything is relative," but that a difference in language, like one in position and velocity, implies a difference in point of view that must be taken into account: not doing so means moving farther from, rather than closer to, the truth.

Politics, presentism, and historicism

For most of the period considered here, most Western discourse took a number of things as given. It assumed the superiority of human over all other kinds of beings and the human right to exploit nature without end; the superiority of the white race, the Christian religion, and Western civilization over all others and the natural right (sometimes seen as a duty) of Europeans and Euro-Americans to rule and exploit everyone else; and the superiority of men over women, with the concomitant right of men to govern women's lives. Many of the scholars discussed here shared these views, which were the views of their societies. What is more, many of the theories presented here, even those that were meant to be and indeed sometimes were progressive or revolutionary in their own time, can be seen from the vantage of the early third millennium to have helped in one way or another to reinforce these assumptions. This motivates a tendency in some of the recent literature on these subjects, including some of the best of it, to present all discourses before our own as part of a single metanarrative justifying inequality and oppression (e.g., the central thrust of Bauman and Briggs 2003 on the history of language ideologies, Zimmerman 2001 on German anthropology of the late nineteenth century). This is not the road I follow here, for several reasons. First, such presentism comforts our current beliefs and tells us that we are better than those who went before. It renders more difficult the – even temporary – suspension of our own assumptions that is, it seems to me, the major contribution that fieldwork-based anthropology has made to Western thought. I am advocating, then, a modest historicism (cf. Stocking 1968). At the same time, the presentism of many recent studies tends to offer an unrealistically unitary and even conspiratorial picture of modern Western culture and society, where every word written over five hundred years, on any topic and expressing any view, is likely to be interrogated to see how it contributed to the great colonialist, classist, racist, and sexist project. This is particularly ironic when such critiques of a supposedly monolithic modern West come from an anthropology that has been undergoing decades of self-criticism for portraying non-Western cultures in too homogeneous a way. On the contrary, I am presuming that modern Western society, like any other, is historically complex and riven with faults and contradictions, and that these social cracks can sometimes give rise to discourses that really are surprising, that really can at least point in unexpected directions.

Such a project, on the other hand, requires a recognition of the fundamental reality of capitalist and colonial expansion over the modern period and the pervasiveness of the ideologies that were (and are) part of this process. The conditions of modern Western society have set limits on what could be said, at least in widely disseminated and influential discourse; it is necessary to trace these limits and in many cases to denounce them. But the world today is shifting in ways that we cannot claim to understand fully. Non-Western worlds are standing up for themselves in unpredicted ways; intellectually we may be seeing the beginnings of a provincializing of Europe (Chakrabarty 2000). In these circumstances, it seems to me that what is called for is a reading of modern Western discourses and discoveries that is neither monolithic nor particulate, but notes historical and ideological fissures and at the same time seeks to recognize broad opposed tendencies where these have existed.

The structure of the argument

The first chapters of the book posit the laying-down of modern Western options and their extensions through the nineteenth century. The first chapter presents some aspects of the non-modern Western world – a feudal world marked by a coherent hierarchical cosmology, its initial transformation into a capitalist world that assumes unique yet equal individuals moving in an empty universe understandable by laws, and the concomitant discovery of linguistic diversity. Chapter 2 sketches out the great options for modern thinking that were articulated in the seventeenth century, starting with the rationalism and mechanism of Descartes, which held that human reason was the same everywhere and always, and the empiricism of Bacon and Locke, which held that whatever we know we learn from the world. While these universalist approaches were phenomenally successful in modeling and transforming the natural world, they were not so good at recognizing diversity, nor at conceptualizing the distinctiveness of individuals or of different languages, civilizations, or historical periods. The great alternative to this universalism was a pluralist essentialism that insisted that humans live in a multitude of personal, linguistic, national, or cultural worlds. The main lines of this position were articulated by Leibniz, again in the seventeenth century. The formulations laid down during this period have continued to be used and reused up to the present.

The third chapter traces the battles between competing universalisms in France and Britain through the eighteenth century in debates that involved the order of words, the role of reason and experience, and the rights of man. Chapter 4 looks at the passage from an initial statement of an essentialist thought-form in Leibniz's monads to the development of full-scale pluralist essentialism by Herder and the German Romantics, who postulated a multiplicity of ethnic worlds each defined through a unity of place, national soul, and language. Some remarkable pairs of brothers were at the heart of this movement: the Brothers Schlegel, who founded both historical and descriptive linguistics; the Brothers Grimm, whose collection of folktales was part of a lifelong project to explore and valorize the soul of the (German) people; and the Brothers Humboldt, who respectively invented systemic ecological geography of the landscape and modern systemic linguistics.

Chapter 5 traces out the back-and-forth through the nineteenth century between essentialism in linguistics and philosophy and the form of universalism that would come to be called positivism, in linguistics but also in the new field of anthropology. A minority linguistics carried on the Romantic concern with language specificities, and one stream in German philosophy continued to insist on the unity of language and thought. It was these philosophers who first introduced the term "linguistic relativity." By late in the century, German linguistics and anthropology were tending toward a highly empirical study of multiple national characters. In Britain, on the contrary, the universalist domination of the human sciences culminated in the rise of evolutionism, which sought to explain all of human history through simple universal laws, everywhere applicable in the same way. Languages proved the most difficult material for evolutionists to assimilate, since languages did not seem to evolve from simpler to more sophisticated forms in the way that weapons or house types did.

The next few chapters turn to the work of Boas and his students and contemporaries during the first decades of the twentieth century. Chapter 6 presents Boas himself, physicist turned psychophysicist turned geographer turned ethnologist-linguist. By the time Boas was being trained, German science had made a distinction between the natural sciences, dominated by explanatory universalist paradigms, and the historical or spiritual sciences, dominated by pluralist and essentialist paradigms. Throughout Boas's career, he balanced on the cusp of this dichotomy. Boas offered a vision of language specificities that asserted the multiplicity and at least partial coherence of linguistic and cultural worlds against the then-dominant evolutionism, but at the same time denied the necessity of a link between a given language and a given mode of thought or national, racial, or ethnic soul. Chapter 7 concentrates on three of Boas's disciples and the articulation of the idea of linguistic relativity: the poet-philosopher-linguist-anthropologist Edward Sapir, the poet-philosopher-anthropologist-translator Dorothy Demetracopoulou Lee, and the natural scientist turned linguist Benjamin Lee Whorf.

Chapter 8 presents the twentieth-century German school of Neoromantic or Neohumboldtian linguistics, whose proponents argued that a people's culture, territory, and especially mother tongue form a distinctive totality that shapes the lived world of the speaking subject, and so constitutes a permanent and inescapable horizon of knowledge. The goal, in this view, must be to deepen understanding and appreciation of the mother tongue. While Boas and Boasian anthropology are often accused of essentialism, a comparison with the truly essentialist parallel world of Neohumboldtian linguistics shows how profoundly different this project was from theirs.

The last chapters are devoted to what has happened in the discussion of linguistic difference since Boas. Chapter 9 tells of the fall of Boasian linguistics: the disappearance of its major theorists, the rise of universalist cognitive science and the dominance of an ancillary philosophy and linguistics from the 1950s on. Part and parcel of these movements was the invention of a "hypothesis" of linguistic relativism or determinism associated with the names of Sapir and Whorf, at first as a hypothesis to be tested, then as a straw man to be burned. Psychologists, linguists, philosophers all proclaimed the unity of the human mind and, over some forty years, presented Whorf, in particular, as an incoherent advocate of the most extreme relativism and essentialism, doctrines they found almost embarrassingly easy to refute. Here I discuss the main critiques and show that they were often based on the attribution to Whorf, sometimes to Sapir, and occasionally to Boas, of positions they would have rejected – but which did coincide with those of earlier essentialist thinkers and with the twentieth-century Neohumboldtian project.

Chapter 10 has three parts. It begins with some other intellectual traditions that, like the Boasian one, sought to give both universals and local systems their due. I concentrate here on structuralism, on symbolic anthropology and on Gaston Bachelard's development of a new epistemology, which shows remarkable parallels, in particular, to Whorf. The second section presents some of the scholars who maintained Boasian perspectives from the 1960s through the 1980s, and the final section looks at the gradual return of serious interest in and research on linguistic relativity, particular within the cognitive sciences themselves, with increasing momentum since the mid-1990s.[6]

Throughout the book I highlight the recurrence of the same arguments across the centuries; the relationship of language attitudes to the importance accorded (or not accorded) to poetic language; and changing theories of translation, often a royal road to the understanding of attitudes toward language difference.

1   A passage to modernity

If I may be so bold as to try to characterize our own lived universe, which seems to have come fully into being in the sixteenth and seventeenth centuries: this is a world of infinite static three-dimensional space and eternal, constantly flowing, one-dimensional time: both of these are measured in terms of quantity (miles, years), not in terms of differential qualities.[1] Things and people exist within this fixed and uniform spatiotemporal frame, which is very big. What we see when we look up on a clear night is vast or perhaps infinite space, with the stars shining so far away that thinking about it gives us a sense of flying rather than of locating, of losing orientation rather than gaining it. We live on a more or less spherical planet, one among a number that circle one such star, which looks bigger than the other stars because it is much closer to us than they are. Things in this world follow immutable natural laws, but in such a way that personal experience is highly varied and often surprising. "Things" include human bodies, but not the human mind. On the contrary, each human being is a unique individual whose appearance and actions give clues to the mind "underneath," which constitutes the real person. Individuals are born free and should, within limits, control their own lives.

This, I think, is a fair characterization of how most modern Western people presume things are. But to put it this way is to presuppose that this is not the only possible way to conceptualize the world, nor the only one to have been held by human beings. In the European Middle Ages the background assumptions about how things work seem to have been profoundly different from the ones I have just sketched.

The rose of the world

In the years AD 611 and 612, two eclipses of the moon and one of the sun were visible across Spain. Sisebut, the learned king of the Spanish Visigoths, requested his subject Isidore, Bishop of Seville, to write a book explaining to his anxious people how the natural world worked. The resulting treatise, called *On the Nature of Things*, lays out a picture of the changing seasons, the transformations of elements, and the reasons for meteorological and astral activity.

It is illustrated with seven images that present the processes of nature; six of these are circular, earning the book the nickname *Liber rotarum*, the book of wheels (Isidore 615 [1960]: 15–18).

In one of the pictures (Isidore 615 [1960]: 202 *bis*), the circle is divided by curved lines into four equal spaces around a central space. In the middle is the word *annus*, the year. The upper space is labelled *uer*, the spring; the other seasons follow clockwise around the circle. Just below *uer* is written *oriens*, the east; summer, autumn, and winter are respectively paired with south, west, and north. Finally, the interstitial spaces also have words in them, these indicating qualities: hot and cold, wet and dry. The disposition of the whole makes it clear that the top sector, spring/east, is wet and hot; summer/south is hot and dry; autumn/west is dry and cold; winter/north is cold and wet, and back to the east and to springtime, hot and wet: we have turned the wheel once.

In this *imago mundi*, space and time are divided into *qualitatively* different regions, each determined by the changing qualities of hot and cold, dry and wet. A fundamental aspect of this picture is something that to us today seems utterly bizarre: spatial and temporal regions echo each other. The image is both a calendar and a map of the world. Calendars and maps are the same thing.

Another circle (Isidore 615 [1960]: 216 *bis*) shows a similar division into four regions and the same four qualities. But here there are some new factors. On the outermost rim, between the names of the qualities, are the elements that manifest them: fire, air, water, and earth, with fire on top, presumably because it was held to be the lightest of the elements. Immediately inward from each element is the name of the season corresponding to it, and the arrangement is the same as in the first image: summer corresponds to fire, and so forth. On a third level inward there is another set of words: beneath fire and summer is not, this time, a direction, but the word *colera*; this is the humor yellow bile, one of the four constituents of the human body and temperament, the corporeal counterpart of the element fire. As yellow bile is listed with fire and summer, so, around the wheel, is black bile (*melancholia*) with earth and autumn, phlegm with water and winter, blood with air and spring. In the middle of the diagram, one above the other, are the words *mundus annus homo*, "the world, the year, the human being." Human natures, in other words, do not vary freely, but depend on the qualities of one's humoral makeup.

Taken together, the two images present a world of "cosmic cohesion" (Obrist 1997: 35) in which elements, regions, periods, humors, characters all move together in a single intricate dance.[2] Circular images of this type were not rare through the Middle Ages. They were sometimes called *rota mundi*, the wheel of the world, *rosa mundi*, the rose of the world, or, when the winds of the different directions were portrayed on them, the rose of the winds, the ancestor of the compass rose. Isidore's text, along with others such as his *Liber numerorum*, which gives the implications of a long series of numbers, make explicit a cosmological system that would remain background knowledge in Europe for a thousand years (Brandt 1966: 1–2, 10).

How seriously can we take this as representative of the way people conceived of the world? Did medieval people really identify time and space in their everyday activities? Is it even possible to speak of medieval people in general, lumping together men and women, peasants, nobles, and clerics, over a thousand years of history? Or is this model of the world a purely abstract construction meant only for high-level conceptualization? I am not a medievalist and will not venture to answer any of these questions. But it is surely remarkable that this kind of world pattern could be accepted, repeated, and recopied even as an abstract model. Most people in the Western world today, of any gender, age, or social class, would find identifying seasons and directions and aspects of the body with each other profoundly *dis*orienting.[3]

The principles behind the images were not secret or occult. For the most part, they were so evident as to remain part of "the vast domain of implicit knowledge ... [of] categories considered essential, but that were not necessarily made explicit" (Obrist 1997: 34). In some domains, however, the underlying principles had to come to the surface. A large part of medieval medicine, for instance, consisted of bringing the humors into balance by adjusting diet and activity to regional climate, season, and stage of life. The system was self-enclosing, both in the mutual reflection of time, space, the elements, and the human being, and in a more concrete sense: the medieval person who gazed up at a clear night sky was looking *through* a series of concentric crystal spheres. The stars were small but very bright orbs hung on the eighth sphere, beyond which were spheres bearing angels and beyond these the infinity of God. The inner spheres, turning at different rates, bore the planets, of which the largest and brightest was the sun. The earth under our feet was the center of this whole turning world.

As the sun ruled the planets, as God ruled the orders of angels, so each domain in the world was hierarchized – literally, since "hierarchy" means a sacred order. The king in the secular world, the pope in the sacred, ruled a hierarchy of human beings, each of whom owed fealty to the representative of the levels superior to his or her own. One's basic type was unchangeable, both in terms of temperament and of status: you were born noble or peasant, and these were fixed, fundamentally different, types of body/mind. Nowhere here was there any notion of free and unique individuals finding their way in an empty world.

Isidore's most famous work, the *Etymologies* or *Origins*, composed late in his life and dedicated to the memory of the now deceased King Sisebut, defines the place of language in this world. The *Etymologies* are an encyclopedia that defines things and explains their origin by revealing the sources and so the true meanings of their Latin names (Henderson 2007). As time, space, and physical processes correspond, so words correspond to the things they name.

In the chapter devoted to "the languages of nations" (9.1), Isidore retells the story of the Tower of Babel.[4] Originally "the whole earth was of one language and of one speech." Human beings got together to build a tower up to heaven; God struck it down, and to make sure nothing like this was ever attempted again, he confounded human tongues so that mankind was divided among many languages (seventy-two according to Isidore).[5] Three of these, Hebrew, Greek, and Latin, are sacred, since they were inscribed above the crucified Christ and are necessary for interpreting holy scripture. They are also representative of the three great types of language in the world, which Isidore defines through another set of correspondences, this one between the macrocosmic geography of the world and the microcosmic "geography" of the human mouth and throat:

All the nations of the East – like the Hebrews and the Syrians – crunch together their speech and words in their throats. All the Mediterranean nations – like the Greeks and the people of Asia minor – strike their speech on the palate. All the Western nations – like the Italians and Spaniards – gnash their words against their teeth. (Isidore 636 [2006]: 191)

Like his picture of the cosmos, the key elements of Isidore's view of language remained dominant for almost a thousand years. Through the Western European Middle Ages Latin was the one prestigious language, and discussions of language were virtually always discussions of Latin. While the schools argued over the relationship between words and things, the idea that languages could be different in important ways does not seem to have arisen. "Grammar is of one and same substance in all languages, even though it may vary in its accidents" (Roger Bacon, in Stankiewicz 1981: 180). The Latin sound system and the eight parts of speech that had been identified for Greek, then applied to Latin most influentially by Donatus (fourth century) and Priscian (sixth century), defined organized language (Hüllen 2001: 211). The ninth-century German monk Otfrid of Weissenburg said that the "barbarism" of High German made it hard to write because, unlike Latin, it was inherently *inculta et indisciplinabilis*, "unaccustomed to being held in by the curbing rein of the art of grammar" (Percival 1975: 248, n. 28).

From the closed world to the magical universe

The medieval picture of the cosmos fitted with a hierarchical social world, an economy based on agriculture and dependent on the seasons, and the open extraction of surplus from producers, necessitating the constant reinforcement of fealty, of knowing one's place in the world, as a cosmological imperative. The rise of capitalism meant the destruction of this system. The one that replaced it would be based not on agriculture, but on industrial production; it required the availability of human beings unattached to particular places and with labor power to sell. In this new system the extraction of surplus is occulted and presented as the by-product of a freely negotiated contract between individuals, a potential employer with the power to pay and a potential employee with labor power to sell, to be measured out in quantitative units of time. It is not surprising that this kind of social structure should correspond to an insistence on individual uniqueness and free choice, which increasingly become the themes of implicit ideologies and explicit philosophies over the next centuries.

Capitalism frees human beings and throws them into a social space defined primarily by negotiation and contract. It was noted by Karl Marx, one of the most perspicacious ethnographers of modern society (1867 [1967]: VIII), that the liberation of the serfs from the great manors coincided with the expropriation of small farmers and the first vagrancy laws – all forcing people off the land, erasing their traditional places in the world, and turning them into unique individuals, free to find a job or die.

In a capitalist system, each producer, in competition with others, must increase production and markets or be driven out of business. This is a tremendous incentive for seeking new markets and new sources of capital, and virtually any discovery or technical innovation would now offer the possibility of yielding a competitive advantage. With the rise of capitalism, then, came both colonialism, as Europe began to conquer the rest of the world, and the scientific revolution. These transformations meant an altered relationship of the subject to space, time, and social life, and, with the increasing rate of scientific discovery and the arrival of massive new input from distant places and the deeper past, to a suddenly expanded world.

By the sixteenth century, Western European societies were in full transition from a predominantly feudal way of producing and living to one that, in its basic structure, remains ours. Yet most sixteenth-century thinkers were still operating in a mode that was fitting less and less well with current circumstances. Instead of simply assuming that the universe is a single great hierarchy that embraces both nature and divine and human society, in which each order reflects the others, this view began to be laid out explicitly and almost defensively; the quest for new knowledge was understood to be a pursuit of signs of God's secret meanings hidden in the appearances of the world. From the well-defined set of correspondences of the medieval rose of the world, we pass to a frenetic quest to interpret what Michel Foucault (1966 [1970], Chapter 2) calls the prose of the world. The new "relationships are not static equations, as with Isidore ... [Now] they become shifting metaphors" (Borst 1988 [1992]: 21).

By understanding the secret signatures of the world, the philosopher/mage/ scientist can have an effect on reality. This was the dream of generations of Renaissance occultists, Hermeticists, and Christian Cabbalists (e.g., Eco 1993

[1995], Chapters 4 and 6). For these schools, as for Isidore, knowing the true name of a thing is to know its real identity. But now the central concern was control and transformation, through what in retrospect looks sometimes like science, sometimes like raving.

The search for secret signs is exemplified in the *De occulta philosophia* (1533 [1992]) of Cornelius Agrippa (1486–1535), which presents lists of hundreds of correspondences, so that one has the impression that everything in the world is a symbol of everything else. Agrippa's tables of numbers read like a *Liber numerorum* run amok, to the point that the wheel of the world starts to go off the rails: here the line-up of elements, seasons, directions, and humors is not quite coherent, with fire and summer identified with the east, air and the spring with the west, earth and autumn with the south (Agrippa 1533 [1992]: 267). Agrippa's goal is not to conform to a given, stable order, but to uncover a true and secret language that corresponds directly to and so controls the hidden springs of the universe.

During this period vernacular languages were gaining in importance, particularly in Italy, where a new merchant class was producing a great vernacular literature. From the fourteenth century on, literary defenses were composed for all the major Western European languages. While medieval grammarians such as Isidore were bypassed in favor of the now available Donatus and Priscian themselves – Lorenzo Valla called Isidore *Hisidorus indoctorum arrogantissimus* (Padley 1976: 17) – the assumption remained that Latin grammar and the eight parts of speech defined language structure.

[T]he idea does not occur to the many authors that languages other than Latin might each have their "own grammar"... Latin was *the* language *per definitionem* ... The grammaticography of vernaculars ... was diversified in the languages covered but ... unified in the method of description ... [T]he old Latin model always loomed in the background. (Hüllen 2001: 213, 216)

To defend other languages, therefore, was to show that they fit this structure – or else they could not be real languages. The first grammars of Western European vernaculars were all attempts to find the eight parts of speech in them (Percival 1975: 248–50; Hüllen 2001: 213–15).

There were two options for those wanting to use vernacular languages. One was to stick with the story of Babel and bemoan linguistic diversity as the punishment for a sin, but argue that we have to use the vulgar tongues nevertheless (the position of John Calvin), or that the original and true language might be recoverable through studying ancient texts, or the Hebrew language, or the "prose of the world." The other option was to embrace multiplicity as part of "the variety of things in the universe" (the title of a work by Louis Leroy, published in 1557). In this sense, "[t]he concept of linguistic diversity is part of the Renaissance discovery of the opulence of nature and of the nearly inexhaustible diversity of man" (Stankiewicz 1981: 180). In this period

[w]e witness a kind of ennobling of the multiple … Multiplication is not corruption, but fecundity. (Dubois 1970: 115–6, 119)

One of the great Renaissance motifs is that each language, each nation, has its own spirit or genius. "Just like individual people, so individual nations have each their own genius" (Erasmus, in Stankiewicz 1981: 184). But the idea was particularly elaborated by Italian authors as part of the debate over which dialect would become the basis of a standard Italian. The Florentine shoemaker-philosopher Giovan Battista Gelli (1498–1562) writes (1551 [1976]: 201–2) that translation is hard because every language has its distinctive caprices (*capresterie*). This word, which suggests the gamboling of young goats, occurs again in a dialogue of Gelli's townsman Benedetto Varchi (*c.* 1502–1565), who says that the genius of a language is to be found in "a certain peculiar or special or particular property," not in the actual words but in the *capresterie* that one can perform with them (in Stankiewicz 1981: 182). Sperone Speroni (1500–1588) locates the distinctive genius of a language in the way it is learned by children not through labor, but through play and in delight (Stankiewicz 1981: 184).

The diversity of linguistic geniuses becomes apparent at the moment of translation. Summing up the idea of language diversity as a *felix culpa*, a lucky fault, Girolamo Cardano (1501–1576) recalls Isidore's geographic phonetics:

[L]anguages are diverse, and ways of speaking are various. This depends on the nature of places: Italians have trouble pronouncing sounds from the chest, while this is easy for Hebrews … The variety of languages is a useful thing, since it allows the expression of all the affects (*affectus*) of the soul. The proof of this is that the phrases of Homer cannot be expressed in Latin or in our mother tongue, nor can those of Virgil in Greek or in our mother tongue, and even less the meaning of the poems of Petrarch either in Latin or Greek. (cited in Dubois 1970: 115, 118–9)

In a posthumously published contribution to the Italian language debate, Varchi makes a defense of diversity in general:

[N]othing is so small or ugly that it does not contribute to the perfection of the universe … [If] there were just one tongue … Virgil could not have equalled Homer, as Dante would not have been conceded to be the equal of both; and the same could be said for all the others, orators or poets, who have been equal to or hardly inferior to each other in diverse languages … This is why … I say that nature could not and perhaps should not have created a single language for the whole world. (Varchi 1570 [1995]: 546)

In his *Defense and Illustration of the French Language*, the poet Joachim du Bellay (*c.* 1522–1560) says that to create a French literature it is not enough to translate ancient works, and in any case it is impossible to render [a translated text] ... with the same grace that was used by the author: for every Language has something indefinable (*je ne scay quoi*) proper only to itself, and if you try to express the native sense (*le naif*) of this in another language, observing the law of translation, which is never to go outside the limits of the author, your style will be constrained, cold, and of ill grace. (du Bellay 1549 [1948]: 36)

Du Bellay's statement raises questions that we will see coming back again and again over the next several hundred years. If languages are different in important ways, how can we locate the specificity of each? And if they are different in a way that is pervasive then how is translation possible?

A new world of languages

In the year 1532, a comet and an eclipse of the moon were visible across France. Things were not going well for the kingdom. Seven years earlier, King Francis I had been captured by his enemy the Holy Roman Emperor and released only upon payment of a ransom that included kingdoms. The conjunction of disruptions in the sky and the state was making people start to panic, a panic that was encouraged by popular astrologers, many of whom were German and so partial to the Emperor. Partly to reassure people, partly to support the France-first politics of his patrons the du Bellay family, the monk and medical man François Rabelais (*c.* 1494–1553), a respected astrologer himself, published a series of parodic prognostications mocking astrological pretensions. For the year 1533, Rabelais predicted:

This year ... Saturn will be retrograde, Venus direct, Mercury inconstant. And a mass of other planets will not proceed as they usually do. So for this year, crabs will walk sideways, ropemakers work backwards, footstools will get up on benches, pillows will be found at the foot of the bed; many men's bollocks will hang loose for lack of a gamebag; the belly will go in front; the bum will be the first to sit down; nobody will find the bean in their Kings' cake ... in sundry places the beasts will speak ... And there will be more than twenty-seven irregular verbs this year, unless Priscian holds them in a tight rein ...

This year the blind will see but little, the deaf will be pretty hard of hearing, the dumb will hardly speak, the rich will keep themselves somewhat better than the poor, and the healthy than the sick. Many sheep, oxen, piglets, goslings, pullets and ducks will die, whilst among monkeys and dromedaries the mortality will be less cruel. Old age will prove incurable this year because of the years gone by. (Rabelais 2006: 175–6; translation modified)

Rabelais' conclusion: don't pay attention to false prophets, but trust in God.

This *Pantagrueline Prognostication* came out just after Rabelais' novel *Pantagruel* (1532). In the novel, the eponymous hero, who represents the ideal prince-scholar-student, even though he is also an enormous terrifying giant – a *grand homme* in every sense of the word – has two linguistic encounters. First

(Chapter 6) he meets a fellow who speaks a French that is incomprehensible because even as he is talking about boozing and whoring, he uses absurdly Latinized terms for everything. Both aspects of his speech, the vulgar content and the high-flown phraseology, turn out to be typical of students at the University in Paris. Pantagruel loses patience; terrified, the student begs for mercy, reverting to his native dialect. He reveals himself to be a bumpkin from the Limousin, now speaking a language equally hard to understand, but this time not because of its fake sophistication but its real cringing rurality.

We know that Rabelais was hostile to the University, then the center of conservatism in the scholarly world (the feeling was mutual), and that he was a proponent of the new learning. Here he is identifying these attitudes with opposed kinds of French: a high-flown, Latinized French for his enemies, marked by a pretentious obscurity that reinforces their privileged control of knowledge; against this, a straightforward, ostensibly natural French for his friends, a French that seems to be an invisible form allowing good sense and interesting information to shine through.

This "normal" and normative French is spoken by the great prince and his followers. The natural speech of the Limousin schoolboy is his own local dialect. The incident reflects the consolidation of the French state, the institution of a standard dialect, and the increasing marginalization of non-standard ways of speaking, i.e., all the regional forms in what had been a multilinguistic territory. In France, the dialect that provided the base for the standard was that of the Loire Valley: and it happened that this was also the home territory of Rabelais, of Descartes, and of Ronsard and du Bellay, the two major language- and style-defining poets of the century.

We should note the acuity with which Rabelais produces extended examples of this triplicity of forms of speech – to make fun of two of them, to be sure, but he could have made fun of them with a couple of words. This is a bit of virtuoso virtual descriptive linguistics, showing to what extent we are now, in the sixteenth century, understood to be living in a world of a variety of languages, dialects, and registers. Rabelais' work itself is marked above all by his play among a multiplicity of styles and forms of expression, just as it is marked by his delight in discovery of a newly opening world.[6]

So right here we have some of the main points of philosophical and political modernity: the constitution of the nation-state with its standard language; the valorization of plain speaking and the linking of honesty with discovery; the opening-up of curiosity about all aspects of the world.

In the second incident (Chapter 9), Pantagruel first meets his companion Panurge, "whom he would treasure all his life." When they come across Panurge, a ragged and miserable figure, the giant's company asks who he is and how he came to this pitiable state. His reply is incomprehensible; one of Pantagruel's followers identifies it as German. They ask him again, and

Panurge goes on to reply in more languages, nine more in the first edition, up to thirteen in that of 1542. The languages used include Greek, Hebrew, Latin, six European vernaculars, and four languages presented as coming from faraway lands, including Utopia and the Antipodes. Finally, after the Latin speech, the frustrated Pantagruel says, "But friend, don't you know how to speak French?" "Of course," comes the reply in perfectly normal French, "it is, thank God, my natural mother tongue, for I was born and brought up in the garden of France, in Touraine," which is to say (no surprise) in the Valley of the Loire (Rabelais 2006: 56, translation modified).

Again, the same joke could have been made with a lot less effort. But Rabelais is not just making a joke: he's showing off, as is Panurge, composing paragraphs in languages real and unreal. This *tour de force* opens up a multi-linguistic world: it bears witness to what J. R. Firth (1937, Chapter 5) called the discovery of Babel.

In this comic piece Rabelais is also showing something of the nature of linguistic diversity. While the gist of Panurge's reply is the same every time – it may be summed up as "I'm starving, give me something to eat!" – the style of presentation varies along with the language. The German is highly allusive, "a gloss on an absent text" (Demonet 1992: 179); the Scots is both flattering and moralizing; the Italian is highly ornamented, the Spanish pompous and bombastic, the Dutch and Danish straightforward, the Basque imperative and nearly rude.

The rhetorical and linguistic work that Rabelais carries out … amounts to giving each language a style, which is at once a content and the definition of the language itself; as a whole, this passage … illustrates not the similarities of languages, but their differences as discourses borne by peoples who are supposedly more or less chatty, obsequious, rude, charitable, etc. (Demonet 1992: 179–80)

If this reading is correct, then Rabelais is offering a panorama of the geniuses of languages and peoples, made manifest through distinctive national styles.

Three vernaculars

As the dignity of vernaculars came to be accepted, so did the idea that each language had its own distinctive and worthwhile qualities. As the discussion of these issues moved from Italy into other lands, we in fact find a divergence among themes and styles of discourse in France, England, and Germany: as we will see in the next chapters, French thinking developed a fascination with a universal reason, British a concern with the external world of things, and German with diversity and distinctive styles. Coherent arguments for the value or even superiority of a national language developed along with nations and national tendencies.

In consonance with the advance of the French national project, as early as the mid-sixteenth century the French had developed a grammatical theory of the superiority of their language over all others, and especially over Latin. To understand their argument requires a brief syntactic excursus.

Like other old Indo-European languages, Latin is highly inflectional, that is, each major word carries markers that indicate its relations to other words in a sentence. In Indo-European languages these markers are usually suffixes. The Latin word *equus*, "horse", for instance, can be divided into a root *equ-*, which indicates that we are talking about a horse or horses, pure equinity if you like; and an inflection *-us*, which gives information on several dimensions at once: it tells us that this horse is masculine (rather than feminine) in gender, singular (rather than plural) in number, and serves as the subject of the sentence (instead of any of five other possibilities). Pronouns and adjectives are marked for the same dimensions, while inflections mark verbs for person, number, tense, and mood. *Equ-* by itself simply does not exist in the language: every noun, pronoun, adjective, and verb must carry its inflection as an integral part of the word.

It is the pervasiveness of inflection that binds the Latin sentence together. A sentence maintains its meaning, designates the same proposition if you like, with its words in virtually any order. To change the relationships among the elements you have to change the word-endings themselves.

The modern languages of Western Europe show a more or less drastic reduction of the inflectional endings. In French and English, and to a lesser but still marked degree in German, individual words carry much less grammatical information than did their ancestors. In these languages, word order has to be more rigid than it was in Latin and other early Indo-European languages. This is a simple syntactic fact; only the French would have the gall to make it into an argument for the superiority of their own tongue.

Their argument drew on a history of philosophical attempts to define a natural or direct order of logical thinking, and therefore of speaking. Starting in Hellenistic times, and through the Middle Ages (Scaglione 1972: 74–96, 105–21), rhetoricians had proposed that there was a single natural or direct order of thought: the mind first posits what it is thinking about, then thinks something about it. In a sentence, this would take the form of a nominal subject coming first, followed by a verb indicating what the subject is doing, followed in turn by the nominal object to which it is being done. Accidental qualities should follow the substances and actions they qualify: adjectives should come after nouns, adverbs after verbs. Most of these theorists spoke Greek, and while Greek had a word order almost as free as that of Latin, the "natural order of thought" pretty well followed the baseline order for the Greek sentence. This was not the base order of the Latin sentence, which tended to put the verb last.

As it happens, among the prestigious languages of sixteenth- and seventeenth-century Western Europe, only French regularly follows precisely the "natural order." This linguistic datum was seized on to claim that French was the language that best reflected the order of reason. In the next century, this view was bolstered by the prestige of rationalism in philosophy. Looking back, the typical word order of the French sentence seems to have been an extraordinary piece of luck for the French rationalists, who were thus permitted to be rationalist nationalists.

The claim that French is better because it follows the natural order was first made (exactly) in the middle of sixteenth century. Drawing on the medieval *ordo naturalis* (Scaglione 1972: 153), Louis Meigret's (*c.* 1510 to *c.*1588) *Tretté de la grammere françoèze*, published in 1550, the year after du Bellay's *Deffence*, argues that the French order subject-verb-object "was given both by the order of nature and by reason" (Ricken 1978: 15–16).

[I]f we carefully consider the order of nature, we will find that the French style fits it much better than does the Latin ... I do not find it reasonable that we should enslave ourselves to [Latin usage], and abandon a much easier and more straightforward way of raising the edifice of our language following the order that nature holds to in her works, and which the usage of speech has tended to follow. (Meigret 1550 [1880]: 195–6)

If there is a single natural order of reason, then any other order is a deviation or inversion. English, which follows the "natural order" pretty well, still puts its adjectives before the noun: an inversion. Highly inflected Greek and especially Latin, at least in their literary manifestations, "invert" to a degree that would render a French or English sentence completely unintelligible. And while German always puts the verb in second place in the main clause and at the end in subordinate clauses, almost everything else can dance around in a way unheard of in either English or French. The license to invert would be taken to mean that the language in question had been led astray by the solicitations of the senses. Inversion is thus often presented as a kind of grammatical moral failing; "inversion" was also, of course, the word used until the late nineteenth century to denote what we now call homosexuality.

Compared to this sophisticated argument for the superiority of French, the sixteenth-century defenses of English and German are still quite modest. They make virtually no reference to word order: the argument is, rather, that English is useful and practical, and that German is unique and rich.

Modern English has a strong tendency to treat words as semantic isolates. One result of this is that nouns and adjectives can be verbed, verbs and adjectives nouned. As Calvin puts it in the comic strip, verbing weirds language (Watterson 1994: 53), but it's a weirding of wording to which English lends itself. English vocabulary is drawn from many different sources; its speakers seem to feel no hesitation in naturalizing foreign words and have had much less concern about language purity than have the French and the Germans.

I certainly don't want to claim that there is any direct determination of ideology, even language ideology, by language type: but it happens that as the French could claim that the syntax of their sentences reflected that of reason itself, similarly English philosophers who were oriented toward a world of distinct *things* could find a direct echo of things in relatively isolate and grammatically unmarked English *words*, potentially at least fairly pure nuggets of meaning. The characteristics of English could be drawn upon in what came quite early to be an ideology not of reason, as in French, nor of a specific texture, as we will see was the case with German, but with usefulness and dispatch. We have a lovely expression of this ideology from a 1582 guide for teaching English by Richard Mulcaster (1531–1611):

I do not think that anie language, be it whatsoever, is better able to utter all arguments, either with more pith, or greater planesse, than our English tung is … For is it not in dede a mervellous bondage, to becom servants to one tung for learning sake, the most of our time, with losse of most time, whereas we maie have the very same treasure in our own tung, with the gain of most time? our own bearing the joyful title of our libertie and fredom, the Latin tung remembring us of our thraldom and bondage? I love Rome, but London better, I favor Italie, but England more, I honor the Latin, but I worship the English. (in Baugh and Cable 1978: 202–3)

English is praised for its pithiness, and the main justifications for learning in English seem to be to save time and to be free of Rome. Again, this practical ideology will reach its full flowering, if you can call it that, in the 1600s.

German is the most highly inflected of the major modern Western European languages, and in this sense looks the most archaic. Its relative grammatical richness permits a flexible word order, but one always anchored by the finite verb. Where French and English line up their clauses one after the other, the inflected nature of German allows the embedding of clauses inside each other, "whereby conceptual contents that 'belong together' are incapsulated within a single phrase or construction, the terminal lexemes thus forming a kind of conceptual boundary" (Erich Drach, in Miller 1968: 94), the verb coming only at the end of all the subordinate clauses. This tendency matched an ideology of organic German profundity (Haroche and Maingueneau 1985: 352–3). The Irish writer Flann O'Brien said that waiting for the German verb is surely the ultimate thrill (1977: 143).

Unlike French, German does not come from Latin; unlike its cousin English, which has included an enormous French vocabulary since the Middle Ages, German does not have a history of linguistic mixing.

In the sixteenth century, we only have hints of what Germans, still inhabiting a chaos of warring states, would mount in the seventeenth as a defense of their language for its distinctiveness, its very German-ness. The 1573 grammar of Laurentius Albertus (*c.* 1540 to after 1583), while still following the Latin pattern of description, praises German for its distinctiveness and purity, as well as its variety and richness: the goal of his work is "that the abundance and marvellous variation of combining words in our language might be shown" (McLelland 2001: 15).

Again, I am not claiming that the structures of these languages somehow directly determined the ideologies associated with them.[7] But certainly these ideologies were flexible enough both to fit national projects – an increasingly absolutist French state, an England increasingly dominated by the bourgeois classes and fascinated with empirical discovery, and a divided and war-torn still-virtual Germany – and to find real aspects of their languages that could be pointed to as reinforcement. Perhaps this relationship between language structure and linguistic ideology (Silverstein 1979) is a case of "the mimetism that can exist between the spirit and the letter of languages" (Marrache-Gouraud 2003: 32). Similarly, the distinctive traits of these languages seem to have been exploited in the development of their respective prose styles, rendering underlying grammatical nuance explicit in the poetics of prose (cf. Friedrich 1979).

The three tendencies I have identified here – French universal reason, English useful correspondence to the world, and German autonomy and richness – will be intensified in the seventeenth century, all reaching a kind of climax in the 1660s.

2   One reason, one world, many monads

> A brief, and sufficiently accurate, description of the intellectual life of the
> European races during the succeeding two centuries and a quarter up to our
> own times is that they have been living upon the accumulated capital of ideas
> provided for them by the genius of the seventeenth century.
> Alfred North Whitehead (*Science and the Modern World*, 1932; exergue to Chomsky,
> *Cartesian Linguistics*)

Many writers of the seventeenth century seem to be relaying first glimpses of
a new world that is, most extraordinarily of all, simply the world as it is, seen
clear for the first time. The articulation of modern experience took different
forms in the main philosophical options then established: Descartes' rationalism for the mechanical world and the reasoning mind, the empiricism of Bacon
and Locke for experiment upon and interaction with the world, the monadism
of Leibniz for the multiplicity and uniqueness of essences and personalities.

Each of these alternatives is closely bound up with a language and style: these
authors are part of the heritage of their respective nations and tongues. For
rationalists, who tended to be French, reason comes first; for empiricists, who
tended to be British, the world comes first. Both of these views are universalistic, seeking general laws that apply everywhere in the same way. In German
thinking, on the contrary, the notion of diversity as a positive good came to be
a central and developing idea in a mode that I am calling essentialist.

Language diversity has always posed a problem for universalistic approaches.
The rationalist solution was to propose a general grammar based on reason and
to judge languages depending on how closely they matched this ideal. The
empiricist solution was to seek to modify and purify existing languages to
make them transparent reflections of the multifarious yet law-ordered reality of
the world. For essentialists, on the contrary, linguistic diversity was one more
expression of the diversity of the world: their tendency was to highlight the
specificity of each language, seeing it as the expression of a unique essence.
There are glimpses of this view of languages in Leibniz's work, but it will
reach its full development only in the later part of the eighteenth century.

Not coincidentally, the seventeenth century was also the period of the fixing
of the prose styles of the French, English, and German standards. Anyone who

has tried to work with more than one of these languages knows how different they are in sound, in syntax, and especially in what is considered normal style. The theoretical options of rationalism, empiricism, and essentialism developed in interaction with the formation of the newly fixed languages, their stylistics and grammars.

The construction of French

Meigret's claim of the conformity of French to the natural order of reason was maintained by a number of authors during the later sixteenth and early seventeenth centuries. This was also the period of consolidation of the French state. By 1635, the French language was sufficiently established to call for policing. This is the year Cardinal Richelieu founded the Académie Française, a state literary institution that had as it goals the regulation of usage and the protection of the language from bad taste. The discourse *On the Design of the Academy and the Differing Geniuses of Languages* by the abbot Amable de Bourzeys (1606–1672) could serve as a charter for French thinking about language for the next hundred-and-fifty years. Bourzeys distinguishes between "the laws of right reasoning," which are "the same everywhere and always," and the laws of pleasing, which "differ according to times and places." Since eloquence aims to please, that of the Ancients will be different from that of the Moderns, and the Oriental style will be different from ours. This is normal,

for who does not know that every language has its own particular air and genius ...? ... [E]very language has ... a certain elegance (*biensceance*) which is peculiar to it ... [W]e would condemn the greater part of foreign beauties if we judged them only by our own. In doing which we would not be committing a lesser fault than he who would hate all flowers that are not similar to lilies. (Dryhurst 1971: 233–5)

This sounds like sixteenth-century discourse on the variety of the geniuses of languages and peoples – but here it is restricted to poetic or eloquent uses of language and emphatically does not apply to the discourse of reasoning, which is the same for all peoples. This set of ideas was evidently very much in the French air when, two years later, Descartes published his *Discourse on Method*.

The Cartesian consolidation

The argument for the naturalness of French found a powerful ally and justification with the rise of philosophical rationalism. The founder-hero of the movement was René Descartes (1596–1650), a soldier, and a brilliant natural mathematician who with a warrior's directness decided to trust only the light of his own reason and so finished off the medieval cosmos and replaced it with a new world (Koyré 1942).

Descartes constructed his world through two heroic experiments in sensory deprivation, described in his intellectual autobiography, the *Discourse on Method* (1637). In the first, the young soldier (today we might call him a mercenary) found himself in winter in Germany separated from his intended command. Unable to continue, he hunkered down by himself in a heated room for some days and, reasonably comfortable, with nothing in particular to distract him, set about wondering about the nature of the universe. His singlemindedness was rewarded with a set of principles providing a rigorous method for understanding all things using the "language" of mathematics.

These long chains of reasonings, each one simple and easy, which geometers use to arrive at their most difficult demonstrations, had caused me to imagine that all the things that come within the scope of human knowledge follow one on the other (*s'entre-suivent*) in the same way, and that, provided only that we … always keep to the order required for deducing one thing from another, there can be nothing so remote that it cannot be reached in the end, nor so hidden that it cannot be discovered. (Descartes 1984: I, 120)

We learn from Descartes' notebooks that this revelation was shored up by three prophetic dreams.

Years later, again seeking relative solitude and the liberty to follow any train of thought without fear of censorship, Descartes moved from absolutist France to the Netherlands, land of free thinking. Here, in relative isolation, he resumed his search for what is unquestionably real in a series of what he calls metaphysical meditations. Anything he could doubt, he decided, he would throw out; he would keep only what cannot be doubted, what is self-evidently true. And the touchstone for such incontrovertible ideas was that they be *clear* and distinct. The French word *clarté* doesn't just mean clarity in the English sense of transparency, but, much more actively, means light, illumination, brilliancy. If you can see the truth, it's because your thoughts are illuminated by the clear light of reason, *la lumière naturelle*. Descartes calls such unquestionable clear and distinct ideas *intuitions*.

So Descartes set about his philosophical housecleaning. Everything he learned in school went out the window; so did all of his perceptions and sensations, including those of his own body, which might have been hallucinations or dreams; out went all of his beliefs, including belief in his personal identity, and all of his memories: all of this could have been planted in his mind two seconds earlier by a malevolent spirit. What is left when everything can be doubted? What is left when everything is provisionally gone, even identity? What is left, says Descartes, is the fact of doubting itself. To be doubting is to be thinking: I know, no matter what, that I am thinking. If I am thinking, then there must be somebody who is thinking: therefore I, the thinker, the doubter, must exist. I simply cannot doubt or deny this. Whence the *cogito* – "I think, therefore I am" – which can be taken as the pivotal point where thought turns in a new direction and something new is recognized.

Once reduced to this point, the world can be rebuilt by pure deductive logic. I know some things absolutely, self-evidently: one and one equal two; God must exist (for this one, you must read Descartes); from such "clear and distinct ideas," ideas that by their very clarity and distinctness must be true, Descartes rebuilt the world in a logically understandable way.

Does this trajectory sound familiar? A gifted and intransigent explorer of warrior status challenges the received understanding of how the world works and insists on discovering, through a practice of moderate sensory deprivation, what is left after everything is gone, who reaches a point of absolute knowledge and from that point reconstructs a new kind of world: Descartes is the Buddha of the West.

Descartes' world was a dualistic one: a material world, defined through its quality of extension and following the universal principles of mechanics, which can be expressed mathematically; against this, a mind or soul, not material, not extended, not mechanical, endowed by God with the gift of reason. All bodies, including human bodies, are machines; we can understand every material event as the result of single causes that are themselves the result of other causes in a linear chain of causation going back to Creation. This is a full world: space itself is the sum of interacting bodies, and time is the process of their movement. The second substance, the reasoning mind, is what allows us to reconstruct explanatory chains and map the workings of the machine.

By the method of universal doubt, says Descartes, I can be assured of my own thinking, my own existence, and my own soul. But how can I be sure that other people are something other than automatons? It is here that language enters the argument: no machine, Descartes says, could have the variety and appropriateness of response that is found in human language. It is language that reveals the existence of a soul. The interest here, as it will be for most French and British philosophers for the next two centuries, is in language in general and its relationship to reason or to the world as such, not in the specifics of different languages. Thought and reason are everywhere the same.

Yet languages are everywhere different. Descartes had faced this question in a series of letters in 1629 and 1630. Ernst Cassirer (1923 [1953]: 128) sums up his argument:

[J]ust as there is a very definite order among the ideas of mathematics ... so the whole of human consciousness, with all the contents that can ever enter into it, constitutes a strictly ordered totality. And similarly, just as the whole system of arithmetic can be constructed out of relatively few numerical signs, it must be possible to designate the sum and structure of all intellectual contents by a limited number of linguistic signs, provided only that they are combined in accordance with definite, universal rules.

While it should be possible to construct such a language, this could only be done once a full-scale analysis of all of human knowledge has already taken place.

The other place where Descartes talks about the variety of linguistic expression is in his response to an objection to his *Meditations* of 1647 articulated by the English philosopher Thomas Hobbes (Descartes 1984: II, 125–6): what if what we call reason is really nothing but a linking of words? In this case, we would not be talking about things, but about the words for them. Descartes answered with the example of language difference, presented as very much *not* a difference in ways of thinking: "For who doubts that a Frenchman and a German can have the same thoughts or reasonings about the same things, despite the fact that the words that they think of are completely different?"

In their *Logic*, Descartes' followers, the grammarians and logicians of the Abbey of Port-Royal, cite this exchange and go on:

[S]ince it appears by their different words, that the Arabs, for example, have no concordance with the French for giving the same meanings to sounds, they could not agree in their judgments and reasonings if their reasonings depended on this convention. (Arnauld and Nicole 1662 [1992]: 36–7)

But they do agree, at least sometimes.

Claude Lancelot (*c.* 1615–1695), the co-author of the Port-Royal *Grammar*, had been the first to propose language-learning methods in which the explanatory prose was in the language the learner already knew; that is to say, the Port-Royal authors produced the first Latin and Greek grammars actually written in French, replacing the earlier method of learning Latin by memorizing Latin examples of Latin rules. The new method presupposed what had seemed so evident to Descartes: that there was a universal order of prelinguistic thought that could be expressed in any language (Foucault 1969: vii), and that language was simply a technique for externalizing and communicating this thought. The Port-Royal *Grammar* is based on the same principle – we might call it the principle of logical universality. It defines language as a way of expressing already-existing ideas, "explaining one's thoughts by signs that men have invented for this purpose" (Arnauld and Lancelot 1660 [1830]: 7), and seeks to show how any language presupposes an innate logical order. So when Noam Chomsky comes up with a theory of a universal innate order underlying all languages, he identifies with what he calls Cartesian linguistics (Chomsky 1966). The Port-Royal *Grammar* is thus no more a grammar of French than Chomsky's *Syntactic Structures*, which draws primarily on English examples, is a grammar of English.

In his Latin grammar Lancelot had taken the fixed word order of French as the only natural one: "The order of words ... should be common to all languages, as we see it in our own: but the Romans were so fond of figurative discourse that they almost never speak in any other way" (in Ricken 1978: 16). The Port-Royal *Grammar* will again point to the inversions in Latin and Greek word order and distinguish this from the naturalness of

French: "There is no language that uses fewer of these figures than our own, since it particularly loves distinctness (*netteté*) and expressing things, as far as possible, in the *most natural* and least encumbered order, while at the same time it yields to none in beauty or in elegance" (Arnauld and Lancelot 1660 [1830]: 108).

Later in the decade, the Cartesian philosopher Gérauld de Cordemoy (1626–1684) sought to elucidate the interaction of mechanical body and rational soul in the production of speech. Cordemoy presents himself as an empirical researcher on child language acquisition. He starts by noting the perversity of small children:

But whatever effort one makes to teach them some things, one often notices that they know the names of a thousand others, which one had no intention at all of showing them.

This part, at least, is clearly the fruit of first-hand participant observation.

And the most surprising thing about this is to see, when they are two or three years old, that by the sheer force of their attention they are able to sort the name of a thing out of all the [verbal] constructions that one gives them that refer to that thing.

After this, with the same application and the same discernment, they learn words that signify the qualities of the things whose names they know.

Finally, extending their knowledge still further, they notice the actions or movements of these same things. (1668 [1968]: 213–14)

Cordemoy then makes the link to the grammarians' doctrine of parts of speech:

[Grammarians'] precepts are nothing but an imitation of those that nature gives to children.

First the Grammarians make known the names that signify things, which they call substantives; then they make known the names that signify qualities, which they call adjectives. And it is only after having clearly distinguished these different names that they make known the words that signify the actions of things, which they call verbs. (p. 214)

In the 1669 edition of his *Avantages de la langue françoise sur la langue latine*, Louis Le Laboureur (1615?–1679) cites Cordemoy to say that all human beings think the same way, whatever language they speak: "[T]he Latins thought in the same way we Frenchmen do ... Since their heads were made no differently from ours, it certainly seems that they must have conceived of things in the same way that we conceive of them" (1669: 162). French respects this order; Latin follows many different ones. The conclusion is unavoidable: the French speak as they think, the Romans thought one way and spoke another. "The Latin sentence, twisted and bound up (*guindé*) as it is, *embarrassait bien souvent leur esprit*" (p. 149), which I am sorely tempted to translate, "often messed with their heads." To understand a Latin sentence, the listener has to go through an extra step of "mentally reconstructing a chain of thoughts that the order of the words does not respect" (Ricken 1978: 19).

Le Laboureur imagines proto-relativistic objections to his theory. Isn't it possible that these differences in word order are simply a question of habit, rather than of nature? Certainly not, replies Le Laboureur: either you follow the natural order, as we French speakers do, or else you don't. Only one side can be the side of reason (1669: 172). But what if the real difference is one of taste, each people taking pleasure in the peculiarities of its own language? "Reason is of every country (*La raison est de tout pays*)," comes the answer; "In this I do not consult the taste that the peoples have, but the taste that they should have."

In the *Entretiens d'Ariste et d'Eugène* of 1671, the Jesuit Dominique Bouhours (1628–1702) cites Le Laboureur to praise French straightforwardness against the twists and turns of Latin. In a return to Renaissance theories, he identifies each language with a national style:

[E]very nation has always spoken according to its genius. The Greeks, who were polished and voluptuous people, had a delicate language, full of sweetness. The Romans, who aspired only to glory, and who seemed born only to govern, had a noble and august language ... In the language of the Spaniards one feels their gravity and that air of pride (*cet air superbe*) that is common to their whole nation. The Germans have a rough and crude language; the Italians have one that is soft and effeminate, fitting their temperament and the manners of their country. It follows, then, that the French, who are naturally brusque, and who have a high degree of fire and vivacity, should have a brief and active language, which has nothing drawn-out about it. (Bouhours 1671 [1920]: 60)

Bouhours is quite nasty about "northern" languages:

French is infinitely distant from the crudeness of all the languages of the North, most of whose words flay the throats of those who speak them and the ears of those who hear them. These double VVs, these double FFs, these double KKs ... all of these consonants piled up on top of each other, are horrible to pronounce, and have a frightening sound. The blend of vowels and consonants in French has an entirely contrary effect. (pp. 73–4)

By the way, English sounds like whistling (*siffler*).

The arguments for the superiority of French, based to some degree on its sound, but essentially on its word order, would be picked up and repeated over the next few decades (see Scaglione 1972: 222–38) in books with titles like François Charpentier's *De l'excellence de la langue françoise* (1683).

Reason in literature and translation

The dominance of rationalism reinforced other tendencies in seventeenth-century French culture. In literature and poetics, seventeenth-century France gloried in a canon reflecting reason, moderation, and the transformation of

passions into beauty through artistic mastery. The ideology of fine craftsmanship and reasoning wit found its expression in the twelve-syllable Alexandrine
couplet with its two equal, semantically balanced hemistiches divided by a
clear syntactic caesura, a form that would dominate French verse for the next
several hundred years. By the end of the century, the canons of this Classicism
were influencing all Western European literatures.

Translation theory in this period reflects the same assumptions about the
world, language, and style. This was the age of *les belles infidèles*, Beautiful
Faithless Ones, in the feminine (Zuber 1968; Bassnett 1980: 58–64), a label
given by the philologist Gilles Ménage (1613–1692) to a translation from Latin
by Nicolas Perrot d'Ablancourt (1606–1664). Perrot's text, remarks Ménage,
reminds him of a woman he once loved dearly in Tours: she was *belle*, but
infidèle (in Horguelin 1981: 76). This does capture something of the character
of much French translation of the period: the aim was to convey foreign texts
ancient and modern in elegant French, eliminating anything in style or content
that would shock contemporary sensibilities; if the original was in verse of any
kind, it was translated either into prose or into Alexandrines. The goal of such
domesticating translation (Venuti 1995), was to produce an assimilated French
text. Sometimes this went very far indeed. In the preface to a 1646 translation,
Perrot d'Ablancourt explains his method:

It is difficult to make a fashionable suit of clothes (*un habit à la mode*) out of a suit in
the antique style without changing some things ... Those who know Eloquence will
understand my reasons for ... abridging some passages that were too slow (*languis-
sants*), besides the fact that this Author is subject to frequent and useless repetitions,
which neither my language nor my style can suffer. (in Horguelin 1981: 93)

In his 1662 version of Thucydides, Perrot presents himself as a necromancer,
bringing the ancient author back to life in a modern French body "as if by a
kind of Metempsychosis." If Thucydides had trouble recognizing himself in
his new French get-up, he would still have no reason to complain, "any more
than a sick man would complain of the Doctor who has given him health and
vigor by the force of his remedies" (in Zuber 1968: 382–3).

The Abbé Perrin boasted that his *Aeneid* of 1648 was the first to dress
up Aeneas "as a French cavalier, with pomp of plumes and bangles" (in
Ladborough 1938: 86).

The justification for this kind of practice could be quite sophisticated.
One wants not primarily to translate the words of a text, it was argued, but
to reproduce in a modern reader the emotions the original text evoked in its
own destined readers (Levi 2000: 127). Were we to stick too closely to the
author's actual style, this would produce a very bizarre text in modern French.
We should therefore translate everything in such a way as to convey the same
impression of normality that the author would have given in his own time, that
is, we should translate him in a good modern French style, offering what the

ancient or exotic author would have written had he been a seventeenth-century Frenchman.[1] Indeed, in the early eighteenth century Madame Anne Dacier's prose translations of Homer would be widely criticized for being too faithful to their author. No less a personage than Voltaire wrote to her that one should "translate for one's own time, not for the past" (in Horguelin 1981: 121).

In philosophy, in aesthetics, in translation theory and practice, seventeenth-century rationalism elevated a single set of principles to universal and trans-historical status. Along with the European conquest of much of the rest of the world, one set of European canons was in the process of being deprovincial-ized (Chakrabarty 2000).

The invention of English

From the Renaissance on, British philosophers seem to have been particularly concerned with the external world where French rationalists were particularly concerned with the internal world. From the beginning of the seventeenth century, the dominant British assumption was that true ideas are not innate in the mind, but come from the interpretation of sensory input. Since humans all have the same senses and live in the same world, the fact of language diversity and, more generally, the diversity of opinions, is as bothersome for this empiricism as it is for rationalism.

The style that comes to be recommended for expository prose in English is an unornamented, simple one that sticks as closely as possible to the relations among things. This was already clear in the work of the founder of British empiricism, Sir Francis Bacon (1561–1626),[2] who insisted that our experience of the world, not abstract reasoning, was the source of true knowledge. Particularly dangerous for knowledge are the words that blind custom has led us to use: we must separate knowledge from language and study things, not words (in Borst 1957–1963: 1240); "Words plainly force and overrule the understanding" (Bacon 1620 [1863]: 49). One possible solution, approved by Bacon, was to develop a new language that would accurately reflect the reality of the world, as the original language of Adam had done. The twin Baconian notions of reforming language or, at the limit, creating a new and better one would be some of the most actively pursued ideas of the British seventeenth century.

But empiricism also means curiosity about human experience, and language diversity is certainly part of that experience. So Bacon himself would propose a comparative study of languages:

[T]he noblest species of grammar, as I think, would be this: if some one well seen in a great number of tongues, learned as well as vulgar, would handle the various properties of languages; showing in what points each excelled, in what it failed. For so ... the several beauties of each may be combined ... for the right expressing of the meanings of the mind. And at the same time there will be obtained in this way signs ... well worthy of observation ... concerning the dispositions and manners of peoples and nations, drawn from their languages. (1623 [1860]: 441–2)

Two grammars from the middle of the century illustrate different facets of British curiosity about language.

Unlike most of the early vernacular grammars, the *Grammatica linguae anglicanae* (1653) of the mathematician John Wallis (1616–1703) does not assume the universality of Latin parts of speech (Constantinescu 1974). Unlike the Port-Royal grammarians, Wallis focuses on surface patterns, from which he was in some cases able to abstract non-surface elements of structure (Isermann 1996), as experimental scientists would discover non-obvious patterns in the world.

Wallis was, in a sense, defamiliarizing his own most familiar language, English. At the other end of the scale is an attempt to explain the working of an utterly unfamiliar language: the *Indian Grammar Begun*, a description of Natick, now usually called Wampanoag, an Algonquian language of Massachusetts, published in 1666 by the Puritan missionary John Eliot (1604–1690). Unlike most missionaries, who more or less assimilated the language of their flock without seeking to analyze it, Eliot "came at it" through a consistent research method.

I diligently marked *the difference of their Grammar* from *ours*; *when I* found the way of them, I would pursue a *word, a noun, a verb*, through all the variations I could think of. And thus I came at it. We must not sit and look for miracles; *Up, and be doing, and the Lord will be with thee*. (1666: 66)

This pursuit of a word through its variations allowed Eliot to produce "the first published attempt ... at a description of an 'exotic' language which can justifiably be called scientific" (Miner 1974: 170).

Bacon's experimental and inductive program was embodied in the Royal Society of London for the Improvement of Natural Knowledge, founded in 1660 by, among others, John Wallis. The Royal Society was the central focus of the rise of experimental science in the seventeenth century. Among the features that marked the interactions of the members, at least in their idealized picture of themselves, was a distinctive way of talking. A chapter of Thomas Sprat's *History of the Royal-Society*, published in 1667, is entitled "On the Language of the Members":

[The Members] have ... been most rigorous in putting in execution ... a constant resolution to reject all the amplifications, digressions, and swellings of style, to return back to the primitive purity and shortness, when men delivered so many *things* almost in an equal number of *words*. They have exacted from all their members a close, naked, natural way of speaking; positive expressions, clear senses, a native easiness bringing all things as near the mathematical plainness as they can; and preferring the language of artisans, countrymen, and merchants before that of wits or scholars. (in Vickers 1987: 170–2)

The concern here is not with propositions and the order of words as for the French theorists, but with single words and their better or worse reflection of things. Note the equivalence of words and things by *number*: strict one-to-one correspondence is offered, offhandedly, as an ideal.

If one reads the actual writings of members of the Royal Society, one in fact finds plenty of rhetoric. Some of their basic scientific arguments depend on the use of analogy and other tricks (Vickers 1987). But the point is an ideological one: this is a style that is meant to give the impression of simplicity, sobriety, and above all of transparency. Ideally, language must be made transparent so the world can show through.

A universal Character

If real languages are the problem, one solution would be to invent a new language that directly reflected not the total organization of knowledge, as Descartes had imagined, but the reality of the world. While this idea was widespread in the seventeenth century, it was among the British empiricists that it really took off. An extraordinary number of universal languages were proposed, in more or less detail, by people associated with the Royal Society, again mostly in the 1660s.[3]

The most ambitious and thorough of these schemes was carried out under the patronage of the Royal Society by its founder and first president, John Wilkins (1614–1672), Dean of Ripon and Bishop of Chester. Wilkins' system is constructed in such a way that each word contains its own definition – if you know the code. And the code was based on a general classification – of everything. The preliminary work for a philosophical language was to consider everything about which humans might have anything to say and categorize it. Wilkins spent decades, with the help of assistants, writing *everything* down on slips of paper and dividing the heaps of slips into categories.

Wilkins' system is described in his *Essay towards a Real Character and a Philosophical Language*, published in 1668. He presents his project as too great in scope for a single man to accomplish; after all, "those great wits of the *French* Academy" had been working for many years to produce their dictionary, "and yet that undertaking is (for ought I can understand) far enough from being finished." And in the French case the task was merely to record and stabilize the usage of arbitrary words. "Certainly then, the Design here proposed, ought not to be thought unworthy of … assistance; it being as much to be preferred before that, as *things* are better than *words*, as *real knowledge* is beyond *elegancy of speech*, as the *general good of mankind*, is beyond that of any *particular Countrey* or *Nation*" (1668, epistle dedicatory).

Wilkins divided things into forty genera; each was subdivided into differences, the differences into species, and so on down. The table of categories takes up over half of his large book. Since the system was first of all a Character, that is, a writing system, meant to be read in any country, each genus was assigned a simple visual mark. The differences were variations on the generic signs, the species variations on the differential signs, and so on down. Someone who knows the system can look at the complex squiggle thus produced and figure out its definition. In order that the Character might be spoken and not only written, toward the end of the book Wilkins assigns syllables, consonants, and vowels to the various categories.

The work here all seems to be done in the relationship between words and things, not in that among words. There is, to be sure, a chapter called "Syntax" (p. 354). Here Wilkins distinguishes between customary and figurative syntax, which allows inversions, and natural syntax, in which "That which governs should precede; The Nominative Case before the Verb, and the Accusative after; The Substantive before the Adjective." For the philosophical language, only the natural order will be used. And that is all; the rest of this chapter is, for some reason, about the length of vowels.

Each sign is its own definition: you can look at a sign or hear the equivalent set of sounds and by reconstructing the meaning according to the system know what it means. Fritz Mauthner said that children who learned the Character as their first language would later discover that it was "a universal key and a secret encyclopedia" (paraphrased in Borges 1942 [1984]).

This transparency of reference is the beauty and the failing of the system. It requires an acceptance of the validity of the classification and more generally of the world as we think we know it (as noted by Borges). An elephant in Wilkins' system is *zibi*: eighteenth genus, *zi*, beasts, first difference, *–b–*, that of Whole Footed Beasts, fourth species, *–i*, beasts "having little prominencies at the end of the foot." Wilkins notes that this is the greatest of all beasts, but his classification of the elephant is based on its toes. And what do you call a woolly mammoth if you should find one frozen in the ice, as someone would for the first time in 1806? Is it a *zibib*, a beast with an affinity for the elephant (as a comet, *dageg*, is something with an affinity for a planet, *dage*), or a *zibisla*, the opposite of an elephant through excess?

In a system such as Wilkins' every change in classification can imply hundreds or thousands of changes in vocabulary; it is the pigheaded opacity of natural language words that shores them up against shifts in knowledge.

Besides these rather grand problems, Wilkins' system was quite cumbersome and, as one might imagine, difficult to use. It was the subject of the following lines from the "Ballad of Gresham Colledge" (Stimson 1932: 115), which made fun of the whole Royal Society:

> A Doctor counted very able
> Designes that all Mankynd converse shall,
> Spite o' th' confusion made att Babell,

By Character call'd Universall.
How long this character will be learning,
That truly passeth my discerning.

The Newton–Locke consolidation: space, time, and the individual

Among those entertaining a universal language scheme in the 1660s was the young Isaac Newton (1643–1727) who, like so many others, was troubled by the diversity of tongues portraying a single world. His conclusion was that of his colleagues: the source for a universal language cannot be existing languages in their multiplicity, but must be the world itself.

The Dialects of each Laguage [*sic*] being soe divers & arbitrary A generall Language cannot bee so fitly deduced from them as from ye natures of things themselves wch is ye same to all Nations & by wch all Laguage was at ye first composed. (in Elliott 1957: 7)

Newton, a member of the Royal Society from 1672, its president from 1703 to his death, would soon abandon the language project and turn to "things themselves" more directly: his overall model of the physical world would remain canonical into the twentieth century. The system was laid out in the *Philosophiae naturalis principia mathematica*, published in 1687, then in his posthumous *System of the World*. One of the things that made Newton's model appealing on both sides of the Channel is that it represents a coherent picture of the world based on experiment, but interpreted through mathematics: it synthesizes experiment and reason, fulfilling both Bacon's desiderata and Descartes' dream.

Gaston Bachelard wrote, "We dwelt in the Newtonian world as in a spacious and well-lighted abode" (1934 [1984]: 44, translation modified). For most modern Western people, most of the time, when we are not actively trying to think about relativity or quantum physics, I would change his verb tense to the present: in our daily experience of the world, we are still living in the house Newton described. The architect's plan of that "abode" is laid out in a famous scholium in which Newton feels called upon to make explicit what he means by space, time, and motion (*Principia*, I, Scholium to the definitions):

I do not define time, space, place, and motion, as being well known to all. Only I must observe, that the common people (*vulgus*) conceive those quantities under no other notions but from the relation they bear to sensible objects. And thence arise certain prejudices, for the removing of which it will be convenient to distinguish them into absolute and relative, true and apparent, mathematical and common.

I. Absolute, true, and mathematical time, of itself, and from its own nature, flows equably (*aequabiliter fluit*) without relation to anything external … [R]elative, apparent, and common time, is some sensible and external … measure of duration by the means of motion, which is commonly used instead of true time; such as an hour, a day, a month, a year.

II. Absolute space, in its own nature, without relation to anything external, remains always similar and immovable. Relative space is some movable dimension or measure of the absolute spaces; which our senses determine by its position to bodies; and which is commonly taken for immovable space ...

IV. Absolute motion is the translation *(translatio)* of a body from one absolute place into another; and relative motion, the translation from one relative place into another ...

VI. As the order of the parts of time is immutable, so also is the order of the parts of space ... All things are placed in time as to order of succession; and in space as to order of situation. (Newton 1687 [1934]: 6–12)

These are our time and space, purely a matter of measure, not of content. They are what things happen inside.

Why did Newton feel he had to tell us what space, time, and motion were? It suggests that the Newtonian world is a construction now taken for granted by most modern Westerners but not necessarily by people in other societies, and that it may still not have been taken for granted by the seventeenth-century *vulgus*, who continued to live in a world of interrelated places and moments, not of absolute space and time.

In the realm of mind and language, the work that had the greatest impact on the next century was that of Newton's friend, the philosopher John Locke (1632–1704). Here I will give a general characterization and point up some important features of his work for the question of linguistic diversity.[4]

While Locke was elected a fellow of the Royal Society in 1668, he was a medical doctor and political philosopher, not a physical scientist, and he does not feel that what he has to say carries the same weight as does that of the explorers of the new sciences. Compared with these "Master-Builders," he presents himself as "employed as an under-labourer, clearing the ground a little, and removing some of the rubbish that lies in the way of knowledge" (Locke 1700 [1975]: 10). This rubbish, which interferes with a clear, i.e., unblocked view of the world, consists mainly of ways of thinking and ways of talking.

For Locke, far from being the locus of reason, the mind in itself is a *tabula rasa*, a blank slate, to be written on by experience. There are "No innate Principles in the Mind" (*Essay Concerning Human Understanding*, 1695, Chapter 1), only the capacity to learn through "the notice, that our Senses take of the constant Vicissitude of Things" (1700 [1975]: 324). While the mind has no initial content, it does have faculties for perception, for remembering what it has perceived, and for combining the ideas thus derived. Human understanding grows out of these straightforward processes.

Locke's presentation of space and time reproduces Newton's, but with more wonder expressed at the enormity of

those boundless oceans of Eternity and Immensity ... uniform infinite Oceans of Duration and Space .... Duration and Space being themselves uniform and boundless, the Order and Position of things, without such known setled Points, would be lost in them; and all things would lie jumbled in an incurable Confusion. (1700 [1975]: 198–9)

The free individual navigates within this empty enormity. Locke had at least as much impact as a political thinker as he did as a general philosopher, and is remembered as one of the founding fathers of liberal individualism.

Like Bacon, Locke saw language as a convenient way of communicating thoughts that already exist about things that already exist: *"the true end of Speech* ... is to be the easiest and shortest way of communicating our Notions" (1700 [1975]: 460). One advantage of language is to group the multitude of things we can experience in the world into a much smaller, and easier to handle, set of categories.

It is impossible that every particular Thing should have a distinct peculiar Name ... We may easily find a Reason, why Men have never attempted to give Names to each Sheep in their Flock, or Crow that flies over their Heads; much less to call every Leaf of Plants, or Grain of Sand that came in their way, by a peculiar Name ... The Number [of things we can meet with] must be infinite, and the Memory confounded with the Plenty, as well as overcharged to little purpose. (pp. 409, 432)

If there is no universal reason imposed on us by God, and if words are simply tools, then "every man has so inviolable a liberty to make Words stand for what Ideas he pleases that no one hath the Power to make others have the same ideas in their Minds, that he has, when they use the same Words, that he does" (p. 408). This means that meaning is problematic and requires deliberate work. While language is very useful, it is also very dangerous, both because of this inherent indeterminacy and because of the uncontrolled historical development of languages themselves.

[Words] interpose themselves so much between our Understandings, and the Truth, which it would contemplate and apprehend, that like the *Medium* through which visible Objects pass, their Obscurity and Disorder does not seldom cast a mist before our Eyes, and impose upon our Understandings. (p. 488)

This is a particularly clear formulation of the British empiricist understanding of what it means to be clear: it's to be free of mist. Might this be an instance of climatic determinism?

For Locke, then, as for Port-Royal, the specificities of given languages, and the differences among languages, were inherently problematic. But for Locke, a voracious reader of travel literature (Paxman 2003: 184–95), language diversity was a more serious problem than it was for the rationalists. The latter took translation to be a simple transfer of a universally understandable meaning from one external form to another; Locke, on the contrary, questioned the very possibility of full translation between languages:

A moderate skill in different Languages, will easily satisfie one ... [that it is] obvious to observe great store of Words in one Language, which have not any that answer them in another ... Nay, if we will look a little more nearly into this matter, and exactly compare different Languages, we shall find, that though they have Words, which in Translations and Dictionaries, are supposed to answer one another; yet there is scarce one of ten, amongst the names of complex *Ideas* ... that stand for the same precise *Idea*, which the Word does that in Dictionaries it is rendred by. (1700 [1975]: 432)

For Locke, this untranslatability is another proof of the general unreliability of words and the need to police them. But note where the problem, and presumably the possibility of a solution, lies: as for the whole empiricist tradition, language is here understood as a set of *words*, which can more or less adequately be made to match the world understood as a set of *things*. The idea that we should worry about how words are put together does not arise.

Two critiques of Whig linguistics

The model of language as set forth by members of the Royal Society reflected the concerns of the rising bourgeoisie: in its ruthless practicality, its assertion of the priority of things as they are, and in the purported absolute freedom of the individual subject, it echoed a wider Whig sensibility. Two of the most famous comic scenes in English-language literature are critiques of these assumptions, both by "Red Tory" Church of England authors who were sharply critical of modern industrial society and its values.

One critique of the ideology of words and things is found in *Gulliver's Travels* (1729) by the Church of Ireland dean Jonathan Swift (1667–1735). In Book III of the *Travels*, Gulliver visits the floating island of Laputa. Here there is a "grand Academy" for the investigation of the world, founded "about forty years" before Gulliver's visit in 1708. Given that "Words are only the Names for *Things*," its members were active with a "Scheme for entirely abolishing all Words whatsoever." Instead, everyone should carry about whatever Things they need to talk about and simply present them to each other. Not only would this language reform give a transparent and true picture of things; it would also provide "an universal Language to be understood in all civilized Nations." A deplorable resistance to this scheme has come, however, from the common people, and especially the women, "constant and irreconcileable enemies to Science," who do not appreciate the progress this improvement represented, and instead of, say, carrying cows (or woolly mammoths) around on their backs in the interest of truth and science, insist on continuing to "speak with their Tongues," and threaten rebellion (cf. Lewis 2007; on Swift's politics, see Montag 1994).

In the nineteenth century, the Oxford mathematician and Church of England deacon Charles Lutwidge Dodgson (1832–1898), aka Lewis Carroll, published two novels ostensibly recounting the dreams of a little girl. In the second, *Through the Looking-Glass* (1872), Alice meets a large egg named Humpty Dumpty (Chapter 6), who is sitting on a wall. Humpty Dumpty presents himself as the free individual who fully exploits his Locke-given liberty to decide the meaning of the words he uses. This requires, however, that his interlocutor, in this case the sane and stubborn Alice, must humbly beg clarification every time the egg wants to exercise his freedom of speech by inventing a new usage.

"There's glory for you!"
   "I don't know what you mean by 'glory,'" Alice said.
   Humpty Dumpty smiled contemptuously. "Of course you don't – till I tell you. I meant 'there's a nice knock-down argument for you!'"
   "But 'glory' doesn't mean 'a nice knock-down argument,'" Alice objected.
   "When *I* use a word," Humpty Dumpty said, in rather a scornful tone, "it means just what I choose it to mean – neither more nor less."
   "The question is," said Alice, "whether you *can* make words mean so many different things."
   "The question is," said Humpty Dumpty, "which is to be master – that's all."

Humpty Dumpty's freedom is that of the owner of capital, not that of his employees. At least he pays fairly:

"When I make a word do a lot of work ... I always pay it extra ... Ah, you should see 'em come round me of a Saturday night," Humpty Dumpty went on, wagging his head gravely from side to side, "for to get their wages, you know."

Here is the free modern individual as egomaniac, unable to conceive, or simply not caring, that his claim on freedom presumes the compliance of others. And we all know what happened to Humpty Dumpty.

Diversity

A purely rationalist–empiricist model does not account for our full experience as denizens of modernity. Seeking to explain decontextualized phenomena in terms of universal laws, it is singularly ill-equipped to account for our daily dealing with real difference, something that is lived most unavoidably in our experience of ourselves and other people: not as machines, and not as expressions of a universal reasoning mind, but as distinctive personalities. We feel that a person's looks, his or her acts, speech, attitude are expressions of a single unique essence. And this essence cannot be explained by dividing it into smaller pieces or performing experiments on it. It is, rather, something that we just know, that we grasp intuitively as a whole.

   Still today, then, there is a domain of our experience that demands a respect for uniqueness, not the application of universal laws; that presumes the presence of an essence which we must interpret, rather than explain; and for which our daily practice is to grasp a complex yet coherent whole intuitively. And this domain of human individualities is not the only one that is treated in this way: we experience nationalities, ethnicities, landscapes, and what we call works of art as expressions of mysterious essences, to be interpreted and appreciated rather than analyzed and explained.

This is a crucial distinction. For rationalism, empiricism, and their various combinations, there is one world of isolated facts that are to be explained through universal laws. For what I am calling essentialism, there are many worlds, each to be grasped as a whole, each to be interpreted as the manifold expression of a unique essence. *Both* of these have been part of daily human experience, as they have been strains in the explicit theorization of experience, at least since the seventeenth century.

At the same time that the British and French were discovering reason and the world, a defense of diversity was being constructed in Germany.

The discovery of German

In the seventeenth century, France and England were making what seemed like enormous progress in economic development and national integration. Looking on from their politically fractured territories, the speakers of German dialects could only feel that they were getting to the party late. Compared to the widespread claims for the clarity and rationality of French, for the usefulness of at least a reformed English, the early descriptions of German have a decidedly defensive tone. Reflecting this sense of urgency, the *Fruchtbringende Gesellschaft*, the Fruitbearing Society, was founded in 1617, well before the Académie Française, for the promotion and eventual unification of the German language.

The lauding of German for its distinctive qualities – rather than for its conformity to reason or its practicality – intensified through the seventeenth century. In 1641, Georg Philipp Harsdörffer, an active participant in the Fruitbearing Society, wrote that German

thunders with the heavens, flashes lightning with the quick moving clouds, radiates with the hail, whispers with the winds, foams with the waves, creaks with the locks, sounds with the air, explodes with the cannons; it roars like the lion, lows like the oxen, snarls like the bear ...

and on and on, including quacks like the duck and clucks like the hen (cited in Eco 1993 [1995]: 99). It's hard to imagine a seventeenth-century Frenchman boasting that his language is capable of clucking like a hen.

Less extreme, but along the same sensory lines, is the praise of German by Justus Georg Schottelius (1612–1676), "the most influential German grammarian of the 17th century" (Faust 1981: 359):

[W]e have as our own such a noble, magnificent language, rich in gentleness, rich in good things, full of thunder, full of lightning, full of laughing, full of weeping, full of quaking and roaring, full of gentle longing, virile ringing out, flowing sweetness. (in Sdun 1967: 20)

In his *Extensive Work on the German High Language* of 1663, Schottelius praises the unified sound of German, its purity, and its ability to touch the listener's heart. Schottelius defines the value of a language not through its word order – there is little on word order in the book (Faust 1981: 360) – but through its body of root words. The roots of German possess "a high degree of perfection" on the basis of five criteria, among which two are of particular interest: "(1) that the root words are made up out of their own natural letters and not of foreign ones; (2) that they have an appealing sound and fully express their object" (Faust 1981: 51). What matters the most here is the distinctiveness and integral authenticity of the materials of a language, its being most purely itself.

Already, then, we have three distinct linguistic ideologies for three modern vernaculars. For the French view, French was valuable because it best corresponded to the *clarté* of universal reason. For at least one important English view, English, while faulty, could be reformed to embody clarity in the sense of transparency and utility – and if it could not be reformed, it could be replaced with an invented language that let the world be seen without interfering fog. For the Germans, German takes on a specific density: with German, language becomes a material, not a mere medium for seeing with or seeing through. The metaphors are auditive and tactile; German has a sound, and what is more, a corporality, a weight.

These ideological stances, all put into canonical form in the 1660s, would continue to dominate discussions of language through the next century-and-a-half. German Romantics would come to praise the depth, darkness, and organic profundity of German, particularly against what they presented as the mechanical and superficial clarity of French.

This German linguistic chauvinism differs from both French and English chauvinism in a fundamental way. French *clarté* and English transparency are universal values. The body of the German language is not a universal value: it is distinctive to German, and it raises the idea that every language has its own specific corporality, its own opacity, its own unique essence.

Leibniz's dispersion: a world of worlds

Omne corpus est mens momentanea. (Leibniz, cited in Boutroux 1881: 42)

Car, comme tout est plein … (Leibniz, *Monadologie*, §61)

The first explicit theorist of essentialism, with all that it implies of a positive valuation of diversity, was the German philosopher, mathematician, historian, diplomat, and librarian Gottfried Wilhelm Leibniz (1648–1716).

Leibniz produced an enormous body of work, mostly unpublished until after his death, on "law, theology, mathematics, physics, engineering, etymology, economics, and geology, as well as philosophy" (Chapman 2005: 179), not to mention politics and something like computer science. The overarching theme in Leibniz's work is that of conciliation: his procedure is typically to identify two opposed sides of an argument and see whether he can find a way to unite them at some higher level – as in his diplomatic initiative to reconcile Protestant and Catholic countries by getting them together to attack Egypt (Stewart 2006, Chapter 5). The ultimate cosmopolitan, Leibniz published mostly in French and Latin, but he also contributed in important ways to the development of German.

Through the dispersion of Leibniz's writings, he lays out his whole system only twice, once at the beginning of his career and once at the end, in short treatises that would be published after his death.

The first version of the system, the *Discours de métaphysique*, was composed in 1685. Leibniz declares his dissatisfaction with both rationalism and empiricism. What we know directly is our own souls, and each of our souls is distinctive: on the model of souls, we should conceive a world not of two basic substances, matter and mind, as in Descartes, but of an infinite multiplicity of "singular substances" or "substantial forms." It's not clear how far Leibniz wants to go with this here, but certainly unique human individuals do represent such substances. From God's point of view, which Leibniz never hesitates to take, knowing a subject means knowing all of its predicates:

God, who sees the individual notion ... of Alexander, sees in it at the same time the foundation and the reason for all the predicates that can be truly said of him, such as, for example, that he would defeat Darius ... something which we can know only from history. And, moreover, if we consider carefully the connection of things, we can say that in the soul of Alexander there are for all time remnants (*des restes*) of everything that has happened to him, and marks of everything that will happen to him, and even traces of everything that happens in the universe, even though it only belongs to God to recognize all of these.

Then comes the punchline: the next section is entitled "That every singular substance expresses the whole universe in its own way ..." It reads:

Every substance is like a whole world and like a mirror of God, or indeed of the whole universe, which each one expresses in its own fashion, rather as the same city will be represented differently according to the different locations of the person who is looking at it. (1998: 60, translation modified)

By the time of the second statement of the complete system, the *Monadology*, composed in 1714, it is clear that this conception goes far beyond the merely human soul. The universe is composed of monads, atoms that are individual both in the sense of being indivisible and in that of being unique. "The *Monad* ... is nothing but a simple substance ... *simple*, meaning without parts" (p. 268). "[E]very Monad must be different from every other. Because in nature there are never two beings that are perfectly alike" (p. 269). A monad is complete unto itself: "Monads have no windows, through which something could come in or go out" (p. 268).

The world is not a machine (Boutroux 1881: 41), since all monads possess perception, force, and desire, although to different degrees. Change in monads occurs not because of bumping into other things, as in Descartes, or because of the action of forces such as Newton's gravity, but from their own motive force, an "internal principle" (Leibniz 1998: 269). And every monad is "a perpetual living mirror of the universe," aware, however obscurely, of everything in the world.

And just as the same city when seen from different sides will seem quite different (*tout autre*), and is at it were multiplied perspectivally; it happens in the same way that because of the infinite multitude of simple substances, it is as if there were as many different Universes, which are, however, only different perspectives on the one universe according to the different point of view of each Monad. (1998: 275)

Central to Leibniz's thinking is the analogy to literal point of view: being willing to move around at least virtually, on the one hand to imagine how things might look to God, on the other to perambulate the town and see that, since you are not God, it looks different depending on where you are. Leibniz appears to have been the first author to introduce the notion of point of view into philosophical discourse (Boutroux 1881: 170, n. 2).

Leibniz's universe of more or less conscious monads offers a direct challenge to Newton's universal spatiotemporal framework:

[For Leibniz] space and time ... are "relative," that is, relative to the things that are ordinarily said to be located within space and time. They are nothing outside of the things that are in them and owe their existence and their nature to the relations of order that come into being among things ... The fact that our universe has a particular kind of spatial and temporal structure is a contingent trait of this world. (Boutroux 1881: 88)

In histories of philosophy, Leibniz is often categorized as a rationalist and universalist (e.g., Cassirer 1923 [1953]), and he had a constant concern for what could be known about human thought in general. In the late 1660s and early 1670s Leibniz, who was in contact with the Royal Society – he became a member in 1673 – was working on his own version of a universal language or *ars characteristica*. With characteristic optimism, he felt that just as any number could be broken down and expressed as the product of primes, so it should be possible to convert any human idea into a combination of a small number of basic concepts. In a direct response to Descartes, Leibniz (1903: 27 ff.) proposed that the constitution of the new language did not need to wait for the completion of an analysis of all knowledge.[5]

The quest for a universal language was particularly acute for Leibniz because of his view of the relationship between words and thoughts. For both rationalists and empiricists, words are more or less adequate ways of externalizing already-existing ideas. For Leibniz, on the contrary, words and other symbols play a role in the elaboration of thought itself: "if there were no signs, we should never think or conclude anything intelligibly" (1677 [1951]). Locke had defined words as "marks for the ideas within [one's] own mind, whereby they might be made known to others, and the thoughts of men's minds be conveyed from one to another" (1700 [1975]: 402). Against this, in a paragraph-by-paragraph response to Locke's *Essay*, Leibniz argues that language "enables man to reason to himself" (1705 [1996]: 275).

Leibniz agreed with Locke on the problem of translatability. Already in one of his earlier pieces on German, he had challenged the transparency of translation: "I don't think that there is any language in the world that can render (*geben*) the words of another language with the same impact (*Nachdruck*) or even with a single word" (2000: 82–3) – note the addition, which seems characteristic, of the *effect* of language to simple questions of referential meaning. Where Locke had seen translation problems as showing how languages can mislead us, Leibniz takes a different tack, proposing, as Bacon had, a comparative grammar of different and distinctive languages:

[S]omeone who wanted to write a universal grammar would be well advised to move on from the essence of languages to their existence, and to compare the grammars of various languages. (1705 [1996]: 302)

Later in the text there is a linguistic confession of faith: "I really believe that languages are the best mirror of the human mind, and that a precise analysis of the significations of words would tell us more than anything else about the operations of the understanding" (1705 [1996]: 333). Note the plural here: not "language" as a general activity, but "languages" (*les langues*) in their diversity. A few pages later comes a passage that prefigures both historical linguistics and psycholinguistics:

Eventually every language in the universe will be recorded, and contained in dictionaries and grammars; and comparisons will be made amongst them. This will be extremely useful for the knowledge of things ... as well as for the knowledge of our mind and of the marvellous variety of its operations. (pp. 336–7)

Why, Leibniz asks in a piece from 1712, do different languages have different words? Because human beings, whose needs and circumstances differ, see things from different points of view and highlight different qualities (in Gensini 1990: 68).

In tracts promoting the use and development of German, Leibniz, like his predecessors, valorizes what makes the language distinctive and unique. He says that it would be an "eternal pity and shame" if "our good old German" should be lost as was Anglo-Saxon (in 1697; 2000: 50), presumably through too much foreign admixture. To save German we must discover its "inner kernel" (p. 56); this will allow us to maintain its "richness, purity, and brilliance" (*Reichtum, Reinigkeit und Glanz*; p. 80). This kind of vocabulary foreshadows the Romantics, and like them Leibniz says that the purest, richest language will be found not among the urban elite, but among peasants (2000: 58).

Jürgen Trabant (1990b: 144) sums up the place of languages in Leibniz's system: "To the pessimism of the myth of the Tower of Babel, which presents the diversity of languages as a curse, a punishment, and an obstacle, Leibniz opposes his optimism about multiplicity, his joy in the diversity of languages ... [which] is ... a linguistic reflection of the monadology. As the plurality of monads serves to reflect and multiply the universe, so the plurality of languages is a source of richness." As Sigrid von der Schulenberg (1973: 4–5) wrote, "To [Leibniz], diversity no longer appears as a curse from the days of the Tower of Babel. For him, the final purpose of linguistic diversity is not confusion but beauty, that of the enrichment of the world."

Conclusion

By the end of the seventeenth century, distinctive ideological and philosophical patterns had been established in France, Britain, and Germany. To a very large degree these were expressed in canonical form during what seems to have been the absolutely extraordinary decade of the 1660s. By this period, distinctive aspects of modern life, all of which are present by this time in Western European societies, had come to be thought of as differentially central for an understanding of the world: in France the human capacity to reason, which is *de tout pays*; in Britain the capacity to know the objective world through the senses, varying as to situation and circumstance, but always subject to the same natural laws and conditions of right perception; in Germany the uniqueness of each individual entity, most clearly the individual personality, but by implication, at least, each language and people.

Yet while rationalism and empiricism dominated French and British thinking respectively in the seventeenth century, there were minority currents developing in both countries. We have seen how close some of Bouhours' formulations were to earlier models of the genius of peoples and languages, and correspondingly to later Romantic models; and, as we will see in the next chapter, the Cartesian idea of the imagination led to increasing admiration for linguistic flexibility. In England, the prevailing empiricism was challenged by a revival of idealism in the work of the Cambridge Platonists starting in the 1670s. As for Germany, the full range of Leibniz's contribution did not become public until the second half of the eighteenth century, and there was no shortage of explicit rationalists, including, one could argue, Leibniz himself. And in all three countries there were important mystical, puritanical, and esoteric strains.

The eighteenth century would be marked by the development of these minority positions, the transmission of theoretical models across national and linguistic lines, and their battles.

3   The world at war with reason: Britain and France in the eighteenth century

Newton published his *Principia* in Latin, so it was immediately available on the Continent. Locke made sure a synopsis of his *Essay* was available in French; a full French translation followed in 1700. Much of the thinking of eighteenth-century France involved the discovery of British thinking or resistance to it. In the view of one French historian of philosophy (Bréhier 1938 [1993]: 275), "The masters of the eighteenth century are Newton and Locke."

In Britain, conversely, we see the acclimatization and increasing influence of rationalism and of an idealism with Renaissance roots. By mid-century, these together form the main alternative to the still dominant empiricism.

The eighteenth century was marked by intellectual war as much as it was by political revolution.

The word order wars

Word order became a fashionable and most lively issue in France between 1600 and 1800, reaching a climax around 1750. The stylistic consciousness of the age fastened on it as a testing ground for some of its most original ideas, in a unique convergence of grammatical, rhetorical, and logical criteria ... Almost everybody thought he had something to add in these debates. Every *philosophe* was somewht of a grammarian, and every grammarian thought of himself as a metaphysician. (Scaglione 1972: 222, 254)

By the end of the seventeenth century, there was a growing tendency in French philosophy to valorize the bodily part of the Cartesian dichotomy, and with it the complexities of sensation, emotion, and imagination, alongside the rigidity of reason. This tendency reacted against the idea that there was only one natural order. The new sympathy for inversion would gain impetus with the incorporation of Locke's ideas, but it was already underway among the Cartesians themselves.[1]

We can see the transformation in succeeding editions of the manual of rhetoric of the mathematician and Biblical scholar Bernard Lamy (1640–1715). The first edition, entitled *De l'art de parler*, a reference to the subtitle of the Port-Royal *Logic*, *l'art de bien penser*, appeared in 1675. Lamy defends the legitimacy of rhetoric, that is, the use of the tricks of emotional language to

persuade one's audience, playing on their bodily feelings and their imagin-
ations. Yet at the same time, he continues to support the priority of the natural
order of thought and grammar. He writes,

As for the order of words ... the natural light shows so clearly (*vivement*) what one
should do ... One cannot understand the meaning of a discourse if one does not first
know what it is about. The natural order thus requires that in any proposition the
noun that expresses the subject should be placed first, if there is an Adjective that this
Adjective follows it closely; that the attribute should be placed after the Verb, which
links the subject to the attribute. (1676: 33)

"This, on the whole, is the natural order, which one should normally follow;"
but he adds, "yet one can sometimes trouble it in a useful way" by using a non-
natural word order to persuasive effect.

The fourth edition of Lamy's book, published in 1701 and now bearing the
title *La Rhétorique*, takes a very different tack on the question of word order.
Under the same heading as above, "On the Order and Arrangement of Words,"
we now read:

It is not as easy as one thinks to say what is the natural order of the parts of speech
... Speech (*le discours*) is an image of what is present to the mind, and the mind ...
envisages a number of things all at once, among which it would consequently be difficult
to determine the place, the rank held by each, since the mind encompasses them all, and
sees them in a single glance (*regard*). The essential thing for arranging the terms of a
discourse is, therefore, that they be connected in such a way as to bring together and
express all at once the thought that we want to signify. Still, if we want to find some
succession of ideas in the mind, since one cannot understand the meaning of a discourse
... (Lamy 1712: 64)[2]

And he goes on as in the earlier editions – for a while. This edition, however,
continues with a comparison of French and ancient languages, which sees the
natural order as more of a necessity than a virtue:

We thus also see that peoples who express their thought without art are subject to this
order. The ancient Franks spoke as they thought. They sought no other order than that
in things themselves, and expressing them as they presented themselves to their minds,
they arranged their words as their thoughts happened to be disposed in their conception
[i.e., subject first, then adjective, then verb, etc.]... This order is natural, and it is one
of the advantages of our language not to stand for any deviation from it. It wants (*Elle
veut*) us to speak as we think ... The beauty of our language is that a discourse in French
cannot be beautiful unless each word reveals each idea one after the other in order. We
cannot bear it if one word is moved far from its place, if we have to wait to understand
what went before ... Our language ... is appropriate for dealing with the sciences, since
it does so with an admirable clarity, in which it is inferior to none ...

But now comes the "but":

But we must also admit that it is not so much a virtue as a necessity for our language to
follow the natural order; this is something it has in common with all languages whose

nouns have neither gender nor case. In a discourse it must show where to put the different parts of which it is composed ... [I]n our language ... it is only the order that distinguishes the one who acts and the one who is the subject [sic] of the action ... Without a given arrangement, the same words have a contrary meaning ...

The Latins and the Greeks are thus not obliged to subject themselves, as we are, to the natural order. We might even question the idea that this is a defect in their language ... When one speaks, one does not simply want to mark each idea one has in one's mind with an appropriate term; one has a conception that is like an image made up of a number of traits which come together for its expression. It would seem appropriate, then, to present this image as a whole, in order to consider all of its traits, connected as they are, in a single view. This is what happens in Latin: everything is connected, as things are connected in the mind. (Lamy 1712: 65–6)

These paragraphs show extraordinary prescience: first, a proto-relativist position on word order; second, a distinction between the simultaneity of complex thoughts and the necessarily linear order of speech, both of which would be central elements in the argument over the natural order that would rage through the eighteenth century.

In 1704 appeared the *Examen des préjugés vulgaires* of Father Claude Buffier (1661–1737), who could not have been farther from the chauvinism of his fellow Jesuit Bouhours. Among the propositions that Buffier argues for in this book are "That women are capable of all the sciences," "That savage peoples are at least as happy as polite ones," and "That every language and jargon that is spoken in the world is, in itself, of equal beauty". In this last dialogue, the fall guy, Timagène, is the mouthpiece for all the received wisdom about the superiority of French, even quoting Bouhours; he is corrected by his interlocutor Téandre, whose main quality seems to be breadth of perspective. Timagène sums up his whole attitude: "'When I hear a German speak, or an Englishman, or a Low Breton, I cannot prevent myself from feeling that these ways of speaking are shocking, and even ridiculous'" (Buffier 1732: col. 995). He goes on to justify his feelings in terms of French clarity:

"[I]t is easy to see that there is no language so clear as ours ... It follows a natural order in its expressions, which are arranged in the same way that ideas are arranged in the mind ... The more I think about it ... the more ... I am shocked by [the] reversal of ideas in most languages, and the more I am persuaded that all in all, French is preferable to them because of its distinctness (*netteté*)."

"You are always a bit too quick to take sides," replied Téandre ... "I'm afraid that the distinctness that we find in our language is not such a great advantage, nor that it should be the factor that allows us to place our language above others. I'd be relieved, at least, if you could tell me first whether you've seen people who know Italian, Latin, German, or English well, and who complain that they can't express themselves as distinctly in these languages as in French? Do we see them making mistakes because they can't understand each other?

"As for the arrangement of our expressions, which conforms, you say, to the arrangement of ideas in our minds, while this prerogative may sound impressive, it has little reality; for ideas appear all together in the mind to make up a proposition, or else they have no determinate meaning, and it is for this reason that even if they put the verb at the end of the sentence, the Latins conceive what they are saying no less quickly or clearly: there is nothing in all this but habit and a bit of imagination." (Buffier 1732: 1007–8)

As for the sounds of language, Téandre says that all languages sound beautiful to their speakers, and concludes, in a phrase that sounds like Boas two hundred years later, "What is true in all this? That they have their habits, and we have ours" (1732: col. 996).

When Buffier comes to write his own French grammar in 1709, he will maintain that a grammar is not a prescriptive manual for how one should speak, but a scientific description of norms that already exist in a speech community: "Languages were not made for Grammar, but Grammar for Languages" (1732: 3). And the place of universal reason in all this? In an extended analogy, Buffier compares language with fashion (*la mode*):

Since every language has its particular, and infinitely varied, ways of expressing these [universally necessary] things, we must regard languages as a mass of expressions which chance or fancy has established uniquely among a certain group of men, or a certain nation, in approximately the same way as we consider fashion. Fashion requires all nations to dress; each one does so through usages that should be seen as pure effects of fancy and chance ... Thus reason, strictly speaking, has nothing to do with a language, except to study it and teach it such as it is; or to invent a way to study and teach it such as it is.
  The proof of this is evident: it is that a language ... is nothing other than the way in which a certain number of men have unconsciously (*insensiblement*) agreed to express their thoughts to each other through speech. (1732: 3–4)

So every language deserves to have its own grammar, and the greatest error made by writers of grammars is to apply the system of one language to others:

Every language, to be properly learned, should have its own particular Grammar; and what makes so many bad Grammars is the wish to apply what is appropriate for one language to another, entirely different, language. (1732: 3)

I don't believe anyone would say anything this relativistic about languages until Wilhelm von Humboldt about a hundred years later.

While Buffier's relativity seems to be an extreme case, things were on the move in the new century. Locke's empiricism and liberalism and Newton's empirically-based mathematical picture of the world were coming to be adopted by progressive thinkers along with a revaluation of sensory experience. Defenders of the senses and the imagination argued that the slavish attachment to a single word order made French prose dry and sterile, and that where it was effective it was precisely because it varied its order. La Bruyère (1645–1696) said that "We are slaves to the construction," i.e., of the sentence (in Ricken 1984 [1994]: 114), and Fénelon (1651–1715) wrote:

Our language has been impoverished, dried out, and encumbered. It dares only to proceed according to the most scrupulous and uniform grammatical method: we always see the substantive noun coming along first, leading its adjective as if by the hand; the verb does not fail to walk along right behind, followed by an adverb that lets nothing squeeze in between the two of them, and the structure immediately calls for an accusative, which can never change its place. This is what excludes all suspension of the mind, all expectation, all surprise, all variety, and often all rich patterning. (1716: 71)

Against these arguments, which were repeated by a number of authors in the 1710s (Ricken 1978: 66–73; 1984 [1994]: 113–15), the literary theorist César Chesneau Du Marsais (1676–1756) defended the regularity of French. Du Marsais distinguished a fundamental construction from the possibility of figurative ones – the latter may be lovely, but they depend for their comprehensibility on the former, and can always be reinterpreted to fit the natural order. Du Marsais put this distinction into practice in his own 1722 manual for learning Latin, in which he reorganized Latin sentences into the "natural order" of French, and only then, once the student had grasped the sense of the sentence, put it back into the "scrambled" word order of the Latin original. Criticized for simply Frenchifying Latin, Du Marsais replied, "You say that I turn Latin into French; I deny it: I simply reduce Latin to the natural order, which is of every country" (in Ricken 1978: 87). Note the repetition of Le Laboureur's phrase, *de tout pays* (discussed in Ricken 1978: 88). As Du Marsais would put it later, all he was doing was "[t]eaching Latin by reestablishing the logical order of Latin sentences which departed from that order because they were ruled by the imagination and the passions" (in Hagège 1986: 212–13).

Du Marsais' distinction of two styles or levels of word order allowed him to collect and classify deviations from the underlying pattern and propound a theory of the effectiveness of figures of speech (1730), which continues to be the most important source for subsequent Western tropologies. Today when Du Marsais' name is mentioned, it is usually as the master of the analysis of figurative language.

In the case of the Jesuit father Joseph-François Lafitau (1681–1746), we have an attempt to describe a language totally unlike French while still paying lip service to the universal order of reason. Lafitau did missionary work in New France, learning good Mohawk and Huron. In 1724 he published a book showing parallels between Iroquoian religion, politics, and customs and those of the ancient world (Lafitau 1724). Lafitau gives little information on the structure of the languages – but what he does give is remarkable. He starts in good rationalist form:

St Isidore of Seville says that Aristotle was the first to distinguish two parts of speech in language, that is, the noun and the verb ... Of the two parts of speech ... the Huron and Iroquois Languages, which are the ones I will be talking about here, since I do not know the others, have only the verb, which dominates the entire language ...

[I]t is necessary ... for the communication of our ideas, which are approximately the same in all men, and which everywhere have the same objects ... that every language

have like ours ... [nouns, adjectives, pronouns, verbs, and so forth] ... or else there must
be an equivalent that can furnish all the signs necessary to make up for the absence of
these different parts of speech ...

The Huron and Iroquois languages have, strictly speaking, only verbs, which make up
the basis of the whole language, such that everything conjugates and nothing declines;
but in these verbs is found an admirable artifice which compensates for all the rest; and
it is this artifice that makes up the whole economy of these Languages, which have their
beauties as do ours. (1724: II, 486–8)

In a passage to break a linguist's heart, Lafitau then says that he would have
liked to give a better idea of one or the other of these Languages, but upon
reflection he decided that he would either have to offer a shortened version that
would not do the language justice, or else go on at such length that he would
become tiresome (*ennuyeux*), since he would have to use

a multitude of barbarous terms, which would be disagreeable to the Public, who are little touched by these foreign Languages, from which even Scholars can draw little light,
and which would only have the effect of showing that these Languages are very distant
from those we know; that they are rich in spite of the defectiveness that is attributed to
them, and that even if they have an economy different from that of our languages, they
do not for all that lack great beauties. (1724: II, 489)

And then we move to the conclusion. But we have in Lafitau a statement that
languages can work perfectly well while violating the rules of natural reason.

Ideas about the nature of language and thinking are never very far from politics. The theory of the reasonableness and clarity of French had arisen as part of
a strengthening of the French state. From the mid-eighteenth century, the word
order wars heated up even as the political crisis deepened and led to revolution.
Attacks on the natural order were grounded in a sensualism closely allied with
Locke's bourgeois-democratic liberalism, and were often taken as attacks on
Church and State; conversely, critiques of Church and State often took the form
of discussions of language. From mid-century, the debate on word order pitted
rationalists, who were generally supporters of the monarchy and who insisted
on the superiority of the "natural order," against neo-empiricists and sentimen-
talists such as Condillac, Diderot, and Rousseau (the three of them used to dine
together once a week; Ricken 1978: 120), reformers and revolutionaries, who
maintained that word order should be flexible to reflect the multiplicity of situations the world presents, and who pointed out the ways in which French does
in fact allow a choice of orders of words. Representatives of both sides wrote
articles on language for Diderot and d'Alembert's *Encyclopédie* (published
from 1751).

It was the sensualist philosophy of the abbot Etienne Bonnot de Condillac
(1715–1780) that offered critics of the "natural order" a philosophical under-
pinning comparable to that which Descartes' rationalism had provided for its
supporters. For Condillac, an admirer of Locke, there are no innate ideas, and

all knowledge grows out of sense impressions. Condillac offered one of the first stage theories of human development: earlier humans were entirely controlled by their senses; the human mind learned only gradually to abstract. This doctrine had to include language, since Condillac, like Leibniz, held that signs, including linguistic signs, are not merely ways of externalizing already-existing ideas, but are a necessary part of human ideation, in particular of memory. In the *Essay on the Origin of Human Knowledge* (first edition 1746), Condillac mocks both Locke and Descartes for imagining a kind of thought that pre-exists any kind of symbolization:

This is what prevented Locke from seeing how necessary signs are for the operations of the soul. He imagines that the mind makes mental propositions in which it joins or separates ideas without the intervention of words ... As for the Cartesians ... they were as far removed as one can possibly be from making this discovery [of the dependence of thought on signs]. How can anyone suspect the necessity of signs if with Descartes he believes that ideas are innate ... ? (1749 [2001]: 91, translation modified)

On this point, Condillac cites the German philosopher Christian Wolff: "Monsieur Wolff has observed that it would be very difficult for reason to operate in a person who does not have the use of instituted signs." Wolff, whom we will discuss in the next chapter, is here maintaining the position of Leibniz.[3]

Condillac's doctrine of developmental stages has thought and languages going through the same progression: a modern language like French, with its rigid syntax, is more abstract than a language like Latin, which is free to foreground what strikes the speaker as most important. But this does not mean that French is better than Latin: since sensory experience and the imagination are as important as reasoning, the strict order of French is a limitation; Condillac, like Fénelon, called for more flexibility to allow greater responsiveness to the diversity of experience and the complexity of ideas.

We flatter ourselves that French has the advantage over the ancient languages of arranging words in our discourse as ideas arrange themselves in the mind ... [But] what is here called natural necessarily varies with the genius of the languages, and in some it covers more (*se trouve plus étendu*) than it does in others. Latin is our evidence; it unites constructions that are the opposites of each other, and which nevertheless seem equally in conformity with the arrangement of ideas ...

On what is the opinion based of those people who claim that in [a] proposition ... the French construction alone would be natural? Whether they consider the matter in light of the operations of the soul, or in light of the ideas, they must recognize that they are caught in a preconception ... [Of] the two Latin constructions ... one is as natural as the other. The mistake we make is that we take as the more natural one an order that is nothing but a habit that the character of our language has caused us to develop ...

For my part, it seems to me that the advantages of the two languages are so different that one can hardly compare them. (Condillac 1749 [2001]: 173–4, 177, translation modified)

Ideas, says Condillac, are non-linear, their many aspects bearing manifold relations to each other: to speak, on the other hand, you have to line elements up in some kind of order. The best order will be found not by obeying pre-given rules but by finding the sequence that most clearly reveals the relationships among the ideas. This echoes, of course, what Lamy and Buffier had been saying some forty years earlier.

In a discussion of the "genius of languages," Condillac writes:

Just as the government influences the character of nations (*peuples*), so the character of nations influences that of languages ... [E]verything confirms that the language of each nation expresses the character of the people who speak it ... I wonder if it is not natural for each nation to combine its ideas according to its own genius ... [C]ombinations authorized by long usage are truly what constitutes the genius of a language. (1749 [2001]185, 193–4, translation modified)

Passages such as these have led some authors (e.g., Aarsleff 1988) to see Condillac as the source of the idea of linguistic relativity. But in Condillac such statements remain isolated: his real interest is not in particular languages, but in language as such as a necessary tool for thought, a tool that has been perfected through stages (cf. Trabant 1986, Chapter 5). This is very different from the delight in diversity and the identification of language with nation and culture that are central themes in Humboldt and the Romantics.

One of the strongest attacks on the natural order came from the priest-rhetorician Charles Batteux (1713–1780), who in his *Letters on the French Sentence in Comparison with the Latin* offered a thoroughly sensualist theory of word order, saying that the "metaphysical" French word order is only a result of habit and that the truly natural, or practical, order would follow the order of importance of the ideas being expressed (Ricken 1978: 111–17). Here he compares the freedom of a Latin speaker, who, upon sighting a serpent, can put the crucially important object first and cry "*Serpentem fuge!*" with the French order, "Run away! A snake!," which is truly an inverted order. "Here is a species of inversion that we may not have suspected" (Batteux 1748: 17).

In his 1751 "Letter on the Deaf and Dumb," addressed to Batteux, Denis Diderot (1713–1784), seeks to show "how complicated is this question of inversions." Diderot plays with the arguments for both sides of the word order debate with characteristic adroitness, tossing and turning them, as it were, and putting all of them in question (Hobson 1976; Ricken 1978: 120–30). Diderot picks up Batteux's example of the serpent, but argues that there is no natural necessity for putting the snake before the verb: this will depend on the attitude of the speaker, and whether his or her primary fear is of the snake or for my welfare: "One is overwhelmed by terror, the other gives me warning" (Diderot 1916: 181). Diderot concurs that French word order is more sober and better for the sciences, while freer word orders are better for poetry. But the French word order is not natural: in an endorsement of Condillac's stage theory, and in a critique of Batteux's lack of any historical dimension, Diderot sees the fixed word order of French as a relatively late development, with nothing natural about it.

Diderot's linking of the word order debate to what can be learned from the deaf seems prescient. The question was whether thinking occurs as a chain of elements following a necessary order, or whether thinking is a complex, simultaneous activity that can be rendered linguistically in many different orders. As I mentioned at the beginning of this book, deaf sign languages show a great deal of simultaneous morphology, giving at least some support to the old arguments, from Lamy and Buffier to Condillac and Diderot, for the non-linearity of thought and the legitimacy of "inversions."

Condillac and Diderot's defense of inversions and their use of stage theory have a critical role: the rigidly ordered Old Regime seems an anachronism, implicitly at least worthy of overthrow.

Provoked by these sensualist attacks, proponents of the natural order of French, led once again by Du Marsais, launched a "rationalist counter-attack" (Ricken 1978: 131). In his 1754 article on "Construction" for the *Encyclopédie*, Du Marsais replied to Condillac that even in pure thought there must be a hierarchy among the various ideas in a proposition, which can be reflected better in some sentence structures than in others. After Du Marsais' death in 1756, his position was extended and reinforced by Nicolas Beauzée (1717–1789), starting in his 1765 *Encyclopédie* article on "Inversion." Beauzée distinguishes the analytic order of words, which is universal and belongs to general grammatical science, from the characteristics of any particular language, giving priority to the former. Echoing Le Laboureur and Du Marsais, he concludes that "the immutability of the original [design of thought] prescribes invariable rules for a [linguistic] copy of it, rules which are consequently available to all men without distinction of times, climates, or languages: reason is of all times, of all climates, and of all languages" (in Ricken 1978: 149).

The main sensualist riposte would come from Batteux in a series of books defending the naturalness of free word order and excoriating "the prejudice about inversion" (1748). In these later writings, Batteux incorporates Diderot's developmental view of language, and he adds a theory of the history not only of languages, but of *theories* about language: "It did not take long for grammarians, who had only made their rules on the basis of a language that had been created and established before they came along, to convince themselves that their rules were Nature herself who had presided over the formation of languages" (1748: 154).

So the debate went on – a debate conducted primarily in French, still the dominant intellectual language of continental Europe. In 1783, the Berlin Academy, an institution founded by the Francophile King Frederick the Great, offered a prize for the best essay on this universality of the French language. It was won by Antoine, (apparently self-styled) Comte de Rivarol (1753–1801) for a splendid rehashing of the old rationalist arguments offered with something like Romantic fervor.

What distinguishes our Language from ancient and modern languages is the order and construction of the sentence. This order must always be direct and necessarily clear. French first names the *subject* of speech, then the *verb*, which is the action, and at the end the *object* of this action: behold the Logic that is natural to all men; behold what constitutes common sense (*le bon sens*). Now this order, so favorable, so necessary for reasoning, is almost always contrary to the sensations, which first name the object that strikes them first; this is why all Peoples, abandoning the direct order, have had recourse to more or less bold turns of phrase, as demanded by their sensations or the harmony of the words; and inversion prevailed upon the earth, because man is more imperiously ruled by the passions than by reason.

In a footnote, Rivarol recognizes the validity of such inversions in poetry and in certain situations: he actually agrees with Batteux that the Latin "*serpentem fuge*", which would have the addressee running at the first word, is preferable to what a "French grammarian" would have you say: "'Sir, take care, there is a serpent that is approaching,' and the serpent would be at you before it is named."

French, by a unique privilege, has alone remained faithful to the direct order, as if it were all reason [Note that *le français* here, meaning the French language, is masculine, and homonymous with *le Français*, the Frenchman] ... It is in vain that the passions upset us and solicit us to follow the order of sensations; the syntax of French is incorruptible. This is the source of that admirable clarity, the eternal foundation of our Language: what is not clear is not French; what is not clear is still English, Italian, Greek, or Latin. To learn inverting languages, it is enough to know the words and their paradigms; to learn the French language, one must also master the arrangement of words. One might say that it is out of a perfectly simple Geometry, that of the simple straight line, that the French language was formed; and that it was curves and their infinite varieties that presided over the Greek and Latin languages. Ours rules and directs thought; these hurl themselves forward and get lost, along with thought, in the labyrinth of sensations, and follow all the caprices of harmony; they were thus marvellous for Oracles, which our language would have repudiated absolutely. (Rivarol 1784: 48–9)

Rivarol's text was attacked by representatives of progressive and revolutionary circles. Hostile reviews appeared by Dominique-Joseph Garat (1749–1833), who in later years would serve as Minister of Justice of the revolutionary government, and by Urbain Domergue (1745–1810), future *grammairien-patriote*, who would identify revolutionary freedom with a free word order. Garat says that where "inverting languages," thanks to their inflections, have twenty ways to express an idea clearly, "direct-order languages" have only one way to express an idea clearly and twenty ways to be obscure (1785: 31). Domergue mocks Rivarol and his rigidity. He repeats the serpent example and chastises Rivarol for attributing dangerously long-winded phraseology to the French (in fact Rivarol had only referred to "the French grammarian"):

What … is the direct order? It is certainly not the successive arrangement of the subject of the proposition, then verb, then object; it is, rather, the arrangement of ideas in the order in which the mind presents them. When I see a snake … the snake being the first thing that my eyes bring to my mind, I follow the direct order, no matter what language I am speaking, if the word "snake" comes first in my proposition.

Whether I cry out in Latin, "*Serpentem fuge!*" or in French, "A snake! Run!" (*Un serpent! Fuyez!*), I am in both cases being faithful to the direct order, and woe to the cold and absurd language that would have you say "Sir, take care, there is a serpent that is approaching!"… Yet this is how the author has Frenchmen talk, this is what he calls the direct order. (Domergue 1785: 886–7)

Come the Revolution, Garat and Domergue found themselves in positions of power, Rivarol in exile. For a time, Condillac would be an intellectual hero. With the Restoration, we once more return to the debate over word order. For the reactionary political theorists Louis Gabriel de Bonald (1754–1840) and Joseph de Maistre (1753–1840) it was the corruption of the direct order of language, as much as anything else, that had led to the horrors of the Revolution.

A language will be more or less analogical [i.e., in conformity with the natural order] depending on whether society obeys more or less natural laws. We have seen how in the storms of the revolution, the French language itself lost its natural quality, and forced inversions, barbarous constructions took the place of its beautiful and noble regularity …

Who was to blame? "That detestable Condillac … The guiltiest of modern traitors," wrote de Maistre in a letter to Bonald (in Ricken 1978:77).

The debate dissipates after this: but during the early part of the twentieth century, French schoolchildren were still being taught that French is the language of *clarté* because it respects the natural order of thought (Maingueneau 1979: 241–60; Haroche and Maingueneau 1985).

For almost three hundred and fifty years, French thinkers worried about the order of words in the sentence. Meanwhile, on the other side of the Channel, British thinkers were worrying about words themselves and whether they fit the world.

Word wars

Just as the eighteenth century saw a strong empiricist influence arriving in France, so it saw the development of a formal rationalism in Britain. The great eighteenth-century British works on language made war over the relative role of innate ideas versus experience of the world (Scaglione 1972: 319–36).

The conversations that led to the composition of Locke's *Essay* had taken place at the home of his patron, the first Earl of Shaftesbury. Locke served as tutor to the earl's grandson, Anthony Ashley Cooper (1671–1713), who would become the third Earl and one of the great philosophers of aesthetics. This third Shaftesbury was strongly influenced by the Cambridge Platonists, a school that rejected the *tabula rasa* view of the mind, insisted on the innateness of reason (which they called "the candle of the Lord," an image close to that of French *clarté*), and held that the perceived universe was an expression of underlying ideal forms. Shaftesbury would develop a view of artistic creation as a revelation of forms that can only be grasped as wholes. As Cassirer (1923 [1953]: 143) sums up his theory:

What the study of every natural organism reveals to us, becomes irrefutable certainty as soon as we consider our own self, the unity of our consciousness: namely, that truly self-subsistent being does not take its form from its parts, but is and operates as a formed whole prior to any division. In his self, each one of us can immediately apprehend an individual principle of form, his own characteristic "*genius*."

Shaftesbury's nephew James Harris (1709–1780) would propose a theory of language based on these ideas in his 1751 *Hermes*. In a letter to his friend Lord Monboddo, Harris complained that the empiricist domination of British thought had "transferred the whole of philosophy from the head to the hands. That is to say from Syllogism and Theory to Air Pumps and the Electric Apparatus" (in Bergheaud 1990: 39). Harris sees language as reflecting a deeper reality than that of sense experiences, a realm of relational ideas that are innate in the human mind. This order is realized in all languages as four classes of words (noun, verb, etc.), and this gives Harris a basis for proposing his own universal grammar.

Harris finishes his book with a discussion of the genius of languages, in each case linked to a kind of political regime:

Nations, like single Men, have their *peculiar* Ideas ... these *peculiar* Ideas become THE GENIUS OF THEIR LANGUAGE ... [T]he *wisest* Nations, having the *most* and *best Ideas,* will consequently have the *best* and *most copious Languages ...*

WE BRITONS in our time have been remarkable borrowers, as our *multiform* Language may sufficiently shew ... Yet we have this advantage to compensate the defect, that what we want in *Elegance,* we gain in *Copiousness,* in which last respect few Languages will be found superior to our own ...

The Eastern World, from the earliest days, has been at all times the Seat of enormous Monarchy. On them fair Liberty never shed its genial influence ... Such was their Condition, and what was the consequence ? – Their Ideas became consonant to their servile State, and their Words became consonant to their servile Ideas ... Nothing was either great or little in moderation, but every Sentiment was heightened by incredible Hyperbole. Thus tho' they sometimes ascended into *the Great* and *Magnificent*, they as frequently degenerated into the *Tumid* and *Bombast* ...

And what sort of People may we pronounce the ROMANS ? – A Nation engaged in wars and commotions ... Hence therefore their LANGUAGE became, *like their*

Ideas, copious in all Terms expressive of things *political*, and well adapted to the purposes both of *History* and *popular Eloquence*. – But what was their *Philosophy?* – As a Nation, 'twas none, if we may credit their ablest Writers. And hence the Unfitness of their Language to this Subject. (Harris 1751: 407–11)

For Harris the high point of world civilization had been achieved by the Greeks:

The GRECIAN COMMONWEALTHS, while they maintained their Liberty, were the most heroic Confederacy, that ever existed. They were the politest, the bravest, and the wisest of men ... one can hardly help considering THAT GOLDEN PERIOD, as a Providential Event in honour of human Nature, to shew to what perfection the Species might ascend.
   NOW THE LANGUAGE OF THESE GREEKS was truly like themselves; 'twas conformable to their transcendent and universal Genius. Where Matter so abounded, Words followed of course, and those exquisite in every kind, as the Ideas for which they stood. And hence it followed, there was not a Subject to be found, which could not with propriety be expressed in *Greek*. (pp. 415–20)

Even in illustrating his own brand of rationalism, Harris's interest remains fixed on words rather than on how they are put together; and even in his proposal of a variety of geniuses of languages, his focus is on word choice and surface style, not, as will be the case in Germany, on their differing characters.

Harris's friend the Scottish judge James Burnett, Lord Monboddo (1714–1799), was thinking along similar lines when he visited Paris in the 1760s and consulted grammars of American languages in French collections. This exposure to the languages of savages provoked Monboddo to come up with a proto-evolutionist theory of the development of language by which he proposed, as he wrote to Harris, "showing the origin and progress of this most wonderful of all the arts of man, the art of speech, a work which would not make a bad second part ... to your 'Hermes'" (cited in Bergheaud 1990: 43). The first volume of Monboddo's book, duly entitled *Of the Origin and Progress of Language*, appeared in 1773.

A key source for Monboddo was the description of the Huron language by the Recollet missionary Gabriel Sagard (d. 1636). Whether it was accident or predilection that led Monboddo to Sagard, it was a choice that was heavy with consequences. Other, more easily available, grammars of Huron gave an idea of the structural complexity of the language – or Monboddo could have turned to Lafitau. Brother Gabriel, on the contrary, is notorious for his self-proclaimed poor knowledge of Huron and his low opinion of the language (Hanzeli 1969: 56–62). Following Sagard, Monboddo sees Huron as "more imperfect, and therefore nearer to the origin of the art, than any language, so far as I know, that has hitherto been discovered" (Burnett 1773: 322–3).

For Monboddo, ideas precede words, and thought gradually developed through stages. Languages provide the best material for understanding this development, "for as there is a necessary connection betwixt thinking and speaking, we trace there the progress of the human mind in its state of infancy" (1773: 348).

Monboddo distinguishes three stages in the history of language. The earliest humans did not speak, but uttered cries. The living example of this stage is a nation of wild men called Ouran Outangs.

They are exactly of the human form ... they live in society; they make huts ... and they carry off negroe girls, whom they make slaves of, and use both for work and pleasure ... But though ... it appears certain, that they are of our species, and though they have made some progress in the arts of life, they have not come the length of language ... I myself saw at Paris one of them, whose skin was stuffed, standing upon a shelf in the King's cabinet of natural curiosities. He had exactly the shape and features of a man; and particularly I was informed, that he had organs of pronunciation as perfect as we have. He lived several years at Versailles, and died by drinking spirits. He had as much of the understanding of a man as could be expected from his education, and performed many little offices for the lady with whom he lived; but never learned to speak. (Burnett 1773: 174–6)

With the gradual development of thought came that of "barbarous languages." Such languages must have a huge mass of words, since savage people cannot be expected to abstract general categories from particular experience. Since they are so numerous, these words will have to be very long so that they can be differentiated. Savage languages will have no adjectives, since their speakers will be incapable of distinguishing qualities from the things that have these qualities (p. 352).

Of the savage languages of the world, "[t]he Huron is the rudest and most imperfect" (p. 364). And Sagard's Huron certainly fits the theory. It has no derivation or composition and therefore has

not attained to that art by which a language is connected together ... The consequence of which is, that if their sphere of life were not very narrow, there would be such a multiplicity of words entirely different from one another, that the memory would be overburdened, and the language become too bulky and cumbersome for use ...

There is no such thing in the language as a quality expressed without the particular substance in which it is inherent: for there is not in the whole language one adjective ... far less have they abstract nouns ...

There is not in the Huron language ... so far as I can discover, any word denoting a higher genus, such as animal or vegetable, and far less matter, space, being, or such like metaphysical entities. This is ... true of all barbarous languages without exception ...

Lastly, With respect to syntax, they appear to have none at all ... These savages therefore, though they have invented words, use them as our children do when they begin to speak, without connecting them together. (Burnett 1773: 363–8)

This last point is a reversal of Cordemoy's, for whom children's language provided evidence of a natural and primordial syntax based on the universal order of thought.

With civilization, writes Monboddo, came givers of law and "artificers of language"; "languages of art" possess, for instance, pure relational terms missing in savage languages. The most highly artistic of all languages was achieved, as we might expect, by the Greeks, whose inflected language was superior to modern European ones, forced as they are to use mere word order to bind sentences together. In fact, while discussing the absence of syntax in Huron, Monboddo admits that

[i]t would seem however, that persons may make themselves understood without syntax. This I think can be done no other way but by the arrangement of the words (which is a considerable part of the syntax in modern languages that have no cases). (p. 370)

But everything happens in stages, and Monboddo recognizes that some savage languages are less savage than others. Even Huron is not entirely primeval, and there are other barbarous languages out there that appear to be highly artificial, to use Monboddo's word. One such conundrum is Albinaquois, i.e., Abenaki, an Algonquian language that was described to Monboddo by one Father Roubaud, a former Jesuit missionary in New France.[4] Roubaud seems to have given Monboddo a pretty good picture of the grammatical complexity of Algonquian languages, according to him the Greek and Latin of the New World. Roubaud described them as structured and elegant – they have conjugations and declensions and even decline their verbs! Monboddo writes:

As to inflection, they have more of it than any other language I have heard of. For not only in that way do they form the cases of their nouns and the tenses of their verbs, but they form verbs expressing so many different modifications of the action, that it is difficult to ascertain the number and variety of them ... By this variety of expression, the forms of their verbs become almost infinite ...

[Roubaud] assured me ... that this almost infinite variety of their verbs was all according to the exactest rule and strictest analogy, without those irregularities and anomalies to be observed even in our learned languages ... [I]f you once know the rules by which those different verbs are formed, you may form as many of them as you have occasion for with great facility. (pp. 387, 391)

At this point Monboddo really should throw up his hands and admit that by his own criteria Abenaki is superior to Latin, maybe even to Greek, and easily to English or French. But instead he switches analogies.

From this account ... I am disposed to conjecture, that in the progress of language ... there has been invented a language too artificial ... before a language of complete art was formed, which is always as simple as the nature of the thing will permit ... Before the art was complete, there was an intermediate stage of a language, too intricate and complex in its structure. And in this respect I imagine the invention of language resembles the invention of machines. At first a machine is contrived very clumsy, and answering very ill the purpose for which it is intended; then art falls to work with it, and makes it better; but so complex, and with so many springs and movements, that it is not easily used. But art ... at last devises a way of simplifying the machine, and making it perform its operations with as few powers and movements as possible: and this is what I call the perfection of art. To this perfection the language of the Albinaquois is not yet arrived: but I cannot doubt, that if the Albinaquois were to cultivate arts and sciences as much as the antient Greeks did, and among other arts the art of language, they would come at last to simplify their language, and make it perhaps as perfect as the Greek. (pp. 393–4)

Between them, Harris and Monboddo launched a powerful attack against empiricist theories of knowledge, using languages to prove their point. The leading exponent of what we might call an empiricist counter-attack was the radical political activist John Horne Tooke (1736–1812), a defender of the rights of man, who was imprisoned in 1777 for too vocal support of the American Revolution and tried for treason in 1794 for his defense of the French one. Horne Tooke thought Locke was too soft. He believed that there were, in the end, no such things as ideas: we have sensations, we apply words to them, we manipulate the words and call it thought.

In 1786 Horne Tooke published *Epea pteroenta, or, The Diversions of Purley*, a book of dialogues among a group of friends meeting at a country house.[5] The evident target of the *Diversions* is Harris, whom Horne Tooke "roasts" (Salus 1976: 93). Harris had entitled his universal grammar *Hermes*, the Greek name for the Egyptian god Thoth, the inventer of language. Horne Tooke recalls, rather, the myth of Hermes and the hundred-eyed Argus, whom the god charmed to sleep and then slew. Horne Tooke sees in this an image of language leading philosophy astray:

Hermes, you know, put out the eyes of Argus: and I suspect that he has likewise blinded philosophy … If therefore Philosophy herself has been misled by Language, how shall she teach us to detect his tricks? (1798:15)

Horne Tooke uses the standard empiricist analogy of clearing away the trash that traditional learning has piled up between us and the truth. The philosophers of universal grammar, he says, have left the true nature of language "in thick darkness."

Yet, I suppose, a man of plain common sense may obtain it, if he will dig for it; but I cannot think that what is commonly called Learning, is the mine in which it will be found. Truth, in my opinion, has been improperly imagined at the bottom of a well: it lies much nearer to the surface; though buried indeed at present under mountains of learned rubbish. (1798: 10–11; cf. Aarsleff 1967: 45)

What is language for? To communicate our thoughts, as everyone has said. But there is a second requirement for language: "to do it with dispatch" (p. 27). What the rationalists call relational words are in fact shorter signs that replace whole phrases that say things concretely. Apparently purely grammatical, that is, relational elements, the cases, tenses, genders, and all the particles that were the rationalists' delight, are merely abbreviations for concrete nouns and verbs.

They allow language to go faster. "Abbreviations are the *wheels* of language, the *wings* of Mercury. And though we might be dragged along without them, it would be with much difficulty, very heavily and tediously" (p. 25). After all, the title of Horne Tooke's book is a formula from Homer that means "winged words" – and Hermes wears winged sandals.

[M]any words are merely *abbreviations* employed for dispatch, and are the signs of other words ... [T]hese are the artificial wings of Mercury, by means of which the Argus eyes of philosophy have been cheated. (p. 27)

This renewed and reinforced empiricism comes from the first part of the book. But the vastly larger part of the *Diversions* is devoted to actual etymologies, some two thousand of them, mostly of English words. Horne Tooke tries to show concretely, over and over and over again, how apparently purely relational and abstract terms are derived by abbreviation from perfectly concrete and sensual originals. The task of etymology is to restore the concrete meanings behind the apparent abstractions. This is necessarily both a historical quest and a theoretical one, and is often a political one: Horne Tooke uses many of his analyses to make political points, such as an often-cited etymology of the word "right" that turns into a ringing endorsement of civil disobedience (pp. 302–11).

Even more than his predecessors, then, Horne Tooke is interested in individual words, not in how they are put together. Where the British language theorists of the seventeenth century sought the link between words and ideas or words and things through reform or replacement, Horne Tooke looked for the same link to real objects through time: in original material meanings now lost in the past, but reconstructible through perspicacious etymologies.

With the rise of a serious comparative and historical linguistics, Horne Tooke's etymological efforts came to look as fantastical as those of Isidore of Seville. Yet his book remained enormously influential well into the nineteenth century, since it gave what for a time looked like an empirical basis to British materialism and philosophical radicalism, and did so "from a quarter which was least expected to produce it, language having provided what appeared to be the most cogent arguments of the opposition" (Aarsleff 1967: 88).

Conclusion

Here I have discussed only a few British thinkers about language. A broader view shows that across ideological differences, one important tendency in the second half of the century was to define poles of language types. At one extreme were languages that were wilder, closer to savagery and nature, that is, the languages of America and of the Celtic fringe. Depending on the debate, these were treated as highly poetic and/or as highly barbarous. At the other extreme were languages that were highly, even too refined, notably French. In a shifting set of valuations, English was usually able to position itself in between these extremes, as a language that was civilized enough, but not too civilized (Lauzon 1996; 2008; and cf. Bauman and Briggs 2003, Chapter 4).

What the British thinkers we have looked at, whether neo-rationalist or neo-empiricist, had in common was an interest in a range of real data as the source for philosophical development: for Harris the comparison of English and classical languages; for Monboddo data coming from the now colonized world; for Horne Tooke the putative history of English words. There was nothing comparable during this period in France, where grammarian-philosophers remained preoccupied with battles on a far more abstract level over natural versus unnatural orders of words in the sentence.

In both Britain and France, considerations of language diversity turned on the relative weight to give to orderly mental patterns versus the multifariousness of experience. Even where comparative data from differing languages was considered, it was used as fuel to support one or another broad philosophical position. Even for those who, like Condillac, saw words as an essential part of thinking, or who, like Horne Tooke, thought words *were* thinking, these activities were conceived of either as *the same* among all peoples or as developing *in the same way* among all peoples. All of these thinkers, rationalists or empiricists, *métaphysiciens* or sensualists, presumed the universality of human thought processes or their universal development through stages, and none of them took linguistic and cultural specificity or diversity as a real factor. In Germany, in the meantime, something entirely different was going on.

4   Multiplicity and the Romantic explosion

Das Wahre is das Ganze.
G. W. F. Hegel

… das Wesen der Wirklichkeit in unendlicher *Vielheit* erkannt wird.
Richard Wagner

The diversity of individual personalities was presumably lived by the French and British as much as by the Germans in the seventeenth and eighteenth centuries: it's hard to imagine more distinctive characters, in opinion, style, language, and even physique and physiognomy than, say, Voltaire or Dr. Johnson. But in the debates we have been considering, the distinctiveness of each person did not carry over into a sense of that of nations or languages as a serious philosophical or political issue. The great question remained whether languages were ruled by universal reason or by a bewildering variety of immediate circumstances that derived from the local workings of equally universal natural laws.

The middle of the eighteenth century saw a new valorization of the particular and the local among many sections of the Western European intelligentsia. Besides being an effect of the increasing questioning of absolutes by French philosophers, a passion for the distinctive and the authentic was spurred on by a fad for local traditions coming largely from the British Isles with James Macpherson's (1736–1796) tremendously popular "translations" of the purported Scottish oral epics of Ossian (Bauman and Briggs 2003: Chapter 4).

In Germany, while the eighteenth century was marked by the continuing influence of rationalism and an attraction for empiricism, elements of Leibniz's system of monads stayed alive thanks in large part to the influence of the major German philosopher of the first half of the century, Christian Wolff (1679–1754). The development of a pluralist valorization of diversity not only of inviduals, but of nations, civilizations, and languages, would take place in Germany from mid-century.

Wolff and language

Wolff, a university professor of mathematics and philosophy, is often seen as the successor to Leibniz. An idea of his philosophical ambition may be gained from the title of his dissertation "A Universal Practical Philosophy, Composed Following the Mathematical Method." Wolff's system maintained a number of Leibniz's themes, including that of a world of monads and the argument that thought requires the use of symbols (Ricken 1990: 211–31). Wolff was the conduit for these ideas to several generations of German writers (Forster 2002: 333), and also, as we have seen, to Condillac. In Wolff, the question is still one of thought and language as such, without a connection being made to the characteristics of particular languages.

Wolff is credited with the creation of a large part of the modern German language. He published his first major writings in German, a project that required forging a philosophical vocabulary where none had existed before. Instead of borrowing words from other languages, Wolff sought to identify the core meaning of each foreign term, proposed German semantic equivalents, and reconstructed German forms on that basis. Thus his German "translation equivalents" often have different semantic fields than do their originals. "Wolff followed the connotation of speech-usage, creating ... the words as if no Latin equivalent existed and without reference to any such existing equivalent" (Blackall 1978: 33, 38). There is implicit in this practice a sense of the distinctiveness of the semantics of different languages.[1]

The Königsberg crucible

Three of the central figures in the transformation of philosophy were friends in the 1760s in Königsberg,[2] a city at the eastern end of the Kingdom of Prussia. The eldest of the three was the grandson of a Mr Cant, a Scottish saddlemaker whose family Germanized the spelling of their name when they moved to Prussia. Immanuel Kant (1724–1804) was born in Königsberg, studied and then taught at the university there, and never in his life travelled more than a hundred miles from his home town. As a student, Kant was trained in the systems of Leibniz and Wolff. He became a versatile philosopher who wrote on morality, theology, mathematics, logic, astronomy, and the existence of God. It was Kant, for instance, who first proposed (in 1755) that the Milky Way might be a mass of stars seen sideways, and that nebulas might be other galaxies seen from a distance.

Despite the range of his interests, Kant did not have much to say about language. But some of his friends had a lot to say. Johann Georg Hamann (1730–1788), born and schooled in Königsberg, was a thinker of rationalist tendencies – until he went on a business trip to London and, in despair at the failure of his enterprise, took to dissolute living, then underwent a religious conversion and became a Pietist and mystic. Back in Königsberg, with Kant's help, Hamann got a job in the tax office. In his free time he wrote tracts in which he attacked rationalism and the universalist assumptions of the Enlightenment.

Hamann insisted on the dependence of thinking not only on language, but on the characteristics of *each* language. His position – found scattered over a large number of often fragmentary pieces – has been summarized:

Language as such … is never simply general, but rather is always the specific language … Each language, … represents its own world, is bound up … with all thinking … No more than there is thought free of language, is there a suprahistorical and ahistorical reason. (Karlfried Gründer, cited in Miller 1968: 17–18)

In the late 1750s, the Berlin Academy offered a prize for the best essay on the relation between people's languages and their opinions. Hamann did not take part, but he gave his own views in 1760.

The lineaments of a people's language will … correspond to the orientation of its mode of thinking; and every people reveals this through the nature, form, laws, and customs of its speech as well as through its external culture (*äusserliche Bildung*) and through a spectacle of public actions. The dialect of the Ionians has been compared with their costume, and the legal punctiliousness which rendered the Jewish people so blind at the time of the divine visitation is obvious [literally "falls into one's face"] through their language. From this orientation of the mode of thinking arises comparative wealth in some areas of the language and poverty … in others … as well as the willfulness that is perceived in idiotisms and all that one understands to be the genius of a language. (Hamann 2007: 13, translation modified)

The idea of each language and people having its own genius goes back at least to the initial flush of Renaissance discovery (Chapter 1). We have seen something of this kind in Bouhours and Harris, and it is referred to by Condillac. But Hamann is offering a whole vocabulary to talk about the relationship. There is an "orientation" or "direction" (*Richtung*) of the "mode of thinking" (*Denkungsart*) of each people, an orientation characteristic of the whole speech community, which is also the national community. The relationship between the "lineaments"[3] – that is, the specific structure – of the language and the orientation of the mode of thinking is one of "correspondence." But the correspondence is not balanced. Speech is audible, publicly (*öffentlich*, openly) available, while the orientation of the mode of thinking is not: it must be revealed, and a people reveals (*offenbaren*, make open, accessible) it through the perceptible aspects of its speech: its "nature, form, laws, and customs." Beyond language, a people also reveals its thought-orientation through externally observable practices, which collectively are called a *Schauspiel*, here translated "spectacle," usually meaning a play, a drama, literally a "show-play." Hamann is rethinking the "genius of a language" according to the model of singular hidden essence and multifarious open expression that Leibniz had used for monads.

The following year, so contemporaneously with the "rationalist counterattack" in France, Hamann wrote on word order in German and French. While Hamann presents himself as simply pointing out relative strengths and weaknesses, German comes out ahead *because* it inverts:

The German language is by its nature more capable than others of these inversions ...

The reason why the syntax of some languages permits this alteration of word order to a greater or lesser degree depends largely on the nature of their grammatical etymology ... The greater the diversity and sensuousness with which the etymology of grammar indicates changes in the movable parts of speech ... the less rigidly bound its syntactic order may be. The etymology of French grammar, however, has features that are neither so numerous nor so recognizable, and therefore the use of inversions in its word order is forbidden of itself ... German in contrast tolerates an alteration of word order without reversing the sense. (2007: 25–6)

Two decades later, Hamann would sum up his view of the relation between language and thought in a letter:

Even if I were as eloquent as Demosthenes, I would have to do nothing more than repeat a single maxim three times: reason is language, *lógos*. On this marrow I gnaw and will gnaw myself to death on it. For me a darkness still hovers over these depths; I am still waiting for an apocalyptic angel with a key to this abyss. (cited in Miller 1968: 16)

Hamann's friend Johann Gottfried Herder (1744–1803), the recipient of this letter, would do the most to launch the linguistic and national pluralism that would reach its full flowering in the Romantic movement. Herder was from a town outside Königsberg, and he arrived in the big city at the age of seventeen to get a medical education. Unfortunately he fainted at his first encounter with actual surgery; after a period of searching for a place in life, he got into the university. His favorite professor was Immanuel Kant. The liking was mutual, and Kant seems to have been a model for Herder of what a clear and open-minded thinker and pedagogue could be. Herder has been described as "a Kantian of the year 1765" (Rudolf Haym, cited in Zammito 2002: 147).

But "besides Kant and more than Kant, longer lasting, deeper, more personal than the latter – more than any other human being was the influence of Hamann on Herder" (Haym, cited in Zammito 2002: 408). Both Hamann and Herder maintained the doctrine that thought requires language, the corollary that different languages will influence thought differently, and a way of conceiving this relationship as one of expressions of distinctive essences.

In 1764, Herder left Königsberg to go even farther east, to teach in Riga, in a job that Hamann had helped him secure. He was ordained a Lutheran priest and followed this vocation through a number of shifts to different parts of Germany, becoming friends with Goethe and helping create the climate that led to Romanticism.

Herder: aspects of the new view

One law for the lion and the ox is oppression. (William Blake)

Herder articulated the idea that each nation, each people (*Volk*), expressed a unique spirit and, by implication, should be allowed to develop that spirit fully.

Thus he has been seen as the theorist on the one hand of cultural pluralism and the defense of minority rights, and on the other of nationalism and ethnic cleansing.

For Herder, the diversity of peoples, customs, and languages represents an unambiguous good (Bauman and Briggs 2000: 166–94; 2003: Chapter 5):

> Whereas [the French *philosophes* and their German disciples] ... believed that reality was ordered in terms of universal, timeless, objective unalterable laws which rational investigation could discover, Herder maintained that every activity, situation, historical period, or civilization possessed a unique character of its own ... [T]he attempt to reduce such phenomena to combinations of uniform elements, and to describe or analyse them in terms of universal rules, tended to obliterate precisely those crucial differences which constituted the specific quality of the object under study, whether in nature or in history. (Berlin 1976: 145)

Michael Forster (2007) describes Herder's "epoch-making insight":

> Enlightenment philosopher-historians ... had still believed that, as Hume put it, "mankind are so much the same in all times and places that history informs us of nothing new or strange." What Herder discovered ... was that this was false, that peoples from different historical periods and cultures often vary *tremendously* in their concepts, beliefs ... sensations, and so forth ... Given such radical difference ... interpretation is often an extremely *difficult* task ... In particular, the interpreter ... needs to resist ... a temptation falsely to *assimilate* the thought which he is interpreting to someone else's, especially his own.

The goal of philosophy must be to consider the largest possible number of human forms: philosophy should become anthropology (Zammito 2002: xii). Cultures, for Herder, "are comparable but not commensurable; each is what it is, of literally inestimable value in its own society, and consequently to humanity as a whole" (Berlin 1976: 181–2).

The image Herder was working from was of a unique national spirit (*Geist des Volkes* or *Nationalgeist*) animating a people (*Volk*) and expressed in their language and customs.[4] This is a new realization of Leibniz's monads. "Herder ... applies to language the same principle which he does to every other form of human culture – the Leibnitzian principle of individuation ... Just as each monad represents the universe as seen from its own perspective, so each language, being the supreme expression of a 'national mentality', in fact, identical with it, reflects the universe in its own characteristic way" (Miller 1968: 21–2). In a 1768 letter, Herder defines his view of history as based on "every human eye [having] its own angle of vision: every one makes a projection of the object before him after his own fashion" (in Zammito 2002: 338).

Herder articulated his view most broadly in reworkings of the philosophy of history in the 1770s and 1780s. The most famous overall statement comes in 1774, in *Yet One More Philosophy of the History of Mankind*:

[A]t bottom all *comparison* proves to be *problematic* ... who can compare the *diverse* (*verschiedene*) satisfaction of *diverse* senses in *diverse* worlds?... Each nation has its center (*Mittelpunkt*) of happiness *in itself*, like every sphere its center of gravity (*Schwerpunkt*)! ... Is not the good on the earth *strewn about*? Because one form of humanity and one region of the earth could not grasp it, it got distributed into a thousand forms (*Gestalten*), it roams forth – an eternal Proteus! – through all parts of the world and all centuries. (Herder 2002: 296–8, translation modified)

Herder's first public statement was the lecture "On Diligence in Several Learned Languages," pronounced in 1764 to inaugurate his position in Riga.[5] Herder begins his talk, and so a lifetime of thinking about linguistic diversity, at the Tower of Babel:

As the children of dust undertook that edifice that threatened the clouds, the chalice of confusion was poured over them: their families and dialects were transplanted to various (*verschiedenen*) points of the compass; and a thousand languages were created according to the climes and mores of a thousand nations. When here the native of the Morn glows under a blazing noon, the rushing current of his mouth streams forth a heated and emotive speech. There, the Greek flourishes in the most sensuous and mild of regions, his body ... is bathed in grace ... his vocal instruments exquisite; and thus there arose among them that exquisite Attic tongue ...

The Romans, sons of Mars, spoke more forcefully ... More masculine yet is the speech of the martial German; the sprightly Gaul invents a skipping, softer language; the Spaniard gives his own an appearance of gravity ... The languorous African mumbles weakly, waning away in broken tones, and the Hottentot, at last, loses himself in a stammer of gibberish. (Herder 1992: 29, translation modified)

The influence of Harris's *Hermes* is clear here; but where for Harris the factor distinguishing languages was political, for Herder it is climatic and moral: there is mutual reflection among *Umwelt*, national character, individual physiology and temperament, and the style of a language, marked by sound, structure, and meaning ("gibberish").

The implication of such a view is to turn inward:

If thus, each language has its distinct national character, it seems that nature imposes upon us an obligation only to our mother tongue, for it is perhaps better measured to our character and coextensive with (*ausfüllet*) our way of thinking. I may perhaps be able to ape haltingly the sounds of foreign nations, without, however, penetrating to the core of their uniqueness. (p. 29, translation modified)

Yet "as long as the plans for a universal language belong among the ... journeys to the moon, so long will many languages remain an indispensable evil and thus almost a genuine good" (p. 31). In fact, it is imperative to learn many languages to have direct access to the thoughts of great writers. Translations are odious:

[Translation] is a shorter path, but an uncertain one, unfortunately; it is too short to reach the goal. There are always beauties that shine through (*durchscheinen*) the veil of language with twofold charms: tear away the veil and they disappear. (pp. 31–2, translation modified)

Great texts "lose everything when I transplant them against their nature." So we must explore other languages: "two or three languages I need to learn, and I hear each of the greatest minds speak in his own tongue" (p. 32). But there is a problem with this approach: there are just too many languages to learn.

But what a limitless sea do I see here before me, where I dare not venture without a Palinurus – a labyrinth of languages where, without a guiding thread, I lose myself! Very well, this guiding thread is my mother tongue ...

Mother tongue and fatherland will give the traveller an identity and a home:

Just as the love of our fatherland binds us to each other by heartfelt bonds of affection, the language of our fathers holds attractions for us also, which ... impressed themselves upon us first and somehow shaped themselves together with the finest fissures of our sensibility ... [O]ur mind clandestinely compares all tongues with our mother tongues ... Thereby the great diversity of language is given unity ... I am afloat on a bark which carries me. (pp. 33–4)

Deeper appreciation of one's own allows wider exploration of other languages, which means of other fields of thoughts:

As long as we keep our native language on our tongue, we will penetrate so much more deeply into the distinctiveness of each language ... For, in what precise relationship do language and mentality stand? Whoever masters the entire scope of one language surveys a field full of thoughts, and whoever learns to express himself precisely in it thereby gathers for himself a treasure of well-defined (*bestimmter*) concepts. The first words we stammer are the foundation stones of our knowing, and our nursemaids are our first teachers of logic. (p. 34, translation modified)

Herder's first widely circulated publication was a series of *Fragments on Recent German Literature* from 1767–1768. Here he makes an argument for the dependence of thought on language.

If it is true that we cannot think without thoughts, and that we learn to think through words, then language gives to the whole of knowledge its limits and contours ... We think in language ... and in ordinary life it is indeed apparent that thinking is almost nothing more than speaking. (SW2.12, 17–18, in Miller 1968: 20–1)[6]

Herder took the unity of thought, language, and feeling and put it together with the diversity of languages to draw the conclusion of a consequent diversity of forms of thought and feeling. Here we have a world of discrete worlds, each unique, each a coherent totality. And the relationship among them is, again, one among different points of view. "Every nation speaks ... according to the way it thinks, and thinks according to the way it speaks: as varied as the viewpoint was from which a nation looked at a thing, it designated it in the same way" (SW2.18, in Miller 1968: 22).

The relationship of language and thought was to be brought to bear on German:

To what degree is the language of the Germans in harmony with their way of thinking? ... How can one know from their way of speaking, its elements, its pronunciation and the measure of its syllables, up to its whole nature, that it was formed (*gebildet*) under the German heaven there to dwell, and to work? (SW2.26–7)

These questions propose an almost mystical unity among a language, its speakers, its literature, and a distinctive landscape.

We have an apparent contradiction in the *Fragments*: at one moment Herder is arguing for the unique and irreplaceable qualities of every language; at the next he is ranking them, almost without exception with his own at the top of heap. We find this for sounds:

"Our language is supposed to have something barbarian about it, because of the many consonants with which it is crowded" [citation from Lessing and Nicolai's *Literatur Briefe*] ... So that our sounds may not dissipate themselves among the consonants, we have more diphthongs and stronger vowels than [the French]; in this manner our language assumes a certain Doric fulness, which fits ... our character ...

We have more aspirated sounds in our language than they, and aspiration is as much a part of the gentle in speech as the sigh is part of the tender words of the lover, as the caressing west wind pleases the spring, for it does bear some kinship to them. Go through the gentle, tender, pleasing words: they all commend themselves through a soft *h* or *ch*, which coarser peoples have such difficulty in emulating, peoples who, like the Russians, must utter the *H* in the form of a sharp *G*, the soft *ch* in a harsh *cch*. (Herder 1992: 128–9)

Herder calls Russian coarse and rough in virtually the same terms Bouhours had used against German.

In a fragment on inversions, Herder, like Hamann before him, sees flexibility in word order as a valuable quality of German:

"The German ... has constructions so bizarre that the metaphysical order of the words is disturbed without reason ... For example: the metaphysical order of the words is disturbed: how ridiculous it sounds ... *vint le Comte ici par* [German word order, instead of normal French *le Comte vint par ici*]; and yet the Germans say ... *kam der Graf herbei*." [Citation from the *Literatur Briefe*] – Who among the Germans is not so struck by this example, as if by a stroke of lightning, that he would immediately take the idiosyncrasy of the French language, and its inflexibility, for the one and only metaphysical word order, and would therefore ... to please the French and for the honor of the philosophy of language, introduce the following order of construction: "Because you to us did not want today to do us the favor, we to you it will do." For that is the genuine French order of construction ... and the idiosyncracy of the French construction is, after all, the metaphysical word order itself. (1992: 130–1, translation modified)

And he will even pick up the analogy of the serpent to argue that German has the same valuable flexibility as Latin, using virtually the same argument as Diderot had seventeen years earlier:

An example; *Flee* the snake, someone calls to me, to whom my *fleeing* is the principal objective, though I did not want to flee. – *The snake*, flee! cries another, who wants nothing more immediately than to call my attention to the snake. I will flee on my own, as soon as I hear of it. (p. 132)

Also like Diderot, Herder goes on to *accept* the identification of French with reason, but pulls a proto-Romantic reversal, giving pride of place to the inversions of oral expression and poetry.

The more any [modern language] has been shaped by grammarians and philosophers, the more rigid the fetters it bears. The closer it is to its original state, the freer it will be. The more it is alive, the more inversions it will have; the more it has become a language of dead letters, the fewer inversions there will be. All of this is confirmed by the French language ... It may perhaps be that, because of this uniform process, because it is so fine a book language suited to reading, it is called a language of reason. But for the poetic genius this language of reason is a curse. (p. 134)

Herder felt that national character was best expressed in spontaneous creation, notably in oral poetry. We have seen the pervasiveness in later eighteenth-century France and Britain of the identification of poeticity with a free, natural state. Herder intensely admired and defended the poems of Ossian and encouraged their translation into German; and he produced one of the great early collections of folk songs from many nations, particularly small nations, a summum published as *Voices of the Peoples in Songs* in 1778–1779.

Herder defended the human, rather than divine, character of language in the 1772 *Treatise on the Origin of Language*, the prizewinner in another one of those contests held by the Berlin Academy. Here we find a remarkable tension between Herder's impulse to defend languages in their specificity and a desire to rank them: he gives as one of his arguments, for instance, that some languages are so poorly made that it is insulting to attribute them to God. Herder lists savage languages with "unnecessary excess" in some things, insufficiencies in others (Herder 2002: 116). "Such a language is rich because it is poor, because its inventors did not yet have enough of a plan to become poor ... The analogies of all savage languages confirm my thesis: each of them is in its way prodigal and needy – only each in its own manner" (p. 117). But there's the rub: each may be "most imperfect," but each is imperfect *in its own way*: which makes it unique, perhaps even precious.

Arabic has lots of words for swords and stones and snakes. The languages of Oriental despotisms (remember Harris) are, "in accordance with [their] people[s'] inclinations, rich in flatteries, titles, and verbal ornamentation" and use different pronouns depending on rank (p. 117). Carib doubles its vocabulary depending on whether a man or woman is speaking, but has "only four words for the colors! What poverty!" (p. 118). Huron, which is entirely based on verbs, uses a different one depending on whether its object has or lacks a soul. And – unless he is being sarcastic, about which one is never quite sure with Herder – this catches his fancy and starts to look more like a richness than a deficiency. "Let one pursue that principle through the whole of nature. What a richness!". Similar richness is found in the Huron distinction between verbs associated with one's own or with another's property.[7] The reader swings back and forth trying to figure out whether Herder is praising or condemning and arrives, exhausted, at his conclusion: "Each of these cases ... is so interconnected with the custom, character, and origin of the people – but everywhere the inventing human spirit reveals its stamp" (p. 118).

Like Buffier at the beginning of the century, Herder takes a wicked pleasure in reversing received wisdom. Here he challenges both the claim that savage languages have long words and the conclusion of one (French) author that this, paradoxically, is a sign of laziness:

[The author] asks "whether ... since ... all human beings love laziness, it can ever be expected of [the] ... Orenocks that they should ... improve their longwinded, eight-syllabled, difficult, and most cumbersome language." And I answer: First, the *fact* is incorrect ... "Their long-winded, eight-syllabled language" it is not. Condamine merely says that it is so unpronounceable and distinctively organized that where they pronounce three or four syllables we would have to write seven or eight, and yet we would still not have written them completely. Does that mean that it *is* longwinded, eight-syllabled? And "difficult, most cumbersome"? For whom is it so except for foreigners? To improve it for an arriving Frenchman who hardly ever learns any language except his own without mutilating it ...? But is it the case that the Orenocks have *not yet* formed *anything* in their language, indeed not yet *formed* for themselves any language, just because they do not choose to exchange the genius which is so peculiarly theirs for a foreigner who comes sailing along? (2002: 146–7)

That Orenock is hard for Frenchmen to pronounce does not mean that it is primitive, but that it is not French. And why should it be? The Orenock language has its own genius.

Herder notes that some languages have very few number terms. The implications of this fact will continue to be debated into the twenty-first century. For Herder, this is not a deficiency, but a reflection of the way the people in question live.

How few [numbers] do most savages have, however rich, excellent, and developed their languages may be! Never more than they needed. The trading Phoenician was the first to invent arithmetic; the shepherd who counts his flocks also learns to count; the hunting nations, which never have work involving large numbers, only know to describe an army as like hairs on a head! Who can count them? Who, if he has never counted up so high, has words for this? (p. 120)

This is the argument Boas would use against the evolutionists.

Kant's critical revolution

We've been discussing Hamann and Herder's work up to the early 1780s. In 1781 there took place one of the monumental events in the history of philosophy: the publication of the *Critique of Pure Reason* by Herder's old teacher Immanuel Kant. This book marks the arrival on the scene of an entirely different Kant, the critical philosopher, who is one of the unavoidable philosophical landmarks. In fact, historians often act as if the real Kant was born in 1781 (Zammito 2002: 5).

If Kant was born at fifty-seven, he had gestated for eleven "years of silence" during which he had published nothing. In 1770, Kant had reread the Scottish philosopher David Hume (1711–1776), a skeptic and empiricist way beyond Locke. Hume's famous case concerned the relationship of cause and effect: if knowledge comes from the senses, all judgments about causation are based on an assumption that things will continue to happen as they always have. Such an assumption cannot be rationally justified. This most elementary bit of reasoning, that a given cause produces a given effect, turns out not to be based on reason at all, but on blind faith. Kant said that Hume had awakened him from his dogmatic slumber.

How do we know things? asks Kant. For Descartes, there had been two kinds of knowledge. One is a priori knowledge, which is self-evidently true. A priori truths are analytic, which is to say that the predicate is implied in the subject, without requiring further input. "I think, therefore I am" is an analytic statement if we agree that thinking necessarily implies existence. But for Descartes any judgment that requires sensory input has to combine analytic primitives: it is synthetic, rather than analytic, and can only be known a posteriori. For Locke, there is no a priori knowledge: all knowledge is both a posteriori and synthetic. Hume, as we have seen, pushes this to the point of questioning the certainty of rational knowledge of any kind. For Leibniz, not surprisingly, it all depended on point of view. From the point of view of God, which Leibniz had no trouble taking, all knowledge is analytic, since for Him *every* substance contains all of its predicates. The rest of us monads, however, while having knowledge of all things past, present, and to come, possess it only obscurely: Leibniz makes a distinction between perceptions, which can be obscure to the point of unconsciousness, and apperceptions, true conscious realizations. The issue here is to allow implicit knowledge, always already there, to become explicit: we might say that for a monad true knowledge is all analytic, but only available through work, i.e., is a posteriori. Herder, we have seen, sees languages and nations as unique and obscure kernels of this kind, waiting to be revealed in their distinctiveness.

But this is not the tack that Kant would take in the *Critique*. In one of those breathtaking acts of modesty that sometimes make revolutions – think of

Copernicus accepting the non-centrality of the earth, and so of himself, in the universe – Kant argues that the issue should not be whether or how we can know the truth, but the *limits* of our knowledge. Where philosophers had argued about the contents of thought, Kant made a sidestep to ask about its form: what conditions must thinking presuppose to be human thinking at all? Can we even conceive of a world that operates with no time, space, or causality? No, says Kant: these are necessary aspects of any human conceptualization; yet they are not analytic or self-evident. Intuitions (*Anschauungen*) such as space and time, fundamental categories such as causality, quantity, quality, existence and non-existence, are both synthetic and a priori – a priori for humans, since they are prerequisites for human thought, although not necessarily for that of all possible beings.

This synthesis of rationalism and empiricism was, like Newton's, enormously successful; and Kant presents precisely Newton's space, time, and causality, not necessarily as the structure of the world in itself (who knows?), but as the necessary preconditions of any human conceptualization.

In performing his synthesis, a whole set of questions that had been central to Leibniz and Herder have been shunted aside: not only are there no monads here, there is no place in the system for linguistic, national, or individual variation. In Kant's system there is only one point of view, which is to say that there are none.

It is not surprising that Hamann and Herder were not pleased with their old friend's new philosophy.[8]

Hamann and Herder react to Kant

Hamann responded in 1784 with a brief *Metakritik*. He argues that reasoning itself depends on language – "the only, first, and last organon and criterion of reason" (2007: 208), and on particular languages. "How is the capacity to think possible? No deduction is needed to prove the genealogical priority of language over the several holy functions of logical propositions and syllogisms" (Benes 2008: 109). The elements of languages were the true "pure forms *a priori*" (110).

Herder, too, would feel that what Kant's universalism missed was the reality of different languages. In his introduction to the 1784 German translation of Monboddo, he wrote that such works provide a first foundation for "a philosophy of human understanding based on its most distinctive work, the diverse (*verschiedenen*) languages of the earth" (SW15.183).

Herder's *Ideas for Philosophy of the History of Mankind*, published from 1784 to 1791, has been read as a pluralist response to Kant's universalism.

In fundamental opposition to the universalist aesthetic of Kant, Herder insisted that the language and poetry of a people be assessed "with respect to time and place"; for each

Volk, the authenticity and vitality of its poetry rests only on its faithfulness to "The genius of their nature, their country, their way of life, the period in which they lived, and the character of their progenitors." (Bauman and Briggs 2003: 181, citing SW14.98–9)

Herder restates that language is the source of all reason (SW13.362) and, more specifically, that "A people has no idea for which it has no word" (SW13.357).

In 1799, Herder published his own *Metacritique* of Kant's *Critique*, stressing the constitutive role of language in human knowledge (Formigari 2003). For Kant, space, time, causality are universal for human beings, without regard to the fact that they have language or that they have different languages. "In answer to Kant's positing of space and time as innate ideas, Herder offers language as the teacher of these ideas" (Penn 1972: 52).

"What is thinking," Herder asks, and answers: "*inner speech*, that is, internalized signs expressing themselve; speaking is thinking out loud" (SW21.88). "The human soul thinks with words; it does not merely express itself (*sich äussern*, literally externalize itself), but designates itself and orders its thoughts by means of language" (SW21.19). "Every man can and must think only in *his own* language" (SW21.32).

A long section of the *Metacritique* questions the Newton/Locke/Kant picture of time and space (Formigari 2003: 138–43). Space, Herder claims, is no a priori intuition: it draws on bodily orientation, movement, and visual cues which pass into language, whose grammatical structures offer an organization for a perceived and cognized space. Time, for its part, is the interiorization of bodily rhythms and the rhythms of nature, rendered manipulable for human thinking through adverbs and tenses in human languages. "There is no time of all times, no infinite time: this is merely an abstraction, just as the idea of infinite space is an abstraction. There are different times that measure the diverse mutations of beings" (Formigari 2003: 139).

The beating of my pulse, the slow or hurried flow of my thoughts, are not a measure of time that is applicable to others; the flow of a river, the growth of a tree, do not serve to measure time for all rivers, trees, and plants. The life of an elephant and of a gnat do not last the same time, and how different is the measurement of time on different planets! We can therefore risk saying that at a given time there are in the universe innumerable other times: the time that we present to ourselves as the measure of all the others is only a relative measure for our thoughts; just as infinite space is such a relative measure for all the particular places in the universe. Infinite time, like its companion space, as the measure and frame for all time, is an illusory image. (SW21.58–9)

Herder goes on to attack the Kantian categories, asserting that they are simply verbal categories that Kant has elevated to universals of human knowledge (SW21.94–5).

Against Kant's new universalism, Herder offers the first fully articulated theory of pluralist essentialism that centers on languages and cultures. By the time of his death in 1803, this model was being taken in new directions by the Romantics.

The Romantic generation

The Romantic movement of the beginning of the nineteenth century admired diversity for its own sake and sought to understand it as a plurality of essences to be grasped as wholes, as against the linear bit-by-bit logic of the rationalists. Instead of a single mechanical world and a single linear order of thought, the Romantics supposed a multiplicity of "worlds," each the expression of a distinct essence. This held for individual personalities, great authors, historical periods, civilizations, landscapes.

Here we are largely speaking about a single generation: most of the protagonists of the next part of this book – Schleiermacher, Hegel, the Brothers Schlegel, the Brothers Humboldt – were born in the years from 1767 to 1772, a period that also saw the births of Beethoven, the poets Hölderlin and Novalis, and the literary theorist Tieck, while the philosopher Fichte was born in 1765, the painter Caspar David Friedrich and the philosopher Schelling in 1775, the novelist Hoffman and the psychologist Herbart in 1776.

As against Classicism, Romanticism admired multiplicity and authenticity and, again, the expression of deep essences. The modern novel, with its display of multiple individuals with their differing voices and its exploration and revelation of deep personality structures, is a Romantic creation. In Goethe, as in Shelley, Keats, and Wordsworth, the ideal for poetry is simple, straightforward and authentic song.

Herder had proposed keeping the mother tongue pure by avoiding translation (Steiner 1975: 81–2). Yet he carried out the prodigious work of translation represented in his collection of folk songs from many lands – translated into German, with the implication that this would enrich German literature itself. The Romantics wanted translations that offered new and unfamiliar aesthetic experiences to the modern public (Berman 1985 [1992]). This was the golden age of what is called foreignizing translation, which is felt to enrich, not distort, the host language by modifying it (Steiner 1975: 339–42). This kind of translation practice was accompanied by theory that directly addressed that of the *belles infidèles*, which, if you remember, held that since exotic authors do not seem exotic in their own languages and settings, we should translate them according to the canons of our own place and time. A. W. von Schlegel criticizes what he calls French translation for making the foreign visitor "dress and behave according to [French] customs" (Lefevere 1992: 79), and Friedrich Schleiermacher (1768–1834), in the period's translation manifesto (1813 [1973]), says that to translate a foreigner as he would have written had he *not* been foreign is like painting a portrait of a man not as he actually looks, but as he would have looked if he had had a different father.

In the study of language, among the most important Romantic figures were the brothers August Wilhelm (1767–1845) and Friedrich (1772–1829) von Schlegel. Friedrich's book *On the Language and Wisdom of the Indians* (1808) championed two ideas that would be the foundation for linguistics through the nineteenth century and arguably up until the present. The first is that Sanskrit, the ancient language of India, is related historically to many languages of Europe, and that it is possible to establish historical relationships among languages by comparing sounds and grammatical structures. This is the beginning of the field of historical linguistics and of the genetic classification of languages. But Schlegel goes on to treat this whole family of languages, which we now call Indo-European, as the exemplar of a single type whose key element, whose inner structure (*innere Bau*), lies in the way it puts meaningful elements together to make words. Schlegel proposed two great categories of linguistic type into which all the languages of the world could be divided. And *this* was the beginning of what is now called typological classification of languages. In a development of his brother's idea, A. W. von Schlegel (1818) came to distinguish the inflectional morphology of Indo-European languages, especially old ones, from two other types: the isolating morphology typical, for instance, of Chinese; and the agglutinating morphology of many Old World languages, including Turkish. The Schlegels and their successors into the twentieth century held the inflectional type to be superior to the others because it is "organic," with words "growing" out of "roots," while in an isolating language meaningful elements simply bump up against each other, and in an agglutinating language they are stuck together mechanically.

In the Schlegels' first formulations genetic and typological categories are assumed to be one and the same: the type of morphology is an expression of the spirit of the language family. In the course of the nineteenth century, genetic and typological ways of analyzing and classifying languages would diverge into two different schools. Historical linguistics, primarily of the Indo-European language family, would increasingly seek to discover universal laws, particularly laws of sound change. This would be the dominant linguistics of the nineteenth and early twentieth centuries. At the same time, a minority linguistics, emerging out of the work of Wilhelm von Humboldt, would seek to analyze the greatest possible variety of language types in order to identify the specific essence of each. It is this Humboldtian movement that will maintain the Romantic interest in the diversity of distinct systems (Trabant 1986: 160–3).

The Brothers Grimm

The great operationalizers of the Romantic program were the brothers Jakob (1785–1863) and Wilhelm (1786–1859) Grimm. The Grimms' project was to document, and in a sense reveal the essence of, German culture. Since, like most Romantics, they felt that the authentic spirit of the people was to be found among the unlettered, ideally rural, common people, they undertook as their first scholarly exploit the great collection of German folk tales for which they are best remembered.

It is worth contrasting the spirit of this publication (first edition 1812–1815) with that of the other famous collection of folk tales, the Mother Goose Stories of Charles Perrault (1628–1703), published in 1697. Very much a seventeenth-century Frenchman, Perrault was a fervent defender of the superiority of French and the natural order of thought. While his stories are authentic French oral tales, apparently learned from his nurse, he presents them in the most elegant language, full of cleverness and double meanings. No greater contrast can be imagined with the Grimms' fairy tales. The Grimms actually went out into rural villages and listened to well-reputed storytellers; they made an effort to transcribe these tellings in a style similar to that of the actual performances, and indeed a number of their *Märchen* are printed in local dialects. Throughout, the stress is on authenticity: these tales *as they actually are told* are treated as irreplaceable treasures, the heritage of the German *Volk* (Belmont 1986: Chapter 3; Bauman and Briggs 2003: Chapter 4).

Together, the Grimms went on to produce an edition of a medieval German epic, the first major edition of medieval German legends, and what remains the great dictionary of the German language. Wilhelm published books on runes and on German heroic legends. Jakob became one of the greatest historical linguists of the century. His German grammar (1819–1837) remains a monument of the comparative-historical method, showing in detail the relations between German and the other Indo-European languages. He also published the first edition of medieval German laws, a *Deutsche Mythologie* on Germanic, including Norse, religion, and a history of the German language.

The Grimms were the first practitioners of the ultimate Romantic project of a single author or small group of authors essentially mapping out the language, folk literature, ancient customs, and ancient religion of a people as part of a national project. In the centuries that followed they would have emulators all over the world. Most such projects, like that of the Grimms, have seen as their mission to reveal and promote the many expressions of a distinctive national and linguistic essence, and so operate in monadic and essentialist forms that go back to Leibniz.

The Brothers Humboldt

I do not see how anyone learning a new way of languaging can escape a pervading sense of exotic pleasure. (A. L. Becker 1995: 12)

The Brothers Humboldt represent the passage from a philosophy of history to a philosophically-inspired geography, anthropology, and linguistics. Herder had called for philosophy to become anthropology; Wilhelm von Humboldt would compose a "Plan for a Comparative Anthropology."

The brothers were well-to-do members of the Prussian nobility. Alexander (1769–1859), the younger of the two, spent five years as an explorer in Latin America and turned himself into one of the great naturalists of all time (Sachs 2006). Alexander von Humboldt took a typically Romantic and holistic view of complex landscapes, trying to understand them as unique totalities, and so is seen as the founder of the disciplines of ecology, environmental studies, and geography as a descriptive or "cosmographic" science, as opposed to sciences seeking only universal laws (Bunzl 1996). In the 1840s, well into his seventies, he published his great opus, the founding bible of geography. A work as immodestly named as Bacon's *Novum Organum*, Descartes' *Le Monde*, or Newton's *System of the World*, it is called *Kosmos*.

Alexander's older brother Wilhelm von Humboldt (1767–1835) was a diplomat, philosopher, and analyst of many tongues. He initially studied law, but like his brother inherited enough money to do more or less what he wanted. He spent several years based in Paris (1797–1801), where he made friends with a number of philosophers[9] and whence he carried out linguistic fieldwork in the Basque country. "It was with his experience of the Basque language that Humboldt discovered a completely novel linguistic universe; the singularity of this experience revealed the diversity of linguistic types" (Thouard, in Humboldt 2000: 23; on Humboldt on Basque, see Chabrolle-Cerretini 2007: 41–7), a theme that would remain Humboldt's central concern. Humboldt then began a diplomatic career representing Prussia on the world stage. From 1809 to 1810 he served as national director of education and in effect founded the modern university system at the University of Berlin (now Humboldt University, named after both brothers).

The politics of the brothers was liberal and progressive. Alexander devoted himself to the struggle against slavery – a bone of contention in his relations with his friend Thomas Jefferson. In 1819, with the authoritarian turn of the Prussian government, Wilhelm left public service and retired to his house outside Berlin, devoting himself thenceforth to his great passion, the languages of the earth. We have a rather cruel portrait of him in retirement by the French writer and diplomat Chateaubriand, who laments that the great man now wastes his time on such trivial pursuits and actually converses with his daughter in Sanskrit at the dinner table (Trabant 1990a: Chapter 2).

In his dabbling, Wilhelm von Humboldt was founding linguistics. If Alexander was the great cosmographer, Wilhelm was, if you like, a cosmographer of languages, the master glottographer. In his brother's words, Wilhelm "was able to penetrate deeper into the structure of a larger number of languages than have probably yet been encompassed by any *single* mind" (preface to 1836 [1999]: 4). He was at the same time the great glottophile, delighting in the diversity and specificity of languages. This is clear in a letter he wrote in 1803:

The sheer pleasure of entering with each new language into a new system of thinking and feeling bring[s] me unending delight. (cited in Swiggers 1985: 729)

Humboldt's linguistics is part of a broader project to understand human self-creation (*Bildung*), both individual and collective. A statement from 1787 epitomizes the spirit of this project: the Enlightenment, he wrote, should spread not only light, but warmth (GS1.2; Trabant 1990a: Chapter 1).[10]

Humboldt presented his general theory of language in lectures at the Berlin Academy in the 1820s and in three unfinished book-length manuscripts. The best known of these, *The Diversity of Human Language Structure and Its Influence on the Spiritual Development of Humanity* (1836 [1999]), was published posthumously thanks to his brother. A large volume in itself, it is the introductory essay for two more large volumes analyzing the Old Javanese or Kawi language and so is often referred to as the introduction to the Kawi Work. Humboldt also wrote, sometimes finished, and occasionally published descriptive analyses or extended discussions of an extraordinary range of languages, including Basque, Sanskrit, Persian, Chinese, and North and South American languages, some of which he knew about thanks to letters home from his brother's travels, as well as comparative studies of Pacific languages such as Kawi.

Humboldt was an admirer of Kant and thought in terms of universal characteristics of humanity and language. One of his central shifts in emphasis, consonant both with his Kantianism and with much Romantic thinking, was from language thought of as a static thing, a product (*ergon*, in Greek) to that of language as an activity (*energeia*) (Fabian 1971). Kant represented a philosophically respectable argument for the active power of the human mind, seen neither as a blank slate nor as a universal logic machine. Humboldt felt that Kant had identified something in human knowing that was beyond all linguistic and cultural variation, and he expressed this in one of his lectures to the Berlin Academy:

The sum of what can be known lies, as the field of activity of the human mind, between all languages and independent of them, in the middle; man can only approach this realm of pure objective knowledge in accordance with his own ways of perceiving and feeling, that is, by a subjective path. (1997: 18, translation modified)

Kant thus offered Humboldt a frame for a wide-ranging comparative project. But with this justification in place, the actual models Humboldt draws on to characterize languages, peoples, and historical periods recall, rather, Leibniz and Herder. Indeed, Humboldt's "Plan for a Comparative Anthropology" of 1797 has been seen as a "synthesis of Herder and Kant" (Trabant 1990a: 52).

Humboldt's actual construction of the diverse linguistic world draws on the thought-forms of pluralist essentialism: this is a world of many languages, each expressing an inner essence, principle, or spirit. The bulk of Humboldt's research "is certainly not universalist in tone. Though [he] believed that the capacity for language is universal, he followed the nationalistic doctrine of Herder in thinking of a particular language as the property of the nation speaking it" (Salus 1976: 98). Humboldt saw each language as an individual to be grasped as an expressive totality, not a mechanical construction based on cause and effect (e.g., 1836 [1999]: 26). As his view is characterized by Emile Bréhier (1938 [1993]: 706):

Language is given all at once as a totality, and not built up from parts; the diversity of languages comes from the obstacles or support that the universal force of language finds in the spiritual force inherent in each people: a hidden and mysterious force, which is not part of the chain of cause and effect that is available to reason.

"[I]ndividuality," Humboldt says in an Academy lecture, "is unity of diversity (*Verschiedenheit*)" (1997: 52, translation modified); Denis Thouard comments on this that "Humboldt is evidently thinking of Leibniz (*unitas in varietate, diversitas*)... *Verschiedenheit* refers back to the Leibnizian *diversitas*, rethought in the domain of languages" (in Humboldt 2000: 130).

For Humboldt plurality and diversity are inherently good:

we haven't done much if we do not ... take account of the diversity (*Verschiedenheit*) of heads ... of the many ways in which the world reflects itself in different (*verschiedenen*) individuals. (GS1.286–7, from 1795)

"Individuals" here, as always in Humboldt (Trabant 1986), indicates not only individual people, but individual nations, historical periods, languages. In the 1797 "Plan for a Comparative Anthropology," Humboldt asserts that human nature as a whole can only be expressed through the individual characters of nations. The objects of anthropological research are "the particularities of moral character of different human types" (GS1.377).

Most of the authors we have looked at up to now simply assumed the superiority of modern European civilization. Humboldt's is a more complex model. In Matti Bunzl's words (1996: 22),

[e]ach individual *Volk* had a *Nationalcharakter*, a distinct *Volk* character, which was embodied in the totality of its outward manifestations: traditions, customs, religion, language, and art. These in turn revealed the degree of *Bildung* attained by a given nation. Since these achievements were based on capacities intrinsic to each national entity, they could not be compared to an external standard, but deserved an unconditional respect. However, some nations, including the Germans, English, French, Italians, and the ancient Greeks, had made the most of their innate potentialities and reached a higher state of self-realization, serving as models by which the rest could learn to maximize their own cultural potential.

Here superiority is based on relative degrees of individuation: certain nations are superior in that they have become more *themselves* than have others. This possibility remains open for all – the implication, however, being a reversal of colonial thinking: to fully realize themselves, non-European nations should go farther in their specificity, which means becoming less, not more, like European ones. Something of the kind was expressed by Herder, as we have seen.

In the practice of linguistics, this valorization of diversity means that one should consider the largest possible number of maximally different languages. In contrast to most of the linguists of his time, Humboldt was interested in all the languages in the world.

Like each individual person, for Humboldt each language possesses a unique inner form and should be understood as a system or a whole expressing a single principle:

A language is a being (*Wesen* [which also translates as "essence"]) determined everywhere by a single indwelling principle (*Prinzip*) that cannot be classified into any general category (*Gattung*), any more than can a human being or a human face. (1829, GS6.356)

Noteworthy here is the turn to the individual face as the model for all individualities, whether of nations, languages, or historical periods. A face is *perceived* as a set of parts, but we *apperceive* it as a single expressive totality. Humboldt will return to this analogy in discussing the "total impression" given by a language:

Now here the ... most distinct *individuality* plainly strikes the eye and is borne inexorably in upon our feeling. Languages, in this respect, can least inaccurately be compared with *human facial forms* (*Gesichtsbildungen*). The individuality is undeniably there, resemblances are recognized, but no measurement or description of the parts separately and in interconnection can sum up (*zusammenfassen*) the particularity in a concept. It rests upon the whole, and in the equally individual conception ... For language, in whatever shape we may receive it, is always a spiritual exhalation (*Aushauch*) of a nationally individual life ... However much in it we may fix and embody, dismember and dissect, there always remains something unknown in it that is left over, and precisely this which slips away from analysis (*Bearbeitung*) is that wherein the unity and breath (*Odem*) of a living thing resides. (1836 [1999]: 50–1, translation modified)

Each language has a distinctive character, which Humboldt likens to the spirit in a living body; "a nation's mental individuality ... imparts to the language a characteristic colour and shading" (pp. 154–5). But where is one to look for the indwelling principle that makes the whole come together? One of the problems of much Romantically-inspired research is that it fails to deliver: one expects to find proposals for what it is that distinguishes a language, but they are extremely rare. Languages are just too complicated and function at too many relatively autonomous levels to lend themselves to portrayal as expressions of a single essence.

In his lectures at the Academy, Humboldt, like the Schlegels at the beginning of the century, finds a key in morphology. Humboldt takes up the Schlegels' categories, as well as their ranking of types, and makes them his own. Within linguistics, Humboldt will be remembered primarily as the great expositor of language typology. Yet Humboldt's goal was not classification in itself, but finding a way into the character of each language as an *Individuum*.

The whole set of studies on the structure of languages is only the basis for the more important linguistic research, the study of character: "This is the keystone of the study of language." (Trabant 2000a: 315, citing Humboldt 1997: 9)

As for Herder, there is a presumption in Humboldt's work that a people and their language have a natural, organic connection.

The *intellectual distinctiveness (Geisteseigentümlichkeit)* and the *language-configuration (Sprachgestaltung)* of a people are so intimately fused with one another, that if one were given, the other would have to be completely derivable from it. For *intellectuality (Intellectualität)* and *language* allow and provide only forms that are mutually corresponding (*gegenseitig zusagende Formen*). Language is, as it were, the outer expression (*Erscheinung*) of the spirit of peoples; the language is their spirit and the spirit their language; one can never think of them sufficiently as identical. How they actually conjoin with each other in one and the same source, beyond reach of our understanding (*Begreifen*, conceptualization), remains inexplicably hidden from us. (1836 [1999]: 46, translation modified)

The perceptible is the expression – *Erscheinung*, from a root meaning to shine or to show forth – of the imperceptible.

Humboldt sees each type or group of languages as operating on the basis of distinctive principles and, as Buffier had claimed a century earlier, the grammarian must grasp these to provide an adequate description, requiring in each case the forging of new analytical tools. It will not do to take Latin grammatical terms and concepts and apply them to Choctaw or Chinese, a procedure that makes Choctaw or Chinese look like poor imitations of Latin, Latin *manqué*. In 1826 Humboldt criticized a Jesuit grammar of Japanese:

He follows ... the system of adapting his grammar to Latin grammar ... We must always carefully distinguish the way in which a given grammatical form is really found in the language from the way in which it is represented by the author. [His] whole scaffolding of moods, gerundives, supines, and participles ... would disappear before a method that was adapted to the real genius of the language. (GS5.238)

If a language corresponds to the spirit of a people, and if thinking depends on language, then each language implies a distinctive construction of the world through thought. Immediately preceding the Kantian- and universalist-sounding passage quoted above about the "objective" being "situated in the middle of all languages," Humboldt had written:

It is self-evident from the mutual interdependence of thought and word that languages are not so much the means to represent truth once established but rather the means to discover truth previously unknown. Their diversity is not one of sounds and signs, but a diversity of world views themselves. (1997: 18 translation modified)

These lines contain two of Humboldt's key terms: diversity (*Verschiedenheit*) and *Weltansicht*, which can be translated world view or, indeed, point of view on the world (detailed analysis of this concept in Chabrolle-Cerretini 2007).

The most famous statement comes from the Kawi introduction:

[S]ince a like subjectivity also affects language in the same nation, there resides in every language a characteristic *world-view*. As the individual sound stands between man and the object, so the entire language steps in between him and the nature that operates, both inwardly and outwardly, upon him. He surrounds himself with a world of sounds, so as to assimilate and process within himself the world of objects ... By the same act whereby he spins language out of himself, he spins himself into it, and every language draws about the people that possess it a circle whence it is possible to exit only by stepping over at once into the circle of another one. To learn a *foreign language* should therefore be to acquire a new standpoint in the world-view hitherto possessed, and in fact to a certain extent it is so, since every language contains the whole conceptual fabric and mode of presentation of a portion of mankind. (1836 [1999]: 60)

This view of language makes translation problematic. In an 1816 text on translation, Humboldt wrote that "[I]f one excepts expressions that designate merely bodily objects, no word of any language corresponds perfectly to a word in another language ... A word is so little the sign of a concept that the concept cannot even come into being, much less be fixed, without it" (GS8.129).

Humboldt was a poet and critic, a friend of many of the German literary figures of his time. One of his major claims was that it was in literary works, notably in poetry, that the potentialities of language could be fully developed: this meant, as Sapir and Paul Friedrich would later argue, that poetic language offered a privileged access into the distinctive nature of a given language-world (Trabant 2000b: 33–4).

Like Herder, even while discovering something unique and precious in each language, Humboldt maintains the superiority of some types over others. While each language or type of language has its own essence, there is also an essence of language as such, and *this* is best expressed by the inflectional morphology of the Indo-European languages. Only through inflection is the true balance maintained between order and freedom:

[T]he *method of inflection* ... alone imparts true inner fixity to the word for both mind and ear, and likewise separates with certainty the parts of the sentence, in keeping with the necessary ordering of thought ... [T]here can be no doubt but that it harbours exclusively the pure principle of language structure ... [I]t elevates the most primary essence (*ursprünglichste Wesen*) of language, articulation and symbolization, to their highest degrees ... Compared with the *incorporative procedure* [of American languages], and that of loose *addition* without true word-unity, the *method of inflection* appears as a principle of genius, born of a true intuition of language. (1836 [1999]: 145, translation modified)

Humboldt continues his condemnation of non-inflecting languages, but, as we saw with Herder, it turns weirdly into praise as the author goes into specific cases. Humboldt begins by listing some deviations from the inflecting ideal and pointing out that these may be present in differing combinations:

The essence of such a language will result from the *mixing* of these principles, though as a rule it will develop a still more individual form from their application. For where the full energy of the guiding power does not preserve the correct balance, it is easy for one part of the language to attain, improperly, a development out of keeping with the rest. From this and other factors, *particular excellences* may also arise in languages in which we cannot otherwise recognize precisely the character of being exceptionally suitable organs of thought. Nobody can deny that old-style Chinese possesses a striking dignity, in that manifestly weighty ideas approach each other directly ... The Malayan language ... is not unjustly renowned for its agility and the great simplicity of its verbal arrangement. (1836 [1999]: 146, translation modified)

Humboldt goes on to the artistry in the play of Semitic vowels, the brevity and boldness of Basque (remember Rabelais on Basque brusqueness?), and the power of combination of ideas in North American languages. And then we swing back to what's wrong with all these treasures.

Humboldt's ranking of languages is merely *actual*: it is not *potential*, which is something that would be far more serious for a Romantic thinker. Any language, any people has the possibility of full development into something unique. It's just that not all of them have gone very far down that road.

[E]very language would be able to indicate everything, if the people it belongs to were to traverse every stage of their culture ... Each [language], like man himself, is an *infinity* gradually developing in time. What glimmers through (*Durchschimmernde*) is therefore something that *modifies* all indications subjectively and even quantitatively. It does not appear (*erscheint*) there as an effect (*Wirkung*); rather, the *effective* (*wirkende*) *force* externalizes itself directly, as such, and hence as merely caressing the effects (*Wirkungen*) with its breath, so to speak, in a distinctive way. (1836 [1999]: 157, translation modified)

Like Herder, Humboldt presumes that under normal circumstances, national character, language, race, world view all fit together. "One might wish to object" to this, writes Humboldt,

that children of any people, if, before they speak, are displaced into a foreign community, develop their linguistic abilities in the latter's language. This undeniable fact, we might say, is a clear proof that language is merely an echoing of what is heard, and depends entirely on social circumstances, without regard for any unity or diversity of the essence (*des Wesens*).

Yes, we would reply today, we would certainly make this objection. Look at how he answers it:

But in cases of this kind it has been difficult to observe with sufficient accuracy how laboriously the native pattern has had to be overcome, and how perhaps in the finest nuances it has still kept its ground unvanquished ... If language, by its origin from the depths of man's nature, did not also enter into true and authentic combination with physical descent, why otherwise, for both cultured and uncultured alike, would the language of the fatherland possess a strength and intimacy so much greater than that of any foreign one, that after long abstention it greets the ear with a sort of sudden magic, and awakens longing when far from home? (1836 [1999]: 58–9, translation modified)

Mustn't there be a sort of continuing bodily nostalgia for one's ancestral tongue – even if all evidence is to the contrary? To anticipate, this desire to understand each language and culture and the minds and bodies of its bearers as a single distinctive and satisfying whole is something that will be rejected by the Boasians. It explains why they kept insisting that there was *no* necessary connection between language, thought, culture, and race even as they were clearly arguing for a close connection between language, thought, and culture – from a certain point of view.

5   Essences and universals through the nineteenth century

Most intellectual genealogies derive Boas's thinking on language and culture, as well as the idea of linguistic relativity, directly from Herder and Humboldt (e.g., "The line of descent from the German cult of linguistic relativity practised by von Humboldt and his followers ... to the work of Whorf is clear and unbroken" [Haugen 1987: 138, referring to Christmann 1967]). This is usually done via a leap from the beginning to the end of the nineteenth century (e.g., Schaff 1964 [1973]; R. L. Brown 1967; Miller 1968: 14–34; Penn 1972: 15–22; Malkiel 1974; Steiner 1975: 89). But the period between the relatively coherent essentialism of Humboldt and the Romantics and the relatively coherent relativity of the Boasians, which is to say most of the nineteenth century, in fact held a series of connecting figures in philosophy, linguistics, and anthropology.

The nineteenth century was marked by increasing confidence in natural science and the method of taking particular phenomena out of their context to regroup, classify, and explain them on the basis of universal laws. In Britain, in particular, the full application of this natural-scientific method to human history led to the rise of evolutionism and the constitution of anthropology as a comparative science. In Germany, the increasing prestige of the natural sciences was offset by the positing of a category of cultural or spiritual or historical sciences (*Kultur-* or *Geisteswissenschaften*) that required the use of different methods: in studying the work of an author or artist, the literature or art of a people, or the spirit of a civilization or a historical period, what mattered was the phenomenon in its context, as part of a unique whole; the goal was to interpret such wholes by seeking to define the spirit that made everything within them intelligible. Philosophy, philology, and the emerging field of anthropology all had different relationships with this division of method. Here I would like to go through each of these fields. Since they fertilized each other, this will necessitate some back-and-forth of our own.

Philosophy: Hegel's synthesis and the "relativity of language"

Although he was a contemporary of the Romantics, the ideas of G. W. F. Hegel (1770–1831) had such an impact on the following generations that I feel justified in including him in this chapter. Hegel was the last of the great philosophical system-builders, and by the time of his death his system was the dominant reference point in German philosophy. Hegel saw his role as that of evaluating and synthesizing all previous thought. He did this by drawing on the essentialist legacy and encapsulating it in a wider developing Reason.

Hegel's idealism encompassed all of human history: he wanted to reread what had been and prophesy what would be. In his system, history realized the development of the world-spirit (*Weltgeist*) through a series of stages, each revealing its own *Geist*. Reality was merely the manifestation of this logic, which is the ultimate reality. Hegel proposed four stages, each of which represented a central theme: the Oriental world expressed despotic subjectivity, the Greek world beauty, the Roman world law, the modern or German world freedom. All aspects of life and thought in each of these historical spheres could be understood only in terms of that sphere and had no meaning outside it. As Althusser sums it up (Althusser and Balibar 1965 [1970]: 186), "The Leibnizian concept of *expression* ... dominates all of Hegel's thought."

For twenty years after Hegel's death there were battles among his followers, which to some extent still continue. Among the "Young Hegelians" was the young Karl Marx (1818–1883), who "stood Hegel on his head" by arguing for the priority of the human species-essence (*Gattungswesen*) over any ideal abstractions. The movement, while radical in its politics, remained within the paradigm of essence and expression and used the vocabulary and the thought-forms of Hegel, and therefore of the Romantics and Herder.

At the same time, there were tendencies that entirely rejected Hegel. One of these, which has come to be labelled "German language philosophy" (*Sprachphilosophie*), maintained that where Hegel had gotten it wrong – in company with most major philosophers since Plato – was in failing to recognize that human thought always implies language. As a result, most philosophical constructions were merely word games with no actual referent. Critiques of this kind kept coming up for some fifty years after Hegel's death, offered by philosophers who are rarely mentioned even in histories of German philosophy.[1] It was these forgotten philosophers who introduced the term "linguistic relativity."

The first was one of Hegel's fiercest critics, Otto Friedrich Gruppe (1804–1876). It is hard to get a grip on Gruppe. Classical philologist, Germanist, philosopher of language and cognition, polemicist, literary theorist, art critic, playwright, poet, bureaucrat, student of some of the greatest scholars of his day, friend of George Eliot and victim of the sharp pen of Karl Marx, Gruppe was until very recently – there has been something of a revival since his bicentenary – remembered, if at all, as a dilettante, unfortunately immortalized by Marx as a *Hanswurst*, a superficial dolt (Cloeren 1988: 112). Immediately after Hegel's death, Gruppe published his epistolary treatise *Antäus*, then three years later *The Turning Point in German Philosophy*. In these books, Hegel incarnates speculative philosophy, which for Gruppe is nothing but building castles in the air when what is required is to get our feet back on the ground. Whence the title of his first book: in Greek mythology Antaeus, the son of the Earth, gained strength through touching his mother. Heracles finally succeeded in killing him by lifting him up in the air, away from the life-giving contact, as Gruppe would have it, with reality. We know reality through concepts and have concepts only through language, and there is no guarantee that language accurately reflects reality. It is in this context that Gruppe makes what I believe is the first use of the term "linguistic relativity" (cf. Gumperz and Levinson 1996: 14, n. 2) with his phrase "the necessary relativity of the whole of language" (*die notwendige Relativität der ganzen Sprache*) (1831 [1914]: 425). Such relativity implies a corresponding relativity of concepts, since "[t]hought is not without language as language is not without thought, both stand in a relationship of mutual exchange (*Wechselbeziehung*). This has never yet been considered in its full importance and with everything that follows from it" (1834: 28, in Cloeren 1988: 101).

Gruppe praises Humboldt and Herder (1831 [1914]: 511); not surprisingly, he doesn't like Kant's abstractions and approves of Herder's *Metacritique* (1831 [1914]: 512). But Gruppe's interest is in language in general more than in particular languages. The examples that he gives – that words have changed their meaning through time, that Aristotle's categories are merely hypostases of Greek grammatical categories (1834: 116 ff.) – do not tell us about any particular language, but about the relativity of language as such.

Gruppe was as much a philologist as a philosopher. Among his many other works is a book on the history of German translation, in which, like the Romantics, he wants to recognize the specificity of "the genius of our language" (1859: 355).

Gruppe's philosophical writings were largely ignored for several decades. In 1854 he came out with a new book restating his approach. A few years after this Conrad Hermann (1819–1897) published his *Philosophical Grammar* (1858), which argues the same basic point as Gruppe – that philosophical abstractions are abuses of more concrete language – but represents a more classically essentialist position. For Hermann, each nation/people/language is a distinctive whole, its language setting *limits* to what can be thought:

Hermann repeatedly states that it makes no sense to speak of thinking as such, but only of thought which is concretized in a specific language. Language as form ... [is] "the autonomous dominating power over our own entire individual thinking itself. Thus thought and language are one and the same." (Cloeren 1988: 140, citing Hermann 1858: 44)

This is why there are thoughts that occur in some languages and not in others (p. 41). Hermann returns to Leibniz's metaphors of mirrors and points of view: "every single language is a mirror ground a particular way (*besonders*) in which, therefore, the intellectual (*geistige*) content of the world is reflected from a particular angle (*von einer besonderen Seite aus*)" (Hermann 1858: 99).

A similar position was taken a decade later by the schoolteacher Gustav Gerber (1820–1901). Gerber's major target is Kant, who failed to be critical enough regarding the language he himself was using.

[W]hat Kant began to investigate as a critique of pure reason must be continued as a critique of impure reason, objectified reason, thus as a *critique of language*. The diversity (*Verschiedenheit*) of scientific, moral, religious concepts, the distinctiveness (*Eigentümlichkeit*) of the whole of a people's way of life (*des Volkslebens*), the diverse (*verschiedene*) historical developments in different nations are in themselves sufficiently clear signs to indicate that a general system of thought is the same abstraction as a general system of language would be. (in Vonk 1999: 289, translation modified)

In 1885, Ludwig Noiré (1829–1889) published a book on the origin of language bringing up many of the same themes. Noiré's work served as the philosophical basis when the Sanskritist, linguist, and mythographer Friedrich Max Müller (1820–1899) gave his lectures on the *Science of Thought*. Müller sees language as essential for thought:

Let anyone try the experiment and he will see that we can as little think without words as we can breathe without lungs ... Should we know of a sky if we had no name for it? ...

[I]f there is no such thing as a mere name, neither is there such a thing as a mere thought or a mere concept. The two are one and inseparable. We may distinguish them as we distinguish the obverse from the reverse of a coin; but to try to separate them would be like trying to separate the convex from the concave surface of a lens. We think in names and in names only.

It is very strange to see how some philosophers are perfectly unable to see the identity of thought and language, while others never doubt it. (1887a: 47, 50)

Indeed. Still, like some semantic universalists of our own time (e.g., Wierzbicka 1992), Müller sees no contradiction between the diversity of languages and the unity of thought, since for him linguistic diversity is only a surface phenomenon. An Indo-European philologist of the old school (see the next section), Müller felt that his science had succeeded in discovering the set of basic roots underlying all Indo-European languages, and therefore probably of all human language (1887b: 59–63).

Georg Runze's (1852–1922) book *Sprache und Religion*, dedicated to Max Müller, was categorical about the identity of language and thought: "Thinking is silent speaking, speaking is thinking aloud; as the thought creates the word, so also the word creates the new thought" (1889: 2).

Besides the relativity of *things (sachliche Relativität)* there also exists *linguistic* relativity (*sprachliche Relativität*), which allows only a recognition of arbitrary oppositions, experimental correlations, approximate totalizations *between* spirit and language, *between* thought and word, sense and tone, idea and sound, idea-representation (*Vorstellungsbild*) and tone-representation (*Tonbild*). (1889: 145)

With the exception of Hermann, when the *Sprachphilosophen* used the phrase "relativity of language" or "linguistic relativity," it was to refer to language in general as a factor in thought and perception, not to differences among languages. They seem to have jumped past Humboldt's central concern with language diversity and reconnected with Wolff.

Language: comparative philology

The historical kinship of Greek and Latin with Sanskrit, and so with each other, was a monumental discovery, and it led to an explosion of research with a first consolidation in the work of Franz Bopp (1791–1867). Bopp felt that languages could be compared as living organisms could. In 1836, he elaborated this: languages are "organic, natural bodies formed according to definite laws, having a life-giving principle within" (in Benes 2008: 79). The idea of the life-giving principle that determines the growth of an entity, that is, the externalization of its potentialities, is evidently close to those of Herder and Humboldt; Bopp was a friend of Humboldt's and his teacher of Sanskrit.

Starting with his 1816 comparative study of conjugation systems, Bopp would go on enlarging and refining his model and bringing in other languages, and within a decade the comparative study of Indo-European was "normal science."

Bopp's book came out the same year as the first volume of the Grimms' fairy tales, and Jakob Grimm, in particular, was one of the main contributors to the new science, proposing, among other things, the first recognized law of sound transformation. Grimm's Law, first formulated in 1822, explains a series of differences between the occlusive consonants of words in many Indo-European languages and the form they take in Germanic. This case illustrates two points. Grimm's Law was presented as part of his grammar of German: where Bopp was looking to the whole field of Indo-European languages, the Grimms kept German at the center, as in all of their other work, and drew on comparisons primarily to illuminate what happened in Germanic. But the fact that Grimm discovered a law points in a different direction: toward a universalist model of research, in which facts – in this case specific sounds – are isolated and explained through the application of general laws. This tendency of historical philology to consider itself a natural science, to think of language as a mass of phenomena individually explicable by laws, would become stronger as the century progressed.

Perhaps the greatest transformation was one that affected all the sciences. Up to the early nineteenth century, most Europeans accepted calculations based on the Bible that concluded that the earth was a few thousand years old. Most of the early comparative philologists therefore presumed that whatever the ancestral form of the Indo-European languages might have been, it had to be close to the original language of mankind. The opening-up to "Deep Time" (Gould 1990) came in the work of the Scottish geologist Charles Lyell (1797–1875). In his *Principles of Geology* (first volume 1830), Lyell adopted the principle of uniformitarianism: the kinds of processes we observe around us today must be used to explain processes in the past; if judging by observable processes a layer of rock must have been formed millions of years ago, so be it. Suddenly the earth, and with it the living world, looked much, much older – old enough, in fact, to think seriously about transformations in living things, and of humans and their languages, over a long period. For August Schleicher (1821–1868), for the first time, the ancestral Proto-Indo-European language was not the primeval voice of origins, but a real human language, albeit a prehistoric one. Schleicher had worked out most of his ideas before Darwin published *The Origin of Species*, and when it appeared Schleicher saw it as a confirmation of his own theories.

This transformation allowed the next great consolidation in linguistics, the rise of the Neogrammarian movement in the 1870s (Tuite 2006: 237–42). The Neogrammarians redefined historical linguistics unambiguously as a natural science, defining laws that operated without exception on isolated phenomena. The best developed laws were those of sound change, of which Grimm's remained the model. By the end of the 1870s, the object was no longer any language as it exists or existed, but a vast field of transformations of isolated sounds and forms. A major aspect of human life had been moved into the natural sciences.

Language: the Humboldtian stream

At the same time, a systemic linguistics continued to develop, carrying on Humboldt's concern with language specificities and the characterization of language types. Against the primary interest of the historical linguists in a single Indo-European family and the transformation of its sounds and words through time, this Humboldtian stream (Koerner 1977) sought to account for the variety of languages of the world and to understand linguistic categories across languages. While linguists of all schools continued to cite Humboldt's general principles, actual followers of his methods remained "a minority opposition current against the historical-comparative current" (Trabant 2000a: 317).

The main representative of this opposition, a living monument of Humboldtian linguistics through much of the nineteenth century, was Heymann Steinthal (1823–1899). Steinthal maintained the main features of Humboldt's work, but tried to state them more clearly and scientifically (Trautmann-Waller 2006; Benes 2008: 251–8). Early on (1848), he tried to ground Humboldt's linguistics in the philosophy of Hegel, seeing the former as an expression of the ideas the latter articulated more broadly.

Humboldt's idea of the "inner form of language (*innere Sprachform*) is the central concept of Steinthal's theory of language" (Bumann 1965: 120); he says that his book on grammar, logic, and psychology "is merely the explication (*Erläuterung*) of this concept" (Steinthal 1855: xx). For Steinthal, "Humboldt's statement of the eternal birth of language from the spirit held the same significance for linguistics that Descartes' *cogito* held for modern philosophy" (Steinthal 1877: 66).

The model for Steinthal's psychology of language was the system of J. F. Herbart (1776–1841), for whom each mind was a distinctive matrix of already-received material which guides the reception of incoming data. However data are *perceived* by the senses, they are only *apperceived* – Herbart used the distinction developed by Leibniz – through the activation of those aspects of this matrix that most resemble them, while at the same time transforming the matrix to some degree. In Steinthal's theory, subjective experience formed a whole which he called an *Anschauung*, the Kantian word usually translated as intuition. But unlike Kant, Steinthal did not believe that form was imposed on this mass as a general property of the human mind. On the contrary – shades of Lamy, Buffier, and Condillac – it was the structure of language that allowed the analysis and sequential presentation of complex intuitions (Mackert 1993: 333). A language imposed form on thought through its own inner form, made up of its "distinctive system of grammatical categories," which are "the forms in which a people (*Volk*) transforms its intuitions into representations" (Steinthal 1860: 316).

Steinthal felt it was part of his job to rank languages,[2] and he did so on the basis of how well they distinguished formal relations in their categories, introducing a division between languages with and without form (cf. Mackert 1993: 333–4). Once again, the Indo-European languages represent the highest achievement.

Steinthal followed Humboldt in his philological approach to languages, an interest in their literatures as well as in their structures. In his book on the Mande languages of West Africa, Steinthal (1867) presents texts along with the grammar, a model that directly inspired Boas and his students (Bunzl 1996: 68–9). And Steinthal's grammars are based on the type of the given language, not on Greek or Latin.

The Mande book typifies Steinthal's contradictions. In the introduction to the first version, he had written:

[T]he author intends to show that in fact there are languages that have no point in common with the category schemas of philosophical grammarians, and which it is as impossible to compare with our highly organized Indo-European languages with regard to their inner structure as it is to compare an insect to a mammal ... Just as the frog and the man both breathe, so both Soso and Sanskrit have words for activity and substance ... But just as human breath is not to be found in the breast of the frog ... in the same way Soso lacks the Sanskrit noun and verb. (Steinthal 1867: vi–viii)

He quotes these lines from 1851 in the new edition, in 1867. Now, while not changing his opinion, he seems honestly upset that these kinds of characterizations might have had an actual effect on people's lives:

That the languages being dealt with here are very low on the scale, that is, that in their organization they are very imperfect, I must express with the inconsiderate impartiality (*Rücksichtlosigkeit*) required by science. Should I have the misfortune of my book being cited by perverse spirits who wish to preserve slavery, this would hurt me, but only as an unhappy accident might hurt me ... These Negro languages ... may well be very imperfect in comparison with the Indo-European languages; but I wonder whether this mechanism of the *a* or *e* affix is not something astonishingly human. (p. xiv)

Steinthal's career parallels that of his contemporary Karl Marx (Marx was born in 1818, Steinthal in 1823). Both were of German Jewish background. Marx's father had converted to Lutheranism, and he himself was of course a devout atheist, but he was always identified as a Jew; Steinthal was a pillar of the German Jewish community. Both were profoundly German in their training and basic tendencies. Both started out as Hegelians who wanted to push the Hegelian envelope in new directions: Marx wrote his revolutionary revisions of Hegel in 1844 at the age of twenty-six, Steinthal published his rereading of Humboldt as a Hegelian in 1848 (the year of the *Communist Manifesto*) at the age of twenty-five. Both were fascinated by developments in the natural sciences, and both spent much of their careers trying to develop more rigorous scientific approaches in the human sciences. Both ended up with models that are pluralist, requiring that given data be understood in the context of a particular historical "field" – Marx's modes of production, Steinthal's basic language types – and at the same time tried to develop rigorous and universally valid ways of establishing the nature of these "fields."

Anthropology: German pluralism

One source for a pluralist view of what would come to be called cultures was a comparative theory of the psychology (-gies) of peoples (*Völkerpsychologie*) developed by Steinthal in collaboration with the philosopher Moritz Lazarus (1824–1903) (Trautmann-Waller 2004). The goal was to elucidate human nature in its diversity:

Because the essence of mankind was expressed by its "division into *Völker*" and its development was "tied to the diversity of peoples," the laws of folk psychology would have to emerge slowly out of data collected from many different peoples; by this means, folk psychology would eventually achieve genuine understanding both of the general nature (*Wesen*) of the *Volksgeist* and its individual expressions among particular peoples. (Bunzl 1996: 28)

These multiple and internally coherent *Volksgeister* represent a historical link between Romantic visions of the unity of a people, its language, and its mode of thought on the one hand and the Boasian concept of cultures on the other.

Humboldt's influence is clear in the psychology of Lazarus and Steinthal, in that of Wilhelm Wundt (1832–1920), and in the ethnography and geography of Adolf Bastian (1826–1905). Bastian's major work, *Man in History* (1860), is dedicated to Alexander von Humboldt, and his discussion of language (I, 380 ff.) is based on Wilhelm (Bunzl 1996: 63). Bastian's Berlin school of anthropology (Zimmerman 2001) included Steinthal and the anti-racist physical anthropologist Rudolf Virchow.[3] As a young scholar, Boas would work with Wundt, Virchow, and Bastian, and he would express regret at not having attended Steinthal's lectures.

Anthropology: evolutionism

In the later nineteenth century, the most important universalist movement in the study of human history was evolutionism, which arose primarily in the English-speaking world from the 1850s. Its impetus came from Lyell's uniformitarianism, which had provided the earth and humanity with time for the gradual development of organisms and institutions. The model, as developed by Herbert Spencer (1820–1903), held that the universe and everything in it showed a general progress toward ever higher levels of complexity and organization. Unlike the earlier stage theories of Condillac and Diderot, which were inherently critical of the current social order as in discrepancy with the stage that humanity had reached, nineteenth-century British evolutionism was predominantly self-congratulatory, seeing existing modern society and the Empire as the apogee of human history.

The evolutionist model was brought into the comparative study of human cultures most famously by Sir Edward Burnett Tylor (1832–1917), who introduced the word "anthropology" for the new natural science of human transformation. All human institutions, in this view, could be located on a single scale of development from the most savage to the most civilized. Apparently savage institutions still existing among civilized peoples – superstitions and folk customs, for instance – were understood as isolated survivals from an earlier age. Peoples who continued to act in a savage way – by dressing in skins or not at all, living in small bands, practising hunting and gathering and lacking agriculture and industrialization – were themselves survivals of the same kind, groups who had not changed over the millennia. The savage is therefore *primitive*, a word that magically combines a condition and a time period. Since

everywhere humanity passes or fails to pass through the same stages, information about hunting and gathering peoples can be used to conduct "researches
into the early history of mankind" (the title of one of Tylor's books); to call
these people "primitive" is to say that they *are* the early history of mankind,
still available for consultation. And on any topic: their religion must still be
close to the original religion, and their languages must be very much like the
original tongues of humanity.

This gives an idea of the sleight-of-hand that this form of evolutionism represents: a voyage in space, say to central Australia, equals a voyage into the
distant past; in a way very different from that of Isidore, space equals time. It is
perhaps not a coincidence that H. G. Wells' story *The Time Machine* was published in 1895, Sir Arthur Conan Doyle's *The Lost World* in 1912, and Edgar
Rice Burroughs' *The Land that Time Forgot* in 1918.

In his book *Some First Steps in Human Progress*, based on lectures on the
Chautauqua circuit, the American evolutionist Frederick Starr (1858–1933)
asks "Why languages interest the anthropologist": "To the anthropologist, who
is seldom or never a linguist," he answers, "language is interesting, (a) in deter-
mining connection or contact between different races, (b) as showing the status of a race of people, (c) as evidence of a grand development and progress"
(1901: 187–8). We are a far cry from Humboldt's view of languages as keys to
world views, not to mention from Starr's contemporary Boas – whom he beat
out for the anthropology job at the newly founded University of Chicago.

Yet languages turned out to be hard nuts for the evolutionists to crack. While
one can always declare that inflectional languages are superior to others,
there is no evidence that speaking an isolating language has slowed down the
Chinese, nor that speakers of agglutinative languages have any trouble thinking and communicating about whatever they want to think and communicate
about. People who have no agriculture or metallurgy also have no trouble talking with an adequacy that cannot be distinguished from that of speakers of any
language. There just don't seem to be any primitive languages.

Reading the manuals of the evolutionists is quite illuminating in this regard.
They are very comfortable talking about the evolution of animal husbandry or
architecture, but in their chapters on language the authors seem to be casting
about for whatever signs of primitivity they can identify. Spencer sees the most
primitive languages as loose ones, with little integration of the words.

But in most inferior languages, the process of "agglutination" ... has gone far enough
to produce some stability in the compound words: there is a manifest integration. How
small is the degree of this integration, however, in comparison with that reached in well-
developed languages, is shown both by the great length of the compound words used for
common things ... and by the separableness of their elements ... That the great length
of ... words implies a low degree of development, and that in the formation of higher
languages out of lower there is a gradual integration, which reduces the polysyllables

to dissyllables and monosyllables, is an inference confirmed by the history of our own language. (1862: 203–4)

The development of language, like that of everything else in the universe, is toward greater and greater integration, and the English monosyllable is the summit of development.

Language equally exhibits [integration] throughout all grammatical development. The lowest kinds of human speech, having merely nouns and verbs without inflections to them, manifestly permit no such close union of the elements of a proposition as results when the relations are either marked by inflections or by words specially used for purposes of connexion. Such speech is what we significantly call "incoherent." To a considerable extent, incoherence is seen in the Chinese language. (Spencer 1862: 205)

When Spencer has to explain the fact that modern European languages such as English are less inflected, and so, one would presume, more like Chinese than were their ancestors, he turns to "integration of another order":

After the development of those grammatical forms which make definite statements possible, we do not at first find them used to express anything beyond statements of a simple kind … In the number of subordinate propositions which accompany the principal one; in the various complements to subjects and predicates; and in the numerous qualifying clauses – all of them united into one complex whole – many sentences in modern composition exhibit a degree of integration not to be found in ancient ones. (1862: 206–7)

The height of integration and, by implication, of civilization, would, then, be realized in the kind of prose represented in the style of this founder of evolutionary thinking, with long sentences put together out of short, highly integrated words that combine in a carefully thought-out way to form tight ranks of qualifying subordinate clauses lined up in such a manner as to reproduce, in their very order, an elaborate construction of thought which is clearly organized and at the same time encompasses multiple strands of ratiocination.

Tylor, for his part, was intensely interested in languages. "In the winter of 1860–1 alone,"

he learnt the elements of Sanskrit, gathered some material for a book on general philology, read a grammar of Greenlandish and "got some knowledge of the language," read Bopp and Porschmann on Malayo-Polynesian, and gained an "elementary knowledge" of Russian. In the next summer, he began Welsh. (Henson 1974: 16–17)

The non-correspondence of words and things bothered Tylor as it had British thinkers in the seventeenth century. Given that the lexicons of modern civilized languages are just as unmotivated as those of any primitive tribe, Tylor is as pessimistic as Bacon or Locke about *any* language as a means to knowledge:

[I]s it not a pregnant consideration that the language of civilised men is but the language of savages, more or less improved …? The development of language between its savage and cultured stages has been made in its details, scarcely in its principle. It is not too much to say that half the vast defect of language as a method of utterance, and half the vast defect of thought as determined by the influence of language, are due to the fact that speech is a scheme worked out by the rough and ready application of material metaphor and imperfect analogy, in ways fitting rather the barbaric education of those who formed it, than our own. (Tylor 1871: 475)

Most of the evolutionists felt obliged to try to indicate what constituted savage characteristics in languages. To do so, any difference between Western European languages and a "primitive" or exotic one, whether in phonetics, grammar, or semantics, was taken as a sign of the primitive character of the latter. If travellers had trouble grasping a sound in an exotic language, the conclusion was drawn that the language itself had poorly defined sounds. Washington Matthews (1843–1905) has a sad chapter on "Some Difficulties in the Study of the Hidatsa Language" with a long section on the unclearness of consonants.

I believe that these Indians do not well appreciate the differences between ... allied sounds as they fall on their ears, and consequently make no effort to distinguish them with their tongues ... Furthermore, when you hear an Indian uttering a sound ... you are often at a loss to select a character to express it. In other words, there are labial, lingual, and dental sounds which *we* have not yet learned to distinguish, and which we have no characters to represent ...

When I first obtained some insight into the extent to which these permutations existed, I could scarcely trust my senses, and often feared that I labored under some subjective difficulties. At other times, when, in the mouth of the same speaker, and almost in the same breath, I would hear a well-known word suddenly change its form, I would puzzle myself by supposing that the change took place in accordance with some inscrutable grammatical rule. But when I came into the possession of vocabularies collected by others, I became better satisfied with the results of my own observations. (1877: 80–2)

The American-Canadian anthropologist Horatio Hale (1817–1896) wrote that "[i]n many languages, as is well known, there are elementary sounds of an indeterminate nature, which seem to float between two, and sometimes even three or four, diverse articulations" (1884: 233).

In grammar, the difficulty of fitting non-Western languages into the eight parts of speech was taken, as it had been in the first studies of the European vernaculars, as a sign of their lack of organization. Matthews tells us that "[w]ords will be considered under the usual eight heads of nouns, pronouns, [etc.]" (1877: 92), and he gives over sections to gender, number, case, only to say in each section that there isn't any obligatory expression of gender, number, or case.

The situation was particularly acute in comparisons of semantic categorization in Western and non-Western languages. If an exotic language made gross distinctions where our languages make fine ones, this was intepreted to mean that it had poorly defined concepts; if it made fine distinctions where ours make gross ones, this meant that it was incapable of abstraction. Edward John Payne (1844–1904) wrote:

Savages will have twenty independent words each expressing the act of cutting some particular thing, without having any name for the act of cutting in general; they will have as many to describe birds, fish and trees of different kinds, but no general equivalents for the terms "bird," "fish," or "tree." (1899: 103)

But only a few pages later, he was saying that these languages "merely gave general, undifferentiated impressions" expressed by "portmanteau words" or "holophrases" (1899: 117). Boas, then Lévi-Strauss (1962), would point out the arbitrariness and unfairness of such a procedure.

Another way of finding primitivity was to focus on those aspects of language that might be seen to evolve in a single direction. Most commonly cited were the use of gesture and the relative elaborateness of number and color vocabulary.

Tylor says that while there is no evidence for this, early language must have been dominated by gestures. He repeats stories of tribes that require gestures as a supplement to their "scanty sentences" (1871: 164). The American anthropologist Lewis Henry Morgan writes, "As we descend through the gradations of language into its ruder forms, the gesture element increases in the quantity and variety of its forms until we find language so dependent upon gestures that without them they would be substantially unintelligible" (1877: 37). He gives no references. Starr, for his part, has no chapter on language as such, but three on "Gesture and Speech." There may be tribes, he says, whose languages are so dependent on gesture that their members cannot speak to each other at night.[4] Certainly, there are primitive groups whose meager languages depend on gestures to allow understanding. Overall, the level of civilization is in inverse proportion to the amount of gesture. The civilized Anglo-Saxon hardly gestures at all; to study this subject, one must go

among peoples who, like the French and the Italians, speak in each of their movements and whose faces show all the thoughts that fly through their minds … among children, who have not yet learned duplicity … among the inferior races – the true children of nature. (Starr 1901: 170)

The evolutionists also found evidence for progress in the greater development of certain vocabulary domains in technologically more elaborate societies. Some languages only have words for one, two, and many, and it is possible to make some correlation between a large-scale society, elaborate technology, and a large set of number terms. In the writings of some evolutionists, language is virtually reduced to number terms. Similarly, the fact that some ancient and exotic languages have few terms primarily denoting colors (as first noted by W. E. Gladstone in 1858) was taken as a sign of their primitive nature (MacLaury 2001; Deutscher 2010).

Those who sought primitivity in language had to contend with reports that continued to come in from missionaries and travellers telling of the remarkable structural complexity and elegance of some "primitive" languages. Frederick William Farrar (1831–1903), the Dean of Canterbury, wanted to make sure this didn't give anybody the wrong idea:

[T]his apparent wealth of synonyms and grammatical forms is chiefly due *to the hopeless poverty of the power of abstraction* ... When the mind has nothing else to work upon, it will expend its energy in a lumbering and bizarre multiplicity of linguistic expedients, and by richness of expression will try to make up for poverty of thought. Many of these vaunted languages ... – which have countless forms of conjugation, and separate words for the minutest shades of specific meaning, – these holophrastic languages, with their "jewels fourteen syllables long," to express the commonest and most familiar objects ... have not even yet arrived at the very simple abstraction required to express the verb 'to be,' which Condillac assumed to be the earliest of invented verbs! The state of these languages ... is an additional proof of primordial and unbroken barbarism. The triumph of civilisation is not complexity but simplicity. (Fastar 1865: 52–4)

Darwin and philology

While today we associate evolution with the name of Charles Darwin (1809–1882), he was an atypical evolutionist, distinctive in proposing not universal progress but a very specific mechanism of random variations trimmed by natural selection, through which organisms tended to evolve to fit their current environment. If the environment changes, a trait that helped a species survive in an earlier period may be the very one that dooms it in this one.

Darwin himself seems to have drawn inspiration from linguistics.

In February 1837 ... Darwin wrote to his sister Caroline, discussing ... Sir John Herschel's idea that modern languages were descended from a common ancestor. If this were really the case, it cast doubt on the Biblical chronology of the world: "[E]veryone has yet thought that the six thousand odd years has been the right period but Sir J. thinks that a far greater number must have passed since the Chinese [and] the Caucasian languages separated from one stock." (Whitfield 2008)

Herschel had expressed the idea in a letter written in 1836 to none other than Lyell. Indeed, Steinthal would continue to claim that the idea of transformation of form was first developed in linguistics and only later borrowed into biology (Kalmar 1987).

The American evolutionists and language

Most of the founders of American anthropology came from a cohort that had served in the Civil War and explored the West. They would typically be experts on all the aspects of a given territory: its geology, flora, and fauna, and, along with this, its native peoples and their languages. Given their taste for natural science, most of these soldier-scholars looked to the British evolutionists for a congenial theory of human history and the place of different human types. The

Introduction to the Study of Indian Languages (1877) of Major John Wesley Powell (1834–1902), founder of the Bureau of American Ethnology, exemplifies this applied evolutionism. Powell adopts the empiricist view that language should be rapid, economical, and effective, to the point that he sees all redundancy in expressions of grammatical relations as a burden. What we need are simple words with all relations expressed by word order.

[A]ll paradigmatic inflection in a civilized tongue is a relic of its barbaric condition. When the parts of speech are fully differentiated and the process of placement fully specialized, so that the order of words in sentences has its full significance, no useful purpose is subserved by inflection ...
   All paradigmatic inflection requires unnecessary thought. (Powell 1880: 74b)

Always having to specify gender in English pronouns is bad enough. But in Ponca the situation is much worse.

A Ponca Indian, in saying that a man killed a rabbit, would have to say the man, he, one, animate, standing, in the nominative case, purposely killed, by shooting an arrow, the rabbit, he, the one, animate, sitting, in the objective case ... Perhaps one time in a million it would be the purpose to express all of these particulars, and in that case the Indian would have the whole expression in one compact word, but in the nine hundred and ninety-nine thousand nine hundred and ninety-nine cases all of these particulars would have to be thought of in the selection of the form of the verb, when no valuable purpose would be accomplished thereby.
   In the development of the English, as well as the French and German, linguistic evolution has not been in vain. (p. 74c)

Conclusion: "It will thus be seen that by the criterion of organization Indian tongues are of very low grade" (p. 74b).
   Powell's dismissal of American languages was a target for the ethnologist Daniel Garrison Brinton (1837–1899):

I should like to combat ... that ... ancient prejudice which led the old Greeks to call all those who did not speak their sonorous idioms barbarians ... Modern civilized nations hold that prejudice yet, in the sense that each insists that his own language is the best one extant, the highest in the scale, and that wherein others differ from it in structure they are inferior.
   So unfortunately placed is this prejudice with reference to my subject, that in the very volume issued by our government at Washington to encourage the study of the Indian languages, there is a long essay to prove that English is the noblest, most perfect language in the world, while all the native languages are, in comparison, of a very low grade indeed! ...
   We may suspect that when a writer lauds his native tongue at the expense of others, he is influenced by a prejudice in its favor and an absence of facility in the others. (1885, in Brinton 1890: 318–19)

Brinton was a great admirer of Humboldt's, and his central concern was with characterizing American languages typologically. He maintained the argument that each language family or each territorial linguistic group would be marked by a single central grammatical mechanism: "every large, connected, terrestrial area developed only one, or scarcely more than one, fundamental linguistic type, and this with such marked individuality that rarely did any of its languages depart from the general scheme" (Brinton 1890: 350, citing Heinrich Winkler). Brinton's conclusion is that the inner development of American languages is based on a single principle that expresses itself in morphology as polysynthesis, that is, the inclusion of any and all grammatical elements in a single construction; in verbs as incorporation of nominal and pronominal elements; and in ideation as holophrasis, the "impulse to express the whole proposition in one word" (Brinton 1890: 359). Yet this principle is less a distinctive essence than a universal stage:

I think there is no doubt but that [polysynthesis and holophrasis point] ... to that primordial period of human utterance when men had not yet learned to connect words into sentences, when their utmost efforts at articulate speech did not go beyond single words, which, aided by gestures and signs, served to convey their limited intellectual converse. Such single vocables did not belong to any particular part of speech. There was no grammar to that antique tongue. Its disconnected exclamations mean whole sentences in themselves.

A large part of the human race, notably, but not exclusively, the aborigines of this continent, continued the tradition of this mode of expression in the structure of their tongues ...

Although I thus regard one of the most prominent peculiarities of American languages as a survival from an exceedingly low stage of human development, it by no means follows that this is an evidence of their inferiority ...

If we apply what is certainly a very fair test, to wit: the uses to which a language is and can be put, I cannot see that a well-developed American tongue, such as the Aztec or the Algonkin, in any way falls short of, say French or English. (Brinton 1890: 322–3)

As we have seen with a number of authors, Brinton moves among condescension, condemnation, and praise. He takes another poke at Powell:

[N]either [polysynthesis nor holophrasis] appears anywhere mentioned in the official "Introduction to the Study of Indian Languages," issued by the United States Bureau of Ethnology! How the author of that work ... could have written a treatise on the study of American languages, and have not a word to say about these doctrines, the most salient and characteristic features of the group, is to me as inexplicable as it is extraordinary ... Steinthal, the most eminent philosophic linguist of the age, still teaches in Berlin, and teaches what I have already quoted from him about these traits. What is more, Major Powell does not even refer to this structural plan ... This is indeed the play of "Hamlet" with the part of Hamlet omitted! (1890: 358)

The rise of race

The general tendency in the intellectual life of the second half of the nineteenth century, across theoretical divisions, was to assume the identity of race and either nation or level of civilization. Even such liberal thinkers as Bastian and the linguist August Friedrich Pott saw languages differing based on the racially distinct physiologies of their speakers (Benes 2008: 207–9). For virtually all of the authors so far considered, Indo-European languages were superior to those of other families, even though this judgment was sometimes challenged in actual analyses. When non-Western peoples were admired, it was usually for their noble savagery, not a quality a modern Westerner could be expected actually to emulate.

During the second half of the century, racist ideologies of varying degrees of scientific respectability flourished across the Western world. One popular model, which found its definitive formulation in the *Essay on the Inequality of Human Races* (1855–1857) of the Count Arthur de Gobineau (1816–1882) – a successor to the counter-revolutionary French thinkers of the beginning of the century – identified speakers of Indo-European languages as the Aryan master race, the source of all that is valuable in world history. This view competed with that of the two "providential races," Aryans and Semites (Olender 1989 [1992]). In his dismissal of savage languages, Dean Farrar takes this latter position to the point of suggesting separate human creations:

These primeval lords of the untamed creation [i.e., early humans as found in archaeological sites], so far from being the splendid and angelic beings of the poet's fancy, appear to have resembled far more closely the Tasmanian, the Fuegian, the Greenlander, and the lowest inhabitants of Pelagian caverns or Hottentot kraals. We believe that in Scripture itself there are indications that they appeared upon the surface of the globe many ages before those simple and noble-minded shepherds from whose loins have sprung the Aryans and Semites – those two great races to whom all the world's progress in knowledge and civilisation has been solely due. (Fattar 1865: 56)

The identification of Africans, Native North Americans, and Pacific peoples as inferior races fit well, of course, into most colonial projects.

In Germany, the concern with national and linguistic purity was racialized and turned particularly against the Jews, seen as a people lacking a distinctive homeland, culture, and language, the Yiddish language being held to be a mere mixture. During the second half of the century, Antisemitism came to be institutionalized in Germany. One example among thousands is that Steinthal, "the most eminent philosophic linguist of the age," could not receive a professorship.

Most American research assumed, and an active program claimed to prove, the superiority of some races over others, with native peoples and immigrants, especially Jewish and Mediterranean immigrants, low on the ladder and Africans at the bottom. In 1916, the well-connected eugenicist Madison Grant (1865–1937) would publish *The Passing of the Great Race*, a tract advocating the culling of inferior races that would serve as "Hitler's Bible" back in Germany.

Antisemitism was largely responsible for driving Boas out of Germany. This was the America to which he was coming.

6   Boas and the linguistic multiverse

The birth of a new concept is invariably foreshadowed by a more or less strained or extended use of old linguistic material ... In most cases the new symbol is but a thing wrought from linguistic material already in existence in ways mapped out by crushingly despotic precedents.

Sapir (1921: 17)

The generation of the 1850s

At the end of the nineteenth century, two options were available in the human sciences. On one side, a natural-science model that sought explanations and universal laws; on the other, a pluralist, essentialist option that sought to interpret multiple wholes. For the first, language differences were epiphenomena to be ignored or corrected. For the second, they were the sign of the multiplicity of worlds constituted by different peoples and cultures. All agreed that peoples, cultures, languages, and, for most, races could be ranked, thus saving even the essentialists from drifting into absolute relativism. All agreed that their domains had clear centers in regard to which others could be ranked, whether it be the conscious speaking subject, the highly evolved (male) European, or the worthy (male) representative of his *Volk*.

Early in the twentieth century, these centers were displaced with the rise of new disciplines with different assumptions. To a large degree, these were the creations of scholars born during the second half of the 1850s. Boas (born 1858) was a near contemporary of other revolutionaries: Freud (1856–1939), Saussure (1857–1913), Durkheim (1858–1917), Planck (1858–1947), Husserl (1859–1938). Each of these was the founder of a new system, indeed a new field of study that would, in one way or another, break with the presuppositions of nineteenth-century thought. The disciplines they founded define some of the main currents of the twentieth century: psychoanalysis, synchronic linguistics, cultural and social anthropology, sociology, quantum mechanics, phenomenology. The new disciplines questioned the validity of considering elements in isolation from their context, and at the same time made explicit and so challenged the unstated centers of the earlier disciplines (cf. Derrida 1967 [1978]).

113

Some of them can be seen as the result of rediscovering aspects of the old essentialism – its systematicity and its assumption that different fields imply different internal rules – while at the same time rejecting essentialist tenets as a whole.

Franz Boas

Franz Boas was the founder of the North American schools of cultural anthropology and linguistics. These vocations, made by him into academic disciplines, were radically new both in their practice and their theory. For the first time, there was a major school of linguistic analysis based on intensive field research with speakers of a range of largely non-Indo-European, in this case mainly Amerindian, languages, exhibiting enormous grammatical variety.

This new practice assumed a new theoretical stance. In an echo of the creation of a pluralist linguistics by the Romantics and Humboldt in the face of Enlightenment universalism, Boas started his anthropological career and defined many of his positions in opposition to evolutionism. He and his students rejected the evolutionist view of language on every level: they held that each language deserves to be treated on its own terms, not with categories borrowed from classical grammar; that the specifics of each language are important; and that to some degree, each linguistic system orients the habitual thought of its users in a way that cannot be identified with general stages of development. These positions parallel Humboldtian ones, and it is not surprising that Boas and his students are often presented as the theoretical heirs to Herder and Humboldt. But at the same time, the Boasians rejected some key essentialist tenets. While they sought coherent patterns in languages and cultures, they did not presume that such coherence was natural: a highly integrated culture or a pervasive linguistic pattern had to be a specific historical product, limited in time as in space, for which there was no necessity in human nature. As apparently essentialist a book as Ruth Benedict's *Patterns of Culture* (1934) is, with its portraits of highly integrated and contrasting cultural styles, it also presents societies whose various institutions seem to go off in different directions, and Benedict points out that even some of the most integrated cultures that she discusses have highly non-integrated pasts (pp. 223–7). In linguistics, the Boasians maintained that speakers of very different languages can be very similar in economic activity, social structure, aesthetics, and/or religion, and that speakers of the same language can differ drastically on these parameters. Any language is capable of expressing any content; the language one speaks does not limit what it is possible to think.

Yet these are the same people who argued through example and in doctrine that the specifics of one's language can be highly influential in the way one conceives the world. This apparent contradiction, maintained throughout the production of Boas and his students, has sometimes been taken as an otherwise unaccountable incoherence. I would argue, however, that such a stable apparent self-contradiction could also be understood as the sign that these authors are struggling to find images adequate for conveying a complex reality within a pre-existing discursive field massively oriented either to universalism or to essentialism.

The Boasians rejected any ranking of languages and cultures according to a fixed standard. This, I think, is a theoretical position imposed on them by their practice, starting with Boas himself. Boas had actually lived in societies called primitive. He had "primitive" friends and collaborators with whom he worked closely, not only on whose knowledge, but indeed on whose persistence and intelligence his whole career, and at one point his life (Stocking 1968), depended. Any anthropologist or linguist of the Boasian school had to collaborate with intelligent "primitive" adults who did not have childlike mentalities, whose languages were not incapable of abstraction, whose beliefs and religious practices did not seem any more superstitious or arbitrary than those of most Christians or Jews. In Boas's case, what he called his "scientific work" allowed what was already a strong democratic and radical tendency to reach a complete reorientation of thinking about human variation. And it is noteworthy that most of his most prominent students were socially marginal characters of one kind or another – relatively recent immigrants, members of minority ethnic groups, a disproportionate number of women for the period; and that in North America, unlike, for instance, in Britain, anthropology was generally felt to be a discipline on the left side of the political spectrum.

Boas stressed that each language or language type should be treated on its own terms:

No attempt has been made [here] to compare the forms of the Indian grammars with the grammars of English, Latin, or even among themselves; but in each case the psychological groupings which are given depend entirely upon the inner form of each language. In other words, the grammar has been treated as though an intelligent Indian was going to develop the forms of his own thoughts by an analysis of his own form of speech. (Boas 1911a: 70)

The terminology here comes straight out of Steinthal. In a letter, he writes that his goal was "a presentation of languages on Steinthal's principles, i.e., from their own, not an outsider's point of view" (in R. L. Brown 1967: 14–15).

But Boas's endorsement of Steinthal comes with a revelatory qualification, one that points to the novelty of his overall conception of language. The source of this caveat is a talk given in 1910 at the International Congress of Americanists in Mexico City in which Boas announces the publication of the *Handbook of American Indian Languages*. Boas wants to point out that the grammars in the *Handbook* are based on the principles of each language itself ("psychological principles"), not on those of traditional Western grammar:

The attempt to describe the psychological principles of various languages is not new. The works of Wilhelm von Humboldt and of Steinthal on the types of linguistic structure are the most important of this type. Steinthal's descriptions of Mexican [i.e., Nahuatl] and Eskimo [i.e., Inuktitut] are certainly the models of what I have tried to do. Naturally, the fundamental ideas are not the same. At the time of von Humboldt and Steinthal, the valuation of languages would have been one of the principal objects of investigation, while today this problem does not interest us; we are attracted, rather, to psychological problems. (Boas 1910: 227)

Here Boas is both confirming and denying his affiliation with the Humboldtian stream in linguistics. By continuing to value some language types over others, Humboldt and his followers had managed to have a plurality that remained ordered on the basis of the fixed center or reference point of inflectional Indo-European. By abandoning the center, Boas precipitated a decentered linguistic and cultural world: not a chaos of relativism, at least not necessarily, but a world in which principles for ordering and for passing between situations had to be worked out from within a given perspective – there was no God's-eye-view – through the practice of moving among perspectives, as much as possible without privileging any one of them. It is not surprising that Sapir and Whorf, weaned on this decentered way of thinking about language and culture, should have seized on Einstein's relativity as a way to conceptualize their new situation.

Boas, science, and linguistics

Boas himself was intensely aware of the tension between the universalist explanatory procedures and goals of the natural sciences and the particularist interpretative procedures of what in Germany had come to be called the spiritual sciences. We have seen something of how this split was reflected in German linguistics, with natural-science models coming to dominance in historical linguistics and Steinthal's attempts to operationalize the pluralist and essentialist linguistics he inherited from Humboldt. Boas's own early choices in training (Stocking 1968; Liss 1996) show someone right on the cusp of this antinomy. He started out in physics but moved to the very distinctive German field of psychophysics, which sought to understand the relationship between natural phenomena as described scientifically and these phenomena as human beings perceive them. With his further move into geography, Boas became interested in how entire human societies perceive space; his first field research, with the Inuit in 1882, compared maps drawn using scientific instruments with those drawn by the people who lived in the territory. Boas's journals show that living with the Inuit profoundly affected his attitude toward cultural difference, causing him to question the superiority of European civilization and to argue that the important thing was the *Herzenbildung*, the heart's construction, of each person, in any cultural setting (Stocking 1968: 148) – an interesting choice of word given the use of the term *Bildung* in Germany, notably by Humboldt, to mean the civilizing improvement of humanity as a whole, with modern European societies being the most *gebildet*.

Upon his return to Germany, Boas got a job in Berlin as Bastian's assistant; here he met Steinthal. In 1886 he emigrated to the United States and began conducting field research on language and culture with Kwak'wala (Kwakiutl) speakers of British Columbia. Boas stayed in America, eventually, after many vocational adventures, including his rejection at Chicago, securing a position at Columbia University in 1896 and there founding the first Ph.D.-granting American department of anthropology (on Boas and the transformation of anthropology and linguistics, see Darnell 1998a).

In 1887 Boas published a paper on "The Study of Geography," in which he saw the field as occupying both natural-science and spiritual-science territory, but ended up defending the importance of the latter and the heritage of Alexander von Humboldt.

[A]ll [the physical] sciences have the one aim, to deduce laws from phenomena. The single phenomenon itself is insignificant: it is only valuable because it is an exemplification of a law, and serves to find new laws or to corroborate old ones. To this system of sciences Humboldt's "Cosmos" is opposed in principle. Cosmography, as we may call this science, considers every phenomenon as worthy of being studied for its own sake. Its mere existence entitles it to a full share of our attention; and the knowledge of its existence and evolution in space and time fully satisfies the student, without regard to the laws which it corroborates or which may be deduced from it. (Boas 1940: 642)

1887 was also the year Boas joined in a debate with some senior American anthropologists on the proper way to organize museum exhibits (Boas 1974: 61–7 and Stocking 1968: 1–3). Citing Bastian, Boas argued against the then-current form of organization by institution, which sought to show the universal development of a single human civilization, in favor of a presentation by culture area, so that museums could reveal the multiplicity of cultures and the "characteristic style" of each (p. 62). His opponents answered that their evolutionary system was scientific, while Boas's proposed arrangement was merely descriptive.

In his 1906 address to the first joint meeting of the American Anthropological Association and the American Philological Society, Boas returned to this linkage of anthropology with the cultural, rather than the natural, sciences.

Up to the present time we [anthropologists] have affiliated with societies representing the natural sciences and psychology. This is due to the development of modern anthropology under the stimulus of the theory of evolution, and to the important incentives that it has taken from the methods pursued by the natural sciences. It has been the endeavor of anthropologists to discover universal laws, like the laws of physics and of chemistry ...

As we have penetrated more deeply into these problems we have observed that the general laws for which we have been searching prove elusive ...

[T]he tendency must increasingly develop of turning away from the comparative methods of the natural sciences, and taking up more and more systematically the methods of history ... [W]e begin to be inclined to view each cultural trait not primarily in comparison with parallel traits found in remote regions, but rather in connection with the direction taken by the whole culture of a tribe or a people [cf. Hamann's use of the term *Richtung*] ...

While hitherto we have been satisfied with disconnected fragments of observations on the customs of the various tribes, we begin to see more and more clearly that the student must have a full grasp of all the forms of culture of the people he studies, before he can safely generalize. (Boas 1974: 183–4)

In the 1887 museum debate, Boas linked this difference in cultural forms with a relativity of ideas: "It is my opinion that the main object of ethnological collections should be the dissemination of the fact that civilization is not something absolute, but that it is relative, and that our ideas and conceptions are true only so far as our civilization goes" (1974: 64).

Boas's position raises the questions that relativist positions still raise. Are our ideas really just a product of our civilization? What does it mean, then, that Boas, by his own theory himself a product of his civilization, has the idea that our ideas are products of our civilization? Is he unfairly giving himself a privileged position, a point outside this circle, which allows him to look in on it?

A lecture given in German in 1888, "The Aims of Ethnology," suggests elements of answers to these questions. We may indeed be able to achieve a point of view outside that of our culture through a comparative critique of that culture, made possible by familiarity with others:

[E]thnology ... alone opens to us the possibility of judging our own culture objectively, in that it permits us to strip off the presumably self-evident manner of thinking and feeling which determines even the fundamental part of our culture. Only in this way can our intellect, instructed and formed under the influences of our culture, attain a correct judgment of this same culture. (1974: 71)

Here Boas lecturing (in German in New York) reads like nothing so much as Marx writing (in German in London) in the 1850s: Marx's critiques of political economy are critiques of the assumptions behind political economy, assumptions almost universally shared in the Western world of his time. Like Marx, Boas presumes that it is a good thing to take a critical distance on one's unexamined ideas; his program is to attempt this through knowledge of human alternatives. What such knowledge offers is not a place to stand that is given or waiting outside all cultures, but one that must be constructed provisionally and largely negatively, through comparison and critique.

Boas rethinks languages

In his first major treatment of linguistic theory, the 1889 paper "On Alternating Sounds," Boas argues against the evolutionists' position that the clarity of speech sounds depends on the level of development of a language. Boas draws on his training in psychology and psychophysics to discuss experimental findings suggesting that the human subject interprets incoming data on the basis of what is already there, in a formulation that clearly goes back to Steinthal and Herbart: "a new sensation is apperceived by means of similar sensations that form part of our knowledge" (Boas 1974: 74; cf. Mackert 1994). If different visitors to a given people transcribe the same local word differently, then, this is not because the word is being pronounced unclearly or inconsistently, but because the travellers, not equipped to hear the relevant distinctions, assimilate the unfamiliar sounds of the language they are hearing to sounds that are familiar in their own: "sounds are not perceived by the hearer in the way in which they have been pronounced by the speaker" (Boas 1974: 73).

In an anticipation of phonological theory, Boas is holding that every language organizes the universe of sounds in its own way, and that this very fact is the source of misperception when one passes between such systems of sound organization. Differences in transcription come from interference between the transcribers' own systems and that of the language in question. True to his psychophysical training, and again channelling Herbart, Boas distinguishes between the way the ear perceives a sound and the way the preformed mind (and ear) *apperceives* it (p. 74): "It is found that the vocabularies of collectors … bear evidence of the phonetics of their own languages. This can be explained only by the fact that each apperceives the unknown sounds by the means of the sounds of his own language" (pp. 75–6). Boas illustrates this with alternative spellings he himself had produced when trying to transcribe words from Inuktitut and languages of the Northwest Coast, showing that when faced with sounds that did not correspond to those of languages he knew, he would typically hesitate between familiar pigeonholes, thus "splitting" the sound. In every case, an adequate grasp of the sound system of the language in question eliminated this phenomenon.

In his conclusion, Boas goes from these specific cases to a universal decentering:

I think, from this evidence, it is clear that all such misspellings are due to a wrong apperception, which is due to the phonetic system of our native language. For this reason I maintain that there is no such phenomenon as synthetic or alternating sounds, and that their occurrence is in no way a sign of primitiveness of the speech in which they are said to occur; that alternating sounds are in reality alternating apperceptions of one and the same sound. A thorough study of all alleged alternating sounds or synthetic sounds will show that their existence may be explained by alternating apperceptions.

Boas follows up on this claim with a double test. First, if the "alternating sound" illusion derives from a speaker's tendency to put an unfamiliar sound into one or another familiar slot, then it should work not only for such "splitting," but also for "lumping": two distinct sounds that are differentiated according to an unfamiliar criterion should be "heard" in a single familiar slot.

There is a crucial test for this theory; if it be correct, it must occur just as frequently that various sounds which resemble one known sound are considered the same, although they are really different. I observed this in Haida and in Kwakiutl, as well as in Eskimo. In the first there occurs a very slight hiatus, which I discovered only with the greatest difficulty when I heard the words for "we" and "you" about twenty times without being able to discover the difference, the one being *d'aléngua*, the other *daléngua*. (p. 77)

This test closes the circle: if some languages are to be defined by their vagueness, the test should only work in one direction; the fact that it works in both directions means that the languages previously so defined in fact make clear distinctions which are simply different from those that we make, and so are hard for us to recognize.

This suggests Boas's second test. If so-called alternating sounds reflect not the low degree of organization of certain languages, but instead interference between organized systems, then the effect should be mutual: a speaker of Tlingit should make the same kinds of mistakes when confronting English as the English speaker does when confronting Tlingit, mistakes which have been taken as evidence for the inferiority of the latter to the former.

The second and better crucial test is to attempt to ascertain whether individuals speaking one of these languages with "alternating sounds" hear sounds of our language as alternating sounds. This is, in fact, the case. Last summer I asked a Tlingit to pronounce the English *l* [a sound that does not exist in Tlingit]. I found that he alternately pronounced the exploded *l* of the northwest coast and *y*. In the same way he pronounced the German guttural *r* alternately as *r*, *w*, and *g* ... I believe that this crucial test is decisive; and it seems to me a sufficient explanation of the phenomenon of ... "alternating sounds," to assume that they originate by "alternating apperception." (p. 77)

The issue here is not centrally one of an ideology of equality or relativism, but of mutuality, of what Sapir and Whorf would later call calibration. This is perhaps the key element in all of Boas's endeavors, certainly in his anthropology and linguistics: the reality of difference among systems and the possibility of mutual calibration together render irrelevant questions of their relative complexity (how do you determine relative complexity?) or of the inherent superiority of some for understanding others (nonexistent).

From the mid-1880s on, Boas undertook a series of descriptive grammars of indigenous North American languages, particularly those of the Northwest Coast. This was one of the most clearly demarcated culture areas in the world, with an absolutely distinctive style in social organization, religion, and visual

art and perhaps a unique type of subsistence base: a primarily hunting, fish-
ing, and gathering economy that still, due to an incredible abundance of game
and especially of fish, produced regular and predictable surpluses allowing the
build-up of great hoards of wealth. The languages spoken in this region were
of extraordinary diversity, representing five or six entirely different language
families. Yet in spite of this diversity, certain common patterns did appear, in
phonology, grammar, and semantics, making the Northwest Coast a classic
linguistic area (e.g., Beck 2000).

Over the next few decades Boas organized a vast program of documentation
and analysis of North American languages (Stocking 1974). This involved both
his own work, leading to the publication of a number of grammatical sketches,
and the training of students, always in his own brand of language description,
which tried to grasp the categories actually at work in each language.

Let's consider two of Boas's mini-grammars here: his notes on Chinook and
his sketch of Kwak'wala. For Chinook, I'll just note that Boas's presentation
of the language is aimed against the argument that North American languages
lack abstract terms:

The language abounds in abstract terms. It is particularly remarkable that many concepts which we use in the form of adjectives occur as abstract nouns only. For instance,
it is impossible to say " a bad man," but this is expressed by "the man, his badness." The
Chinook does not say "I am sick," but "my sickness is on me"; he does not say "I shoot
him," but "the action of shooting him I perform it against him." Abstract concepts of this
character are very numerous. (Boas 1893: 57)

Chinook was disorienting enough to be the language on which Boas's students
usually "cut their teeth" in his linguistics class, "which met Tuesday evenings
at his home around the cleared family dining table" (Kroeber 1943: 7).

Boas began the 1900 Kwak'wala sketch by noting that the Reverend Alfred
J. Hall had recently published a grammar of the language which "has not succeeded in elucidating its structural peculiarities" (Boas 1974: 167). What was
it about Hall's book that did not succeed? When we look at Hall's grammar, it
is quite clear: he analyzes Kwak'wala (1889: 61) in terms of the classic eight
parts of speech. Hall's definitions of these are the conventional ones: "A Noun
is the name of any person, place or thing, as in … *siMtlum*, snake; *egialaziM*,
goodness." And so forth. Hall gives us an old-fashioned English grammar with
Kwak'wala glosses.

After some pages on the sounds of the language, Boas gets to what would
later be called morphophonology, how their role in word construction modifies
sounds. That topic leads him in turn to word construction itself and grammar.
Immediately after presenting the way adding suffixes changes final sounds,
Boas goes on (p. 170): "Grammatical relations are expressed by means of suffixes and by reduplication." Then there is a brief presentation of how these two

processes affect the sounds of a word. As yet, we have heard *nothing* about nouns or verbs or adjectives. Instead we move into what Boas calls "the groups of relations expressed by grammatical processes." Here Boas is taking one of those big steps back, a Copernican step: instead of knowing in advance what relations this language, like any language, *should* express and looking to see which processes express them, he lets the language itself guide him, starting with the grammatical processes as actually observed and using them to specify what the "groups of relations" are.

Boas begins his discussion of forms with pronominal relations. And almost immediately we run into an aspect of Kwak'wala which Boas feels is pervasive and important in the language, but which fits no easy label from English or Latin: "The language has a strong tendency to define every action and every object in all its relations to the persons conversing." Personal pronouns distinguish the speaker, the addressee, and the person spoken about; the demonstrative pronoun, in a "perfect homology" with the personal pronouns,

indicates the location of an action or of an object as near the speaker, near the person addressed or near the person spoken of. This strict homology appears in many American languages, but in few is the expression of location so rigidly demanded as in Kwakiutl. The location of object or action in relation to the three persons – speaker, person addressed, and person spoken of – must always be expressed. These three positions are further subdivided into two groups, the one expressing objects and actions visible to the speaker, the other expressing those invisible to the speaker. (p. 170)

This constant specification of relation to persons pervades the language, and certainly seems distinctive, at least for a speaker of a Western European language. But this is not taken to be some kind of an essence, a general principle that explains the whole language.

Next Boas looks to pronominal relations and notes that they are usally "incorporated" into the verb. And this is how we get to the verb. As we have seen with Brinton, the notion of incorporation (*Einverleibung*) was central for a long history of studies of American languages, going back to the generation of Humboldt. To call American languages incorporating was to say that they were more agglutinating than agglutinating languages: not only were elements indicating grammatical relations expressed as bound morphemes, but so were elements expressing what we would think of as independent nominal or adjectival meanings. Something we would express as an independent noun, for instance, might only appear in an incorporating language as a suffix attached to a verb.

Boas starts with incorporated pronouns, then moves to nouns: "When substantives are introduced in a sentence of this kind, they are placed following the pronoun which indicates their function" (p. 171). That is, "the man struck the child with the stone" would be expressed with the construction *strike-"he" man-"him" child-"with it" stone*, each word including a suffix that indicates the syntactic relations of the *following* word. Boas at first proposes that this might look like the way another language (German!) could mark syntactic relations in the article, but concludes that something very different is happening here: "we have here really an incorporation of the noun in the verbal expression" (p. 172).

And this conclusion allows a bit of comparative typology:

The construction of the sentence is therefore analogous to that found in other American languages, most of which incorporate object and indirect object, although the degree and character of incorporation vary ... Chinook, Sioux, and many other languages incorporate only the pronominal representative in the verb, and place the noun as apposition at the end of the sentence. Kwakiutl pursues the same method as Chinook, but, instead of placing the nouns as appositions, it places them immediately following the representative pronoun, thus creating a word-complex held together by pronominal particles.

What about the verb? Here again we have a general characterization that points to a broad difference in structure between American and European languages:

The verb generally consists of a stem and numerous adverbial suffixes, which modify or limit the meaning of the verbal stem. These adverbial expressions may be limitations of time, of cause, of manner, of object. They embrace, therefore, our tenses, conjunctions, adverbs, and even objects or prepositional expressions. The lack of distinction in the method of expressing grammatical relations and material ideas, which is found in most Indian languages, manifests itself in the variety of ideas expressed by these suffixes. (p. 173)

Is this "lack of distinction" a sign of the primitive character or incapacity of "most Indian languages"? On the contrary: in the context of Boas's overall work, it is clear that this is part of a broad critique of the arbitrariness of our own unreflective division between grammatical relations and material ideas.

History and philology

Boas was not, of course, only a descriptive linguist. With the founding of the new department of anthropology at Columbia, Boas launched a program for the widest possible documentation of languages and cultures. Two aspects of the Boasian program stand out.

First, Boasian anthropology was posited as the documentation of the human record, and particularly of the history of peoples whose history had not entered the curriculum. This contrasts, for instance, with the view of Malinowski that what mattered was to study people who were as different as possible from Western societies and from each other. For Boas, what mattered was that a people existed or had existed and so was part of the human heritage (Bunzl 2004).

Second, and congruent with this concern, the documentation of a language also implied that of a literature, that is, the constitution of a corpus of texts (Bunzl 1996). Here Boas followed the example Steinthal had set in his Mande grammar. Among Boas's first publications was a large collection of Northwest Coast myths (Boas 1895 [2002]), and he and his students regularly included texts as parts of their grammars and ethnographies. The address to the philologists justifies this practice:

It would seem ... that the classical archeologist or ... philologist must always have an indulgent smile when he hears of serious anthropological studies carried on by investigators, who have neither the time, the inclination, nor the training to familiarize themselves with the language of the people whom they study. According to the canons of philological research, would not the investigator who is not able to read the classics be barred from the number of serious students? ... I think it is obvious that in this respect anthropologists have everything to learn from you; that until we acquire the habit of demanding such authenticity of our reports as can be guaranteed only by philological accuracy of the record, can we hope to accumulate material that will be a safe guide to future studies.

The time must come when we must demand ... from the serious student the same degree of philological accuracy which has become the standard in your sciences ...

If we acknowledge the correctness of the requirements here outlined, the work that is before us is stupendous ... The psychological foundation and morphological developments of American languages are so peculiar that their study must be a revelation to the student of Indo-European or Semitic languages. Well-known problems which you have discussed for years appear in new aspects, and broad points of view for discussion of linguistic questions present themselves readily to the student who takes up the types of language peculiar to our continent. (Boas 1974: 184–5)

Boas's 1911 Introduction

Boas's language program culminates with the publication of the first volume of the *Handbook of American Indian Languages* in 1911. The grammatical sketches presented here represent at least eight language families (depending on how you classify Haida and Tlingit); Boas wrote three and co-wrote one one them, and he closely supervised them all. The introduction to this volume remains the major statement of his linguistics.

At the beginning of the "Introduction" Boas says that there is no necessary link among a people's language, biological inheritance, and culture. Near the end he says that there is no necessary correlation between language and thought, in that one's language does not limit what one can think. All languages allow abstraction; "it would seem that the obstacles to generalized thought inherent in the form of a language are of minor importance only" (Boas 1911a: 67).[1]

As an example, Boas takes on the evolutionists' treatment of number. Counting one, two, three, many, writes Boas, tells us nothing about the cognitive capacities of the person doing the counting. All it tells us is that he or she lives in a society that does not require counting in the abstract.

On the other hand, just as soon as these same people find themselves in contact with civilization, and when they acquire standards of value that have to be counted, they adopt with perfect ease higher numerals from other languages and develop a more or less perfect system of counting … [C]ounting does not become necessary until objects are considered in such generalized form that their individualities are entirely lost sight of. For this reason it is possible that even a person who has a flock of domesticated animals may know them by name and by their characteristics without ever desiring to count them … In short, there is no proof that the lack of the use of numerals is in any way connected with the inability to form the concepts of higher numerals. (p. 66)

A cowherd who does not have the vocabulary to say that he has twenty-seven cows can still tell when Honeybee is missing.

Here is a little thought experiment which, admittedly, will not work for all readers but may work for you. Quick, dear reader, answer the following question without counting: including uncles by marriage, how many uncles do (or did) you have? Is the number of your uncles something that you know? Second task: name your uncles. A great many North American and Western European readers will be unable to give a number for the uncles without going over and counting them one by one in their heads. Number of uncles, unlike number of siblings or number of years of age or number of one's year in school, is simply not a number that most of us feel we need to know. Yet the same people who cannot immediately say how many uncles they have have no trouble naming every uncle, up to an impressive… number. If the members of a society live in such a way that they deal with the world mostly as if it were made up of uncles instead of, say, dollars, this tells us a lot about the world they live in but nothing about their ability to think.

Cradled between Boas's two negative affirmations, of the lack of necessary correlation between language, race, and culture and between language and thought, is the actual presentation of language. Here we have a picture of coherent structure at a number of levels: phonetics, lexicon, grammar.

In phonetics, Boas argues that the potential production of sounds by the human vocal apparatus is unlimited. A child who learns to speak is learning to suppress most of the sounds he or she is capable of making, thus allowing clear distinctions to arise among a limited number of sound types.[2] The set of contrasting sounds used in any language forms a coherent system, and one different from other such systems. Boas repeats the argument from the "Alternating Sounds" paper that the apparent fluidity of sounds in exotic languages comes not from their lower level of evolution but from interference among systems.

When Boas turns to lexicon and grammar, his argument is the same: out of the potentially unlimited complexity of experience and ideation, each language must define and foreground certain configurations rather than others, whether by labelling (lexicon) or by turning the attention to some domains of experience rather than others through grammatical devices.

Since the total range of personal experience which language serves to express is infinitely varied, and its whole scope must be expressed by a limited number of phonetic groups, it is obvious that an extended classification of experience must underlie all articulate speech.

As with sounds, the limited and systemic nature of lexicon and grammar means that

[l]anguages differ not only in the character of their constituent phonetic elements and sound-clusters, but also in the groups of ideas that find expression in fixed phonetic groups. (1911a: 24)

The section of the "Introduction" devoted to the lexicon includes a manifold discussion of vocabulary examples meant to show the variety of ways different languages delimit fields of experience. Boas presents English words for different forms of water, then the famous example of Inuktitut words for snow: there are three, indicating what we call falling snow, snow lying on the ground, and drifting snow. This example was expanded by subsequent writers and in anthropological folklore to hundreds of words for snow (Martin 1986; uncharacteristically, Whorf appears to have been quite sloppy on this point), allowing subsequent revisionists to make hay with the "Eskimo vocabulary hoax" (Pullum 1989 [1991]). But three words are enough to illustrate Boas's point: their presence suggests, at least, that Inuktitut speakers conceive three different "things" where we conceive one, just as English speakers conceive raindrops, rivers, and oceans as different "things" even though we know perfectly well that they're all water. On the other hand, does this tell us very much beyond this fact? One presumes that mariners will have lots of nautical terms, that serious skiers, like the Inuit, will have a pretty discriminating vocabulary of snow. In a closely subsequent passage, Boas himself relativizes his lexical relativity:

It seems fairly evident that the selection of such simple terms must to a certain extent depend upon the chief interests of a people; and where it is necessary to distinguish a certain phenomenon in many aspects, which in the life of a people play each an entirely independent role, many independent words may develop, while in other cases modifications of a single term may suffice.

Yet it remains that differences in such patterning, like the differences in the patterning of sound, imply shifts in what Boas will here call point of view:

Thus it happens that each language, from the point of view of another language, may be arbitrary in its classifications; that what appears as a single simple idea in one language may be characterized by a series of distinct phonetic groups in another. (1911a: 26)

From the apparent confusion of sounds we have moved, with the lexicon, to the apparent arbitrariness of classifications. Boas is supposed to have said, after all, that "the seeing eye is the organ of tradition" (cited in Sahlins 1977: 65).

Besides the "phonetic groups" that carry meaning – what we call morphemes or, in some cases, words – every language has "formal elements which determine the relations of the single phonetic groups." Such formal elements include, for instance, affixes such as the English /-s/, which on its own indicates only the sound made by a snake or an angry cat, but indicates plurality when attached to certain nouns. How easy is it to distinguish between potentially independent words and these formal elements which indicate grammatical relations within the sentence and in discourse? This is the old question of particles, debated at least since Locke and Leibniz (McRae 1988). For a hundred years before Boas, the difference had been held to be fundamental: it is what allowed everybody from Schlegel on to distinguish among isolating languages (all independent words, no affixes), agglutinating languages (mostly affixes mechanically stuck together), and inflectional languages (a nice organic balance of meaningful stem and qualifying affixes). Boas maintains instead that the difference between a word and a grammatical affix is not absolute, but involves a sliding scale of relative independence or dependence, concreteness or abstraction. This effectively blows the earlier typological schemes out of the water, precipitating a much vaster field of structural variation. It also removes one of the bases for claiming the superiority of Indo-European languages.

One result of this shift is that formal affixes no longer look purely formal, but can be understood to convey meaning in themselves. Grammatical categories, in other words, have meaning too. In modern Western European languages we are familiar with grammatical categories of tense, person, number, case, gender, each of which at least potentially is more than a formal indicator of word arrangement, since it adds to or specifies the meaning of words. Many of these categories are obligatory, as the ones just listed are for nouns, verbs, or both: the speaker of the language does not have the choice not to use them. In speaking English, for instance, we do not have the option of not using tense in our verbs or number in one of our two types of nouns (count nouns as opposed to mass nouns); and we must use tense or number with these kinds of words whether or not it is relevant or important to specify the temporal relation between the event referred to and the situation of speaking, or to specify the singularity or plurality of the referent(s) of the noun. English speakers have to do this; if [they-he-she] [do-did-will do] not, [they-he-she] [are-were-will] not [speaking-be speaking] real [English-Englishes].

Boas's point here, probably his major single contribution to linguistic theory (Jakobson 1971: 490), is that the key difference among languages lies less in what they allow you to say – as Boas kept insisting, any language will allow you to say anything you want – but what domains a given language *obliges* you to refer to.[3] Different languages have different obligatory grammatical categories requiring attention to different aspects of experience.

In discussing grammatical categories, Boas follows a scheme of argumentation that is typical for him and later for his followers. He starts by posing and problematizing what is familiar to us:

Grammarians who have studied the languages of Europe and western Asia have developed a system of categories which we are inclined to look for in every language. It seems desirable to show here in how far the system with which we are familiar is characteristic only of certain groups of languages, and in how far other systems may be substituted for it. It seems easiest to illustrate this by discussing first some of the characteristics of the Indo-European noun, pronoun, and verb, and then by taking up the wider aspects of this subject. (1911a: 35)

Boas chooses to use the standard Indo-European categories as an initial organizing structure precisely to show how inadequate these categories are when faced with languages of very different structure. Here he shows how differently a number of Amerindian languages treat the relevant grammatical categories. We have seen that English will not let you not refer constantly to time and number; Kwak'wala requires specification of how you know what you are talking about (a category that Roman Jakobson would name evidentiality) – you must, as Boas pointed out in his Kwak'wala grammar in the *Handbook*, choose among suffixes "expressing the source of subjective knowledge – as by hearsay, or a dream" (1911b: 443). In a number of American languages, nouns have tense (1911a: 39). After pages of examples, Boas concludes:

The few examples that I have given here illustrate that many of the categories which we are inclined to consider as essential may be absent in foreign languages, and that other categories may occur as substitutes ... We conclude from the examples here given that in a discussion of the characteristics of various languages different fundamental categories will be found, and that in a comparison of different languages it will be necessary to compare as well the phonetic characteristics as the characteristics of the vocabulary and those of the grammatical concepts in order to give each language its proper place. (1911a: 42–3)

Note how different this linguistic relativity is from the views of Herder, Humboldt, and, as we shall see in Chapter 8, of the Neohumboldtians. Boas has not assumed that every language–culture–people is or should normally be a seamless whole. On the contrary. But he does hold that the observable facts of distinctive phonetic patterning, lexical classification, and obligatory grammatical categories in every language mean that a shift from language to language is potentially a shift in point of view, a real difference that must be taken into account.

Boas continued to work on languages and linguistics until the end of his life. In some of his later publications, he made stronger claims for the relationship between linguistic patterns and patterns of thought, largely due to the unconscious and so unexamined character of linguistic categories, as in a paper from 1920:

The general concepts underlying language are entirely unknown to most people. They do not come into consciousness until the scientific study of grammar begins. Nevertheless, the categories of language compel us to see the world arranged in certain definite conceptual groups which, on account of our lack of knowledge of linguistic processes, are taken as objective categories and which, therefore, impose themselves upon the form of our thoughts. (Boas 1940: 289)

In his last publication on language, Boas tries to clarify the extent of such imposition:

It is another question in how far the categories of grammar and the general classification of experience may control thought ... The obligatory categories of language differ fundamentally ... It is obvious that the mental picture aroused by a spoken sentence will be fundamentally different according to these categories ... The form of our grammar compels us to select a few traits of thought we wish to express and suppresses many other aspects which the speaker has in his mind and which the hearer supplies according to his fancy ...

There is little doubt that thought is thus directed in various channels ... Such a tendency pervading the language may well lead to a different reaction to the incidents of everyday life and it is conceivable that in this sense the mental activities of a people may be in part directed by language. I should not be inclined to overestimate this influence because devices for expressing ... [various ideas] are ever-present, and may rise into idiomatic use. In this sense, we may say that language exerts a limited influence on culture. (1942: 181–3)

Integration and calibration

For such a visible public figure, one who was always giving out opinions on things, Boas as a thinker remains remarkably mysterious. His reception among anthropologists over the last fifty years has been utterly divided, and not particularly friendly. Many have seen him as a pure empirical particularist, an identifier of isolated traits uninterested in general laws (e.g., Harris 1968) or holistic analyses (Verdon 2006). Others present Boas as the opposite of this, the cultural holist par excellence (e.g., Sahlins 1977). Correspondingly, social anthropologists and postmodernists attack Boasian "culturalism" for its purported assumption that cultures are isolated wholes, externally bounded and internally homogeneous. Oddly enough, these views can all be defended on the basis of some of Boas's language.

I have argued that Boas represents something that was not present either in the Descartes–Locke universalism or in Herderian essentialism. In this regard it is striking that one recent presentation sees him as a hybrid of precisely these approaches, a "hybrid construction ... of Lockean and Herderian conceptions of language and tradition" (Bauman and Briggs 2003: 257, 267).[4]

A thinker who provokes such opposed reactions is at the least an interesting thinker.

Is there in fact any coherence to be found in Boas's overall approach to languages and cultures? I think two central themes stand out, both involving his view of the interaction between systems.

Boas really did believe that there existed a plurality of languages and a plurality of cultures – he seems, in fact, to be the first person to have used the English word "culture" in the plural (Stocking 1968).[5] He saw each language and culture as having a tendency toward coherence, and he felt that such distinctive tendencies became perceptible through contrast and interaction. His phonetics, inspired by his training in psychophysics and through Steinthal's linguistics, itself largely inspired by Herbart's psychology, presumed that each language had an already-present system of sounds, that new sounds would be heard in terms of the old ones, and that the integration of new sounds would contribute to changing the system (Mackert 1994). Sounds, words, grammatical patterns could be borrowed, but would be transformed as they crossed a linguistic boundary. The existence of such boundaries and the broad characteristics of the domains they enclose became perceptible precisely through such crossing and transformation. Because of his focus on this process, Boas became one of the founders of the study of linguistic areas, regions in which languages of different origins have interacted long enough to influence each other, so that all share certain traits. It also made him skeptical of the reconstruction of large-scale language families without regard to areal context, a bone of contention between him and Sapir.

This model, of areas with definable tendencies that become perceptible as material passes into and out of them, is precisely the one Boas used for culture areas. As I have noted, a number of commentators have seen Boas as a mere collector of arbitrary assemblages of traits. But the traits are consistently of interest to him as they cross linguistic or cultural boundaries and are integrated – that is, transformed in ways that reveal the tendencies of the receiving whole – while at the same time maintaining something of their inherent quality. Boas had stated this overall project as early as 1889:

Besides the historical point I try to approach a psychological question by this study: how is foreign material when taken up by a people, modified by preexisting ideas and customs? (cited in Boas 1974: 134)

These lines are from a letter to Tylor, the most important anthropological evolutionist of the time, and they propose a program that is neither evolutionist nor diffusionist, but "psychological" in the Herbartian sense: the important thing about tracing the movements of traits is what happens when they enter what we might call a new field of relations.

A second key to Boas's shift of emphasis may lie in the analogy of calibration.[6] While this is not a term that Boas himself uses, it comes up repeatedly in the work of his students. Remember that Boas came out of the natural sciences. The easy options available to him at the end of the nineteenth century, as I have been arguing throughout this book, were twofold: either to reject linguistic specificity as of little importance, or to embrace a full-scale plurality with each language as a universe unto itself. If this second view were not to slip into chaos, an unacceptable alternative for most thinkers of the nineteenth and twentieth centuries, a general framework must be imposed using some form of ranking – whence would come the various classifications of languages with organic Indo-European as the highest form. This kind of Romantic model, fixed up with the trappings of objective science, remained that of Steinthal. One key element in Boas's shift, as we have seen him state explicitly, was the rejection of such ranked models, not in favor of generalized chaos, nor of a return to a simple universalism, but in favor of a non-centered plurality that allowed the possibility of what we can call mutual calibration.

The key moment for Boas, and I would argue for Sapir and Whorf, again involves what happens at the boundaries. It is the moment of mutual misunderstanding due to the interference of systems, of what we might call *understandable misunderstanding*: the speaker of German mishears the phonemes of Inuktitut in a way that is distinctly German and reveals the presence of both Inuktitut and German sound systems; the speaker of English misunderstands a semantic distinction in Hopi that crosscuts his own, and does so in a way that is distinctly English or at least modern Western European. In practice, linguists since Herder had noted and successfully analyzed such moments of misunderstanding, but drew only the conclusion of difference. Boas took a step back and noted that it remained possible to raise such difference to the level of consciousness, and so grasp the specificity of a phoneme, a grammatical pattern, or a figure of sense. Why was it that Humboldt, Steinthal and company were in fact able to produce what seemed to be *adequate* renditions of non-European distinctions in European languages? The presumption had generally been that this was possible because the analytic languages involved, modern Western languages, were advanced and scientific: the simpler could be analyzed by means of the more complex. From the paper on alternating sounds onwards, Boas replaces this hierarchical model with one of calibration between languages, which, like synchronizing watches, is always potentially mutual. The very notion of calibration implies that it can go either way, that distinctions proper to the systems in contact can be grasped adequately starting from *either* of the systems involved. It is just as possible to render a German distinction in Inuktitut as an Inuktitut distinction in German, just as failures of rendering are mutual and go both ways.

Boas's assumptions of integration and calibration involve four corollaries, all of which are at work in his rethinking of language and culture. First, they imply the existence of distinct systems. Second, they imply diversity: systems are different in important ways. Third, calibration presumes the possibility of the adequate rendering of one system in terms of another. Fourth, it implies that such rendering is mutual: calibration in one direction necessarily implies its possibility in the other.

7   Linguistic relativity: Sapir, Lee, and Whorf

We thus free ourselves from the distasteful conception that the natural universe
ought to possess something of the nature of a centre.

Albert Einstein (1916)

The Boas program was carried on and extended by his students through the
1920s and 30s. It collapsed with the deaths of some of its main figures and came
to be miscognized, I will argue, after the War. Here I want to present three of
its practitioners: Boas's students Edward Sapir and Dorothy Demetracopoulou
Lee, and Sapir's student Benjamin Lee Whorf.

Edward Sapir

Edward Sapir (1884–1939) was born in Germany and came to the United
States as a child. He was initially trained in literature and did his Master's
thesis on Herder's *Treatise on the Origin of Language* (Sapir 1907). This early
text already reveals some important aspects of Sapir's approach to language
and culture. Sapir contests Herder's assertion that the languages of peoples of
nature "lack true grammatical sense" and concludes that

[t]oday … owing to the vast stock of comparative and historic linguistic material at
our disposal, we … can admit, with a clear conscience, that many typically "original"
languages, to adopt Herder's now unserviceable terminology, possess *truly* grammatical features of incredible complexity, as in the case of the Eskimo verb or Bantu noun.
(1907: 129–30)

This is the standard Boasian view. What Sapir himself adds to it is a central interest in the role of poetic figures in language structure, an interest he
shared with Herder and Humboldt, and that we have seen anticipated in the
Renaissance and in some figures of the French Enlightenment.

[Herder] saw clearly the perfectly natural, and, indeed, psychologically inevitable, play
of metaphor that runs through the history of language. This was remarkable at a time
when figures of speech were thought to be the artistic flowers of polite literature. The
modern semasiologist can, however, be bolder than Herder. He recognizes clearly that
metaphor operates with equal power at all periods in the development of a language, not

chiefly in the relatively older phases, as Herder thought, but just as well in times nearer the present. (Sapir 1907: 128)

It was a now legendary conversation with Boas that determined the direction of Sapir's life. "For every generalization he had before believed was certain and exceptionless, Boas could summon indubitable contrary examples from American Indian languages he knew" (Mandelbaum in Sapir 1949: vii). Sapir did his doctorate under Boas and would soon become the most brilliant practitioner of Boasian field and theoretical linguistics (Darnell 1990), spending his life recording and analyzing an enormous number of languages, most of them Amerindian. Sapir's analyses are often cited as models of non-ethnocentric analysis of languages very different from English, French, or Latin.

In 1910 Sapir accepted a post with the Canadian government and spent the next fifteen years at the Museum of Man in Ottawa, then (as now) a smallish city on a very large northern frontier. In 1925, he moved to the Department of Anthropology at the University of Chicago, a new university in a large frontier town, and in 1931 he accepted a position in linguistics at Yale. Yale was a problematic experience after the easy acceptance Sapir had experienced both at the intensely urban Columbia and on the frontiers. One of the centers of the academic, economic, and political establishment, Yale was still pervaded by a snobbishness that manifested itself as, among other things, Antisemitism. The entrenched Yale program on Science and Society was one of the last evolutionist holdouts and sharply hostile to Boas. At Yale, however, Sapir was able to create one of the great circles of linguistics of the 1930s (Darnell 1998b). But it was not to last. He died in 1939 at the age of fifty-five.

Sapir possessed a personal style and a set of concerns very different from those both of the physicist-turned-geographer Boas and Sapir's own student, the scientist Whorf. He had a deep sense of the poetry of linguistic sound and patterning and, unlike Boas, an abiding concern for individual experience, for how languages were lived by human subjects. He published poetry and hung out with psychoanalysts.

Sapir's manual *Language* (first published in 1921 and still in print) extends themes found in Boas's 1911 "Introduction" and represents a re-foundation of Boasian linguistics.

The book is dazzling and disorienting in its constant recourse to examples from an array of languages from all over the world, while continually coming back to English and Latin. Following the Boasian model, here a discussion of the sounds of language is succeeded by one of "grammatical processes," and only then, guided by the processes, do we come to a discussion of the concepts conveyed by the grammar.

With characteristic verve, Sapir attacks the whole history of ranking languages:

[A]ny classification that starts with preconceived values or that works up to sentimental satisfactions is self-condemned as unscientific. A linguist that insists on talking about the Latin type of morphology as though it were necessarily the high-water mark of linguistic development is like the zoölogist that sees in the organic world a huge conspiracy to breed the race-horse or the Jersey cow ... We must ... accustom ourselves to look upon English and Hottentot with the same cool, yet interested, detachment. (Sapir 1921: 124)

He takes aim specifically at Steinthal:

[I]t is clear that we cannot now make the distinction between form languages and formless languages that used to appeal to some of the older writers. Every language can and must express the fundamental syntactic relations even though there is not a single affix to be found in its vocabulary. We conclude that every language is a form language. (p. 125)

In a chapter on linguistic typology, Sapir attacks the relatively simple classifications that had prevailed since Humboldt.

To take, as the sum total of our material, Latin, Arabic, Turkish, Chinese, and perhaps Eskimo or Sioux as an afterthought, is to court disaster ... [T]he strong craving for a simple formula has been the undoing of linguists. (p. 122)

Sapir's own model will be far more complex, based on three different dimensions of variation, and will not fit into a small number of easily defined categories.

Like Boas, Sapir denies any necessary connection among language, race, and culture (1921: Chapter 10). Yet throughout his work there emerges a sense of each language as a coherent whole possessing a "general form" (p. 120), although not one that can be defined by a single essential feature:

[I]t must be obvious to any one who has thought about the question at all or who has felt something of the spirit of a foreign language that there is such a thing as a basic plan, a certain cut, to each language. This type or plan or structural "genius" of the language is something much more fundamental, much more pervasive, than any single feature of it that we can mention, nor can we gain an adequate idea of its nature by a mere recital of the sundry facts that make up the grammar of the language. When we pass from Latin to Russian we feel that it is approximately the same horizon that bounds our view, even though the near, familiar landmarks have changed. When we come to English, we seem to notice that the hills have dipped down a little, yet we recognize the general lay of the land. And when we have arrived at Chinese, it is an utterly different sky that is looking down upon us ... Languages are more to us than systems of thought transference. They are invisible garments that drape themselves about our spirit and give a predetermined form to all its symbolic expression. (pp. 120–1, 221)

The metaphor of a language as a garment or skin goes back to Herder and Goethe. Here Sapir is accepting a notion of languages as stylistic wholes and is interested in how the individual speaker lives a language-guided experience of the world.

Sapir developed the concept of the phoneme, an element of patterning for him as it was for Boas; unlike Boas, however, Sapir was able to make a clear distinction between the sounds themselves as acoustic or articulatory entities and the phoneme as an element of a system. Sapir insisted particularly on what he called "the psychological reality of phonemes." In a 1933 paper of that name (in Sapir 1949), he illustrates the theory with a series of examples in which Nootka and Southern Paiute are presented alongside English, all as equally arbitrary.

Here again, Sapir was interested primarily not only in the system as such, but in the system as perceived by human subjects. This developing concern led him into a close association with psychoanalysis, and it also led him into a much closer questioning of the implications of differences in grammatical patterning for speakers themselves. In phonology, Sapir writes of the "pattern feeling" which predisposes a speaker to perceive sounds in certain ways. He would become increasingly convinced that the specifics of grammatical patterning, too, would lead the user of a given language into unconscious patterns of expectation, typical ways of putting things together (Erickson *et al.* 1997).

Was Sapir a linguistic determinist?

Overall, Sapir's expansion maintains the coherence of a Boasian comparative linguistics, which presents the real differences among languages yet presumes the continued possibility of their mutual calibration. Yet among the most commonly repeated quotations from Sapir are some that sound highly deterministic, as if he did believe that thought was determined by language and that all possible personal experience was trapped within a single language. This may be a result of his strong feeling for form and his affinity for Herder and the early Romantics. We already have something of the kind in *Language*:

[N]o matter how sophisticated our modes of interpretation become, we never really get beyond the projection and continuous transfer of relations suggested by the forms of our speech. (1921: 11)

In a letter of 1921, he wrote, "I quite frankly commit myself to the idea that thought is impossible without language, that thought is language" (Darnell 1990: 99). In *Language*, he writes:

From the point of view of language, thought may be defined as the highest latent or potential content of speech, the content that is obtained by interpreting each of the elements in the flow of language as possessed of its very highest conceptual value ...[1]

It is, indeed, in the highest degree likely that language is an instrument originally put to uses lower than the conceptual plane and that thought arises as a refined interpretation of its content. (1921: 14–15, cited in Lucy 1992a: 19–20)

On two occasions, Sapir uses the term "incommensurable" to describe the relationship between the lived experiences of speakers of different languages.

In one of the earliest uses of the term "relativity" by a Boasian, in his 1924 essay "The Grammarian and His Language," Sapir (1949: 159) cites

incommensurable analyses of experience in different languages. The upshot of it all would be to make very real to us a kind of relativity that is generally hidden from us by our naïve acceptance of fixed habits of speech as guides to an objective understanding of the nature of experience. This is the relativity of concepts or, as it might be called, the relativity of the form of thought. It is not so difficult to grasp as the physical relativity of Einstein nor is it as disturbing to our sense of security as the psychological relativity of Jung ... but it is perhaps more readily evaded than these. For its understanding the comparative data of linguistics are a *sine qua non*. It is the appreciation of the relativity of the form of thought which results from linguistic study that is perhaps the most liberalizing thing about it. What fetters the mind and benumbs the spirit is ever the dogged acceptance of absolutes.

To speak of incommensurable analyses may be to say, as critics have claimed Sapir and Whorf are saying (Chapter 9, below), that no passage is possible between two languages. Yet this reading goes against one of the most fundamental tenets of Boasian thought, including most of Sapir's own. The rest of the passage makes it clear that this is not what Sapir had in mind: on the contrary, whatever he means by "incommensurable" in no way precludes movement back and forth or the possibility of a liberating "appreciation" of both analyses. But this is not something that happens automatically or easily; it takes work.

The other use of the term "incommensurable" apparently occurred in a talk given at the National Academy of Sciences in 1931, for which all we have is a one-paragraph published summary. The tone of this paragraph is extremely deterministic:

Language ... actually defines experience for us by reason of its formal completeness and because of our unconscious projection of its implicit expectations into the field of experience ... Such categories as number, gender, case, tense, mode, voice, "aspect" and a host of others, many of which are not recognized systematically in our Indo-European languages, are, of course, derivative of experience at last analysis, but, once abstracted from experience, they are systematically elaborated in language and are not so much discovered in experience as imposed upon it because of the tyrannical hold that linguistic form has upon our orientation in the world. Inasmuch as languages differ very widely in their systematization of fundamental concepts, they tend to be only loosely equivalent to each other as symbolic devices and are, as a matter of fact, incommensurable in the sense in which two systems of points on a plane are, on the whole, incommensurable to each other if they are plotted out with reference to differing systems of coordinates. (Sapir 1931 [1964])

This is a statement of the implications of obligatory grammatical categories as they had been identified by Boas, albeit stated in terms reminiscent of Roland Barthes' "language is fascist" (see Chapter Six, note 3); it has been taken to mean that different languages imply entirely different universes between which no passage is possible.

In mathematics, however, incommensurability has a very specific meaning: it refers to the relationship between rational and irrational numbers, since an irrational number can never be represented by any number of integers, no matter how many decimal places you include.[2] The word "incommensurable" appears in some discussions of Herder, but the only place he himself uses the word *inkommensurabel* seems to be in the *Treatise on the Origin of Language*, where it refers not to human languages, but to an incommensurability between all human language and that of other animals (Herder 2002: 156). There is a clearer parallel to Sapir's usage in Leibniz's "Dialogue on Human Freedom" (1695 [1989]), which uses the analogy of mathematical incommensurability to explain the existence of evil: as the existence of shapes such as circles and triangles necessarily implies that of irrational numbers such as pi and the square root of two – "the irregularity of incommensurable lines arises from the very essence of figures" – so the only way God could have avoided irrational evil would have been to abandon the greater good of having shapes in the world.

In this stricter mathematical sense, incommensurability means something very different from untranslatability or mutually sealed universes. To say that two languages are incommensurable can be taken to mean that while no *exact* common measure can be established between forms, still, as in the cases of pi and the square root of two, closer and closer approximations remain possible, to the point that equivalents *can* be established for all practical purposes. The implication carries both a sense of ultimate difference and of provisional equivalence.

Probably the most famous statement of Sapir's supposed linguistic determinism comes from "The Status of Linguistics as a Science," a talk published in 1929:

Human beings do not live in the objective world alone, nor alone in the world of social activity as ordinarily understood, but are very much at the mercy of a particular language which has become the medium of expression for their society. It is quite an illusion to imagine that one adjusts to reality essentially without the use of language, and that language is merely an incidental means of solving specific problems of communication or reflection. The fact of the matter is that the "real world" is to a large extent unconsciously built up on the language habits of the group. No two languages are ever sufficiently similar to be considered as representing the same social reality. The worlds in which different societies live are different worlds, not merely the same world with different labels attached ... We see and hear and otherwise experience very largely as we do because the language habits of our community predispose certain choices of interpretation. (Sapir 1949: 162)

This is the passage that is most commonly quoted to demonstrate the putative linguistic determinism of Sapir and of his student Whorf, who cites some of it (1956: 134) at the beginning of "The Relation of Habitual Thought and Behavior to Language," a paper published in a Sapir Festschrift in 1941. But is this linguistic determinism? Or is it the statement of an observed reality that must be dealt with? Note that the passage does not say that it is impossible to translate between different languages, nor to convey the same referential content in both. Note also that there is a piece missing here, between "labels attached" and "We see and hear." In fact, the way I have presented it, with the three dots, is how this passage is almost always presented (e.g., Lucy 1992a: 22); otherwise, the quote usually ends at "labels attached." If we look at what has been elided, we find two examples, coming in a new paragraph immediately after "attached." In a typically Sapirian way, one is poetic, the other perceptual. He begins:

The understanding of a simple poem, for instance, involves not merely an understanding of the single words in their average significance, but a full comprehension of the whole life of the community as it is mirrored in the words, or as it is suggested by the overtones.

So the apparent claim of linguistic determinism is to be illustrated by – a poem (Friedrich 1979: 479–80), and a simple one at that! In light of this missing piece of the passage, what Sapir seems to be saying is not that language determines thought, but that language is part of social reality, and so is thought, and to understand either a thought or "a green thought in a green shade" you need to consider the whole.

The second example is one of the relationship of terminology to classification:

Even comparatively simple acts of perception are very much more at the mercy of the social patterns called words than we might suppose. If one draws some dozen lines, for instance, of different shapes, one peceives them as divisible into such categories as "straight," "crooked," "curved," "zigzag" because of the classificatory suggestiveness of the linguistic terms themselves. We see and hear ...

Again, is Sapir here arguing for a determination of thought by language or simply observing that in cases of sorting out complex data, one will tend to use the categories that are available? In the latter case, he would be suggesting to his audience of professionals (the source is a talk given to a joint meeting of the Linguistic Society of America and the American Anthropological Association) that such phenomena may extend beyond simple classification tasks.

Here it is important to distinguish between claims of linguistic determinism and the observation of the utility of available categories, an observation that in itself in no way questions the likely importance of the non-linguistic salience of input or the physiological component of perception. Taken in the context of the overall Boasian approach to language and thought, this is clearly the thrust of Sapir's comments here. Remember that this was the same man who did the famous "Study on Phonetic Symbolism," which showed that there are what appear to be universal psychological reactions to certain speech sounds (his term is "symbolic feeling-significance"), regardless of the language or the meaning of the word in which these sounds are found (in Sapir 1949).

This evidence against linguistic determinism, as it happens, was published the same year as "The Status of Linguistics as a Science," but in the *Journal of Experimental Psychology*.[3]

The metaphor Sapir uses most regularly for the relation of language patterning to thought is not that of a constraint, but of a road or groove that is relatively easy or hard to follow. In *Language*, he proposed that languages are "invisible garments" for our spirits; but at the beginning of the book he had already questioned this analogy: "But what if language is not so much a garment as a prepared road or groove?" (p. 15); grammatical patterning provides "grooves of expression, (which) have come to be felt as inevitable" (p. 89; cf. Erickson *et al.* 1997: 298). One important thing about a road is that you can get off it; of a groove, that you can get out of it. We will see that this kind of wording permeates Whorf's formulations as well.

Dorothy Demetracopoulou Lee

Sapir's theoretical claims, made for the most part in general studies using examples drawn from his vast linguistic experience, were carried into an extended case study by another one of Boas's students, Dorothy Demetracopoulou Lee (1905–1975), in her work on Wintu, a Penutian language of northern California, and on the remembered traditional culture of its speakers. Like Sapir, Lee trained in literature and practised poetry. Among her early publications are some extraordinary translations of Wintu songs (Demetracopoulou 1935).

Lee published a series of articles (e.g.,1938; 1944) seeking to formulate the "unformulated philosophy" of the Wintu based on the grammar of their language. She looked at a number of obligatory grammatical distinctions made in the Wintu noun, which has no obligatory gender or number, and in the verb, which has no obligatory tense. One of the most distinctive things about Wintu, not only in comparison with Western European languages but with other languages of the same family and the same geographical area, is its development of an obligatory system of data-source or evidential markers that characterize several different parts of speech. As in Kwak'wala, it is quite impossible to speak anything like normal Wintu without at every point specifying the source of one's data, how one knows what one is saying. Lee linked this pervasiveness of evidentiality in Wintu with basic verbal categories (each verb has two forms, one used for what cannot be known directly, the other for what the speaking subject can access in some way) and nominal categories (each noun can take a generalized or a particularized form, the latter implying direct relevance for the speaking subject) to try to render explicit Wintu presuppositions about human agency and the nature of the world.

These presuppositions stand out in part because they contrast so strongly with modern Western presuppositions, which they in turn help to make explicit.

For Lee, it is clear, the Wintu are a people who have collectively developed a coherent underlying unstated philosophy that has come to be crystallized in the grammar of their language – this is evident, for instance, in the title of her paper "Linguistic Reflection of Wintu Thought." The key datum for her is the kind of obligatory grammatical category whose existence was indicated by Boas; the assumption is that at least some obligatory categories will carry meaning which by virtue of their constant use become a salient part of the speaker's orientation; the method is contrastive comparison of Wintu categories with our own.[4]

Lee has been accused of tautology in basing her assertions about the relationship between language and world-conception only on linguistic evidence (Lucy 1992a: 70–2). Since some of the evidence she used comes from the content of myths, this seems unfair: to say that myths, because they are delivered in language, represent linguistic evidence of the same kind as, say, grammar, seems a mere play on words. The specific imagery, content, and events of a myth can be portrayed in any language and in a variety of media: it is this myth content, not the grammar of the language used to convey it, that Lee was drawing on to make her comparisons with Wintu grammar.

Benjamin Lee Whorf

Since the early 1950s, Sapir's student Benjamin Lee Whorf (1897–1941) has most often been presented as the very epitome of extreme cognitive relativism and linguistic determinism. Indeed, as the name attached to the "linguistic determinism hypothesis," a hypothesis almost never evoked but to be denied, Whorf has become both the best-known ethnolinguist outside the field itself and one of the great straw men of the century. This fate is undeserved; he was not a self-made straw man, as Marshall Sahlins once called another well-known anthropologist. While Whorf certainly maintained what he called a principle of linguistic relativity, it is clear from reading *Language, Thought, and Reality*, the only generally available source of his writings, published posthumously in 1956, and even clearer from still largely unpublished manuscripts, that he was also a strong universalist who accepted the general validity of modern science. With some re-evaluations since the early 1990s (Lucy 1992a; P. Lee 1996), we now have a clearer idea of what Whorf was about.

In spite of sometimes deterministic phraseology, Whorf presumed that much of human thinking and perception was non-linguistic and universal across languages. In particular, he admired Gestalt psychology (P. Lee 1996) as a science giving access to general characteristics of human perception across cultures and languages, including the lived experiences that lie behind the forms that we label time and space. He puts this most clearly in discussions of the presumably universal perception of visual space:

A discovery made by modern configurative or Gestalt psychology gives us a canon of reference, irrespective of their languages or scientific jargons, by which to break down and describe all visually observable situations, and many other situations, also. This is the discovery that visual perception is basically the same for all normal persons past infancy and conforms to definite laws. (Whorf 1956: 165)

Whorf clearly believed there was a real world out there, although, enchanted by quantum mechanics and relativity theory, he also believed that this was not the world as we conceive it, nor that every human being conceives it habitually in the same way.

Whorf also sought and proposed general descriptive principles for the analysis of languages of the most varied type. And along with Sapir, he worked on sound symbolism, proposing the universality of feeling-associations to certain speech sounds (1956: 267). Insofar as he was a good disciple of Sapir and Boas, Whorf believed, like them, in the universality of cognitive abilities and of some fundamental cognitive processes. And far from assuming that language determines thought and culture, Whorf wrote in the paper for the Sapir volume that

I should be the last to pretend that there is anything so definite as "a correlation" between culture and language, and especially between ethnological rubrics such as "agricultural, hunting," etc., and linguistic ones like "inflected," "synthetic," or "isolating." (pp. 138–9)

He illustrates his point in a footnote:

We have plenty of evidence that this is not the case. Consider only the Hopi and the Ute, with languages that on the overt morphological and lexical level are as similar as, say, English and German. The idea of "correlation" between language and culture, in the generally accepted sense of correlation, is certainly a mistaken one.

Like Lee, Whorf actualized Sapir's views in extended analyses of a small number of languages, in his case primarily of Hopi, a Uto-Aztecan language spoken in Arizona. Thanks in part to his dynamic writing style and his promotion of linguistic relativity, Whorf became the best-known proponent of the idea.

Whorf, a chemical engineer by training and profession, studied with Sapir to become a passionate amateur linguist – amateur only in the sense that he never took an academic degree in the subject: he was a highly accomplished descriptive linguist, particularly of Uto-Aztecan languages, with an engineer's grasp of complex structures. Whorf ended up as part of Sapir's research group while keeping his day job with Hartford Fire Insurance, and indeed filled in for Sapir at Yale when the latter was ill. Whorf's work on Hopi was carried out primarily with a speaker living in New York City.

In his view of language and human conception, Whorf shares the basic Boasian tenets: that you can say anything in any language; that one cannot rank languages or judge them by a single yardstick of values; that languages are differently structured, at every level; that the constant use of certain forms rather than others, whether these are phonological patterns, lexical arrays, or grammatical patterns, predisposes the user to attend to certain domains rather than others.

Whorf made three major contributions to the Boasian paradigm. First, he distinguished clearly between what is *possible* to think, which is in principle unlimited for speakers of any language, and what people *habitually* think, which may be strongly influenced by their language. Second, he helped push the analysis of language beyond that of explicitly marked parts of speech, introducing the concepts of covert category and cryptotype, distinctions that are often only recognizable through contextual comparison (P. Lee 1996: Chapter 4). Finally, Whorf moved between linguistic and non-linguistic data to talk more specifically than had his predecessors about possible influences of language on culture and thought (Lucy 1992a).

Whorf's most famous analyses are of the conceptual universe of the Hopi using Hopi grammar as a starting point. These are presented, along with general statements about the relationship between language and the lived world, in a small number of scholarly articles, a series of popularizing essays, and some manuscripts that were found after his death. While Whorf sometimes considers vocabulary, the bulk of his analysis of Hopi is based on grammatical categories; one of the distinctive aspects of these analyses is that they are always comparative attempts to calibrate between Hopi and modern Western languages, which he finds have common basic structures and which he accordingly groups as Standard Average European (SAE) (Whorf 1956: 138).[5] I will not attempt an overall characterization of Whorf's presentation of Hopi (but see P. Lee 1996), but merely indicate some salient points. Two stand out:

First, where SAE distinguishes between count nouns (bottle, cat, star) and mass nouns (air, rice, grief),[6] Hopi does not: it has only count nouns, and all Hopi nouns imply some kind of boundary (Whorf 1956: 141). Conversely, there are no imaginary plurals or countables. Where SAE languages treat, for instance, temporal durations as mass nouns that can be cut up into units (an hour, a month, a year are spoken of as if they were slices out of an unbounded mass of time), Hopi treats them only with ordinals: in Hopi, you would not use the same form for "three days" that you would for "three bottles," as if days could be lined up in a row and looked at together, but rather say something like "on the third day" (p. 140). One aspect of this is that the Hopi do not see each sunrise as bringing a new day, to be added to the ones already in storage, but as the same day come back again. And that has implications for Hopi philosophy and religious practice (pp. 148–52).

Second, Hopi verbs do not have obligatory tense. All verbs in Hopi are, however, either unmarked or marked with either the suffix *–ni* or the suffix *–ŋwe*.

These resemble tenses but refer to realms of validity rather than of time. The reportive (zero form) reports an actual occurred or occurring fact; it corresponds to past and present tense. The expective, *–ni*, declares an expectancy, and corresponds to future or incipiency ... The nomic, *–ŋwe*, declares a general or customary truth. (Whorf 1946: 176)

So this choice among three obligatory forms has centrally to do *not* with time relative to the moment of speaking, but with mode of knowing what you are saying (although they're not evidentials). These categories are the main issue in the short manuscript essay, "An American Indian Model of the Universe," where they are presented as indexing the "two great forms" that in Hopi play more or less the role of tenses in SAE. Here Whorf leaves out the gnomic and distinguishes between the unmarked form indicating what he calls the "manifested," which includes our past and the present as it is laid down before us by the past, and the *–ni* form indicating the "manifesting," which covers our future and the becoming-ness of the present. It is crucial to note that these are not in fact a present–past versus a future: different aspects of what we call the present are handled by both of them.

As I have stressed, Whorf was no integral relativist, and he presumed that all human beings have the same bodily experience of "it becoming later and later" (1956: 139); this serves as a basis for cultural and linguistic conceptualizations that can differ greatly. Given his Boasian assumption of mutual calibration, Whorf's presentation of Hopi categories required that he also make explicit the "great forms" that typify his own and our own SAE understandings of time. And here he gives quite a remarkable picture of a world in which time is thought of as a substance that can be divided up and even traded or sold; in which the past and the future are conceived as virtual spaces, the past "behind" the subject and the future "in front," with the subject facing into the future and moving forward along a steadily flowing stream of time.

When I first read Whorf, I found his presentation of the assumed categories of a Hopi universe remarkable, but not inherently unlikely or weird. More extraordinary was the revelation that I, too, was operating in a world just as "constructed" as that which Whorf attributes to the Hopi: Whorf essentially says that I should be feeling that I live on the borderline between an infinite or very large virtual past space occupied by memories and records, somehow located behind me (even though no matter how fast I turn around I can't see it), and a corresponding infinite or very large virtual future space occupied by projections and plans (in fact by hopes and fears), somehow located in front of me, yet invisibly, with the present the infinitely thin interface or moment of passage between them. This exotic construction does in fact match my conception of time. It's a conception that is reflected constantly in linguistic usage, not only in tenses but in turns of phrase: a new day has dawned; tomorrow is another day; forward into the past!

"I find it gratuitous to assume," Whorf writes at the beginning of the "American Indian Model" manuscript (1956: 57), "that a Hopi who knows only the Hopi language and the cultural ideas of his own society has the same notions, often supposed to be intuitions, of time and space that we have, and that are generally assumed to be universal." The use of the word "intuitions" here is a telling one; as we have seen, it comes from Kant, and much of Whorf, like much of Herder and Humboldt before him, can be understood as a response to Kant's reprise of Newtonian space, time, and causality – static empty space, unidirectional flowing time, formless substance, substance-filled form, linear causality – as a priori forms that frame all possible human conceptualization. For Whorf, on the contrary, while there are universal forms of perception and to some degree of conception, these lie at a deeper level of form recognition than do Kant's space and time. Such universal forms of human experience had, he felt, been identified by the cross-culturally valid science of Gestalt psychology. As he put it in one of the popularizing essays, "there is a universal, *Gefühl*-type way of linking experiences, which shows up in laboratory experiments and appears to be independent of language – basically alike for all persons" (1956: 267). Space and time *as they are conceptualized*, on the contrary, vary depending on the cultural and linguistic position of the observer. This distinction between, on the one hand, immediate experiences and "a universal, *Gefühl*-type way of linking" them, and on the other hand more highly elaborated and culturally distinctive conceptualizations, is essential for Whorf. He calls the latter "habitual thought worlds," "the microcosm that each man carries about within himself, by which he measures and understands what he can of the macrocosm" (p. 147; cf. the distinction between a universal experience of space and differing conceptualizations of space on p. 158).

Etymologically *Anschauung*, the word usually translated as intuition, is a looking on or a point of view: the term *Welt-anschauung*, usually translated into English as world view, could, then, be rendered as an intuition of the world or intuition-formation. Herder had claimed that the intuitions and categories that Kant had identified as necessary prerequisites for any human perception or imagining could be seen as elements of *one* way of constructing a world among a multitude of possibilities. Whorf, following Kant, continued to use intuition as a universal term; yet since for him Kant's intuitions and categories, Newton's space and time, Euclid's geometry were not universal properties of the world or of human perception, he would say that they are "no intuitions; they are recepts from language and culture. That is where Newton got them" (1956: 153). We, on the other hand, given the relationship between *Anschauung* and *Weltanschauung*, might speak of world-intuitions that can differ across cultures and languages.

Whorf sometimes uses the word "metaphysics" for these uncritically assumed language-and-culture-dependent conceptualizations of the world:

The metaphysics underlying our own language, thinking, and modern culture (I speak not of the recent and quite different relativity metaphysics) imposes upon the universe two grand COSMIC FORMS, space and time ... Just as it is possible to have any number of geometries other than the Euclidean which give an equally perfect account of space configurations, so it is possible to have descriptions of the universe, all equally valid, that do not contain our familiar contrasts of time and space. The relativity viewpoint of modern physics is one such view ... the Hopi Weltanschauung is another. (pp. 59, 58)

In this passage from the "Model" manuscript, Whorf distinguishes among (1) initial bodily experience of extension and duration, which can be gotten at through Gestalt experiments and which are presumably universal to human beings; (2) our own commonly lived metaphysics, with static space, flowing time, etc., a "recept" from culture and language; (3) the commonly lived metaphysics (in the plural) of peoples speaking other tongues. He thus posits a potential multitude of world views, all of which are recepts from culture and language; and further, a distinction between *all* such world views and (4) the startling world that is revealed by the sciences of the twentieth century, which presume a new, non-commonly-lived but explicitly constructed, metaphysics. For Whorf, certain scientific disciplines – elsewhere he names "relativity, quantum theory, electronics, catalysis, colloid chemistry, theory of the gene, Gestalt psychology, psychoanalysis, unbiased cultural anthropology, and so on" (1956: 220), as well as non-Euclidean geometry and, of course, descriptive linguistics – were exemplary in that they revealed aspects of the world profoundly at variance with the world as modern Westerners habitually assume it to be, indeed as the members of any human language and social group habitually assume it to be.

Since Whorf was concerned with linguistic and/or conceptual patterns that people almost always follow in everyday life, he has often been read as a determinist. But as John Lucy pointed out (1992a), Whorf's critiques clearly bore on habitual thinking, what it is *easy* to think; his ethical goal was to force us, through learning about other languages, other ways of foregrounding and linking aspects of experience, to think in ways that are not so easy, to follow paths that are not so familiar. Whorf's argument is not fundamentally about constraint, but about the seductive force of habit, of what is "easily expressible by the type of symbolic means that language employs" ("Model," 1956: 55) and so easy to think. It is not about the limits of a given language or the limits of thought, since Whorf presumes, Boasian that he is, that any language can convey any referential content.

Whorf's favorite analogy for the relation of language to thought is the same as Sapir's: that of tracks, paths, roads, ruts, or grooves. Even Whorf's most determinist-sounding passages, which are also the ones most cited, sound very different if we take the implications of this analogy seriously: "Thinking ... follows a network of tracks laid down in the given language, an organization which may concentrate systematically upon certain phases of reality ... and may systematically discard others featured by other languages. The individual is utterly unaware of this organization and is constrained completely within its unbreakable bonds" (1956: 256); "we dissect nature along lines laid down by our native languages" (p. 213). But this is from the same essay in which Whorf asserted the universality of "ways of linking experiences ... basically alike for all persons"; and this completely constrained individual is evidently the unreflective (utterly unaware) Mr. Everyman (Schultz 1990), and the very choice of the analogy of traced lines or tracks, assuming that they are not rail-way tracks – that they are not is suggested by all the other road and path meta-phors – leaves open the possibility of getting off the path, if only we had the imagination and the gumption to do it. We can cut cross-country. In the study of an exotic language, he wrote, "we are at long last pushed willy-nilly out of our ruts. Then we find that the exotic language is a mirror held up to our own" (1956: 138). How can Whorf be a determinist, how can he see us as forever trapped in these ruts, if the study of another language is sufficient to push us, kicking and screaming perhaps, out of them?

The total picture, then, is not one of constraint or determinism. It is, on the other hand, a model of powerful seduction: the seduction of what is familiar and easy to think, of what is intellectually restful, of what makes common sense.[7] The seduction of the habitual pathway, based largely on laziness and fear of the unknown, can, with work, be resisted and broken. Somewhere in the back of Whorf's mind may have been the allegory of the broad, fair road to Hell and the narrow, difficult path to Heaven beloved of his Puritan forebears. It makes us think of another New England Protestant: "Two roads diverged in a wood, and I, / I took the one less travelled by, / and that has made all the difference."

The recognition of the seduction of the familiar implies a real ethical program:

It is the "plainest" English which contains the greatest number of unconscious assump-tions about nature ... Western culture has made, through language, a provisional ana-lysis of reality and, without correctives, holds resolutely to that analysis as final. The only correctives lie in all those other tongues which by aeons of independent evolution have arrived at different, but equally logical, provisional analyses. (1956: 244)

Learning non-Western languages offers a lesson in humility and awe in an enormous multilingual world:

We shall no longer be able to see a few recent dialects of the Indo-European family, and the rationalizing techniques elaborated from their patterns, as the apex of the evolution of the human mind, nor their present wide spread as due to any survival from fitness or to anything but a few events of history – events that could be called fortunate only from the parochial point of view of the favored parties. They, and our own thought processes with them, can no longer be envisioned as spanning the gamut of reason and knowledge but only as one constellation in a galactic expanse. (p. 218)

The breathtaking sense of sudden vaster possibility, of the sky opening up to reveal a bigger sky beyond, may be what provokes such strong reactions to Whorf. For some, he is simply enraging or ridiculous. For others, reading Whorf is a transformative experience, and there are many stories of students coming to anthropology or linguistics largely because of their reading of Whorf (personal communications; Alford 2002).

Sapir, Whorf, and Einstein

Sapir and Whorf held that the findings of twentieth-century linguistics and anthropology pointed to a new principle of linguistic relativity, by ana-logy to Einstein's principle of relativity (discussion in P. Lee 1996: 86–8). In this view, differing cultural and linguistic forms implied differences in point of view comparable to those that Einstein correlates with differences in relative velocity. This relativity of point of view is as far from a "hypoth-esis of linguistic determinism" as Einstein's is from a hypothesis of velocity determinism; and like Einstein's, Whorf's relativity, in particular, only makes sense on the basis of general principles which he identified with twentieth-century Western science.

In one of his popularizing essays, Whorf (1956: 213–14) lays out the relativ-ity analogy in its canonical form:

We cut nature up, organize it into concepts, and ascribe significances as we do, largely because we are party to an agreement to organize it in this way – an agreement that holds throughout our speech community and is codified in the patterns of our language. The agreement is, of course, an implicit and unstated one, BUT ITS TERMS ARE ABSO-LUTELY OBLIGATORY; we cannot talk at all except by subscribing to the organization and classification of data which the agreement decrees.

This fact is very significant for modern science, for it means that no individual is free to describe nature with absolute impartiality but is constrained to certain modes of interpretation even while he thinks himself most free. The person most nearly free in such respects would be a linguist familiar with very many widely different linguis-tic systems. As yet no linguist is in any such position. We are thus introduced to a new principle of relativity, which holds that all observers are not led by the same physical evidence to the same picture of the universe, unless their linguistic backgrounds are similar, or can in some way be calibrated.

In the next essay in this series (1956: 235), Whorf writes:

The point of view of linguistic relativity changes Mr Everyman's dictum: Instead of say-ing, "Sentences are unlike because they tell about unlike facts," he now reasons: "Facts are unlike to speakers whose language background provides for unlike formulation of them."

When Einstein formulated his theories, relativity itself was not a new idea; but Newtonian relativity still assumed an absolute space and a fixed passage of time giving coordinates by which events could ultimately be located. There remained a God's-eye view of the whole that is easily grasped in the terms of classical mechanics. Einstein's relativity makes this fixed spatiotemporal frame vanish, so that all measurements become relative to the situation of the measuring entity. The principle of relativity becomes a general condition of observation, and the world thus disclosed is one that requires a new physics that is not easy for twentieth- or twenty-first-century Western humans – or maybe for any human – to conceptualize.

Note that this is no relativism, not Locke's "incurable Confusion." Coherent relations continue to hold among different situations; they can, if you like, be calibrated. Similarly, for Sapir and Whorf languages represent frames of reference that orient the speaker, point him or her in certain directions rather than others. In neither case does this deny the possibility of getting an idea of other frames of reference, in astrophysics or in linguistics (Alford 1981; Heynick 1983; Jakobson 1985: 254–64). On the contrary: that's the work that has to be done. The Boasians were on the lookout for general frames that would facilitate such calibration, whether these were phonetic (Mackert 1994; Bauman and Briggs 2003: 263–4) or perceptual.

Linguistics and physics

We have seen that the word relativity was already being used in reference to language in German philosophy from the early nineteenth century. There are, in fact, suggestions that Einstein himself might have been influenced in his early thinking by a linguistic use of the idea. The adolescent Einstein, having done poorly in college in Germany, went to Switzerland to continue his studies. He lodged with the family of one Jost Winteler (1846–1929), a local schoolmaster. Winteler had once been a promising linguist. His dissertation (1876) was a phonetic analysis of his own dialect of Swiss German of a rigor and thoroughness that was a model for the Neogrammarians (Koerner 1976: 340–1), which the linguist Leonard Bloomfield (1933: 331) said was "perhaps the first adequate study of a single local dialect," and which, according to Jakobson, prefigured phonological theory, giving "the first concrete phonological analysis and classification of speech sounds" (1971: 414).

I don't know whether Winteler read the German language philosophers. But he, too, talks about relativity in language. In his discussion of the contextually determined voicing or unvoicing of occlusives in the Kerenzer dialect, Winteler describes his solution of the problem as based on the recognition of "the relativity of relations" (*Relativität der Verhältnisse*) among speech sounds (1876: 27).

By the time Einstein met him, Winteler was on the margins of scholarly life. Einstein had long talks with his landlord and continued to refer to him with respect and gratitude (Jakobson 1985: 258–60); for a while he was in love with Winteler's daughter, and his sister ended up marrying Winteler's son. While there is no direct evidence for it, Jakobson raised the possibility that linguistic relativity may have inspired the physical. Others have debunked the idea (Kohrt 1984). The best conclusion I can draw is the one Konrad Koerner once offered in this regard (personal communication): *Se non è vero, è ben trovato.*

What were the Boasians doing?

The novelty of the Boasians was to insist on keeping two apparently contradictory thoughts in their heads at the same time – contradictory not necessarily for actual language and thought, but for the ideologies with which most modern Westerners think about language and thought. Virtually all major theorists of language diversity, as I have tried to show through most of this book, either saw language specificities as mere surface effects, since thought or experience is universal and pre- or non-linguistic, or develops through universal stages; or else saw each language as part of a unique whole that also included a race and national spirit. The Boasians, in contrast, insisted that there was no necessary link between language, race, culture, and thought processes while at the same time demonstrating links between language, culture, and ways of thinking. Both of these were true, and they held to the truth of both rather than sacrificing a part of the truth to an overarching requirement of consistency.

A key to what they were doing may lie in the difference in levels of argument, something the Boasians themselves did not stress. The claims of lack of link between language and other aspects of life are made on a very high level of generality, and in explicit opposition to the evolutionist identification of language and thinking as both representing levels of development, and at the same time to the racist and essentialist identification of each language with a national spirit. On the other hand, the Boasian approach is a historical one (Bunzl 2004), and human history shows many examples of correlation, mutual influence, or one-way influence between otherwise autonomous language structures and modes of thought and cultural practice. For an essentialist, such examples represent the norm, the way things ought to be. For the Boasians, on the contrary, they no more represent the natural state of things than do examples of the lack of such influence: all are historical products, brought into being through specific combinations of circumstances and liable to be dispersed if conditions change. Yet this approach is not necessarily atomistic: nothing in it excludes large-scale patterning, and indeed the Boasians regularly demonstrated patterning in language and "patterns of culture." Such patterning can exist at different levels (e.g., broad Northwest

Coast tendencies versus specifically Chinook or Kwak'wala ones; broad tendencies of Chinookan versus Wakashan languages), and widespread patterns can crosscut each other. To use structuralist language, what the Boasians seem to be getting at is the activity of structures on each other, in interaction and at many levels.

While this may sound vague, remember that nothing like this could have been said about Boas's predecessors on the question of language diversity. Even Humboldt and Steinthal, with their very real concerns for universals, kept coming back to the relatively simple model that we might caricature as "Ein Volk, ein Geist, eine Sprache," while universalists from Port-Royal to the Neogrammarians and evolutionists judged languages by a single yardstick and sought to explain fragmentary phenomena by general laws, with little sense of differing fields or systems.

Precursors?

Where, then, might we look for predecessors to this quest for coherence in complexity? Two philosophers stand out, neither of whom in fact had much to say about language diversity, but who offered such models in other domains.

One is Benedict de Spinoza (1632–1677), whose philosophy represented a seventeenth-century alternative to rationalism, empiricism, and essentialism in positing that God and Nature, mind and body are one substance which we perceive and conceptualize as dual because of our own nature. This radical identification of mind and body never became a pillar of Western theoretical thought, caught as it has been in debates between philosophies of a mechanical law-governed universe/body and those of a multiplicity of self-referring minds/cultures.

In rejecting both transitive and expressive forms of causality as inadequate to grasp the complexity of the single world, Spinoza was forced to propose other kinds of relationships between parts and wholes. In his discussion of different forms of causality, Althusser (1965 [1970]: 187) identifies Spinoza with what he calls structural causality, the complex causality of a whole on its parts (cf. Leavitt 1991a; 1996).

Spinoza was a paradigmatic multilingual, and among other things he wrote a grammar of Hebrew, but his thinking specifically about language remains a topic of debate (see recently Vinciguerra 2005).

The Boasians' other theoretical precursor may be Marx. In the 1857 manuscript introduction to the first version of *Capital*, we see him struggling to articulate a conception of universal laws and distinctive wholes *together*. Here is how he tries to characterize the role of agricultural production, which had dominated the feudal economy, as part of the new mode of capitalist production, dominated by industry:

In all forms of society there is a specific production which assigns (*anweist*) rank and influence to all the others and to their relations. It is a general illumination which bathes all the other colours and modifies their particularity (*Besonderheit*). It is a particular (*besonderer*) ether which determines the specific gravity of every being which has come into being within it. (Marx 1857 [1973]: 106–7, translation modified; passage discussed in Althusser, 1965 [1970]: 188 ff.)

Marx periodizes history into modes of production, each of which implies fundamental rules that mark, or give a tonality to, structures at different levels within it. Marx's presuppositions here are historical and not essentialist, in that modes of production, like the social formations they mark, include, and partially define, are not sealed universes: they may be expected to intersect and overlap. While this may sound either like mystical hocus-pocus (if you are a hardnosed universalist) or Stalinist determinism (if you are a free-spirited individualist), it is a rare attempt to think through a more complex model for human history than simply universal laws, sealed cultural personalities, or random events.

Compare Marx's struggling for a way of conceptualizing relations, drawing for possible analogies on what he could know of the natural science of his time – illuminations and ethers, shifting centers of gravity – with, on the one hand, Herder's earlier essentialist analogies ("every nation has its center of felicity in itself alone, as every sphere has its center of gravity") and Whorf's quest for analogies in relativity physics, quantum mechanics, and non-Euclidean geometry.

The Boasians and the War

Relativity is not necessarily relativism. While Boas and his students did not consider some languages or cultures to be superior to others, and while they saw each language type as requiring terms appropriate to it, they did not try to live in a way that was free of all values. Their own were clear: they were democrats and progressives.[8] Precisely because they had strong political values, Boas and his students felt that modern Western society should be pushed in certain directions rather than others, and that the greatest exposure to the widest range of ways of living, speaking, and interpreting the world would help to further this goal (Roth Pierpont 2004). Boas himself had an important career as an anti-racist physical anthropologist, a position that up until the 1940s was very much in the minority; and he wrote anti-Nazi tracts in German that were circulated clandestinely within the Third Reich. In reading some of Whorf's more extreme statements, most of which were published in the MIT alumni magazine and so aimed at a broad audience largely in the physical sciences, I would argue that we should see him both as a scientist and, like Boas himself, as an engaged anti-Fascist propagandist. This would account for some of the hyperbolic style that some readers find irritating, others inspiring (Schultz 1990; Ridington 2006: 127–47).

8 The other side of the mirror: a twentieth-century essentialism

The most common accusation levelled against the Boasians and their successors has been that they were "culturalists" who believe that every culture is a seamless and sealed whole, fully integrated and impermeable from outside: this is essentialism, a cardinal sin for the last few decades. How many times have we heard, since the 1980s in particular, that North American cultural anthropology takes the internal homogeneity of cultures for granted, consistently minimizing personal agency and differences of class, race, and gender within cultures, and equally consistently underestimating the role of hybridization and colonial penetration? In the more restricted domain of language, the Boasians are presented as seeing thought as trapped and determined by language. Whorf in particular, as we will see in detail in the next chapter, is accused of linguistic determinism and conceptual relativism.

It is salutary in this regard to compare the Boasian movement, which to some degree does look back to Humboldt, with a parallel and contemporary movement in Germany, that of Neohumboldtian linguistics. This was a true essentialism, and by contrast shows to what degree Boasian anthropology and linguistics were not.

Philosophical and philological precursors

The immediate precursors to Neohumboldtian linguistics can be found in some German philosophers and literary historians of the early twentieth century. In the early 1920s the philosopher Ernst Cassirer (1874–1945) propounded and promoted a Herder–Humboldt stream in philosophy and linguistics. The first volume of his *Philosophy of Symbolic Forms* (1923 [1953]), which deals with language, was enormously influential. With his emigration to the United States as a refugee, Cassirer's renewed pluralism influenced American students and became a source of inspiration for the symbolic anthropology of the 1970s.

Like Humboldt, Cassirer remained a Kantian while reversing some of Kant's central points. For Cassirer, too, the essential lesson from Kant was the formative power of the human mind; but Cassirer maintains that human minds come into being only through systems of symbols. There are different systems – language, scientific thought, mythic thought, artistic thought – each of which implies a somewhat different kind of lived experience. To understand human beings requires a philosophy that accepts the centrality of sign systems.

Cassirer sums up the basic lesson he draws from Herder and Humboldt:

[W]e do not simply seize on and name certain distinctions that are somewhere present in feeling or intuition; on the contrary ... [W]e draw certain dividing lines, effect certain separations and connections, by virtue of which distinct individual configurations emerge from the uniform flux of consciousness. (1923 [1953]: 280; cf. Miller 1968: 47)

Another precursor of the Neohumboldtians was the neo-idealist philology of the Romanist Karl Vossler (1872–1949), a sharp critic of the isolating methods of historical linguistics in favor of a more global consideration of a language's overall style:

A history of language according to so-called historical grammar is, roughly speaking, what a history of clothing would be without a concept of fashion or of the taste of a period: a chronologically and geographically arranged list of buttons, clasps, stockings, hats, and garters. In historical grammar, these buttons and ribbons would, for instance, correspond to stressed a in an open syllable, k and l in initial position, etc. (1910 [1923]: 19)

Vossler's most general statements are in his book *Geist und Kultur in der Sprache* (1925 [1932]), the title of which, a manifesto in itself, was toned down in translation to *The Spirit of Language in Civilization*. For Vossler, particular languages determine thought and experience; the first language learned, the mother tongue, creates a horizon of possibilities beyond which it is virtually impossible to go. Vossler "maintains that we are all enslaved by the 'inner nature' of our language, 'out of which we neither can nor wish to escape'" (House 2000: 72, citing Vossler 1925 [1932]: 197). Concomitantly, each language is a world unto itself; ideas that come into being within this world cannot really be transferred into another. The most important aspect of language, "the inner language form," he writes, "is untranslatable" (p. 182). I have argued that the doctrine of Boas, Sapir, and Whorf makes neither of these claims. They would, however, be an integral part of Neohumboldtian doctrine.

Vossler's formulation on French language and character is an essentialist charter:

[I]n the final instance [the differences between French and German] are connected with the type of mind predominating in that particular language community, that is, with "the national character" ... [T]heir national character is embodied and realized in what we call the French language. The same national character manifests itself in other ... ways as well, such as the economic political, judicial, moral, scientific attitudes of the French ... Each of these facets shows a different picture of one and the same thing, and each represents in its *own* way the whole thing, the whole Frenchman ... The French language, therefore, is the *whole* of the French mind; but only in the light of language ... Through practice and habituation [the Frenchman] may achieve citizenship in any number of languages; but his spiritual home remains French, which he may deny or forget, but which he can no more lose than he can lose the experiences of his childhood. (pp. 115–6)

This means that in normal circumstances there is a perfect congruence of one person, one language, one culture, one race. Multilinguisticality and multiculturality can only be aberrations.

Only now does it become clear how each race fashions its own Weltanschauung, or rather the potentialities of a Weltanschauung; how by their language and through their language nations unfold their spiritual characteristics into living relationships and interactions; and how there rests in the lap of each language a kind of predestination, a gentle urge to this or that way of thinking. (p. 131)

Vossler continued to publish through the Nazi years. The "mother tongue" of each *Volk* was "its inner eye, its forms of thought with all its possibilities of constructing the world. It is the voice of the childhood of the people, and of its future, its memories and its longings" (Vossler, from 1936, cited in Hutton 1999: 143).

The Neohumboldtian movement

The refurbished essentialism represented by Vossler would mark the new approach in German linguistics. The creation of a group of scholars born in the 1890s and trained for the most part as philologists, it took as its central task the rendering explicit of meanings that were implicit in the vocabulary and to a degree in the grammar of specific languages. The movement has had a number of names, all characteristic: the favored ones since the War have been *Wortfeldlehre*, "word-field theory," *Inhaltsforschung*, "content-research," and *inhaltbezogene Grammatik*, "content-oriented grammar"; it has also been labelled Neoromantic and, most characteristically, Neohumboldtian (overviews in Basilius 1952; Öhman 1953; Bynon 1966; Miller 1968; Seiffert 1968).

The first statement of the new view was the 1923 paper "The Concept of the Inner Form of Speech" by the Indo-Europeanist Walter Porzig (1895–1961). Porzig begins by citing Humboldt: "Language is, as it were, the outer expression of the spirit of peoples; the language is their spirit and the spirit their language." This is an idea that Porzig wants to see returned to a central place in linguistics and the philosophy of language. After criticizing alternative formulations of the idea of the inner form of speech, including the positivist, the psychological, and the phenomenological, Porzig observes that each person grows up with and *inside* a particular language and concludes that "[f]or the individual the forms of his mother tongue are thus truly *a priori* forms of apperception" (Porzig 1923: 165).

But how is one to get a scientific idea of forms of apperception that are already presupposed in one's every experience? The obvious place to look is one's own mother tongue, "[b]ut this is as impossible as trying to see one's own face without the help of a mirror. For these forms are in fact nothing other than the always trusted 'objective' outer world of the naive person." The only way to do this – and here Porzig is paralleling Sapir and anticipating Whorf – is through comparison. "Through comparison of entirely different types of languages, the naive faith in one's own world view is shattered and the groundwork is laid for insight into the inner form of one's own language" (p. 166). This is a parallel, but also a reversal: for Whorf, the consideration of very different languages makes our own linguistically-guided forms perceptible, which in turn helps clarify the specificity of the other language, in a dialectic of mutual calibration. For Porzig, exotic languages are a tool for a better understanding of one's own, and that is the goal.

The best-known figures in the Neohumboldtian tradition were Jost Trier and Leo Weisgerber. In their writings of the 1920s, in terminology derived from Humboldt and the Romantics, these authors speak of each language as representing a world picture (*Weltbild*) characterized by an inner form.[1] This form is semantic: to understand a language in its specificity, one must reconstruct not only its form, but the semantic fields, the word-fields, that make up its contents.

Weisgerber (1894–1970) had been trained as a Celticist and an Indo-Europeanist. In his first papers, he attacks the Neogrammarians for their exclusive interest in isolated phenomena and argues for a holistic study of the organization of meaning in each language. As Boas had done in the alternating sounds paper, Weisgerber (following Cassirer and expressing admiration for Saussure) cites psychological studies, in this case to argue that memory for colors depended as much on language as on the functioning of the eye and brain. "In that one learns and applies such terms as red, green, yellow etc. the riotous chaos of our sense perception of colour is clarified and takes on a fixed orderliness" (1926: 247–8, cited in Hutton 1999: 109). This ordering function of language holds for all of thought. Weisgerber calls German "the language which generally thinks for us" (in Hutton 1999: 109–10). This would be the first of a lifetime of investigations into different sensory domains, notably smells and tastes, as well as colors. Weisgerber argued in each case that one must distinguish among the physical correspondents to the experience, the perceptual reception of the stimulus, and the conceptual construction of a lived field, the latter achieved largely through words (discussion in Miller 1968: Chapters 3–5).

In 1929, Weisgerber summed up his approach to language and its role in defining and unifying the *Volk* in a book with the characteristic title *Muttersprache und Geistesbildung*.

Throughout his long career, Weisgerber's analytic vocabulary shows how indebted he remained to essentialist models:

Characteristic items in Weisgerber's terminological apparatus are *Kraft* ("potency") and *Wirkung* ("effect"); the insistence on a "total" (*ganzheitlich*) view of language; and the notion that language, as energeia, "words" (*wortet*) the world and indeed shapes it by making it the object of language-"grasps" (*sprachliche Zugriffe*). (Seiffert 1964: 74 f.)

Jost Trier (1899–1985) became a major international figure in the study of semantics with his development of the concept of the semantic field. Trier introduced the idea in his first major publication, a 1931 analysis contrasting the vocabularies of knowledge in medieval and modern German, suggesting that a complete reorganization of this semantic field took place between the thirteenth and fifteenth centuries.

Semantic fields, to cite one of the standard introductions (Ullmann 1962: 245), are

closely-knit sectors of the vocabulary, in which a particular sphere is divided up, classified and organized in such a way that each element helps to delimit its neighbours and is delimited by them ... In each field, the raw material of experience is analysed and elaborated in a unique way, differing from one language to another and often from one period to another in the history of the same idiom. In this way, the structure of semantic fields embodies a specific philosophy and a scale of values.

For Trier, the implications bore directly on how language influences the construction of the world:

Every language is a system of selection over and against objective reality ... [and] creates a self-sufficient and complete image of reality. Every language structures reality in its own manner and thereby establishes the components of reality which are peculiar to this given language. The language-reality components of one language never recur in quite the same form in another, nor are they simply a straightforward copy of reality. They are instead the linguistic-conceptual realization of a view of reality proceeding from a unique but definite structuring matrix which continuously compares and contrasts, relates and distinguishes the data of reality.

In relation to the speaking subject, writes Trier,

Every language and every level in language divides up (*gliedert*) the world differently, and so gives forth the world differently, and the speech community, and through it every individual, receives (*haben*) the world in the way the language gives it. (in Basilius 1952: 100)

George Steiner sums up the contributions of Weisgerber and Trier and links the basic thought-form that inspired them back to Leibniz:

Weisgerber ... sought to apply the "monadic" or relativity principle to the actual, detailed features of German syntax and, correspondingly, to the history of German attitudes ... [For] Trier, every language structures and organizes reality in its own manner and thereby determines the components of reality that are peculiar to this given

language … Thus, in a distinctly Leibnizian way, each tongue or language-monad constructs and operates within a total conceptual field … Speakers of different languages
therefore inhabit different "mediary worlds" (*Zwischenwelten*). The linguistic world-
view of a given community shapes and gives life to the entire landscape of psychological and communal behavior. (Steiner 1975: 86–7)

A central concern of the Neohumboldtian project has been the deep and
pervasive power of one's first language, the language in which one first comes
to consciousness, and the specificities of which are inextricably bound up with
one's most profound values. Weisgerber, in particular, held that learning other
languages cannot be of much help in expanding one's horizons, since one
learns them through the mother tongue, and they remain marginal to it (Bynon
1966: 472). The project, then, in spite of what Porzig had suggested, would
not be one of opening up the possibilities of thought through exposure to non-
familiar ways of organizing experience, but the reverse, moving not out, but
in. In spite of Weisgerber's training as a Celticist and Porzig's as a Romanist,
the bulk of the work of this school was about German. The goal was to enrich
understanding and appreciation of the German language, with others cited primarily by way of contrast.

This turning back to the mother tongue marks Weisgerber's contributions to
education theory, one of his consistent interests. In a 1927 paper on the culti-
vation of concepts (*Begriffspflege*) in primary school, Weisgerber argues that
instead of seeking to find some universal language-free way of thinking, which
is illusory, children should be trained to fit their thoughts accurately into the
conceptual categories of their mother tongue (in Hutton 1999: 111).

Linguistics in the Third Reich

Its championing of German and its emphasis on the mother tongue as the lov-
ing matrix of normal human development made the Neohumboldtian view of
language congenial to the Third Reich. Through the 1930s we can see a progressive harmonizing of linguistic and political views. A case in point was
that of the linguist Georg Schmidt-Rohr (1890–1945), a German nationalist
who argued for many years that a people's identity came essentially from their
language. His 1932 book *Language as the Educator of Peoples* (*Bildnerin der
Völker*) called for a "Copernican revolution" in recognizing the centrality of
speech for human thought (p. 8). The table of contents of this volume lays out
a whole program. An example: a section entitled "Language as a power that
creates the group soul"; first subsection: "Every language teaches its speakers
a distinctive way of thinking." Schmidt-Rohr explicitly puts himself into the
essentialist tradition:

The Romantics and Herder and Fichte certainly already recognized and expressed what
Wilhelm von Humboldt showed with such overpowering clarity: that a language is the
soul of a people, which also forms our individual souls. (1932: 11)

We only have concepts, says Schmidt-Rohr, because our language has picked them out for us. And since languages are different, so will be our ways of conceptualizing the world. The way to discover this is to compare languages:

Diverse languages thus represent *diverse* conceptual networks. Even the most closely corresponding concepts from two languages will never encompass the same group of phenomena. – And this expectation will in fact be realized in the fullest measure if we compare two real languages. (p. 19)

Schmidt-Rohr goes on to dicuss colors, divisons of time, and kinship categories, all of which, he says, are arbitrarily defined by languages. Boundaries of classes of objects are determined essentially (*ganz wesentlich*) by linguistic categories.

This brand of what has been called "mother-tongue fascism" (Hutton 2005) remained perfectly essentialist, but located the hidden essence in a language, not in a racial type. That is, anyone whose mother tongue was German was part of the German community – and this included German-speaking Jews, a view that became problematic when Hitler came to power in 1933. The second edition of Schmidt-Rohr's book, now renamed *Mother Tongue: On the Task of Language in the Becoming of the People* (1933) added pages pointing out that his argument was meant primarily to help protect German-speakers living outside Germany. But it quickly became clear that this kind of linguistic, rather than racial, essentialism would not be acceptable. Schmidt-Rohr revised his views, accepted racial determinism, and joined the National Socialist Party. Porzig and Trier were also Party members, and while Weisgerber was not, he, like them, was an active participant in the National Socialist regime and the war effort (Hutton 1999).

In a review of Indo-European linguistics published in 1936 and evidently in line with National Socialist thinking, Kurt Stegmann von Pritzwald sees Neoromanticism and Weisgerber in particular as harbingers of a new generation that rejects the cold science of the old historical linguistics and seeks to aid actively in the self-realization of the German nation.

And now enters a new generation. Almost one hundred years after the appearance of Bopp's *Comparative Grammar* appears Weisgerber's *Muttersprache und Geistesbildung.* The proclamation that linguistics is *Volkstheorie* has liberated the efforts of linguistic philosophy for the last decade. (Stegmann von Pritzwald 1936: 1)

Weisgerber, for his part, did try to maintain the distinction between the natural and the spiritual sciences. He came to accept race as the defining factor for a people, but argued that language was a cultural phenomenon. A language represented the wisdom and the world view of a people accumulated over many generations (Weisgerber 1939; cf. Hutton 2005: 202–3). This model allowed Weisgerber's to be both the dominant linguistics of the Third Reich, and, with the correlation to race removed, of the Federal Republic into the 1970s.

What happened to linguistics under the Nazis becomes clear in successive issues of the journal *Wörter und Sachen*, "Words and Things." The journal had been founded at the beginning of the century. From 1933, which is also when Weisgerber joined the editorial board, the tone of the articles became increasingly *völkisch*. In 1938 a new series was started, with the title now printed in Fraktur to look more distinctively German. The new editor-in-chief was Hermann Güntert (1886–1948), a respected Indo-Europeanist. His editorial launching the new series is entitled "A New Time – A New Goal." Güntert begins by attacking the very notion of a general linguistics.

The concept of a "general linguistics," so beloved these days, seems to me to be ambiguous and unclear, insofar as false ideas can easily hide behind it. For it leads quickly to a "general humanity" with its "language," and that is a fictive, suppositional construction without reality ... We refuse it absolutely, since behind every language must stand the nature of the people (*die Volkheit*) that forms it; we reject the idealistic-humanistic human ideal, the individual as well as the idea of humanity. There is no such thing as plain "language," but only many very diverse (*verschiedene*) languages with their diverse kinds of effectiveness (*Leistungsfähigkeit*). (Güntert1938: 2)

Any attempt to speak of language in general is illusory; the (no doubt French or English) philosopher who does so is merely elevating his own mother tongue to the status of a universal standard (p. 3). See how the discourse of diversity can be turned to defend racism and fascism! I suppose by now this shouldn't surprise us – we've seen so many examples of it at the end of the twentieth and beginning of the twenty-first century.

This strong view of language differences means that translation "in the strict sense of the word" is impossible. And what of individual agency? The only choice is whether to be a loyal supporter or a traitor to your mother tongue.

The journal would continue to concentrate on the Indo-European languages and on what justifies linguistics, the study of Indo-European peoples such as Germans. So is there any point in studying non-Indo-European languages? Yes, there is: comparison with non-Indo-European peoples will allow us to define the distinctive quality (*Eigenart*) of Indo-Europeanness better (p. 4).

And Güntert here, in this linguistics journal, endorses the derived nature of language from biological factors:

Even if a language can operate a pervasive influence on the individual member of the speech community with its own way of conceptually grasping the world – language alone can never make someone a member of the people (*Volksgenossen*). For each language is the expression (*Ausdruck*) of the distinctiveness (*Eigenart*) of a people, and is dependent on much deeper-working biological powers, flowing from the depths of the unconscious: race, genetic makeup, predisposition, personality type, living space, common history, all powers that determine not only language, but also customs, usages, the sense of what is right, world view, and so forth ... So it is completely clear: A *Volk* forges a language to its own measure, but not the reverse! The *Volk* is the power that rules all the life of language, to which all linguistic activity and existence is subject. (p. 6)

Among the articles in this first issue of the refounded journal were one on "The World View of Indo-European Sentence Structure" and one on "The Inner Form of Speech of Japanese in Comparison with That of the Indo-European Languages."

By the 1943/44 issue the editorship was in the hands of SS-Standartenführer Walther Wüst (1901–1993), a leading Nazi Indo-Europeanist and rector of the University of Munich, "in collaboration" with Güntert and an editorial board of five, which included Porzig, Stegmann von Pritzwald, and Weisgerber.

After the War

We have seen Weisgerber as the leader of the new linguistics during the Nazi ascendancy, and he will be labelled retroactively as the "key linguist in Nazi Germany" (Hutton 2005: 202); yet only a few years after the end of the War, he was being described quite warmly in an American journal as "the recent unofficial spokesman of the Humboldtian view [who] has formulated a more or less comprehensive plan of linguistic research" (Basilius 1952: 99). What happened?

What happened is that after the War, Porzig, Trier, and Weisgerber maintained their respectability and continued to teach and publish (on Weisgerber and politics, see Knobloch 2000). Weisgerber, in particular, became the center of a renewed Neohumboldtian school. In 1959 he received a Festschrift; in 1965 his papers from the 1920s – but not those from the 1930s – were collected and published in book form. In a review of the Festschrift, we read that renewed interest in Humboldt "is ultimately due almost solely to the efforts of Leo Weisgerber, who has even been called *Humboldt redivivus*" (Shetter 1962: 318).

Weisgerber's magnum opus, published in several volumes and several editions between 1948 and 1962, bears the characteristic title *The Powers of the German Language*. Here Weisgerber sums up his work on language, the senses, and problems of translation. There is a discussion of the role of gender in German grammar that praises the flexibility in word order that it permits (1950: 79 ff.). In chapters on syntax (1954: 190–200; 1962: 383–90; Miller 1968: 94–7), Weisgerber points out the conceptual effects of the German tendency to encompass large amounts of material between the modifier and the head of a given syntagm, requiring the speaker or hearer to hold a highly complex pattern of relations in mind simultaneously.

Weisgerber's student Helmut Gipper (1919–2005) carried the Neohumboldtian tradition on into a new generation. Unlike the "classical" Neohumboldtians, Gipper showed interest in a range of languages. And unlike them, Gipper started out as a philosopher. His first publications were a discussion of color classification as determined by language and a contrast between the world view based on a mother tongue and one based on science (1956). Gipper went on to develop his own system of language philosophy, which connects elements of Kant's critical model with the Humboldtian view that distinct languages have an impact on the construction of thought.

For Gipper, there is a difference between thinking based on what he calls "common language" (1972: 248) and thinking in a scientific mode. The latter allows a distancing from and indeed a critique of the former. Yet he maintains the Neohumboldtian view that it is never possible to escape entirely from the world view of one's common tongue.

Abstract thinking on a higher level can, through the creation of artificial symbol systems, emancipate itself from common language, without, however, thereby coming to be completely independent of language. For in the end there is no going back behind the horizon of understanding of the common language (*Allgemeinsprache*).

This kind of "relativity" does not mean determinism, since, through scientific thinking, one can provisionally and partially think otherwise than in the categories of one's language. This view has direct implications for the place of German and other modern European languages among the languages of the world. Given the possibility of a partial emancipation from the mother tongue through scientific and philosophical thinking, and the fact that such thinking is not found everywhere, Gipper also sees a difference between the relative transparency or opacity of languages at different stages of cultural development.

In the case of "simple" primitive peoples (*Naturvölker*) ... the relationship between what is linguistically given and what is thought, between the "linguistic world view" and the secondarily conceived world view, is certainly essentially closer than it is in large-scale modern civilizations and industrial societies. In simple relations that are close to nature, the connection of thought to language is a self-evident reality, and no critical distance on language is achieved. Such distance is achieved in societies that have progressed farther, which control a whole spectrum of critical sciences to gain insights that cross the prescientific horizon of understanding of common languages and can lead to the conception of diverse scientific interpretations of the world. (p. 238)

Gipper's philosophical construction thus leads him to a new version of stage theory. In both cases, whether as the natural beloved mother tongue for the Neohumboldtians, or as one of a select group of civilized languages, German remains on top.

Starting his professional career in the 1950s, Gipper was very much aware of what came to be called the Sapir–Whorf hypothesis, which he felt was to all intents and purposes a restatement of things Humboldt had said a hundred years earlier. In his 1972 book *Is There a Linguistic Relativity Principle?*, Gipper discusses Whorf's writings both on theoretical grounds and through reinterpretation of Hopi material. Since this project has been the source of a series of criticisms of Whorf's Hopi data and his analysis of it, I reserve its discussion for the next chapter.

Conclusion

The Neohumboldtian school has sometimes (e.g., Miller 1968; Steiner 1975) been presented as a European twin of Boasian ethnolinguistics – or rather, it has been assumed that the latter represented an American version of Humboldtian essentialism. While this reading is understandable, it fails to recognize that the two schools took Humboldt's legacy in opposite directions. The Neohumboldtians started with the idea of a necessary and normal unity of language, thought, and culture, and pushed it to its limits: valorization of a single language and virtual abandonment of the equally Humboldtian project of large-scale comparison. While the Boasian school hearkens back to *Geist*s and *Volk*s, it draws the opposite moral. Its commitment to contrastive comparison and to the critique of modern Western values forced the abandonment of the unity of language–thought–culture.

The Neohumboldtians show what real twentieth-century linguistic essentialism looks like; by contrast, they show how different the Boasian project is. The comparison, as we will see, suggests that many of the attacks against the "Sapir–Whorf hypothesis" would in fact be directed more appropriately against the Neohumboldtians precisely for the ways in which they differ from Sapir and Whorf. We might even be justified in speaking of a Right-Humboldtianism and a Left-Humboldtianism (cf. the Right-Hegelianism and Left-Hegelianism of the 1840s), except that the Boasian problematic represents a serious enough shift away from some of Humboldt's positions to put this into question.

While these kinds of essentialist models, like anything else, can be abused, in some cases a great variety of phenomena do seem to present themselves as diverse expressions of a single essence. At the same time, it is unlikely that most human languages or cultures or societies can be grasped adequately in this way. It is equally unlikely that a human language or culture or society can be adequately understood using the great alternative to essentialism, linear causal arguments.

In the face of the overwhelming dominance of universalist modes of explanation, Boas and company are often drawing on the evident alternative, essentialist phraseology, to express what are in fact new perceived patterns.

9　The rise of cognition and the repression of languages

Sapir died in 1939, Whorf in 1941, Boas in 1942. Dorothy Lee published some papers on language and world view after this time, as did Harry Hoijer (1904–1976), who worked primarily on Athabaskan languages, notably Navajo (discussion of his work in Lucy 1992a: 75–82). A collection of Sapir's papers was published in book form in 1949, some of Whorf's in 1952, with the definitive volume of his papers appearing in 1956. But that was pretty much it. From the 1950s on, the scholarly world would be going in a direction hostile to relativist ideas.

The cognitive revolution

Much of American academic thinking from the 1920s on accepted the behaviorist assumption that the mind was an inaccessible black box, and therefore that the only thing one could study scientifically was externally observable behavior. In linguistics, the shift in emphasis from Sapir's culturally connected and open linguistics to the much more limited descriptive analysis of his Yale colleague Leonard Bloomfield (1887–1949) took place the 1930s. Bloomfield had experienced a conversion to behaviorism: language was to be redefined as verbal behavior (Bloomfield 1933). He and the several generations of American linguists who followed him sought to create a science of pure description. One result was that linguistics as a separate field grew closer to psychology and farther away from anthropology, which maintained an interest in questions of meaning and context.

With the rise of computing from the 1950s there appeared a new possibility: if we could successfully program a computer to do what humans do, in any domain, then we can use our very programming as a hypothesis for what is going on in the human mind. At least hypothetically, we could get a glimpse inside that black box. This led to the phenomenal rise of new fields of cognitive psychology and, more broadly, of the new family of disciplines that came to be known as the cognitive sciences.

The analogy one has chosen to clarify an idea tends to develop a life of its own: the servant can easily become the master. What are computers good at?

Computing and calculating. Not terribly surprisingly, the computer model reinforced a tendency to define human thought as a form of computing or "processing." Steven Pinker puts this well: "'the physical symbol system hypothesis' or the 'computational' or 'representational' theory of mind ... is as fundamental to cognitive science as the cell doctrine is to biology and plate tectonics is to geology" (1994: 78).

Cognitive science is one of the great success stories of recent times and has led to major discoveries about human thinking, particularly in the area of child development. But the very universalist program that has proven so effective also peripheralizes diversity. Whatever the discipline, cognitive science approaches have massively presumed that "cognition" or "thinking" is a universal process, inherent, perhaps innate, in each individual human, and that linguistic and cultural specificities are mere surface effects, foam on the ocean of mind. Cognitive science "combines tools from psychology, computer science, linguistics, philosophy, and neurobiology to explain the workings of human intelligence" (Pinker 1994: 17) in a universalist toolbag that characteristically leaves anthropology out.

With his usual clarity, Pinker states the attitude of classical cognitive science toward the question of language specifics.

A famous hypothesis, outlined by Whorf ... asserts that the categories and relations that we use to understand the world come from our particular language, so that speakers of different languages quite literally conceptualize the world in different ways. This is an intriguing hypothesis, but virtually all modern cognitive scientists believe it is false. (1990: 200)

On the next page, however, Pinker states the following, apparently seeing no contradiction with what he has just said:

[L]earning different languages does require one at least to pay attention to different aspects of the world ... [L]earning a language does involve learning to categorize the world in particular ways, even if only for the purpose of using language itself: an English speaker must think of a table as being more like a board than a forest when referring to it in a sentence. (1990: 201)

This is characteristic: one defines linguistic relativity in such an extreme way as to make it seem obviously untrue; one is then free to acknowledge the reality of the data at the heart of the idea of linguistic relativity – without, until quite recently, proposing to do any serious research on these data.

Taking linguistic and cultural differences seriously would seem to put the whole cognitive project in jeopardy, at least as this project was understood by most practitioners, at least well into the 1990s. Some cognitive scientists seem really haunted by the specter of relativism. Here is the philosopher and psycholinguist Jerry Fodor, one of the major figures in conceptualizing cognition:

The thing is: I *hate* relativism. I hate relativism more than I hate anything else, excepting, maybe, fiberglass powerboats. More to the point, I think that relativism is very probably false. What it overlooks, to put it briefly and crudely, is the fixed structure of human nature. (Fodor 1985: 5)

There is something startling about hearing this late-twentieth-century American scholar declaring that he hates relativism worse than, say, racism or Nazism or mass murder or any other hateables. His hatred is, however, understandable: real relativism implies a total absence of rules and potentially a war of all against all with might making right. Because of this, everyone, except perhaps for some nihilists, *poètes maudits*, and sociopaths, has always avoided real relativism. The only way to have a relative relativism has been to presume a hierarchy of values, with some kinds of worlds superior to others – the essentialist option; or to seek ways to calibrate among worlds, the Boasian option, as it is the Einsteinian one: relativity rather than relativism.

As we will see in this chapter, the rise of cognitive science was accompanied by a restating of what came to be called the "Sapir–Whorf hypothesis" in the most extreme terms. Three arguments came to the fore repeatedly:

Determinism. The Sapir–Whorf hypothesis says that the language you speak, and nothing else, determines how you think and perceive. We have already seen how false a characterization this is: the model the Boasians were working from was only deterministic in cases of no effort, of habitual thought or speaking. With enough effort, it is always possible to change your accent or your ideas.

Hermeticism. The Sapir–Whorf hypothesis maintains that each language is a sealed universe, expressing things that are inexpressible in another language. In such a view, translation would be impossible and Whorf's attempt to render Hopi concepts in English an absurdity. In fact, the Boasians presumed, rather, that languages were not sealed worlds, but that they were to some degree comparable to worlds, and that passing between them required effort and alertness.

Both of these characterizations are used to set up a now classic article on linguistic relativity by the psychologist Eleanor Rosch (1974):

Are we "trapped" by our language into holding a particular "world view"? Can we never really understand or communicate with speakers of a language quite different from our own because each language has molded the thought of its people into mutually incomprehensible world views? Can we never get "beyond" language to experience the world "directly"? Such issues develop from an extreme form of a position sometimes known as "the Whorfian hypothesis" ... and called, more generally, the hypothesis of "linguistic relativity." (Rosch 1974: 95)

Rosch begins the article noting how intuitively right the importance of language differences first seemed to her, then spends much of the rest of it attacking this initial intuition.

Infinite variability. A third common characterization is that Boasian linguistics holds that, in Martin Joos's words, "languages can differ from each other without limit and in unpredictable ways" (Joos 1966: 96). This would mean that the identification of any language universal would disprove the approach. In fact, the Boasians worked with the universals that were available to them – these were mainly derived from psychology – but opposed what they saw as the unfounded imposition of false universals that in fact reflected only modern Western prejudices. Joos's hostile formulation has been cited repeatedly as if it were official Boasian doctrine (see Hymes and Fought 1981: 57).

For over fifty years, these three assertions have largely defined the received understanding of linguistic relativity. Anyone who has participated in discussions and/or arguments about the "Whorfian hypothesis" has heard them over and over again.

New universalisms in linguistics

The late 1950s and early 1960s saw the rise of major new orientations in linguistics. The best known of these is Noam Chomsky's rethinking of syntax. For Chomsky, the miracle that requires investigation is that any speaking human can produce an infinite number of sentences out of the limited means of a given language. This infinite productivity is a matter of form, of syntax, not of semantic content, and it holds for speakers of any language. What is of interest, then, is the language faculty in itself, not the specifics of any particular language. Chomsky himself sees the deep structures of language and thought as innate in the human mind, and so, appropriately, finds precursors in the Cartesian linguistics of the seventeenth century (Chomsky 1966).

Equally important for the development of linguistics, however, was a rethinking of the question of language universals, initially in the work of Joseph Greenberg (1915–2001). Greenberg compared surface structures in a vast range of languages, and found a hitherto unnoted series of implicational universals: if a language has a given feature (say object-verb sentence structure) it is statistically more than likely to possess some others as well (in this case, for instance, postpositions rather than prepositions). Greenberg's findings led to a whole new kind of linguistic typology, now closely bound with the study of language universals (see, for instance, Comrie 1989; Haspelmath *et al.* 2001), which has been one of the most important growth areas in linguistics since the 1960s. Effort has concentrated on finding reasons for the co-occurrence of features in many languages. The overall goal is the universalist one of identifying "general principles governing variation among languages" (Comrie 2001: 25). Explanations have largely been psychological or experiential – general aspects of human cognition or experience are looked to for explanations of commonly occurring correlations among features. In John Lucy's (1992a: 88) characterization,

[t]he basic argument has been that the observed commonalities among languages demonstrates the existence of common cognitive and semiotic processes at work in all known languages. A marked relativity in conceptual worldview simply cannot be sustained, the argument goes, in the face of this evidence.

If Chomsky's transformational grammar represents a return to a locus of explanation in the universal human mind, which is to say a new rationalism, much of the new typology represents a return of a locus of explanation in an equally universal human experience. In this "implicitly reductionist view,"

[g]rammar is derived from (a conventionalization of) semantics, as semantics is from pragmatics (or discourse), as pragmatics is from "reality," as – for some people – such reality is from physical reality. Such an epistemic hierarchization is predicated on a radical empiricism. (Friedrich 1985: 186)

The implications of these new linguistic models for language diversity are clear, whether you take an innatist or evolutionary view (Kenneally 2007) or the view that language reflects general human experience. For all of these, compared to the importance of language universals, the differences are so minor as to be of little interest in themselves.

Psychologists and linguistic anthropologists kill Whorf again

In the 1950s, anthropologists and psychologists were interested in experimentation and the testing of hypotheses on what was taken to be the model of the natural sciences. At a conference on language in culture, Harry Hoijer (1954) first named a Sapir–Whorf *hypothesis* that language influences thought.

To call something a hypothesis is to propose to test it, presumably using experimental methods. This task was taken on primarily by psychologists. A number of attempts were made to prove or disprove experimentally that language influences thought (see Lucy 1992a: 127–78; P. Brown 2006). Both "language" and "thought" were narrowed down to make them more amenable to experiment: the aspect of language chosen was usually the lexicon, presumably the easiest aspect to control in an experimental setting; thought was interpreted to mean perceptual discrimination and cognitive processing, aspects of thinking that psychologists were comfortable testing for. Eric Lenneberg defined the problem posed by the "Sapir–Whorf hypothesis" as that of "the relationship that a particular language may have to its speakers' cognitive processes ... Does the structure of a given language affect the thoughts (or thought potential), the memory, the perception, the learning ability of those who speak that language?" (1953: 463). Need I recall that Boas, Sapir, and Whorf went out of their way to deny that different languages were likely to be correlated with strengths and weaknesses in cognitive *processes*, i.e., in what someone is capable of thinking, as opposed to the contents of habitual cognition?

If language influences thought, Lenneberg's argument went, speakers of languages with many terms for a given domain should be able to make finer perceptual distinctions in that domain than speakers of languages with few terms. In the most influential studies, the domain chosen was that of color, one that had interested an essentialist tradition for centuries, but that had not been central to the Boasians. Some post-Boasian linguists had turned to colors as a domain illustrative of the great variation in construal of the world through vocabulary. The view that color classifications are unlimited and arbitrary is clearly stated in Bloomfield's *Language*:

Physicists view the color-spectrum as a continuous scale ... but languages mark off different parts of this scale quite arbitrarily and without precise limits. (Bloomfield 1933: 140)

This view was carried on as part of American linguistic lore for the next several decades. As the anthropologist Verne Ray put it, "[t]here is no such thing as a 'natural' division of the spectrum. Each culture has taken the spectral continuum and has divided it into units on a quite arbitrary basis" (1952: 258). In what came to be a standard manual of the descriptivist school, H. A. Gleason uses the diversity of divisions of a continuous spectrum of colors as the initial example of how language works (1961: 4–5).

Initial experimental findings suggested that speakers of English and some other languages found it easier to remember colors for which they had words (e.g., Brown and Lenneberg 1954 [1970]). This was taken to mean that "codability" enhanced memory, an apparent effect of language on cognitive processing. Yet by the 1960s there had been little follow-up on actual psychological testing of the implications of vocabulary differences and a notable lack of breakthrough in the search for "Whorf effects" on perceptual or cognitive processes. Further studies on color seemed, on the contrary, to deny the importance of language differences. In the late 1960s the linguistic anthropologists Brent Berlin and Paul Kay carried out a survey of languages, shifting the focus from color language in general to what they called basic color terms, that is, terms that refer primarily to what we call colors rather than to anything else ("the terms in each language which have specialized reference to what English-speaking researchers would call colors," Lucy 1992a: 177). "Red" is a basic color term, "salmon" is not. If we restrict the acceptable data to such terms, then some languages have more than others; some have as few as two.

Berlin and Kay started by rephrasing Sapir and Whorf as saying that the search for semantic universals was "fruitless in principle" because "each language is semantically arbitrary relative to every other language" (1969: 2; cf. Lucy 1992a: 177–81). If this is what we are calling linguistic relativity, then if any domain of experience, such as color, is identified in recognizably the same way in different languages, linguistic relativity must be wrong. As we have seen, this fits the arguments of Weisgerber and Bloomfield, but not of Sapir or Whorf.

What Berlin and Kay found was anything but arbitrary. First, while boundaries between examples associated with a given term could be very fluid, there was a tendency to agree cross-culturally on focal "centers," i.e., on which red was the reddest red. These were also the quickest hues to be recognized and the most easily remembered. Second, they discovered a uniform attribution of focal colors depending on the total number of color terms: if there were two basic color terms the best representatives of them were what we call black and white, when there was a third term it was best represented by what we call red, and so forth, allowing the construction of a universal color hierarchy. Beyond this, they found unexpected support for models of cultural and linguistic evolution: languages spoken by people in small-scale, low-tech societies had few basic color terms, which, in an apparent correlation with cultural evolution, increased to the eleven found in English. So not only was there no relativity effect; on the contrary, color terminology seemed to confirm our own feelings of cultural advancement.

A few years later Eleanor Rosch Heider (1972) performed a set of tests to see whether focality, rather than codability, could explain the fact that English speakers had an easier time with colors for which they had names. She compared English-speaking subjects with speakers of a New Guinea language with four basic color terms. The result: virtually no difference in color recognition and memory, regardless of the number of basic terms available. In other words, the important factor was the universal fact of focality rather than the diverse facts of vocabulary. "Rosch's finding were seized upon by advocates of universality, who said terminology doesn't affect cognition: color transcends culture" (Olin 2003).

The work on color was one contribution to a movement that gained increasing momentum from the 1960s through the 1980s. While new discoveries were being made on language universals, even work directly bearing on language diversity seemed to show that it simply didn't matter. Summing up generations of breakthroughs in the study of what all languages have in common, Pinker (1994: 59–67) concludes that while language differences can lead to "interesting anecdotes," these are ultimately "canards" or "bunk," of which the supreme example is the Whorfian "hypothesis of linguistic determinism."

Some apparent support for linguistic relativity came from a consideration of grammar rather than vocabulary. In 1981, the psycholinguist Alfred Bloom published a comparison of the comprehension of counterfactual statements among English- and Chinese-speakers ambitiously entitled *The Linguistic Shaping of Thought*. Where English has inflections that mark counterfactuals, Chinese does not, and Bloom felt that this was correlated with the lower degree of success in the task among the speakers of Chinese. Let us note first of all that Bloom's experiment deals with "thought processing," not the construal of the world central to Boasians (DeBernardi 1997). And his findings were quickly challenged: in a debate in the journal *Cognition*, the psychologists Terry Kit-Fong Au and Lisa Garbern Liu were able to show that a rephrasing of the test statements into more idiomatic Chinese virtually erased the difference between the two groups. Thus this sequence of arguments, too, came to be taken as yet more evidence against linguistic relativity (e.g., Pinker 1994: 66–7).

A characteristic study was reported recently in my own university's in-house newspaper under the title "Language and Perception Are Not Connected" (Baril 2004). The article starts by saying that according to the "Whorf–Sapir hypothesis ... language determines perception," and therefore that "we should not be able to distinguish differences among similar tastes if we do not possess words for expressing their nuances, since it is language that constructs the mode of thought and its concepts ... According to this hypothesis, every language projects onto its speakers a system of categories through which they see and interpret the world." The hypothesis, we are told, has been "disconfirmed since the 1970s" by research on color. The article reports on the research of Dominic Charbonneau, a graduate student in psychology. Intrigued by recent French tests in which professional sommeliers, with their elaborate vocabulary, did no better than regular ignoramuses in distinguishing among wines, Charbonneau carried out his own experiment on coffee – this is, after all, a French-speaking university, and we take coffee seriously. Francophone students were asked to distinguish among different coffees; like most of us, they had a minimal vocabulary for distinguishing them (words like "strong," "smooth," "dishwater"). The participants made quite fine distinctions among the eighteen coffees served, well above the possible results of chance, showing that taste discrimination does not depend on vocabulary. Conclusion: "Concepts must be independent of language, which *once again* disconfirms the Sapir–Whorf hypothesis" (my italics). And this of course would be true if there were such a hypothesis, if it was primarily about vocabulary, and if it said that vocabulary determines perception.

The Boasians and color

We have seen that Bloomfield and his successors in linguistics maintained the unlimited arbitrariness of color classifications, and so could have served as easy straw men for the cognitivist return to universals. But what did Boas, Sapir, Whorf, or Lee actually have to say about color? Did they in fact claim that color perception or recognition or memory was determined by vocabulary? Sapir and Lee are easy: as far as I have been able to ascertain, neither one of them talked about color at all. Steven Pinker attributes a relativist and determinist view of color classifications to Whorf:

Among Whorf's "kaleidoscopic flux of impressions," color is surely the most eye-catching. He noted that we see objects in different hues, depending on the wavelengths of the light they reflect, but that the wavelength is a continuous dimension with nothing delineating red, yellow, green, blue, and so on. Languages differ in their inventory of color words ... You can fill in the rest of the argument. It is language that puts the frets in the spectrum. (Pinker 1994: 61–2)

No he didn't. Whorf never noted anything like this in any of his published work, and Pinker gives no indication of having gone through Whorf's unpublished papers. As far as I can ascertain, Whorf talks about color in two places; in both he is saying the opposite of what Pinker says he is saying. In one instance (1956: 209) Whorf makes the not very startling point that if a group of people could see only the color blue, they wouldn't develop much of a color vocabulary. In other words, the existence of a lexical domain depends on that of an enabling physiology. In the other (1956: 163), he is talking about "color blindness and unequal sensitivity to colors" as exceptions to the universal perceptual realities discovered by Gestalt psychology. This passage is to be found on the page on which Whorf looks to psychology to offer a "canon of reference for all observers."

The only mention of the word "hue" in Whorf's published work is a discussion of how the pronunciation *hyuw* illustrates his analysis of English phonology (1956: 227).

In fact, whenever Whorf or Boas talked about color perception or discrimination, they did so with due regard to non-linguistic factors. Boas's doctoral dissertation of 1881 ("Contributions to the Understanding of the Color of Water") had been a study of the absorption of light in water, and in doing his experiments Boas was struck by "the difficulty of judging the relative intensities of two lights that differed slightly in color" (Stocking 1968: 142). Boas dealt with the problem with a psychophysical definition of thresholds below which discrimination is impossible. One effect of this for Boas, as he reminisced almost sixty years later, was to convince him "that there are domains of our experience in which the concepts of quantity ... are not applicable" (1939: 20). We can see how this early work was leading toward greater interest in the mind as a factor in perception; but there is no hint here of linguistic or cultural determinism.

Boas also discusses color in the article on alternating sounds. And it's a highly instructive passage. Boas has clearly distinguished perception from apperception and categorization. He is talking about psychological experiments in distinguishing between sensations in different modalities. "As this is the most important part of our considerations," he writes,

we will illustrate it by a few examples. It is well known that many languages lack a term for green. If we show an individual speaking such a language a series of green worsteds, he will call part of them yellow, another part blue, the limit of both divisions being doubtful. Certain colors he will classify to-day as yellow, to-morrow as blue. He apperceives green by means of yellow and blue. We apperceive odors in the same way, and classify new odors with those to which they are similar. (1974: 74–5)

But is this or is it not an argument for the linguistic determination of perception or discrimination? It is not. He continues:

It will be understood that I do not mean to say that such sensations are not recognized in their individuality, but they are classified according to their similarity, and the classification is made according to known sensations.

In other words, vocabulary may play a role in categorization but should not be expected to affect perceptual discrimination.

Color comes up again in Boas's address at the 1909 Clark University conference on psychology. Speaking to an audience that included Freud, C. G. Jung, and some of the founders of modern experimental psychology, Boas presented his view of a specifically cultural and linguistic unconscious, using color as an example of the diversity of categorization and conceptualization:

Differences [in categorization] ... appear very clearly in the domain of certain simple sense-perceptions. For instance, it has been observed that colors are classified according to their similarities in quite distinct groups without any accompanying difference in the ability to differentiate shades of color. What we call green and blue are often combined under some such term as "gall-like color," or yellow and green are combined into one concept, which may be named "young-leaves color." The importance of the fact that in thought and in speech these color-names convey the impression of quite different groups of sensations can hardly be over-rated. (1974: 249)

Here the differences in classifying colors are seen as important precisely because they *do not* have a direct correlation with "the ability to differentiate shades of color," something that is presumably part of the human heritage as such.

Finally, in a comment parallel to his argument about numbers, Boas noted that American languages have no trouble distinguishing colors – but that they do so by naming objects of the given color, without fixing a single standard (cited in Woodworth 1910: 327–8). As all of these examples show, the Boasians always accepted, indeed insisted on, the autonomy of perception. They were never linguistic determinists.[1]

There is, however, a school of thought that did claim that vocabulary determines perception: not surprisingly, the Neohumboldtians. It is Weisgerber who says that vocabulary determines the perception of color (e.g., 1950: 141): we cannot translate color experience from one language to another. "The vocabularies of taste and of smell in various languages reveal the same kind of translation difficulty and can be studied and explained intelligently only by the neo-Humboldtian assumption" (Basilius 1952: 102).

Reseeing colors

By the early 1960s, there was plenty of ethnographic data on a variety of systems of naming what we call colors from different parts of the world.

What stands out is the variety of dimensions used to categorize visual experience. An exemplary study was that of color language among the Hanunóo of the Philippines, carried out by Harold Conklin (1955 [1964]), one of the eminent practitioners of ethnosemantics (see Chapter 10 below). By starting with language and its uses in real situations, rather than with a presumed universal domain of "color," Conklin shows that in Hanunóo, the four "basic" categories can best be glossed as dark versus light and dry versus wet. For the Hanunóo, in other words, dryness and wetness are essential qualities in defining a lexical domain that overlaps largely with what we call "color." This kind of situation, in which a language defines semantic domains in a way that only partially overlaps with ours, is not rare; there is nothing surprising about it unless we assert that our own semantic domains must be universal and necessary ones.

This opens up the fundamental criticism of most of the work on color terms, articulated forcefully by John Lucy (1997a). "Color" itself is a Western category. The words that many languages use to refer to what we call colors also, and sometimes primarily, index what we consider non-color qualities such as shininess or wetness or smoothness. An experiment that offers people an array of samples distinguished solely by our idea of "color" is only testing how easy it is for them to reconstruct what from their point of view is a perfectly arbitrary set. If general patterns emerge, this is an artifact of the proposed task.

[W]hat about the success of the approach? After all ... it works! These color systems are there! ... I would argue that *what is there is a view of the world's languages through the lens of our own category*, namely, a systematic sorting of each language's vocabulary by reference to how, and how well, it matches our own. This approach might well be called the radical universalist position[2] since it not only seeks universals, but sets up a procedure which guarantees both their discovery and their form ... No matter how much we pretend that this procedure is neutral or objective, it is not. The procedure strictly limits each speaker by rigidly defining what will be labeled, which labels will count, and how they will be interpreted ... Is it any wonder, really, that all the world's languages look remarkably similar in their treatment of color and that our system represents the *telos* of evolution? (1997a: 331–2)

If a language takes shininess as a defining quality along with hue, this fact will simply disappear:

[A] whole level of analysis is missing from the basic color term tradition, namely, no attention whatsoever is paid to what the various terms actually mean in the sense of what they typically refer to, their characteristic referential range. Yet somehow a tradition that ignores these issues is supposed to provide a way of discovering semantic universals. (p. 335)

The obviousness and assumed universality of what we call color is an example of what Bachelard called an epistemological obstacle (see Chapter 10). The idea of "pure" color is reinforced for us, in our society, by the pervasiveness of paint and crayon technology. Steven Pinker gives us the Crayola analogy for the role of focal colors:

[H]umans the world over (and babies and monkeys, for that matter [Query: Aren't babies human?]) color their perceptual worlds using the same palette, and this constrains the color vocabularies they develop. Although languages may disagree about the wrappers in the sixty-four crayon box ... they agree much more on the wrappers in the eight-crayon box – the fire-engine reds, grass greens, lemon yellows. Speakers of different languages unanimously pick these shades as the best examples of their color words, as long as the language has a color word in that general part of the spectrum ... Languages are organized a bit like the Crayola product line, the fancier ones adding colors to the more basic ones. (Pinker 1994: 62–3)

The history of humankind in a couple of crayon boxes. What could be more obvious to us, and at the same time more homey and normal and comforting, than a box of crayons, the childhood tools of pure color, which are an easy pleasure to use precisely because they have already been designed to exclude all the hard-to-draw complexities – wetness, ripeness, roughness, shine – of real visual experience? You could hardly find a more seductive or misleading analogy for the actual visual categories coded in the languages of the world.

Replacing whole language systems with basic color terms is comparable to the evolutionists' replacement of whole languages with numerals, which we could just as easily call basic number terms: "like the fingers on one hand" is not a basic number term, while "five" is. With both numbers and colors we find an increase in the number of terms in societies whose members are required to handle more elaborate technologies. This says nothing about the sophistication of thought processes in general, but a lot about the necessity in some circumstances of having an array of easily transposable terms that can be abstracted from actual situations. To paraphrase Boas's reply to the evolutionists on numbers: the way people live in some societies means that they do not need very many basic color terms. If their way of living changes they pick up or invent new ones; nor, as Boas actually said about color, should we expect the number of terms to affect perception as opposed to common habitual classification. None of this tells us very much about cognition or about how different peoples construe the world.

It may be answered that the real discovery made by Berlin and Kay was not simply that basic color terms increase as people require them to, but that they always do so following the same pattern, one presumably based not on any language, but on the nature of the human eye and brain. I would not dispute this. But I would point out that here, too, the parallel to number vocabulary is very telling. Number terms, too, increase as people require them to, and they, too, always do so following a single pattern: always from one, two, many, to one, two, three, many, to one, two, three, four, many, and so forth; nowhere do we find a counting system of four, seven, one, three, nine, many, or even of one, three, six, many. The development of number terms, then, also seems based on an extralinguistic reality. The difference is that in the case of numbers this fact is so glaringly obvious as to be invisible, while in the case of colors it had to be discovered. But the principle is exactly the same. In both cases, people develop more extensive terminological arrays when the need arises, and in both cases the pattern of development depends on non-linguistic factors: the facts of human physiology and perceived salience in the case of color terms, the facts of ordinal sequence in the case of number terms.

The philosophers kill Whorf again

During the period of the rise of cognitive science some philosophers were discovering "the Whorfian hypothesis," and they did not like it. The philosophically minded sociologist Lewis Feuer (1953) says that Whorf's theory is based on the comparison of vocabularies between languages: he gives the example of Inuktitut words for snow. Feuer points out, as Boas had, but without citing him, that we must expect people to develop an elaborate vocabulary on a topic that is of great interest to them. A distinctive vocabulary would not, then, be a feature that defines a language, but a mere result of circumstance. Since Feuer has already presented linguistic relativity as being entirely about vocabulary, this view would logically eliminate the possibility of linguistic relativity. Feuer goes on to say that "[t]he 'principle of linguistic relativity' argues that there are incommensurable cultural universes. An incommensurable cultural universe would be an unknown one. The fact of linguistic communication, the fact of translation, belies the doctrine of relativity" (p. 95). It's as simple as that: the fact that we can translate at all, that is, that we can use one language to denote referential information expressed in another – exactly as the Boasians said we should be able to do – belies the Boasians' own doctrine. How could the Boasians have missed this for forty years?

Feuer's arguments were picked up by Max Black (1959 [1962]), who presents Whorf as believing that the "real world" is totally unstructured, and that any apparent structure it has is imposed on it by language. If this were true, translation would be impossible, and Whorf's own effort to render the Hopi world in English would be a non-sense (arguments repeated in at least one general introduction to semantics: Palmer 1976: 57). Black (p. 255) consequently cites the "amateurish crudity" of Whorf's project (on Feuer and Black, see de Fornel 2002).

In a 1970 article, John McNamara again attributes a kind of linguistic solipsism to what he calls "a strong Whorfian hypothesis," proceeds to repeat the translation argument, and extrapolates that according to Whorf a bilingual person would be unable to communicate with him- or herself: "in switching to language B, he would never be able to understand or explain what he had just communicated in language A" (paraphrased in House 2000: 78).

Donald Davidson (1974) presents the Whorf hypothesis as representing "conceptual relativism" and linguistic determinism, and as claiming that different languages cannot be calibrated: "Whorf, wanting to demonstrate that Hopi incorporates a metaphysics so alien to ours that Hopi and English cannot, as he puts it, 'be calibrated,' uses English to convey the contents of sample Hopi sentences" (p. 6). Davidson gives no page reference for his apparent citation, just the name of one of Whorf's papers – not, as it happens, one in which the word "calibrated" appears. In the place where Whorf does talk about calibration, the passage that we cited on a new principle of relativity (Whorf 1956: 214), he says the opposite of this: that "speakers of different languages will not be led by the same physical evidence to the same picture of the universe *unless* their linguistic backgrounds are similar or can somehow be calibrated" (my emphasis). Far from contradicting himself by writing about Hopi in English to prove that the two cannot be calibrated, Whorf's efforts are attempts to calibrate them.

Davidson goes on to equate difference in world view or conceptual scheme with untranslatability: "We may identify conceptual schemes with languages, then, or better, allowing for the possibility that more than one language may express the same scheme, sets of intertranslatable languages" (p. 185). If it is possible to translate from one language to another, then the two must form a "set of intertranslatable languages," and their conceptual schemes must be the same. Given the universal possibility of translation, Davidson concludes that all languages must fit in a single set, and therefore by definition the very idea of conceptual scheme is of no use. It is worth setting this oft-repeated claim that the possibility of translation proves the irrelevance of language differences against the reverse claim, drawn by Theodora Bynon from the writings of Weisgerber, that *any* difficulty in translation proves that languages represent different worlds. "If in fact words in different languages were simply referring to 'the same objective reality' there would be no translation problems, no so-called untranslatable words, and the distribution of 'words and objects'... would form neat patterns" (Bynon 1966: 472, based on Weisgerber 1963). But both complete translatability and radical non-translatability are fantasies. In reality, as translators have found for millennia and translation theorists have said for centuries, translation from any human language to any other is always possible but always problematic; it depends on what aspects of the original you are trying to convey and how much you are willing to burden your translation in order to do so. A constant shift in point of view, a dual or multiple perspective implying a kind of practical linguistic relativity, seems to be a prerequisite for the very act of translation (Becker 1995).

It is certainly unfair to present these philosophers solely in terms of their misreadings of the texts. The point they want to make is fair enough: it is that thought and experience derive from more than language alone; that the human brain, the rest of the human body, the world, and social life all influence thought in a way not directly dependent on language, and indeed also influence language.

These critiques – the questions of vocabulary, of sealed language-worlds, of translation, and of a social influence on thought – would probably hit the mark if they were aimed at the Neohumboldtians, but it is not at all clear that they touch the Boasians.

The Neohumboldtians visit the Hopi and kill Whorf again

One of Whorf's most startling claims is that the grammar of Hopi suggests a different construction of time and space than do those of Western European languages. He accepts that there is a universal human experience of time as duration and succession of events, but asserts that this in itself is no warrant for the modern Western conceptualization of time as divided into three "spaces" of past, present, and future, with the subject constantly moving at an unchanging pace from the past through the present into the future. Whorf correlates this conceptual model, which is Kant and Newton's model, with some pervasive traits of modern Western languages, notably the importance of tripartite tense categorization in the verb. As we have seen, Hopi has two "forms" that cover the experiential material Western languages divide into tenses: experiences are divided into the "manifested" (the unmarked form of the verb), which includes both what we would put into the past and the objective, already-there aspects of what we would call the present; and the "manifesting" (marked with the suffix –ni), which includes the transformative and volitional aspects of the present and all of what we put in the future. Whorf concludes that this distinction implies a very different conceptualization of the world and its processes from the three modern Western temporal "spaces." While this presentation does not take account of other aspects of Hopi grammar which Whorf saw as integral to his total argument (Whorf 1956; P. Lee 1996), this point would be the center of controversy for decades.

In an ironic twist, Neohumboldtian linguistics itself intervened in a way hostile to the idea of linguistic relativity precisely on this issue of time in Hopi.

Helmut Gipper was happy with Whorf's overall characterization of the relationship between language and thought but disturbed by what he took to be some of his extreme formulations. Most shocking was the claim that Hopi had no linguistic expressions for "time":

After long and careful study and analysis, the Hopi language is seen to contain no words, grammatical forms, constructions or expressions that refer directly to what we call "time"... Hence, the Hopi language contains no reference to "time," either explicit or implicit. (Whorf 1956: 57–8)

This quote is from the paper "An American Indian Model of the Universe," which Whorf left unpublished during his lifetime, although it is one that has given rise, as Gipper notes (1994: 283), to a popular idea of a "timeless Hopi language." But to some degree, at least, this idea is based on a misreading. We have to recognize (as does Lucy 1992a: 286) that Whorf does not write time, but "what we call 'time'," doubly qualifying the word with scare quotes and with a "what we call." How important are quotation marks? Absolutely essential here, since a few lines above and a few lines down Whorf defines what he means by "what we call 'time'": it is the constructed, spatialized model of time typical of the modern West, with the past conceived as a "space" that is behind us, the future as an analogous space "in front" of us. Whorf makes it clear in the same text that this construction is not to be confused with the universal experience of temporal change, of it "always getting later."

In Gipper's case, however, there is a legitimate philosophical difference here as well. It is crucial for Whorf's argument that one be able to distinguish general and immediate human experience that is largely bodily-based – something that fits with Whorf's fondness for Gestalt psychology – and the varying construals that languages and cultures can put upon this experience. For a Kantian such as Gipper, diversity can only go so far "down": unidimensional flowing time and three-dimensional static space are necessary aspects of human understanding. Elsewhere, in comparisons with ethology, Gipper relates them to human bodiliness in the world (1963). If you share this view, then to claim that the Hopi language implies a very different kind of time and space from the Newtonian ones is to say that the Hopi are not really human, or at best that the Hopi language lacks means to express some of the fundamentals of human experience. On the contrary, since Whorf does *not* share this view, he is saying, to Kantians and Newtonians in particular (1956: 153), that being human is more profoundly various than they allow, that, to abuse Hamlet a bit, it includes "more heavens and earths than are dreamt of in your philosophy."

Gipper was sufficiently curious and dedicated first to publish a detailed study of Whorf's terminology (1963), then to undertake several periods of linguistic field research in Hopi territory in Arizona. He found (1972: 213–35) that Hopi possesses the means to refer to what we call past, present, and future, something he showed through German translation equivalents of Hopi sentences. He also pointed out cases in which days and other temporal units can be counted, and that months can be treated using the same kinds of numerotation as objects. On what one would assume is the crucial point of verb forms, Gipper agrees with Whorf that there are two, not three (1972: 223–4), but argues that these are in fact based on the same tripartite division of time that everyone intuitively possesses, except that instead of having separate forms for past, present, and future, the Hopi have a present-past opposed to a future.

Some of Gipper's students, most extensively Ekkehart Malotki, continued to work on Hopi. Malotki conducted long-term field research and published on the Hopi language of space (1979), then on time. In his 1983 book *Hopi Time*, he documents temporality in Hopi and says that Whorf's claims for the time-lessness of Hopi show that he did not have an adequate understanding of the language. In nearly 700 pages, Malotki massively demonstrates Hopi usages, in all parts of speech, that he says show the omnipresence of concepts of time. He does this sometimes by challenging Whorf's characterizations directly, more often by showing that the best English translation equivalent of a given phrase involves past–present–future distinctions.

The first page of Malotki's book carries only two quotes, one from Whorf and one from Malotki's Hopi field notes. The Whorf quote is the one we have already considered, saying that Hopi has no words for "time"; the field note, a Hopi text with interlinear glosses and an English translation, appears to be about nothing but time.

The only way to judge this juxtaposition is to take it philologically. I have already pointed out that the distinction between the word time with and with-out quotation marks, between the word time used without qualification and what Whorf calls "what we call 'time'," is crucial for understanding what Whorf meant to say in this manuscript. But here, floating on the page, we have Whorf apparently saying that Hopi lacks the means of expressing any kind of temporality.

Here is the sentence that follows on the same page – the English translation of a sentence from Hopi: "Then indeed, the following day, quite early in the morning at the hour when people pray to the sun, around that time then he woke up the girl again." See all the time words? How could Whorf have pos-sibly missed all this?

In fact, this begs the question entirely. Whorf never said that the Hopi can't or don't talk about time; he said that they don't conceptualize time in the same way we do, and that language is a source of conceptualization, both theirs and ours. No one would deny that the most appropriate translation of a given Hopi sentence into normal English might involve English time words. The question is whether the forms that convey given referential information in Hopi work the same way as do English forms, conveying the same background assumptions and, presumably, the same "metaphysics" of a spatialized past, present, and future. These are empirical questions which I cannot answer. But Gipper's lists of German translation glosses, Malotki's lists of English ones, do not answer them either (cf. P. Lee 1996: 140–1).

While Gipper's book got relatively little attention among English-speaking linguists, Malotki's was greeted with jubilation as putting the final nail in Whorf's coffin, the proof that his upsetting claims were based on his incom-petence as a linguist. In his review, Bernard Comrie (1984: 132), one of the major figures in linguistic typology, wrote that "Malotki's presentation and argumentation are devastating. At the end, one is left only with the question ... how Whorf could have been led to make the generalisations about Hopi time expression which he did make." Steven Pinker (1994: 63) cites Malotki to attest to Whorf's "limited, badly analyzed sample of Hopi speech." Even anthropologists of a symbolic persuasion accepted that Malotki had demonstrated that Whorf's presentation was fundamentally flawed or perverse (see Dinwoodie 2006: 329).

Not everyone has taken this line, however. Penny Lee (1991) offered a defense of Whorf's analysis of what he calls tensors, which, she argued, is consistently misrepresented by Malotki. David Dinwoodie (2006: 332) points out that in many cases we do not know in what contexts Malotki gathered his data, nor what came from whom in what situations, in terms of age, activity, or knowledge of English. He then gives a detailed analysis of Malotki's chapter on the ceremonial calendar (Malotki 1983: 451–80), arguing that the examples given are either not explained or in fact fit into Whorf's interpretation.

I am not a specialist of Hopi, of Uto-Aztecan, or of Amerindian languages. But besides the questions Dinwoodie has raised, some other parts of Malotki's book seem problematic simply based on the evidence he presents.

One of Whorf's claims is that while modern Western languages spatialize time, talking, for instance, about durations as being "long" or "short," Hopi does not (1956: 146). Malotki's counterclaim that Hopi does use spatial metaphors for time (1983: 13–27) seems to boil down to the fact that the same word is used respectively for "here" and "now," for "there" and "then," and for "yonder" and "a long time ago," plus a medial term. The terms, in other words, seem to denote what we would call relative "proximity" in both space and time, without distinguishing between the two. Simply on the evidence of meaning and usage, one doesn't know whether these are spatial metaphors for time, temporal metaphors for space, or, as Whorf himself suggests in the "Model" manuscript (cf. P. Lee 1996: 100–1), space–time deictics.

Malotki, for his part, simply asserts the priority of space over time as a fact of human psychology. When the actual linguistic evidence is not clear, he will impose a solution based on a putative universal psychology – that is reflected in, or perhaps reflects, modern Western languages. Whorf's approach is the opposite: he relies on what the language seems to be saying and tries to reconcile his construction of the world to that. This is an imaginative construction, but one that stays close to the data.

Another point in Whorf's presentation is that in Hopi time units are not counted as if they were objects. Malotki's Chapter two, on units of time, seems to support Whorf more than to contradict him: while Malotki indicates some units of time that can be counted, and that Whorf may have missed, these are isolated and do not seem to form anything like the pervasive pattern that is found in modern Western languages.

But as we have seen, Whorf's central argument bears on the difference between verb forms with and without the suffix *–ni*. This obligatory distinction between what he calls "manifested" and "manifesting" is the main issue in the "American Indian Model" manuscript, the paper that provoked the whole Neohumboldtian attack on Whorf. This is one of the key arguments he uses to claim a difference between Hopi and SAE constructions of time; it is the one that immediately justifies his "extreme" position that Hopi has no forms that correspond to "what we call 'time'." Surely his presentation of this part of the language would have to be a major target, if not *the* major target, in an attack on his interpretation of time in Hopi. Yet when Malotki comes to talk about these forms, which he calls "the Hopi tense system," something odd happens. One would think that a book about time in the Hopi language would devote a lot of space/time to tense. But unlike the long discussions of other topics, with pages of Hopi examples, here there is a presentation of four and a half pages, with one of the pages a chart and the half page a citation. Not a single Hopi example is given (in his review, Comrie insists on the large number of examples Malotki offers, as against the few given by Whorf). And Malotki does not get to this crux of all the arguments until page 622 of the book, in the last section of the last substantive chapter (the next and last one is called "Conclusions"), which bears the title "Miscellaneous."

Malotki's argument is simple:

The unidirectional flow of time out of a "before-now" or "already" via a "now" into an "after-now" or "not-yet", often diagrammatically represented by a one-dimensional time line drawn from left to right and featuring an arrow tip pointing into the future, may actually mirror time reality as experienced by human beings; however, there is no compelling or intrinsic reason to find this "natural" state of affairs reflected in the tense categorization of a language. (1983: 624)

This universality and naturalness of a spatialized three-part conceptualization is expressed in a diagram on page 626 which contrasts "the time system" of past–present–future ("the time system," not any particular time system) with the "Hopi tense system" which Malotki calls nonfuture (unmarked), which "generally allow[s]" past or present time interpretations, versus future (*–ni*). In other words, it is possible, if you try hard enough, to find present, past, or future in the referents of Hopi sentences, even though these are not the grammatical categories that are being marked.

Malotki begins his discussion by trying to define tense. He quotes from John Lyons (1968: 305): "Many treatments of tense have been vitiated by the assumption that the 'natural' division of time into 'past', 'present', and 'future' is necessarily reflected in language." Lyons puts "natural" into quotes;

he, in fact, is very careful not to say whether or not he thinks that "past, present, future" is natural, only saying that it has often been suggested that the directionality of time is given in "nature" (his scare quotes) and that "past, present, future" in tense comes from the traditional grammars of Greek and Latin (p. 304). What does Malotki himself think about three-part division? He accepts it as natural, as characteristic of human experience before or beyond language, adding that languages do not necessarily reflect it directly.

So we are back to arguments about naturalness that we thought we had left behind at the end of the eighteenth century: some languages directly reflect the natural state of affairs, others fall into inversion and require extra work. Languages that codify time in a tripartite way (past-present-future) are natural, while those that are different on this score are unnatural. Hierarchy has just been reintroduced among the languages of the world.

Malotki asserts, on the evidence of his translation equivalents, that for –ni "the temporal function is primary" – it's a future marker – but it also has "secondary, atemporal functions." This is his way of recasting Whorf's apparently uncontested observation that –ni indexes a form that includes both what we call the future and some aspects of the present. The difference in interpretation is due to a difference in method. Malotki starts off by separating out meanings into primary and secondary ones, with the primary one corresponding to those we are familiar with. Whorf, on the contrary, starts with the language itself, *its* indexed grammatical categories and the range of their meanings, without defining some as primary and others as secondary based on Western categories.

For Malotki, the two Hopi forms indicate the difference between a future and an unmarked "nonfuture." On page 625 he shows how you can find a past or present force for any unmarked verbs if you try. This is based on producing serviceable English translation equivalents and then asserting their priority over the actual language forms of Hopi. "Perfective verbs generally admit a past tense translation, imperfective verbs a present tense rendering, although a past tense reading for the latter and a present tense reading for the former is also possible under special syntactic and contextual conditions." Does Malotki now go on to spell out these conditions and give dozens of examples, as he has done for all kinds of bits of Hopi language for the last 600 pages? No, he does not. Instead there is a reference: "For more specifics concerning the Hopi tense situation ... see Voegelin *et al.* 1980: 582 [it's really 1979], who concur in the view that Hopi sentences are not restricted to a minimum division of time into future and nonfuture tenses."

The Voegelins' discussion does indeed question Whorf's formulations. Their argument, like his, assumes the universality of time deixis in verbs and the possibility of finding it in Hopi forms, although in the form of combined tense and modality. On the page cited, they note that the addition of non-obligatory elements "make possible a further distinction of the nonfuture tense into present time and past time."

Malotki calls this a function of disambiguating present from past. Hopi, in other words, is ambiguous, but it has tricks that allow disambiguation. What is being disambiguated? The natural and "universal time system" that just happens to be our three-part division, but which is poorly represented by the Hopi tense system.

Malotki goes on to refute claims of linguacentrism such as the one I have just made by saying that in fact Whorf was also wrong in seeing Western languages as expressing a three-part time system. The last half page of this discussion is a quote – from whom is not clear – saying that English is really a two-part system, since what is called the future tense is not morphological but is built up out of other forms: since forms with "will" "are not strictly part of the 'basic' tense system," English can only be said to have a past and a non-past. So our feeling of having a three-part system is not linguistic, but experiential.

The argument has a respectable history (Lyons 1968: 306; Chomsky, preface to Schaff 1964 [1973]; see Alford 2002), but here it seems specious: it amounts to saying that analytical grammatical forms are necessarily less clear semantically than synthetic ones, that "j'irai" is somehow a "real" future where "I will go" is not, when in fact in both semantics and usage, both forms carry a clear future sense, opposed both to present and past.

Malotki really does appear to believe, and deeply, in the universality of our three-part system of imagining time. His idea of proving its pertinence in this case is to show that it is possible to use contextual and other clues to determine whether someone speaking Hopi is in fact referring to past, present, or future, even though the language-forms themselves do not indicate this. But we could as well argue that it is usually possible to infer whether someone speaking English, a language without grammatical evidentiality, is in fact referring to something he or she experienced directly, knows by hearsay, or is concluding based on evidence. Does this mean that English speakers are secretly orienting themselves constantly in a world of evidentiality, but are hiding it? Are all the grammatical categories that have been identified in every language in the world to be treated as universal categories most of which most languages just hide?

Near the end of his glowing review of Malotki's book, even Comrie finds that he cannot swallow its argument about tense.

It is possible that individual claims made by Malotki may be subject to revision or even rejection ... [H]is claim that Hopi has a tense system based on the opposition between future and non-future ... strikes me as questionable: given the wide range of modal uses of the so-called future, it is at least plausible that this is a modal rather than a temporal distinction, with the result that Hopi would have no tense distinctions.

(It does, however, have a profuse system of aspectual distinctions, and the absence of grammaticalisation of time reference as tense says nothing about the ability to conceptualise location in time – one hesitates to ask what conclusions Whorf would have drawn from the absence of gender as the grammaticalisation of sex in many languages.)

The admission is necessary, while the accompanying parenthesis is both characteristically snide about Whorf and characteristically unjustified. Whorf was talking about Hopi grammar and the forms it makes it easy to conceive, not about whether Hopis had the "ability" to refer to what Comrie is calling "location in time," i.e., to distinguish events in temporal relation to each other and to specify the temporal relationship between the event being referred to and the situation of enunciation. *Like any Boasian*, Whorf would presume that speakers of any language have the ability to conceive and convey *any* referential information, including information about what we call "time" and what we call "sex."

The difference between Malotki's and Whorf's approaches to the same distinction (presence and absence of *–ni* in the verb) makes sense in terms of overall philosophical divisons. Where Gipper looked to Kant for his universals, Malotki looks to psychologists; but their arguments are identical. Both are believers in the universal, necessary quality of the three-part temporal distinction, which Malotki calls "the time system" without qualification. For a Kantian, past–present–future "spaces" are simply the form of the human intuition of time. A given language need not, certainly, reflect this directly: those that have three-part tense are, however, natural reflections of this intuition, while those that do not must use other means, sometimes rather cumbersome ones, to convey this universal presupposition. When Malotki asserts that "the temporal function is primary" for the suffix *–ni*, even though it has other "secondary, atemporal functions," this is as much as to say that his method for analyzing Hopi forms is to identify the universal semantic core conveyed by each form (*–ni* is primarily temporal), then explain away usages that do not fit this (*–ni* also has non-temporal functions).

For Whorf, by contrast, since the basic human experience of time is not necessarily spatialized, there is no reason to assume that the three-part spatialized model of time separated from space that is typical of modern Western languages should represent the only possible human conceptualization of space–time. So when Whorf meets a Hopi form, instead of asserting a "primary function" based on a Western category and then listing "secondary functions," he tries to let the form itself speak directly and proposes a category, perhaps a surprising one to those used to Western grammars, that covers all of its functions (on Whorf's descriptive method, see P. Lee 1991; 1996). As we have seen, this respecting of the specificity of each language in creating a descriptive metalanguage, and in drawing conclusions from the analysis, is the linguistic method Boas was proposing at the beginning of the twentieth century.

There is another issue that marks the difference between the two approaches. The whole point of Sapir and Whorf's analogy to Einstein is that his relativity, like quantum mechanics, shows that the world that science can glimpse is *different* from the world as we experience and construe it through "habitual thought." It is what is sometimes called a discontinuist position in the philosophy of science (see the discussion of Bachelard in Chapter 10). Gipper, however, was a convinced continuist: he saw Einstein, whom he admired to the point of having a large photo of him on display in his office (Ralf Thiede on LINGUIST List 2.567, 1991), as having provided a firmer foundation for Newton's universe (Gipper 1972: 2), which therefore remained both absolute reality and the necessary lived world of any human subject.

In reading Malotki telling us what all humans are supposed to presuppose about time, I am reminded of passages from two linguists, one French, one American. In his book *L'homme de paroles*, Claude Hagège writes of rationalist grammarians such as Le Laboureur:

They purely and simply declared that since all men had received the same logical principles as a gift, speakers of Latin, who regularly practiced inversion, therefore had to be speaking differently from the way they thought, while for the French conception and expression coincided. (1986: 206)

Some years later, A. L. Becker gave the following warning, which reads like a retrospective critique of Malotki:

Our general tendency is to "read into" our experience of a distant language the familiar things that are missing, all the silences, and then we claim that all these things are "understood," "implied," or "part of the underlying logical structure" of those languages ... It takes a while to learn that things like tenses, and articles, and the copula are not "understood" in Burmese, Javanese, or Malay ... In Burmese these things aren't implied; they just aren't there. (1995: 7–8)

The great resonance of Malotki's odd demonstration, the sense of palpable relief that he had (finally!) killed off the revenant Whorf, are understandable in terms of the philosophical divisions we have been discussing. For most linguists and cognitive scientists of the period, this was a welcome elimination of a troublesome and potentially devastating claim of human conceptual variability.

The reinforcement of divisions

The 1950s through the 1980s saw the progressive triumph of universalist cognitive science. From the 1980s, one saw the concomitant rise of relativistic postmodernism. By the end of the 1980s there had been a massive return to the old split between universalizing natural sciences and their ancillary social sciences on the one hand, particularizing humanities and their ancillary cultural studies on the other. Some things, in the prevailing view, were universal, others so particular as to call for treatment as fiction or anecdote. Nothing in between was of very much interest, and North American anthropology, the discipline that had been founded upon and achieved a sort of identity in crossing the natural-science/humanities divide, faced an identity crisis. Symptomatically, one noticed many scholarly bookstores disappearing their linguistics sections into "cognitive science," their anthropology sections into "cultural studies."

In this climate, linguistic relativity was heresy, Whorf, in particular, a kind of incompetent Antichrist. The "Whorfian hypothesis" of linguistic relativism or determinism became a topos of any anthropology textbook, almost inevitably to be shown to be silly. Otherwise serious linguists and psychologists (e.g., Pinker 1994: 59–64) continued to dismiss the idea of linguistic relativity with an alacrity suggesting alarm and felt free to heap posthumous personal vilification on Whorf, the favorite target, for his lack of official credentials, in some really surprising displays of academic snobbery. Geoffrey Pullum, to take only one example, calls him a "Connecticut fire prevention inspector and weekend language-fancier" and "our man from the Hartford Fire Insurance Company" (Pullum 1989 [1991]: 163). This comes from a book with the subtitle *Irreverent Essays on the Study of Language*. But how irreverent is it to make fun of somebody almost everybody has been attacking for thirty years?

10   The return of the repressed

> What has collapsed has not necessarily been superseded.
> Trabant (1986: 206)

The previous chapter sought to set the record straight on what I take to be mis-representations of linguistic relativity over several decades from the 1950s. In this chapter we look at some ways in which key elements of the Boasian project survived and eventually grew again. The chapter has three parts: we look first at some other schools of thought that sought to account for sociocultural and linguistic diversity without falling into either universalist or essentialist patterns; we then look at ways in which the Boasian heritage came to be preserved through the height of cognitive hegemony; and finally we examine how this heritage has been revived dramatically, notably within cognitive science itself, especially since the late 1990s.

Once in a while during the period just considered, someone from outside would look at the controversy and wonder about the heaps of condemnation of linguistic relativity and particularly of Whorf. A case in point is the literary theorist George Steiner, who in 1975 called Whorf's work "the crowning statement" of the Leibniz–Humboldt "monadist" case, a theory

of great intellectual fascination. The "metalinguistics" of Whorf have for some time been under severe attack by both linguists and ethnographers. It looks as if a good deal of his work cannot be verified. But [his] papers ... constitute a model which has extraordinary intellectual elegance and philosophic tact. They are a statement of vital possibility, an exploration of consciousness relevant not only to the linguist but also to the poet and, decisively, to the translator. (1975: 88)

Parallels: structuralism and symbolic anthropology

Other twentieth-century schools of thought posed questions comparable to those of the Boasians about the nature and implications of linguistic and cultural diversity.[1] Here I will concentrate on European structuralism and its developments in the Prague School of the 1930s and the Paris-based structuralism of the 1960s and 1970s, the last of which drew equally on a primarily

French non-positivist tradition in epistemology; then on the school of symbolic anthropology that developed in North America in the 1960s and' 70s.

Structuralism. European structuralism in its various forms, like Boasian linguistics and anthropology, posits a plurality of contexts, fields, or systems, each of which must be taken into account in defining the elements that make it up. Beginning with the Swiss linguist Ferdinand de Saussure in the 1910s, it developed in a number of schools, some of which sought to formulate relations between language, thought, and culture in ways that were compatible with those of the Boasians. From the 1960s through the 1980s, in particular, the relative prestige of structuralism helped keep these ideas alive.

Saussure trained in Germany and was himself a brilliant practitioner of Neogrammarian linguistics, but brought to it an almost obsessive sense of system. As we have seen, the Neogrammarians, like the evolutionists, made a methodological virtue of considering only isolated facts in a vast field of law-governed transformations. On the contrary, for Saussure the most important aspect of any real language was its systemic nature. There are points in the *Course in General Linguistics* (published posthumously in 1916 from Saussure's students' notes) in which language, with its necessary difference among signifiers, is presented as inducing corresponding distinctions into the "mass of thought": "there are no preestablished ideas, and nothing is distinct before the appearance of language" (1916 [1972]: 155). This does appear, at least, to represent a real linguistic determinism. Just how much Saussure thought or continued to think this, and how much is to be attributed to the editors of the *Course*, remains under discussion, but it is clear that his notion of linguistic value (Gadet 1990) pushes the systematicity of language to include a language-specific articulation and organization of meanings.

Saussure was a direct inspiration for the Prague Linguistic Circle, which flourished between the two world wars. The Prague School developed the theory of phonology – theirs paralleled Sapir's, but made more explicit the back-and-forth between a universal application of laws to given phenomena and systemic analysis – and was centrally interested in language use and poetics. Whorf's contemporary Roman Jakobson (1896–1982) was one of the main figures in the Prague School, and indeed a leader in three of the great linguistic movements of the twentieth century: Russian formalism, Prague structuralism, and the structuralism that was born in New York during the Second World War and then established in Paris. This is not the place to attempt an outline of his prodigious work (but see Caton 1987), except to note that he drew regularly on that of the Boasians, and in essays in the 1940s and 1950s (e.g., 1971: 490–1) gave Boas credit for the discovery of the importance of obligatory grammatical categories. Jakobson's poetics (1960) recognizes the distinctiveness of each language in its organization of sound and meaning, and this underlies his theory of translation (1971: 260–6).

Jakobson is most famous for his phonological theory, which identifies a small set of universal oppositions on which each language draws to constitute its phonological repertoire (Jakobson and Halle 1956). This recalls the back-and-forth between the acceptance of the likelihood of universals and the insistence on respect for specifics that we found in Boas's phonetics, in Sapir's poetics, and in Whorf's use of Gestalt psychology.

As a result of meeting and collaborating with Jakobson in New York in the 1940s, the French anthropologist Claude Lévi-Strauss (1908–2009) developed his own form of structuralism. Lévi-Strauss's project was to use the basic systemic stance of Jakobsonian linguistics to reconceptualize other domains, notably those of kinship, myth, and what we might call comparative epistemology. For Lévi-Strauss, linguistics usually served as an overall model, not as a field of practice or a source of examples. One important exception is at the beginning of *La pensée sauvage* (1962), Lévi-Strauss's most ambitious presentation of his theory of human thinking. He opens the book with a critique of the procedure, typical of the evolutionists but by no means limited to them, of looking for evidence for the relative primitivity of a language indiscriminately in the breadth or narrowness of reference of terms. What Lévi-Strauss points out, in a semantic argument that echoes Boas's, is that there are two such kinds of claims. If an exotic language has terms that cover broad swaths of experience but lacks finer discriminations (e.g., a word for tree but none for particular kinds of trees), this will be presented as evidence of grossness of classification and so of the primitive character of the language. Conversely, if an exotic language has terms that make relatively fine distinctions but lacks a broader term (e.g., a word for oak, elm, maple, but none that corresponds to "tree"), this will be taken as an indication of the inability to abstract from immediate experience and so of the primitive character of the language. The result is that every way in which a language differs from that of the analyst, whether in greater or less fineness of discrimination, which is to say in lesser or greater abstraction, will be taken as a sign of its primitivity. This initial argument sets up Lévi-Strauss's discussion of modes of classification across societies. Among the examples drawn on is one from Boas's grammar of Chinook.

Another great linguistic structuralist, the major synthesizer of historical linguistics and Saussurean systemics, was Emile Benveniste (1902–1976). Given the frequent accusation of linguistic determinism levelled against the Boasians, we should note Benveniste's paper "Categories of Language and Categories of Thought" (Benveniste 1958 [1966]) – "language" here translating *la langue*, that is, a particular language, not the language faculty. Benveniste cites Aristotle's list of fundamental categories of thought, the precursors of Kant's intuitions and categories. He claims – like Gruppe before him – that Aristotle's categories are in fact projections of the parts of speech of the Greek language, and he says so in some extremely deterministic language. Benveniste's thesis remains controversial among classicists and philosophers (see, for instance, the dossier in Ildefonse and Lallot 2002). Yet neither Benveniste's nor Saussure's apparent linguistic determinism has provoked anything like the outrage that is so often directed at the putative linguistic determinism of Sapir and Whorf.

Symbolic anthropology and cultural approaches. The structuralist wind blowing from Europe contributed to the rise of a North American school of symbolic anthropology in the 1960s and 1970s, centered at least some of the time at the University of Chicago around the figures of Clifford Geertz (1926–2006), David Schneider (1918–1995), and Marshall Sahlins (1930–). During this golden age of cultural approaches, all of these authors claimed allegiance to the Boasian paradigm; but from the vantage point of the new millennium, the theories they developed during this period looks a great deal like the pluralist essentialism of the Romantics. Schneider's "cultural approach" treats cultures as symbol systems organized in galaxies around key symbols and separable from the complexities of social life. Geertz's overall cultural styles, ethea calling for interpretation allowing the identification of fundamental principles multifariously reflected, and which may be assumed to characterize any culture, sound like Benedict without her careful counter-examples. Sahlins' (1977) defense of Boas and "cultural projects" sounds equally essentialist. The static nature of these presentations, their focus on cultures as distinct and unique wholes and lack of concern for diversity within cultures, the sometimes selective use of data to present suspiciously super-coherent portraits of cultural wholes, led to a period of high-energy optimism followed by increasing despair and the rise of the contrary idea that after all culture is constructed – by the ethnographer, as a kind of fiction. As a result, while some anthropological tendencies, along with linguistics and psychology, emulated the natural and cognitive sciences and grew increasingly universalistic and "hard," another emulated travel writing, fiction, and postmodernist philosophy and grew more and more individualistic, confessional, and expressive. Some anthropology departments have split in two over this division.

The major symbolic anthropologists were not linguistic anthropologists, and they have had relatively little to say directly about language and languages. A real language, in its multiple layering, does not lend itself to portrayal as the expression of a small number of key symbols.

Whorf and Bachelard

Another body of work that calls out for comparison with the Boasians is that of the French school of epistemology founded by Gaston Bachelard (1884–1962). Bachelard's work directly influenced several generations of philosophers and historians of the sciences, the best known of whom in the English-speaking world is Michel Foucault, but which also included Althusser, whose Marxism,

often called structuralist, is quite evidently Bachelardian. This "new epistemology" (Fichant 1973) presumes the multiplicity and diversity of sciences, and
above all asserts the difference between our daily experience of life and the
world as the contemporary sciences allow it to be glimpsed.

I would like to spend a little time here pointing out a series of parallels
between Bachelard himself and Whorf, in life as in doctrine. A comparison
of the two will give a fuller idea of the complexity, and yet the coherence, of
Whorf's project and therefore of the Boasian one more broadly.

To begin with the surface parallels: both Whorf and Bachelard were trained
as engineers; each came late to the scholarly work for which he is primarily
known; both had careers outside the academy, either concurrent with or preceding their scholarly lives. In both cases, these careers were on the margins of
research in the natural sciences. After his scientific training, Whorf got a job as
a fire prevention engineer with an insurance company, and became an expert
descriptive linguist during the last decade of his life. Bachelard, born the same
year as Sapir and Malinowski, had a first career as a postal employee in Paris
and studied to become an engineer in the telegraph service. Laid off when
he came back from World War I, he was able to get a job teaching science in
the secondary school in his home town, and during eleven years as a science
teacher he studied philosophy, earning a doctorate in 1927 at the age of forty-
three. In 1930 Bachelard was appointed to his first university position. From
1927 to his death he published twenty-three books, a lot of articles, and several
pamphlets on printmaking. By the 1950s he was a well-established academic
figure and noted Parisian character. In his slouch hat and long white beard, he
looked like a cross between Walt Whitman and Father Christmas. One always
thinks of Bachelard as old, the archetypical wise old man.

One always thinks of Whorf as young, of course, because that's all he ever
was. Whorf started his scholarly career late, died young, and did not found a
school; he has been rejected both by cognitivists as a relativist and by symbolic
and postmodern anthropologists as a determinist and essentialist. Bachelard
also started late, but he survived into a lovable old age and remains very much
part of the French philosophical canon.

Like Whorf, Bachelard came to maturity in an intellectual milieu dominated
by a doctrine that claimed that there was no break between habitual common sense and scientific discovery. In his case this was not behaviorism, but
spiritualisme, a distinctly French idealism that was the major academic philosophy from the late 1800s through the 1930s. The chief spiritualist of the
sciences, Emile Meyerson, argued – as would Helmut Gipper more recently –
that Einstein's relativity could be deduced from Newtonian mechanics, which
reproduced the human lived world. Meyerson was Bachelard's *bête noire*;
Bachelard picks on him in most of his books on epistemology. For Bachelard,
as for Whorf, relativity, quantum mechanics, and non-Euclidean geometries

represent breaks from common knowledge. It was against Meyerson's continuism that Bachelard invented the term "epistemological break." In his last book on epistemology, Bachelard sums up his doctrine:

> It has seemed more and more evident in the course of our studies that the contemporary scientific mind cannot be understood as continuous with simple common sense ... We believe, in fact, that scientific progress always represents a break, perpetual breaks, between common knowledge and scientific knowledge. (1953: 207)

Also like Whorf, Bachelard identified common knowledge with Newtonian mechanics, Kantian static space and flowing time, and Euclidean geometry. For Bachelard, these "intuitions" correspond to our way of constructing the world, but not to the world as it can be glimpsed by the new sciences. Listen to how he foreshadows Whorf's very vocabulary:

> The science of the last century presented itself as ... the science of our own world, in contact with daily experience, organized by a stable and universal reason ... The scientist ... lived in our reality, manipulated our objects ... discovered the obvious in the clarity of our intuitions. He developed his demonstrations following our geometry and our mechanics ... But now contemporary physics brings us messages from an unknown world. (Bachelard 1932 [1970]: 12)

Earlier I cited Bachelard's statement that "We dwelt in the Newtonian world as in a spacious and well-lighted abode." This passage continues: "Newtonian thought was from the first a marvelously clear example of a closed system of thought; the only way out was to break out" (1934 [1984]: 44, translation modified).

Whorf sought to make these obvious intuitions explicit, basing himself primarily, but not exclusively, on language structure. His discoveries were contrastive: by going abroad and reconstructing habitual ways of world-making that seem strange to us, Whorf could turn around and identify from a distance what he felt were our own habitual patterns, those typical of the modern West, as one possibility in a wider field of possibilities, "one constellation in a galactic expanse." Bachelard, for his part, frequently refers to *us*, to *our* intuitions, but it is never made explicit just who *we* are: does the first person plural refer to humankind in general, or to modern Western humankind in particular? We may, I think, assume the latter, since Bachelard does seem to associate Newton, Kant, and so forth specifically with the modern West.

Whorf and Bachelard were both centrally concerned with linguistic and/or conceptual patterns that people almost always follow in everyday life. Because of this it is possible, but I think wrong, to treat both of them as determinists. I have argued that this is misleading for Whorf, who in fact was centrally interested not in constraints on thinking, but in the difference between habitual, and so easier, and less habitual, and so harder, paths for thinking to follow. Bachelard, for his part, bases his whole philosophy on the assumption that it is possible – with effort – to get out of the patterns and imagery of common knowledge, and at the same time he is quite explicit about its power to fascinate and to seduce.

Whorf was ironic about the limitations of habitual thinking, poking fun at "'hard, practical common sense'" (1956: 152), a phrase that he puts in scare quotes. Whorf's famous, and much-targeted, set of stories of how linguistically-based common images can be a fire hazard (1956: 135–7; cf. the mockery in Pinker 1994: 60–1 and the appreciation in Schultz 1990) is only the best known of these rhetorical sallies. Bachelard, for his part, based his whole epistemology on a critique of common knowledge and imagery, immediate experience, as the source of blocks to scientific discovery. The second famous term he invented was "epistemological block," *obstacle épisté-mologique.* "A scientific experience" (or "experiment," since French uses the word *expérience* for both) "is ... an experience that contradicts common experience" (1938: 10), but the images and patterns of common experience are always there, easy and enticing lures. In this, again like Sapir and Whorf, he was writing not of constraint or determinism but of seduction. "Whether deliberately or not, metaphors seduce reason" (1938: 78).

The parallel between Whorf and Bachelard goes deeper than anything I have indicated so far. Both, in fact, felt and responded to the seductive power of the patterns and images of common knowledge. What is more, both gave in: these rigorous and uncompromising critics of our own – their own – ordinary construction of the world were at the same time deeply and I would say poetically or mystically in love with that world, with its experienced forms and surfaces. Both devoted much of their energy not just to critiquing, but to mapping common patterns of thought, and did so with what can only be called love, expressed in charged language comparable to that of novelists or religious writers. The result is that in content and style both Whorf and Bachelard appear as apparently contradictory dual thinkers, provoking much head scratching in several generations of students.

Whorf, it seems to me, fell in love not only with the patterns he identified in Hopi, but also with those he was identifying contrastively in our own – that is, in his own – conceptualization of the world. What was background patterning for Mr. Everyman, the easy and reasonable path to follow, became foreground patterning for Whorf, ground become figure, to cite his favorite Gestalt process (citations and discussion in P. Lee 1996: 96–109). More specifically, Whorf intersperses his scientific prose with passages of highly charged descriptive language. These passages give his writing both power and, as Emily Schultz has noted (1990), apparent inconsistency. The son and brother of visual artists, Whorf's most passionate language typically marks visual experience: what do different languages do, he asks, "with the flowing face of nature in its motion, color, and changing form; with clouds, beaches, and yonder flight of birds?"

(1956: 241). John Crespi (1997) has called this passage Emersonian; it is a tiny New England epiphany.

Bachelard, for his part, started producing a new kind of writing, almost antithetical to his epistemological style, at a specific moment in his life, in 1938, at the age of fifty-four. This is the year of publication of what became his most famous epistemological book, *The Formation of the Scientific Mind: A Contribution to a Psychoanalysis of Objective Knowledge*, which fiercely attacks first impressions, general knowledge, and common sense in general, and is essentially made up of a collection of cases of common images and assumptions that proved historically to be epistemological blocks to the development of scientific thinking. My own favorite example is the sponge, which turns out to have been a source of metaphors for all kinds of mixing processes from the sixteenth well into the eighteenth century. "In Descartes," Bachelard writes, "the metaphysics of space is the *metaphysics of the sponge*" (1938: 79). Let's face it, this is funny; and you can sense how the author, trying to keep his face straight, is getting interested, drawn in, tickled by the richness and subtlety of error. As he writes of another author, "We are never completely immune to the prejudice that we spend a great deal of time in attacking" (1938 [1964]: 65). Now *this* line comes from the second book Bachelard published the same year, ostensibly a sort of coda to *The Formation of the Scientific Mind*. It is an extended study of a more or less connected system of epistemological obstacles, namely our common notions about fire – more shades of Whorf – but in fact this book, *The Psychoanalysis of Fire*, Bachelard's other bestseller, is itself as much a reverie as an analysis. For today's science, says Bachelard, fire is a secondary epiphenomenon, a non-entity; in our daily lives, on the contrary, fire retains the glamor of a fundamental cosmic element – shades of Isidore. Beginning with a critique of our fascination for fire as an obstacle to scientific advance, Bachelard finds himself more and more entranced as he remembers the hearth of his childhood and conducts field research by sitting and gazing into the flames. The book critiquing daydreams turns into a daydreaming book.

This will become Bachelard's second philosophical style; for the rest of his career he will intersperse tough epistemological books with dreamy ones about the four elements, poetics, and reverie, books in which the critic of common thinking allows himself to linger in the realm of epistemological obstacles with evident delight. This second series of books gives elements of a philosophy of reverie, this being the state of explicit emergence of otherwise only semi-conscious images and sensibilities that haunt – one can hardly say that they "structure" – our first impressions and common knowledge.

In these writings Bachelard gives innumerable examples of the clarity and intensity of his largely non-visual sensory memories: the crunch of a fresh waffle, hot off the fire, as if fire itself were crisp and melting in his mouth; the sound of water running through the many streams of the tiny well-watered region of his childhood. Through a certain amount of discursive argumentation, but mainly through the evocative power of his thick and juicy descriptions, he stakes out a space for common knowledge, for what he calls the autonomy of symbols.

There remains an important vectorial difference between Whorf and Bachelard. Whorf sought to *map* common knowledge, basing himself primarily, but not exclusively, on the patterning of language. By contrast, when Bachelard decides to give attention to common knowledge as an autonomous realm, he jumps all the way "across" the possibility of mapping it, to the other side, to relatively unstructured reverie.

Related to this leap to reverie is Bachelard's apparent lack of interest in cultural difference. As I said, one is never sure whether Bachelard is talking about humankind in general or modern Western humankind in particular. In his elemental books, Bachelard's materials are all drawn from modern Western sources: his own memories, modern Western literature, and the modern Western understanding of Euclid, Newton, and Kant. As it happens, he offers the sympathetic space of symbols to the anthropologist, in contradistinction to the psychologist who wishes to explain rather than live among images. "The anthropologist," writes one of Bachelard's disciples and commentators, "the friend of man, must enter into images, dwell among them, ressuscitate their movement; but psychology, disdainful of dreams, soon takes them for lies and replaces them with its own interpretations" (Dagognet 1965: 33, paraphrasing Bachelard 1938). Bachelard's constant use of the first person plural and the fact that his examples are drawn from his own memories and from Western literature allow us to take this work as a first lining-up of typical modern Western fancies, an initial fragmentary ethnography of the modern Western imagination. The method used would have been a combination of exploration and introspection by a man who was both a gifted observer and a brilliant informant, Griaule and Ogotemmêli in one.

Preserving the heritage

Structuralist and symbolic anthropology and the new epistemology paralleled aspects of the Boasian project, but they did not focus on linguistic diversity except as an analogy for other kinds of cultural and ideological difference. In North America, however, despite the increasing triumph of universalism, linguistic anthropologists continued to work on linguistic specificities and their relationship to broader cultural and social patterns, establishing new approaches that each developed a distinctive aspect of the Boasian legacy (see Hill and Mannheim 1992; Lucy 1997b).

Ethnosemantics and tagmemics. The movement in North American anthropology variously known as ethnosemantics, ethnoscience, or cognitive anthropology (P. Brown 2006), which had its heyday in the early 1960s, represented a continuation of the attempt to operationalize a holistic view of language and thought, again by strictly limiting the data to what can be easily mapped. The major studies in this field took vocabulary domains – animals, plants, skin diseases – and used the mutual delimitation of terms to construct models of speakers' classification systems (Tyler 1969). Ethnosemanticists offered what remain classic analyses of unexpected ways of organizing kinship terms and categories of plants, animals, and diseases; we saw in the previous chapter how this kind of approach to color naming challenged our own received categories.

Closely linked to ethnosemantics was the tagmemic theory of Kenneth L. Pike (1912–2000), a student of Sapir's who developed descriptive methods to catch the structural specifics of any kind of language. It was Pike who generalized the distinction between a universalist phonetic analysis of particular sounds and a systemic phonological, or phonemic, analysis of the field of sounds of a particular language into the broader labels of etic and emic, which have had such a varied history in anthropology and in other human sciences. Looking back at the genealogy of tagmemics and Pike's own training, it is clear that this very set of issues maintains central concerns of the Boasians.

Relativity of use. In the 1960s, Dell Hymes (1927–2009) sought to define a typology of cognitive styles characterizing different languages (1961) and proposed what he called a second kind of linguistic relativity, a relativity of language use (1966) as distinct from the primarily referential interests of Boas and Whorf, but overlapping with the poetic interests of Sapir. Not all societies, he observed, use language in the same way, and these specificities of use should be part of any ethnography. The field Hymes thus launched came to be called the ethnography of speaking, later the ethnography of communication. Besides strictly ethnographic analyses of language use and language attitudes, the field has also developed into a forum for reflection on the nature of performance, including poetic performance, across cultures (Bauman 1974; Leavitt 2010).

The ethnography of speaking also includes a tradition of ethnolinguistics in the strict sense: a comparative study of theories of language and language genres (Lucy 1992a: 89–93, 105–12), with some major studies on systems of classifying ways of speaking (e.g., Sherzer 1983). There is a parallel to this tradition in French Africanist ethnography, notably in the work of Geneviève Calame-Griaule (1987) on West African theories of the powers of language.

Grammatical nuance and ethnopoetics. Since the late 1970s, the linguist-anthropologist-poet Paul Friedrich (1927–) has been defending a "reformulation of the Sapir hypothesis" that puts poetic language back in the center of the argument – as indeed it was for Humboldt and Sapir. "Poetic language and language use," Friedrich wrote,

should be the locus and focus of the hypotheses that are concerned with language, "mind," and "reality," and, more specifically, with the theory of linguistic relativity … Language most affects the imagination of the individual under conditions of poetic usage and it is under these conditions that the imagination operates most directly and significantly on language. (Friedrich 1979: 441, 493)

Since poetic language draws on and maximizes the specific characteristics of each tongue, it provides "the locus of the most interesting differences between languages" (1986: 17; cf. Hill and Mannheim 1992: 397–8; Friedrich 2006). Friedrich has developed his approach through work on a large number of traditions, starting with Tarascan, an isolate Mexican language with an obligatory system of shape-marking: in Tarascan, you must assign a shape to everything you want to talk about, including abstractions. Friedrich saw such categories as implicit metaphors that reveal a "network of associations" inherent as a "semantic geometry" in the language itself (Friedrich 1979). This implicit poetics, he has argued through studies in traditions as diverse as Sanskrit, Homeric Greek, modern Russian, classical Chinese, and American English, represent an aesthetic force specific to any language and at least as powerful as the purely referential structuring usually associated with the idea of linguistic relativity.

Friedrich's work reconnects linguistic relativity with the historically important concern with poetic potentiality, and so has served to bring linguists, poets, and anthropologists together to work on what he calls "linguaculture," "a domain of experience that fuses and intermingles the vocabulary, many semantic aspects of grammar, and the verbal aspects of culture" (1989: 306–7; see the essays in O'Neil, Scoggin, and Tuite 2006).

Semiotic functionalism. In a research progam starting in the 1970s, Michael Silverstein (1945–), like Friedrich a student of Roman Jakobson's, sought to clarify the relationship between the structure of a language and the explicit or implicit ideas about language held by its speakers (1977; 1979). Silverstein (1981 [2001]) proposes a hierarchy of aspects of language that would be more or less available to speakers' awareness, thus giving a basis for some of the effects the Boasians had noted: lexical items, for instance, are close to awareness and so easily replaced or discarded, while pervasive grammatical categories are generally far from awareness and less amenable to conscious manipulation.

Throughout his work, Silverstein has continued to draw the implications of the fact that reference, the conception and conveying of information, is only one of many functions involved in language use. Of particular interest to him has been the way languages anchor the speaker in a given context through the use of deictics, such as personal pronouns or verb tenses, that both convey referential information and change depending on who is talking, where, or when. Silverstein's concentration on indexicality offers a mechanism to link what is said into the situation of saying and so opens up linguistic analysis to social analysis and sociolinguistics (Hill and Mannheim 1992: 395–7; Lucy 1992a: 96–101, 115–26). This point of view has been brought to bear on linguistic relativity itself as a socially situated theory (Silverstein 2000).

Relativitas rediviva

Meanwhile, however, things were shifting again. Since the late 1970s, a small band of brave souls (e.g., Alford 1978; 1981; Friedrich 1979) had been challenging the prevailing interpretation of linguistic relativity as relativism and determinism. Whorf's work, in particular, played a central role in the theory of social semiotics being developed from the 1980s by a group of scholars, including Silverstein and John Lucy, at the Center for Psychosocial Studies (e.g., the essays in Mertz and Parmentier 1985). The Sapir centenary in 1984 was an occasion for scholars to meet to re-evaluate his heritage (e.g., Cowan *et al.* 1986). In 1987, as part of a major study of categorization, the linguist George Lakoff reviewed the controversy over linguistic relativity, sought to sort out the various parameters of argument used in the debates on the issue, argued that much of the criticism was based on misreadings, and concluded that "Whorf was right in observing that concepts that have been made part of the grammar of a language are used in thought, not just as objects of thought, and that they are used spontaneously, automatically, unconsciously, and effortlessly" (1987: 335). In 1990 Emily Schultz proposed a Bakhtinian rereading of Whorf's text as largely ironic and fully engaged in the controversies of its time, and by the early 1990s a critical mass had developed for rethinking linguistic relativity. From about this point new cognitive work based on more serious reading of Sapir and Whorf began snowballing (see below), and the relative success of these efforts gave the whole enterprise a new legitimacy. In 1992, John Lucy offered a revised history of linguistic relativity that made it seem like an interesting and provocative idea; some years later, Penny Lee produced the first monographic study of Whorf's thought as a whole, drawing largely on unpublished material (P. Lee 1996). Since 1997 in particular, the year of the Whorf centenary and of several symposia and conferences on the topic, research has been rolling in a number of domains.

Linguistics and poetics

Typology. In linguistics proper, work on grammatical categories across languages has developed in continuity with the great tradition of linguistic typology. The tension between the prevailing universalism and some of the non-universalist implications of the data was evident, for instance, in a volume on evidentiality subtitled "the linguistic coding of evidentiality" (Chafe and Nichols 1986). The majority of chapters in the book presume the existence of a universal set of ideas about knowing that may be "coded" differently in different languages. But some (e.g., Alice Schlichter on Wintu, Martha Hardman on Jaqi) explore the relationship between distinctive evidential systems and the conceptualization of knowledge (Leavitt 1991b).

With consideration of a wider variety of languages, more and more features seem to challenge postulated universals (e.g., Foley 2005 on the non-universalisty of the noun/verb distinction). Laying out this case in his paper "Pre-Established Categories Do Not Exist," Martin Haspelmath uses language and terminology referring directly to the Boasians.

[T]he cross-linguistic evidence is not converging on a smallish set of universal (possibly innate) categories. On the contrary, almost every newly described language presents us with some "crazy" new category that hardly fits existing taxonomies. (Haspelmath 2007: 121–2)

As a result,

descriptive linguists still have no choice but to adopt the Boasian approach of positing special language-particular categories for each language. (p. 121)

Here is one sign of how much things have turned: in 2009, the august journal *Behavioral and Brain Sciences* published an article provocatively entitled "The Myth of Language Universals" (Evans and Levinson 2009). The authors claim that it is precisely the diversity of human languages that makes them of most interest for cognitive science. They criticize (pp. 440–1) approaches that assume the universal relevance of constituent order and so must hold that languages such as Latin, which tag each word and so allow a comparatively free word order, produce sentences that are at a further remove from the underlying pattern than do languages such as English or French. The reader will remember that this position virtually reproduces Le Laboureur's seventeenth-century attack on Latin and will find that its critique here recalls that offered by Lamy and Buffier in the eighteenth.

Such critiques of universals remain a minority approach in linguistic typology; Haspelmath's article appeared in the same journal issue as one entitled "Linguistic Typology Requires Crosslinguistic Formal Categories."

Context. Following the lead of sociolinguistics, Silverstein's pointing to the situation of speech, and a growing movement to interpret linguistic material in the context of its utterance, a good deal of recent work has shown the relativity of linguistic ways of marking social and other kinds of situation. As William Hanks puts it, these are "approaches which push context dependency deeper into the language ... [M]eaning ... derives from the fusion of language form with context" (Hanks 1996: 232). The context in question may be social and interpersonal, or it may be a physical space, as appears to be the case in some Australian languages. But the overall implication is that it is a mistake to isolate lexicon or grammar from the social life of language. Much of the research in this vein has focused on deixis, the means the language provides to link the interlocutors into the speech situation and the world. And along with Silverstein's continuing investigations of the relationship between language structure and ideas about language, there is now a field of the study of linguistic ideologies (Schieffelin *et al.* 1998; Kroskrity 2000). Overall, this nexus of sociolinguistics and ethnolinguistics is probably the most active part of linguistic anthropology today (Duranti 2003).

Poetics and ethnopoetics. Ongoing work in ethnopoetics (Leavitt 2010), performance theory, and the theory of translation (e.g., A. L. Becker's [1995] efforts to go "beyond translation") deals directly with the implications of linguistic specificity. This seems appropriate. If poetic language makes all levels of a language resonate (Jakobson 1960), then, as Diderot, Humboldt, and Sapir believed, it is through poetic language that the specificity of a language is most intensely rendered (Friedrich 1986). Phonetics and phonology represent unavoidable sound-worlds. Choice of words and their semantic fields, explicit or suggested, becomes essential: think of all the uses of river, stream, brook, the sea, raindrop, teardrop – all just water – in English poetry and song. In this kind of context, the specific words and grammatical categories of a language are the unique working material of art and evocation. As are the figures of speech, explicit or implicit, that a language deploys. One effect of the linkage of grammar, poetics, and culture (Friedrich 1996) has been the development of studies of the implications of such figures across cultures in a developing comparative tropology (e.g., Fernandez 1991, 2006, and Bate 2009).

For the poetically awake ear, even just plain syntax becomes not only a key to deep structures or the sign of a language universal, but a source of rising suspense and falling relief. Here Weisgerber's observations on German nesting syntax are perfectly appropriate, not as an argument for the superiority of the intellectual architecture of German, but as elucidating a specific rhythm of ideas, an intellectual poetics. It seems evident that poetic possibilities depend on the limits of word order, on what is expected and what is surprising. In strictly modifier-head languages such as most of the those of South Asia, of whatever linguistic family (it's one of the traits of this particular language area), adjectives come before nouns, there are postpositions instead of prepositions, and the verb always comes at the end: this means you hear of something's qualities before you know what it is, you know what's being talked about before you know where it is or in relation to what, you know all about all the participants in a sentence and find out only at the very end what they are doing.

This is exploited in poetry (cf. the mini-analyses in Ramanujan 1985: 313 and Leavitt 2006b: 99–104); what might it mean for daily talk and thought?

People who think about translation have to face these issues constantly. Even during the periods when cognitivist universalism was at its most dominant, translation theorists (e.g., Steiner 1975; Bassnett 1980) were recognizing the reality and the potential impact of language differences. Their distinction between what they call domesticating strategies (e.g., *les belles infidèles*) and foreignizing ones (e.g., the Romantics) parallels the one that I have been proposing between universalism and various brands of relativity (see Venuti 2004). The conclusion must be that the specifics of the source-language text be respected in the target language: "Insofar as foreignizing translation seeks to restrain the ethnocentric violence of translation, it is highly desirable today" (Venuti 1995: 20).

The greening of cognitive science

The most remarkable shift of interest has been in cognitive science itself. While the new opening up of the field to language specifics has been a broad tendency, here I will just note what seem to have been two important launching points.

Starting in the late 1960s, the psycholinguist Dan Slobin had set up comparative programs on child language acquisition in a variety of languages (Slobin 1985–1997). As these data mounted, they began to show a real impact of language specifics on how children learn, leading Slobin himself to distinguish different kinds of thought processes and propose an influence of language on what he called "thinking for speaking."

Starting in the late 1970s, John Lucy, trained jointly in psychology, anthropology, and linguistics, reread Sapir and Whorf seriously and tried to use their actual ideas, rather than the 1950s revised version, in designing cross-cultural psychological experiments, first on color, then in a major study on noun classes and number in a Mayan language and in English. In the second case, he worked on the basis of the comparison of pervasive obligatory grammatical categories, not vocabulary. This study (Lucy 1992b) showed an influence of grammatical categories on short-term memory. In combination with his rereading of what Whorf really had to say, Lucy's studies, the first convincing psychological experiments to show "Whorf effects," helped launch a general re-evaluation of linguistic relativity within psychology.

The findings of these new research programs were too solid, and too well defended, to be ignored. By the early 1990s, a critical mass had developed as linguists, anthropologists, and psychologists collaborated in "rethinking linguistic relativity," the name given to a major international conference held in 1991, the first on the topic in many years.

A couple of quotes illustrate what has happened. In the book from the 1991 conference, the editors sum up the situation as it existed at that time:

The idea that language could determine (however weakly) the nature of our thinking nowadays carries more than a faint whiff of anachronism; rather, it seems to belong to an altogether different age, prior to the serious study of mind as an information processing device. (Gumperz and Levinson 1996: 22)

Indeed, in a review article on studies that appeared to support some form of linguistic relativity, Paul Bloom and Frank Kiel (2001: 365) ended up dismissing most of it, arguing that the idea that language could have much influence on thought was an intuition based on the mere surface differences of languages: "We think the intuition here is wrong ... [A]lthough there is a strong impression that the language one speaks must influence how one thinks, we think that this impression is more seductive than it is instructive." Yet the same year, another psychologist wrote in a collection of papers on the subject, "If there is one clear conclusion to be drawn from this volume it is that, after decades of obloquy, Whorf is back" (Gopnik 2001: 45). There is even talk of a "neo-Whorfian renaissance" (Evans 2003: 13; Reines and Prinz 2009: 1027).

In the meantime, universalist-inspired studies have gone on apace, and the body of knowledge about what children know before they can speak has grown dramatically. "Nativist theorizing is thriving," write the editors of an ambitious series of volumes on *The Innate Mind* (Carruthers, Laurence, and Stitch 2005: 3).

As the assertions just quoted attest, we now have a complex, multisided debate going on over the relative roles of universals and linguistic particulars, the salience of which can no longer be denied. Melissa Bowerman and Stephen Levinson point to the new situation:

Two kinds of recent development have radically changed the way we think about this area ... [T]here has been a revolution in our knowledge of infant cognition: new techniques ... have revealed striking early abilities ... Over a similar period there have been parallel changes in the study of language acquisition ... new techniques provide increasingly sophisticated ways of probing linguistic knowledge even before production begins ... In addition, the study of language acquisition in non-European languages and cultures ... has come at last to a point where we have a significant range of information ... and these data have challenged many earlier theories and presumptions about universal processes. (2001: 1–2)

Here I can do nothing but skim some recent work on topics that have been coming up repeatedly in the history of these debates. I will point to five domains of research: the relations of language specifics to the conception of space, time, number, gender, and our old friend color.

Space. Combined ethnographic and experimental research on the conception of space has been carried out for some years. On the basis of preliminary work, Penelope Brown, Stephen Levinson, and their colleagues distinguished three frames of reference for spatial orientation that appear to have relevance across languages and cultures: a relative frame, such as our own left and right; an absolute frame, using, for instance, the cardinal directions; and an intrinsic frame, using relations among objects (Levinson 1996; 2003). Looking back, the battles over the nature of space that pitted Descartes, Leibniz, and Herder against Newton and Kant can be reread as between proponents of intrinsic and absolute frames.

The Australian language Guugu Yimithirr, to give an example that has received extensive study, has an absolute system, with terms, and constantly used terms, for the cardinal directions but none corresponding to our left and right (Haviland 1998) – so that one says something like "There's a fly on your northern knee" – and in experiments comparing speakers of this language to those of European languages, differences have appeared in spatial orientation (Levinson 2003; see Foley 1997, Chapter 11; P. Brown 2006).

A research project on ten languages and cultures (Levinson and Wilkins 2006) has found correlations between the frame that is dominant in a language and the frame its speakers use to solve cognitive tasks. "[P]eople think, remember, and reason in the system they most use for speaking with. This is a prime example of a Whorfian link between language and non-linguistic cognition" (P. Brown 2006: 109). Levinson and Wilkins draw the overall conclusion in a footnote. Most psychologists, they write, have been holding onto semantic uniformitarianism for a variety of reasons. "But, as shown in this volume, semantic diversity is a fact, and the theories need to adjust to the reality" (2006: 514, n. 2).

None of this is without controversy, of course. Psychologists of a more universalist persuasion have tried to show that non-linguistic factors, such as the spatial setting of the people speaking the language, are more important than linguistic ones, and the debate goes on (for instance, Li and Gleitman 2002 versus Levinson *et al.* 2002).

That major findings are being made in the domain of spatial relations is ironic, given that Whorf, with his admiration for Gestalt psychology, believed that space was a domain that was likely to be conceptualized in the same way regardless of language (1956: 159; P. Lee 1996: 102 ff.).

Time. In research on time, Lera Boroditsky's comparisons of Mandarin and English, which both spatialize time but in different ways, have shown significant divergences in handling time-related questions depending on the metaphor with which the test is congruent (2001). Boroditsky also found differences in short-term memory for time relations versus personal relations between Indonesian speakers, whose language does not have tense but codes for interpersonal deixis, and English speakers, whose language has obligatory tense and a much less stringent form of person-marking (summary in Kenneally 2007: 106–7).

Number. Old arguments about the implications of number terms have come back to the fore in the ongoing debate over the Pirahã language of Amazonia, which is said to lack a number of what are generally taken to be universal features of human languages. While the scholarly debate (e.g., Everett 2005) bears on phonology, prosody, vocabulary, and grammar, the initial explosion of interest was based on the apparent identification of a language without numbers, a discovery said to support Whorf's "hypothesis ... that language is more a 'mold' into which thought is cast than it is a reflection of thought" (Holden 2004: 1093). First experiments (Gordon 2004) suggest that Pirahã adults do have difficulty with mathematical tasks, difficulty that can be correlated with the lack of an appropriate symbolic toolkit. Such tasks, of course, have up until now formed no part of normal Pirahã life.

Gender. Many languages have obligatory gender marking. In French class when I was a kid we were assured that gender in French was purely a matter of form with absolutely no implications for meaning. As Brown and Lenneberg (1954 [1970]: 241) put it,

In French ... it is not clear that the gender of a form signifies anything to a speaker. Certainly it is difficult to find any common attributes in the references for French nouns of feminine gender. Not even the majority of them manifest feminine sexuality.

But is this really true? Or is gender what Whorf called a cryptotype, whose latent meaning could emerge under some situations? One study (Ervin 1962) suggested that male/female connotations to words with masculine/feminine gender could be activated in Spanish. Such salience of gender was found in some studies in the 1990s (Konishi 1993, Sera et al. 1994). In a recent radio interview (report in Krulwich 2009), Boroditsky reported on research on this topic. She and her collaborators (Boroditsky *et al.* 2003) compared speakers of Spanish and German on the adjectives they would use to describe a "bridge," an item designated by a masculine noun in Spanish, but a feminine noun in German. The Spanish *puente* was described as big, strong, sturdy, towering, the German *Brücke* as elegant, beautiful, slender, and fragile. Reverse the genders, as with the word for "key" in the two languages, and you reverse the connotations. What's more, these effects were found when native speakers of German or Spanish were interviewed *in English*. When the interview aired it provoked an impassioned response, much of which seemed to signal a release of long-bottled-up frustration. The title of one blog, appearing the day of the interview (at www.altalang.com/beyond-words/?s=Boroditsky): "Chew on this, Whorf-haters."

Colors again. Color, of all things, turns out to be another area where "Whorf effects" are in fact showing up. There has been a major return to research on color in the last decade. In particular, the World Color Survey (www.icsi. berkeley.edu/wcs/), covering 110 unwritten languages, has provided a wealth of new information, some of which supports forms of linguistic relativity.

Here I will mention two particularly striking studies. Since language functioning occurs primarily on the left side of the brain, the side that controls the right visual field, one recent study hypothesized that color discrimination might be more affected by language if one half of the visual field was focused on rather than the other. This is exactly what was found. Conclusion: "It appears that people view the right (but not the left) half of their visual world through the lens of their native language, providing an unexpected resolution to the language-and-thought debate" (Gilbert *et al*. 2006: 489). If so, the only resolution can be that there *is* an influence of language on thought, at least in people who are using both halves of their brains.

Another series of experiments tested for color discrimination after correcting for differences in brightness and hue, something that had not been done in Rosch's study. This time, in a comparison of English speakers with speakers of languages with four basic color terms, researchers found that memory was best for the colors for which there were terms. In addition, categorical perception was better when two succeeding color samples crossed a linguistic category boundary, e.g., a blue sample followed by a green sample were discriminated more easily by English speakers than were two shades of what we call blue; conversely, speakers of the other languages had improved categorical perception when the samples crossed boundaries established in *their* languages (Roberson and Hanley 2009).

Overall, the wealth of new information coming in, but above all the new willingness to pose old questions in new ways, have added at least a tint of linguistic relativity to cognitive studies. As was the case for the Boasians, recognition of the reality of variability does not require a denial of the reality of specific universals. Indeed, nativist universalism is still the dominant paradigm in cognitive science. But the tone has become less triumphalist, and universalist positions no longer seem self-evidently and exclusively right. In this light it is significant that a great nativist compendium recently appeared in three volumes (Carruthers, Laurence, and Stitch 2005–2007). The volumes give a compelling case: but clearly, at this point, defenders of universals feel the need to make their case.

Lera Boroditsky sums up the current situation in an article on linguistic relativity from the *Encyclopedia of Cognitive Science*.

Languages appear to influence many aspects of human cognition: evidence regarding space, time, objects, and substances have been reviewed in this article, but further studies have also found effects of language on people's understanding of numbers, colors, shapes, events, and other minds. Considering the many ways in which languages differ, the findings reviewed here suggest that the private mental lives of people who speak different languages may differ much more than previously thought. (2003: 920)

It's true that the author of this article has, as we have seen, been quite sympathetic to the idea of linguistic relativity. But it is still an encyclopedia article, and it is saying things that no encyclopedia article would have said a few years earlier.

Forward into the past?

Since the 1990s, then, efforts have been made to recognize the possibility of the importance of linguistic difference, bringing a more sympathetic reading of linguistic relativity into already constituted paradigms; the cognitive sciences, as well as such fields as ordinary language philosophy or microsociology, now seem ready to consider differences among languages while maintaining their own assumptions and methods. At the same time, we continue to see the dominance of cognitivist paradigms in thinking about language differences. In the words of *Rethinking Linguistic Relativity*, the book that as much as any other put linguistic relativity back on the intellectual map, "in the light of the much greater knowledge that we now have about both language and mental processing, it would be pointless to attempt to revive ideas about linguistic relativity in their original form" (Gumperz and Levinson 1996: 7).

Let us dwell on this for a moment. It is saying that what we now know about language and mental processing makes a revival of the original, Boasian, form of linguistic relativity pointless. But the Boasian version of linguistic relativity was quite explicitly not about thought in the sense of mental processing or potential, but in that of conceptualization of the world. Testing the cognitive abilities or processes of speakers of different languages when performing different tasks, while perfectly likely to add to our understanding of human nature and thought, is in fact outside the Boasian project, which was also the Whorfian project. Yet the dream of such testing has dominated orthodox readings of linguistic relativity since the 1950s and, as we have just seen, is experiencing a more sophisticated rebirth today. Most of the great battles in the field have been fought on this terrain. Well and good; but it is not Boasian terrain.

On the Boasian terrain of the *fact* of linguistic difference and the principle of linguistic relativity, both the dismissal of the "Whorfian hypothesis" for lack of experimental support and its recent return as an inspiration for experimental paradigms seem somewhat beside the point. Testing for "Whorf effects" in cognition may be like seeing whether people travelling at two different velocities are better or worse at cognitive tasks; or, perhaps more fairly, and to use one of Whorf's own examples (1956: 58), like testing someone who has always used Euclidean geometry against a hypothetical person who was raised using a non-Euclidean system. Each is likely to be better at solving some kinds of problems than others, and this difference might offer roundabout evidence confirming the fact that the two are using two different kinds of geometry. But we already knew that. The alternative non-relativity hypothesis here would have to be that both subjects are secretly using Euclidean geometry to do the work, but that the ostensible (surface?) non-Euclidean is quietly adding an extra step and restating his or her findings in non-Euclidean terms. And this again recalls Le Laboureur's claim that the Romans thought like modern Frenchmen, then had to scramble their ideas to make them into Latin sentences. Similarly, we know already that Yucatec uses numeral classifiers differently for animate and inanimate nouns, that Guugu Yimithirr uses cardinal directions in most situations for which English uses left and right. That such a pervasive aspect of one's language should have some incidence on the organization and remembering of input is, it seems to me, to be expected; positive experimental results give roundabout support to the idea that speakers of Yucatec and Guugu Yimithirr are actually using the resources offered by their language to help in problem-solving and memory tasks. It would be more surprising if they weren't.

Cognitivist assumptions and methods are different from those of the Boasians, the people who started to draw the full effects of taking language specificities seriously. What, then, might be the tasks of a linguistic anthropology refounded on "the original form" of the idea of linguistic relativity? What might a Boasian or, hideous neologism that is now gaining currency (Bashkow *et al.* 2004), a Neo-Boasian research program look like? It would necessarily be very different from the kind of essentialist program that has so often been attributed to the Boasians themselves.

A Neo-Boasian ethnolinguistics would take account of the evidence about cognition, development, and language universals that has been amassed since the 1950s. Like the "original form," it would not assume a natural unity of language, culture, and thought or a norm of monolingualism, but would pay attention to bilingual and multilingual situations.

Most urgently, it would be far more conscious and explicit than was the "original" form about the conditions of its own production of knowledge, about differences not only in grammar, but in power. Sapir may urge us to look upon English and Hottentot with the same cool, yet interested, detachment, but these languages and their speakers do not occupy the same situation in a colonized world. Actually practicing mutual calibration presupposes an interlocutor who is in a position to talk back.

It would have to attend to the impossible reality of translation and bring on board the recent, and perfectly compatible, reflections of translation theorists. True to Sapir's poetics, it would have to attend to all forms of speech without privileging the declarative sentence spoken in sober adult didactic mode. Poetry, passionate speech, divine oracles and demonic ravings would be accepted as data just as much as a conversation, an extended monologue, or isolated made-up sentences (Leavitt 2001). Valorization of a variety of linguistic styles, and particularly of poetry, has been part of the defense of linguistic diversity since the Renaissance, and it was very much part of Boasian ethnolinguistics "in its original form." While poetic language has been brought back to the fore in some recent work, notably that of Paul Friedrich or emboldened by his example, it seems remarkably absent from the "neo-Whorfian revolution" in cognition.

Instead of simply exemplifying them, a Neo-Boasian linguistics would have to try to understand the motivating phenomena of language love, language hate, language curiosity, and delight in language(s).

Like the "original form," a Neo-Boasian linguistics would start with language as a whole, not with thought or meaning. The pervasive systematicity of phonology and phonetics, non-semantic aspects of language, would be treated with the same respect as its semantic aspects. Phonological systems are elaborate dances that every human speaker and listener has to master and which determine habitual ways of producing and receiving speech sounds. This level of language does not involve meaning directly, and so claims of its influence seem less threatening than those involving "thought." Yet the Boasians always seem to have treated the patterning of non-meaningful elements as comparable to that of meaningful ones: Boas attended to sound systems, Sapir developed phonology, and one of Whorf's illustrations is of restrictions on the phonology of English monosyllables (1956: 223). Sound patterning certainly has effects on feeling, if not directly on ideation, effects that are heightened and valorized in poetic language. If we could get past the cherishing of thought over feeling, mind over body (Leavitt 1996), and begin to think of habitual thought, like the habitual production of speech sounds, as a kind of habitus, we would give more mind to phonology's choreography of speech organs and ear, bringing Winteler's "relational relativity" back into linguistic relativity.

This has a corollary for the relation between language and thought. We all know that learning a first language means that it becomes difficult to master the sound system of another in a perfect way: this is what is called accent, and recognizing the systematicity of accent has never been controversial. John Lucy has proposed that "the language-influenced rendering of the meaning system of another language" could be reframed as a "semantic accent effect" (2003: 5). Like sounds, a language organizes *meanings* in a way that comes to be perceptible particularly when one passes from one system to another. Semantic accent would thus parallel phonetic accent in a way that would be congruent with the broad Boasian picture.

In many ways, grammatical categories remain mysterious. What does it mean to speak a language that in every sentence requires you to locate yourself in time, or specify your source of knowledge, or the shape of what you are talking about? We still don't know. But putting the question like this suggests a clear and limited way of interpreting the idea that different languages represent different worlds.

And this whole idea of worlds ... The work on deictics and context has opened up one of the central aspects of human language; yet it remains the case that one of language's important functions – a function it shares, to be sure, with other media – is to *define* a world and to project aspects of it on the mind's eye (and ear and nose ...). This is the good old referential function, not as propositional truth value, but as the delineator of virtual things and images: as the imagination. Not only do humans not live only in "the objective world," as Sapir put it: the perceived real world is, for any human being, only one piece of a greater manifold of imagined or remembered virtual scenes. How these scenes are typically structured, how they are connected to each other and to the situation of speech, are likely to vary as much as any other aspect of language use and to depend to some degree on the specifics of the language being used.

The goal would be to overcome the essentialist tendencies that may have continued to be present in the Boasian approach, and particularly in reinterpretations of this approach, without once again throwing the baby out with the bathwater and reverting to what are, in the end, equally limited universalisms.

Conclusion

Language is the most massive and inclusive art we know.
Edward Sapir (1921: 220)

The main purpose of the [proposed] book would be to lead to a freer conception of linguistic phenomena.
Sapir, postscript to a letter to C. K. Ogden, 1923,
(cited in Joseph 1996: 382, n. 13)

The history we have been following has shown alternating sets of images replacing each other periodically in a swinging of attitudes between wonderment at and denigration of the diversity of languages. Renaissance delight in human diversity and attempts to characterize different types, with a recognition of the troubling complexity of translation, gave way to the universal reason or world of the Enlightenment, for which the human task was everywhere and always to follow chains of reasoning or seek to see the world clear. Here the specifics of different languages could only be distractions or dangers. In turn, using forms Leibniz had explicated to allow an admiration of multiplicity, Herder and the Romantics launched a movement for the liberation of particularity, authenticity, and diversity, seeing Descartes' "chains of reasonings" as chains indeed. The later nineteenth-century admiration for the natural sciences drew attention away once again from languages as specific systems in favor of the search for universal laws of human language or human history. The twentieth century saw the appearance both of a new essentialism in Neohumboldtian linguistics and of what I am arguing is something more complex in Boasian linguistics: an apparently contradictory attempt to refuse to follow either of the available thought-forms and so to offer a way of conceiving language differences that is pluralist but not essentialist. In North America, the Boasian fascination with diversity gave way in its turn to behaviorist, then cognitive universalism, which over the last decade or so has started to fray around the edges, if not quite giving way. In these swings, some national cultures, like some disciplines, seem almost congenitally prone to one tendency or the other and can be expected, therefore, to anticipate or retard what on a wider scale look like more general movements in Western thought.

The forty-year gender gap

The most recent set of swings is starkly illustrated in research on grammatical gender.

In 1959, the Russian-born-and-raised American linguist Roman Jakobson, a professor at MIT, published an article on translation pointing out situations in which grammatical gender comes to be semantically "activated," so that, for instance, a French-speaker tends to personify the moon as feminine, a German-speaker as masculine. He called this the mythology of everyday life.

In 2009, the Russian-born-and-raised American psycholinguist Lera Boroditsky, formerly a professor at MIT, gave the radio interview I cited above, telling about procedures that semantically "activate" grammatical gender in speakers of German and Spanish.

Given Jakobson's argument, one would have thought that gender was an obvious place to look for possible effects of language on conceptualization. Yet for almost fifty years, years during which there was more research done on "language and thought" than at any previous time in history, grammatical gender was hardly considered.[1] As psychological precursors, Boroditsky *et al.* (2003) could cite only the one study from the 1960s and two from the 1990s, all of which tended to *confirm* a relationship between grammar and conceptualization.

Why had so few researchers done this kind of experiment for almost half a century, and why *this* half-century?

I won't try to answer this question in terms of the history of science, but in terms of the history of images. The people doing the work on language and cognition through most of this period were inspired by a universalist thought-form that saw human thinking as a kind of pre- or non-linguistic processing. The way to look for "language–thought interactions" was by defining an independent, apparently language-free domain such as color and seeing how that crosscut with apparently easy-to-compare aspects of language, whence a focus on vocabulary. Grammatical categories such as gender are poor candidates for a universalist program for a number of reasons: they do not obviously index an easily defined realm outside language/thought itself (gender does not equal sex); they are not found in all languages; they differ greatly among the languages in which they are found; and they are likely to be "activated" in mythopoetic and imaginative registers, hardly those favored in experimental protocols. Above all, they are intimately bound to other aspects of a particular language. This means that it is very difficult to consider grammatical categories without going into the characteristics and even the poetics of the language as a whole, and to do *this* means at least provisionally to accept the possibility that languages differ in important ways. Enter too deeply into any actual language and you start raising all the questions of commensurability. You run the risk of relativism.

Going too far

This failure to recognize the pertinence of gender, it seems to me, is an example of how hard it is to resist following out the implications of an image. Guided by the beauty of their explanatory tools, proponents of both universalist and essentialist views have found themselves tempted by some symptomatic extreme positions. Such outcroppings mark an author who is being carried away by analogy.

Their central image of the causal chain will tempt people looking for universals toward a number of extreme claims:

They will be tempted to argue, first of all, that since what matters in language is referential content, translation is a straightforward process of conveying the same information from one form of externalization into another. The fact of translation would prove that the differences among languages do not matter.

Second, they will be drawn toward the idea that since thinking occurs independently of language, the language of one's expression might as well be the most convenient or widespread one. There would, then, be no real need to learn other languages than Latin or French in the past, or English today.

Finally, they would be drawn to arguments that one can compare languages with reference to a single universal external measure.

As we have seen, we find these ideas expressed or assumed by French and British philosophers in the seventeenth and eighteenth centuries and again by cognitive scientists and philosophers in the twentieth, with a stage-theory variant developed in the French and Scottish eighteenth century and in nineteenth-century evolutionism. We can sum up these clearly excessive claims as "translation is easy; either everybody thinks just like you, or those who don't don't think as well you do; stay at home and look outward."

Conversely, people leaning toward a pluralist view will be tempted by arguments symptomatic of "hard" essentialism:

They will find themselves wanting to say that translation is impossible, since no two languages map the world in the same way. The fact that translations never say exactly the same thing would prove that the differences among languages are crucially important.

Second, they will tend to argue that thinking depends on the specific language one speaks, and even that if your language lacks a term for a concept, you lack that concept.

Finally, they will tend to feel that the mother tongue represents a horizon from which you can never really escape, or a home to which you continually return. Learning other languages is not a bad thing, but what is important is to deepen your appreciation of your mother tongue.

We find these clearly excessive ideas formulated by Herder and some Romantics and language philosophers in the eighteenth and nineteenth centuries, by the Neohumboldtian program in the twentieth, and to a large extent they typify nationalist and ethnic movements, and a good deal of popular wisdom, today. We can sum them up as "translation is impossible; no word equals no concept; speakers of other languages live in alien universes from yours; stay home and look inward."

There is, of course, plenty of evidence that all of these claims, on both sides, are wrong. The Boasian position proposes something more complex and better suited to what we actually know about these questions.

Translation, first of all, is always possible, but it is never evident; it is possible to translate any referential meaning if one is willing to devote enough words to it.

A language is tendentious in that it requires you to make certain kinds of sounds and to attend to the domains of experience indexed by obligatory or hard-to-avoid grammatical categories. In habitual thinking and talking, the subject rests within these constraints, but it is possible to get out of them if one is willing to put in the effort to do it.

Consequently, learning other languages means defying habitual talking, and so is one good way of challenging habitual thinking.

These claims can be summed up: "Translation is possible but hard; language offers easy-to-follow, but not inescapable, patterns for thinking; the world is likely to be full of surprises."

These propositions, derived directly from the work of the Boasians in the early twentieth century, still seem not only adequate, but advanced signposts for rethinking language and mind.

To reiterate the themes with which we started this book: human beings live in language; they speak and listen constantly to speech, and at least an important part of their silent thinking, imagining, and problem solving takes place in some transform of spoken language. Since there is no language in general, only particular languages, speaking, listening to speech, and thinking in words take place only in the medium of particular languages and must bear the imprint of their peculiarities. Given these facts of life, one can either say that for one reason or another the differences among languages are not important and can be put aside; or one can say that they need to be taken into account. The latter is what I am calling a relativist position on language. There have been two main relativist positions available in the modern West. One of these, the older, sees each language as the expression of a unique essence. The more recent sees each language as a complex representing a distinct "point of view" for the speaker/hearer. Its model is the relativity of Einstein; it is necessarily a more off-center and perhaps contradictory position than the others, but it is one that seems to me to give a better account of its object. Not surprisingly, proponents of the non-importance of language differences have repeatedly taken the second of these positions, the relativity model of the Boasians, to be the first, an essentialist model, and have criticized it on that basis, as linguistic relativism or linguistic determinism.

Einstein's relativity was neither a determinism nor a relativism; it wasn't an ism at all, a doctrine or a moral philosophy, but a principle that allowed a more complex – but still coherent – way of thinking the world than did the alternative: the earlier unstated principle of privileging a single fixed viewpoint. Similarly, linguistic relativity is no ism, but a principle requiring a more complex consideration of human conceptualization than do the alternatives. These, too, are usually unstated, and I count three possibilities: (1) the way speakers of Western European languages conceive the world is right, everyone else is wrong; (2) everyone in the world conceives the world in the same way; apparent differences in language are mere surface patterning, of no real consequence; or (3) each language–culture–nation is a unique universe that must be preserved in its purity. Linguistic relativity should not be identified with the last of these views; rather, it destabilizes all of them, potentially prying open enough room for a more adequate account of human unity and diversity.

Notes

INTRODUCTION

1 Noteworthy exceptions are Parmentier (1985), which re-places linguistic relativity in a succinct history of revolts against succeeding dominant schools, and Schlesinger (1991). Haugen (1987), for his part, cites this history to identify Whorf with Romanticism: "Whorf's one-sided view of the language–thought relationship was not original with him. The general disregard of European linguistic thought by many American linguists in the 1940s kept them from realizing that these views had been debated by European linguists for some two centuries … [M]en of the Enlightenment were inclined to think of reason as prior to language, making language a mere vehicle of thought … Coincident with and as a part of the development of literary Romanticism, the emphasis shifted towards the priority of language over thought."

2 The classic list of immediately observable language universals is Hockett (1966).

3 Nicholas of Cusa's image of God. Compare this with Althusser's further claim that the modern notion of the free, unique subject is a "little lay god" (Althusser 1973 [1976]: 44).

4 On the theory of ramifying metaphor, see the work of George Lakoff, starting with Lakoff and Johnson (1981).

5 On the variety of philosophical relativisms, see Krausz (2009).

6 The literature on virtually every topic treated in this book is large and multilingual, and it's growing like weeds on a wet spring day. I have hacked a path through it as best I could.

1   A PASSAGE TO MODERNITY

1 For conceptions of space and time as made up of qualitatively diversified directions and periods, see, for instance, Granet (1934), Ramanujan (1989).

2 There is an anthropological tradition of looking at common patterning across conceptual domains, perhaps starting with Durkheim and Mauss (1902 [1963]); among the best studied traditions of this kind are those of the humoral medical systems of Europe, India, and China. Traditional Chinese thought, in particular, appears to presume a vast patterning, comparable to that of medieval Europe, of space, time, the elements, and the human body/mind into corresponding domains. Might this kind of putting things together characterize agriculturally based ideologically centralized feudal societies? In China, writes Marcel Granet, "it is probably because this society remained essentially feudal that Space never ceased to be imagined as a hierarchized federation of heterogeneous territories. Characterized by a sort of coherent diversity, it is not the same *everywhere*. Nor is it *always* the same" (1934: 60).

3 Exceptions to my claim that modern people do not think like this may be represented by the practices of traditions of ceremonial magic, such as the Golden Dawn, and in those of adherents of Wicca and other Neo-Pagan religions.

4 As Eco notes (1993 [1995]: 9–10 and *passim*), the Babel story of *Genesis* 11 contradicts the statement in *Genesis* 10 that the children of Noah "divided in their lands, every one after his tongue, after their families, in their nations." If we follow *Genesis* 10 rather than 11, linguistic diversity is both older than Babel and an apparently natural result of dispersion, not a punishment for the sin of pride. The Babel story is part of the J text, and so belongs to the oldest stratum of the Bible, while that in *Genesis* 10 is part of the later P text.

5 On Babel, the seventy-two languages, and the history of ideas about linguistic diversity, see Arno Borst's monumental construction *Der Turmbau von Babel* (1957–1963).

6 The works of Shakespeare (1564–1616), a couple of generations after Rabelais and Agrippa, show parallels to both of them. Like Agrippa, Shakespeare keeps looking for order in a world that seems out of control, offering some of the most pathetic portrayals of how the hierarchical world ought to work and what happens when it doesn't (e.g., Ulysses' speech in *Troilus and Cressida*: "Take but degree away, untune that string, and, hark, what discord follows!"). Like Rabelais, Shakespeare revels in a variety of styles and registers. To critics of the later seventeenth and eighteenth centuries, this was a sign of inferior craftsmanship, but it was taken by the Romantics as showing Shakespeare's naturalness and authenticity.

7 Such a position, that these three traditions show a direct influence of grammar on philosophical doctrines, is argued in Harvey 1996.

2   ONE REASON, ONE WORLD, MANY MONADS

1 The argument was not limited to France. In 1697, John Dryden wrote that in his translation of Virgil he "endeavour'd to make *Virgil* speak such *English*, as he wou'd himself have spoken, if he had been born in England, and in this present Age" (in Venuti 1995: 64). And the American poet Robert Lowell gave English versions of poems from other languages, trying "to do what my authors might have done if they were writing their poems now and in America" (Lowell 1961: xi). But Lowell had the grace to call these *Imitations*. On the debate, see, inter alia, Leavitt (2006b).

2 On Bacon and language, see Bauman and Briggs (2003: 20–26), Dawson (2007: 97–102), Paxman (2003: 54–7, 90–4).

3 On the universal language schemes, see Subbiondo (1992), Eco (1993 [1995]: 209–68), Dawson (2007: 104–7), Lewis (2007), Paxman (2003: 131–44).

4 On Locke on language, see Bauman and Briggs (2003, Chapter 2), Dawson (2007).

5 On Leibniz's universal language, see Eco (1993 [1995], Chapter 14), Paxman (2003: 135–44).

3   THE WORLD AT WAR WITH REASON

1 Here I give only what seem to me particularly telling points in these debates. For a more thorough treatment, see Scaglione (1972) and Ricken (1978, 1984 [1994]).

2 Quotations are from the fifth edition, 1712. I have not had access to the fourth edition; these remarks are based on Ricken 1984 (1994): 113–14.

3 Noticing parallels between Condillac's *Essai* and Leibniz's *Nouveaux essais* – which were not published until 1765, meaning that Condillac could not possibly have read them before writing his *Essai* – Jacques Derrida (1973 [1980]: 120, n. 24) asked: "Does Condillac write, without knowing it, in the margins of a book he has not read?… Will Condillac have plagiarized from Leibniz without knowing it?" While in his published work Condillac, like most of the French eighteenth century, was hostile to Leibniz, it turns out that he had anonymously written quite a sympathetic essay on monads (Condillac 1747 [1980]).

4 I presume this is the same Pierre-Joseph-Antoine Roubaud (1724 to after 1789) who is remembered as a spy for the British, then a convert to Protestantism, who spent much of his adult life seeking favors from the powerful in London and moonlighting as a literary forger.

5 References are to the second edition of Volume I, published in 1798.

4   MULTIPLICITY AND THE ROMANTIC EXPLOSION

1 Both Leibniz and Wolff showed a degree of relativism in their admiration of Chinese thought; at one point in his career, Wolff's open-mindedness got him chased out of his university chair.

2 Now Kaliningrad, a scrap of Russian territory between Lithuania and Poland.

3 In this period the word "lineaments" suggests a structure, but with artistic and erotic connotations; cf. Blake's "lineaments of Gratified Desire."

4 Herder did not use the compound *Volksgeist*, which was introduced by Hegel in 1801 (Rotenstreich 1972: 492).

5 On the construction of this text, see Morton 1989.

6 SW refers to the volume and page in Herder's *Sämmtliche Werke*, Bernard Suphan, ed., Berlin: Weidmann, 1877–1913.

7 Herder's source is the Huron grammar of the Jesuit Pierre-Joseph-Marie Chaumonot (1611–1693).

8 The post-critical Kant seems to have seen language as generally adequate for conveying ideas, and so not a subject worthy of discussion. To the extent that a particular language might influence the presentation of ideas, it should be reformed (Terezakis 2007: 132–5). On the back-and-forth between Herder and Kant, see Sikka 2007.

9 Aarsleff has claimed (e.g., 1988) that Humboldt developed his basic ideas during his years in Paris, and that they were derived from Condillac and the French *Idéologues*. This has raised cries of protest, justifiably, it seems to me, from a range of specialists (e.g., Trabant 1990a, Harden and Farrelly in Humboldt 1997).

10 GS refers to the volume and page in Humboldt's *Gesammelte Schriften*, Albert Leitzmann *et al.*, eds., Berlin: Behr, 1903–1936.

5   ESSENCES AND UNIVERSALS THROUGH THE NINETEENTH CENTURY

1 We know of this tradition primarily thanks to the efforts of Hermann Cloeren and Siegfried J. Schmidt. Unfortunately for our concerns, they are interested in these authors primarily as precursors of twentieth-century language philosophy.

2 Ivan Kalmar (1987) has presented Steinthal and Lazarus as cultural and linguistic relativists. But he does not mention the hierarchical aspects of Steinthal's linguistics.

3 On the liberal and humanistic character of nineteenth-century German anthropology, see Penny and Bunzl 2003.

4 The same claim was being made about the Bushmen in a French school manual in 1904 (Maingueneau 1979: 256).

6   BOAS AND THE LINGUISTIC MULTIVERSE

1 Bauman and Briggs (2003: 285) write that "Boas … asserted that 'primitives' do not abstract and generalize – their speech and thought focus on the concrete, on their immediate environments, rather than on philosophical speculation; primitive languages accordingly lack abstract categories (Boas 1911)." But throughout his career, and particularly in the 1911 "Introduction" here referred to, Boas asserted the opposite of this.

2 This claim had a future. In her book *Patterns of Culture*, Boas's student Ruth Benedict would cite exactly this argument, then extend it to other aspects of human culture: "It is in cultural life as it is in speech: selection is the prime necessity" (Benedict 1934: 23). And it is the same argument from phonetics that Lévi-Strauss uses to set up the *Elementary Structures of Kinship* (1949 [1969]: 93–94). Lévi-Strauss makes no mention of either Boas or Benedict here; he cites Jakobson, who for his part references Anne Grégoire's study of 1937 and says that the reduction of available sounds when learning a language is something that "all observers acknowledge with great surprise" (Jakobson 1941 [1968]: 21).

3 This is what provoked the famous statement of Roland Barthes – who cites Jakobson but not Boas – that "a speech-system is defined less by what it permits us to say than by what it compels us to say … [L]anguage … is neither reactionary, nor progressive; it is quite simply fascist; for fascism does not prevent speech, it compels speech" (Barthes 1978 [1982]: 460–1). Deutscher (2010, chapter 6) sees the recognition of the importance of grammatical categories as a "Boas-Jakobson" hypothesis, as opposed to a "Sapir-Whorf hypothesis" that your language constrains what it is possible to think. It will be evident in what follows that I read Sapir and Whorf, on the contrary, as developing implications of Boas's program.

4 Cf. Joseph (1996), which sees some strains of analytical philosophy as "immediate sources" for Sapir and Whorf, who were therefore "trapped between two very different views of the nature of linguistic influence on thought" (p. 395), namely the "metaphysical garbage" view, typical of Locke and empiricists, and the "magic key" view of Herder and Humboldt.

5 Kalmar (1987) points to some German uses in the nineteenth century and proposes that the semantic content of Boas's "cultures" reproduces that of Lazarus and of Steinthal's plural use of the term *Volksgeister*.

6 I am grateful to an anonymous reader for suggesting that much of what was new in Boas becomes intelligible through the notion of calibration.

7   LINGUISTIC RELATIVITY: SAPIR, LEE, AND WHORE

1 Ezra Pound, born the year after Sapir, would define great literature as "language charged with meaning to the highest possible degree" (Pound 1934: 36).

2 Many thanks to Kellie O'Connor Gutman and Douglas Hofstadter for their suggestions on this point.

3 On sound symbolism see Hinton, Nichols, and Ohala (1994).

4 For a more recent interpretation of Wintu evidentiality, see Schlichter (1986).

5 SAE has been criticized as an arbitrary construction, but is now looking like the recognition of what might be called a semantic *Sprachbund* (Haspelmath 2001).

6 Violating the boundaries between count and mass nouns can give phrases of the effectiveness of James Thurber's (1950) horror: "It's made of lip."

7 Compare this to Herbart's psychology, which sees already-existing material as creating a pattern that guides the assimilation of new material, or the pre-psychoanalytic Freud's project of interpreting mental functioning as the fixation of habitual associative pathways in the brain through ever-easier repetition (Freud 1895 [1954]).

8 In this compare them with Freud and his followers during the same period: bearers of what they felt was a new human science, many of them were also political activists (Danto 2005).

8 THE OTHER SIDE OF THE MIRROR: A TWENTIETH-CENTURY ESSENTIALISM

1 Waltraud Bumann (1965: 126–8) notes that Porzig and Weisgerber virtually reproduce Steinthal's wording to define the *innere Sprachform*. Neither acknowledges this; on the contrary, Porzig says that Steinthal's conception had no followers, and Weisgerber says that from Humboldt to Porzig, linguistics was so preoccupied with externals that nobody made any contributions to the idea of the inner form of speech. This seems extraordinary to Bumann, as it already did to Otto Funke, who wrote: "Porzig's 'inner form of speech' is only a recycling (*Auffrischung*) of Steinthal's definition" (in Bumann 1965: 126, n. 31). Both attribute this disappearing of Steinthal from the history of linguistics to the fact that he was Jewish.

9 THE RISE OF COGNITION AND THE REPRESSION OF LANGUAGES

1 For an early balanced rethinking of the color controversy, see Sahlins 1976.

2 Lucy (1997a: 339) is also critical of what he calls radical relativists, who take vocabulary as somehow more real than what we can know about perception.

10 THE RETURN OF THE REPRESSED

1 The limits of this book make it impossible to discuss other alternatives to the Boasian movement. But other movements did indeed seek to break the hold of the universalism/essentialism opposition. Among the tendencies that should be considered in this way are Russian formalism, with its extension into the Bakhtin school; the social psychology launched by L. S. Vygotsky; some strands of analytical philosophy and British social anthropology drawing on the work of Malinowski and culminating in the later writings of Wittgenstein (Chatterjee 1985); and American transcendentalism and pragmatism, especially Peirce's development of a general semiotics.

CONCLUSION

1 As this book went to press, I learned (Lera Boroditsky, personal communication) of the work of Alexander Guiora and his collaborators (e.g., Guiora 1983), who through the 1970s and into the 1980s carried out studies showing an influence of grammatical gender on the development of gender identity. This work went virtually uncited in discussions of language and thought. While Guiora's work is an exception to the claim made here, it looks like an exception that proves the rule.

References

Aarsleff, Hans. 1967. *The Study of Language in England, 1780–1860.* Princeton University Press.

1988. Introduction. In Wilhelm von Humboldt, *On Language.* Cambridge University Press.

Agrippa von Nettesheim, Cornelius. 1533 (1992). *De occulta philosophia libri tres.* Vittoria Perrone Compagni, ed. Leiden: Brill.

Alford, Dan Moonhawk. 1978. The Demise of the Whorf Hypothesis. *Proceedings of the Annual Meeting of the Berkeley Linguistics Society* 4: 485–99.

1981. Is Whorf's Relativity Einstein's Relativity? *Proceedings of the Annual Meeting of the Berkeley Linguistics Society* 7: 13–26.

2002. *The Great Whorf Hypothesis Hoax.* www.enformy.com/dma-Chap7.htm (last accessed 29 July 2010).

Althusser, Louis. 1973 (1976). Reply to John Lewis. Trans. Grahame Lock. In *Essays in Self-Criticism*, pp. 33–99. London: New Left Books.

Althusser, Louis, and Etienne Balibar. 1965 (1970). *Reading Capital.* Trans. Ben Brewster. London: New Left Books.

Arnauld, Antoine, and Claude Lancelot. 1660 (1830). *Grammaire générale et raisonnée.* Paris: Delalain.

Arnauld, Antoine, and Pierre Nicole. 1662 (1992). *La logique ou l'art de penser.* Paris: Gallimard.

Bachelard, Gaston. 1932 (1970). Noumène et microphysique. In *Etudes*, pp. 11–24. Paris: Vrin.

1934 (1984). *The New Scientific Spirit.* Trans. Arthur Goldhammer. Boston, MA: Beacon Press.

1938. *La formation de l'esprit scientifique: contribution à une psychanalyse de la connaissance objective.* Paris: Vrin.

1938 (1964). *The Psychoanalysis of Fire.* Trans. Alan C. M. Ross. Boston, MA: Beacon Press.

1953. *Le matérialisme rationnel.* Paris: PUF.

Bacon, Francis. 1620 (1863). The New Organon. In *Works*, VIII. Ed. and trans. James Spedding, Robert Leslie Ellis, and Douglas Heath. London: Longman.

1623 (1860). Of the Dignity and Advancement of Learning. In *Works*, IV, pp. 275–498. London: Longman.

Balibar, Renée. 1984. *Galilée, Newton lus par Einstein.* Paris: PUF.

Baril, Daniel. 2004. Langage et perception ne sont pas liés. *Forum, Université de Montréal* 39(2), September 7, 2004.

Barthes, Roland. 1978 (1982). Inaugural Lecture, Collège de France. Trans. Richard Howard. In Susan Sontag, ed., *Barthes: Selected Writings*, pp. 457–78. Oxford: Fontana.

Bashkow, Ira, Matti Bunzl, Richard Handler, Andrew Orta, and Daniel Rosenblatt. 2004. A New Boasian Anthropology: Theory for the 21st Century. *American Anthropologist* 106: 433–4.

Basilius, Harold. 1952. Neo-Humboldtian Ethnolinguistics. *Word* 8: 95–105.

Bassnett, Susan. 1980. *Translation Studies*. London: Methuen.

Bastian, Adolf. 1860. *Der Mensch in der Geschichte. Zur Begründung einer psychologischen Weltanschauung*. Leipzig: Wigand.

Bate, Bernard. 2009. *Tamil Oratory and the Dravidian Aesthetic*. New York: Columbia University Press.

Batteux, Charles. 1748. Lettres sur la phrase françoise comparée avec la phrase latine. In *Cours de belles lettres*, II. Paris: Dessaint et Saillant.

Baugh, Albert Croll, and Thomas Cable. 1978. *A History of the English Language*. Third edition. Englewood Cliffs, NJ: Prentice-Hall.

Bauman, Richard. 1973 (2001). Verbal Art as Performance. *American Anthropologist* 77: 290–311.

Bauman, Richard, and Charles L. Briggs. 2000. Language Philosophy as Language Ideology: John Locke and Johann Gottfried Herder. In Paul V. Kroskrity, ed., *Regimes of Language*, pp. 139–204. Santa Fe, NM: School of American Studies Press.

  2003. *Voices of Modernity: Language Ideologies and the Politics of Inequality*. Cambridge University Press.

Beck, David. 2000. Grammatical Convergence and the Genesis of Diversity in the Northwest Coast Sprachbund. *Anthropological Linguistics* 42(2): 1–67.

Becker, A. L. 1995. *Beyond Translation: Essays toward a Modern Philology*. Ann Arbor, MI: University of Michigan Press.

Bellay, Joachim du. 1549 (1948). *La deffence et illustration de la langue françoyse*. Paris: Marcel Didier.

Belmont, Nicole. 1986. *Paroles païennes: mythe et folklore*. Paris: Imago.

Benedict, Ruth. 1934. *Patterns of Culture*. Boston, MA: Houghton Mifflin.

Benes, Tuska. 2008. *In Babel's Shadow: Language, Philology, and the Nation in Nineteenth-Century Germany*. Detroit, MI: Wayne State University Press.

Benveniste, Emile. 1958 (1966). Catégories de pensée et catégories de langue. In *Problèmes de linguistique générale*, pp. 63–74. Paris: Gallimard.

Bergheaud, Patrice. 1990. Entwicklungen der sprachtheoretischen Reflexion im Großbrittanien des 18. Jahrhunderts. Trans. Ulrich Ricken. In Ulrich Ricken *et al.*, *Sprachtheorie und Weltanschauung in der europäischen Aufklärung*, pp. 38–65. Berlin: Akademie-Verlag.

Berlin, Brent, and Paul Kay. 1969. *Basic Color Terms: Their Universality and Evolution*. Berkeley, CA: University of California Press.

Berlin, Isaiah. 1976. *Vico and Herder*. London: Hogarth Press.

Berman, Antoine. 1985 (1992). *The Experience of the Foreign: Culture and Translation in Romantic Germany*. Trans. S. Heyvaert. Albany, NY: SUNY Press.

Black, Max. 1959 (1962). Linguistic Relativity: The Views of Benjamin Lee Whorf. In *Models and Metaphors*, pp. 244–57. Ithaca, NY: Cornell University Press.

Blackall, Eric A. 1978. *The Emergence of German as a Literary Language 1700–1775*. Second edition. Ithaca, NY: Cornell University Press.

Bloom, Alfred. 1981. *The Linguistic Shaping of Thought: A Study of the Impact of Language on Thinking in China and the West.* Hillsdale, NJ: Erlbaum.

Bloom, Paul, and Frank C. Keil. 2001. Thinking through Language. *Mind and Language* 16: 351–67.

Bloomfield, Leonard. 1933. *Language.* New York: Holt, Rinehart and Winston.

Boas, Franz. 1893. Notes on the Chinook Language. *American Anthropologist* 6: 55–63.

1895 (2002). *Indian Myths and Legends from the North Pacific Coast of America.* Trans. Dietrich Bertz. Vancouver: Talonbooks.

1910. Publicaciones nuevas sobre la lingüística americana. In *Reseña de la segunda sesión del XVII Congreso Internacional de Americanistas*: 225–32. Mexico: Museo Nacional.

1911a. Introduction. In *Handbook of American Indian Languages*, pp. 1–83. Washington, DC: Government Printing Office.

1911b. Kwakiutl. In *Handbook of American Indian Languages*, pp. 423–557. Washington, DC: Government Printing Office.

1939. An Anthropologist's Credo. In Clifton Fadiman, ed., *I Believe*, pp. 19–29. New York: Simon & Schuster.

1940. *Race, Language, and Culture.* New York: Basic Books.

1942. Language and Culture. In *Studies in the History of Culture*, pp. 178–84. Menasha, WI: George Banta.

1974. *The Shaping of American Anthropology 1883–1911: A Franz Boas Reader.* George W. Stocking, Jr., ed. New York: Basic Books.

Borges, Jorge Luis. 1942 (1984). The Analytical Language of John Wilkins. In *Borges, Other Inquisitions, 1937–1952*, trans. Ruth L. C. Simms. Austin, TX: University of Texas Press.

Boroditsky, Lera. 2001. Does Language Shape Thought? Mandarin and English Speakers' Conceptions of Time. *Cognitive Psychology* 43: 1–22.

2002. Interview with Todd Munt, Michigan Radio Ann Arbor and NPR, 20 March 2002.

2003. Linguistic Relativity. In Lynn Nadel, ed., *Encyclopedia of Cognitive Science*, pp. 917–21. London: Nature.

Boroditsky, Lera, Lauren A. Schmidt, and Webb Phillips. 2003. Sex, Syntax, and Semantics. In Dedre Gentner and Susan Goldin-Meadow, eds., *Language in Mind*, pp. 61–79. Cambridge, MA: MIT Press.

Borst, Arno. 1957–1963. *Der Turmbau von Babel. Geschichte der Meinungen über Ursprung und Vielfalt der Sprachen und Völker.* Stuttgart: Hiersemann.

1988 (1992). *Medieval Worlds.* Trans. Eric Hansen. University of Chicago Press.

Bouhours, Dominique. 1671 (1920). *Entretiens d'Ariste et d'Eugène.* Paris: Bossard. [Collection des Chefs-d'œuvre Méconnus.]

Boutroux, Emile. 1881. Notice sur la vie et la philosophie de Leibnitz. In G. W. Leibniz, *La Monadologie*, pp. 1–134. Paris: Delagrave.

Bowerman, Melissa, and Stephen C. Levinson, eds. 2001. *Language Acquisition and Conceptual Development.* Cambridge University Press.

Brandt, William J. 1966. *The Shape of Medieval History.* New Haven: Yale University Press.

Bréhier, Emile. 1938 (1993). *Histoire de la philosophie. Le XVIIIe siècle.* Paris: PUF.

Brinton, Daniel Garrison. 1890. *Essays of an Americanist*. Philadelphia, PA: Porter and Coates.

Brown, Penelope. 2006. Cognitive Anthropology. In Christine Jourdan and Kevin Tuite, eds., *Language, Culture, and Society*, pp. 96–114. Cambridge University Press.

Brown, Roger Langham. 1967. *Wilhelm von Humboldt's Conception of Linguistic Relativity*. The Hague: Mouton.

Brown, Roger, and Eric H. Lenneberg. 1954 (1970). A Study in Language and Cognition. In Roger Brown, *Psycholinguistics*, pp. 235–57. New York: Free Press.

Buffier, Claude. 1732. *Cours de sciences sur des principes nouveau & simples*. Paris: Cavelier et Giffart.

Bumann, Waltraud. 1965. *Die Sprachtheorie Heymann Steinthals*. Meisenheim am Glan: Hain.

Bunzl, Matti. 1996. Franz Boas and the Humboldtian Tradition: From *Volksgeist* and *Nationalcharakter* to an Anthropological Concept of Culture. In George W. Stocking, Jr., ed., *Volksgeist as Method and Ethic*, pp. 17–78. Madison, WI: University of Wisconsin Press.

2004. Boas, Foucault, and the "Native Anthropologist": Notes toward a Neo-Boasian Anthropology. *American Anthropologist* 106: 435–42.

Burnett, James, Lord Monboddo. 1773. *Of the Origin and Progress of Language*, I. Edinburgh: Kincaid and Creech.

Bynon, Theodora. 1966. Leo Weisgerber's Four Stages in Linguistic Analysis. *Man* n.s. 1: 468–83.

Calame-Griaule, Geneviève. 1987. *Ethnologie et langage. La parole chez les Dogon*. Paris: Gallimard.

Carruthers, Peter, and Jill Boucher, eds. 1998. *Language and Thought: Interdisciplinary Themes*. Cambridge University Press.

Carruthers, Peter, Stephen Laurence, and Stephen Stitch, eds. 2005–2007. *The Innate Mind*. 3 volumes. Oxford University Press.

Cassirer, Ernst. 1923 (1953). *The Philosophy of Symbolic Forms. I. Language*. Trans. Ralph Mannheim. New Haven, CT: Yale University Press.

1932 (1951). *The Philosophy of the Enlightenment*. Trans. Fritz C. A. Koelln and James P. Pettegrove. Princeton University Press.

Caton, Steven C. 1987. Contributions of Roman Jakobson. *Annual Review of Anthropology* 16: 223–60.

Chabrolle-Cerretini, Anne-Marie. 2007. *La vision du monde de Wilhelm von Humboldt. Histoire d'un concept linguistique*. Lyon: ENS Editions.

Chafe, Wallace, and Johanna Nichols, eds. 1986. *Evidentiality: The Linguistic Coding of Epistemology*. Norwood, NJ: Ablex.

Chakrabarty, Dinesh. 2000. *Provincializing Europe: Postcolonial Thought and Historical Difference*. Princeton University Press.

Chapman, Siobhan. 2005. Gottfried Wilhelm Leibniz. In Siobhan Chapman and Christopher Routledge, eds., *Key Thinkers in Linguistics and the Philosophy of Language*, pp. 178–81. London: Routledge.

Chatterjee, Ranjit. 1985. Reading Whorf through Wittgenstein: A Solution to the Linguistic Relativity Problem. *Lingua* 67: 37–63.

Chomsky, Noam. 1966. *Cartesian Linguistics: A Chapter in the History of Rationalist Thought*. New York: Harper & Row.

1988. *Language and Problems of Knowledge: The Managua Lectures*. Cambridge, MA: MIT Press.

Christmann, Hans Helmut. 1967. *Beiträge zur Geschichte der These vom Weltbild der Sprache*. Wiesbaden: Franz Steiner.

Cloeren, Hermann J. 1988. *Language and Thought: German Approaches to Analytic Philosophy in the 18th and 19th Centuries*. Berlin: de Gruyter.

Comrie, Bernard. 1984. Review of Ekkehart Malotki, *Hopi Time*. *Australian Journal of Linguistics* 4: 131–3.

1989. *Language Universals and Linguistic Typology*. Second edition. Oxford: Blackwell.

2001. Different Views of Language Typology. In Martin Haspelmath *et al.*, eds., *Language Typology and Language Universals*, pp. 24–39. Berlin: de Gruyter.

Condillac, Etienne Bonnot de. 1747 (1980). *Les Monades*. Laurence L. Bongie, ed. Oxford: Voltaire Foundation.

1749 (2001). *Essay on the Origin of Human Knowledge*. Trans. Hans Aarsleff. Cambridge University Press.

Conklin, Harold. 1955 (1964). Hanunóo Color Categories. In Dell Hymes, ed., *Language in Culture and Society*, pp. 189–92. New York: Harper & Row.

Constantinescu, Ilinca. 1974. John Wallis (1616–1703): A Reappraisal of His Contribution to the Study of English. *Historiographia Linguistica* 1: 297–311.

Cordemoy, Gérauld de. 1669 (1968). Traité physique de la parole. In *Œuvres philosophiques*, pp. 201–56. Paris: PUF.

Cowan, William, Michael K. Foster, and Konrad Koerner, eds. 1986. *New Perspectives in Language, Culture, and Personality*. Amsterdam: Benjamins.

Crespi, John. 1997. Wallace Stevens and Benjamin Lee Whorf: The Uncertain Business of a Poet, a Linguist, and a Jar. Paper presented at the Annual Meeting of the American Anthropological Association, Washington.

Dagognet, François. 1965. *Bachelard. Sa vie, son oeuvre*. Paris: PUF.

Danto, Elizabeth Ann. 2005. *Freud's Free Clinics: Psychoanalysis and Social Justice, 1918–1938*. New York: Columbia University Press.

Darnell, Regna. 1990. *Edward Sapir: Linguist, Anthropologist, Humanist*. Berkeley, CA: University of California Press.

1998a. *And Along Came Boas: Continuity and Revolution in Americanist Anthropology*. Amsterdam: Benjamins.

1998b. Camelot at Yale: The Construction and Dismantling of the Sapirian Synthesis, 1931–39. *American Anthropologist* 100: 361–72.

Davidson, Donald. 1974. On the Very Idea of a Conceptual Scheme. *Proceedings and Addresses of the American Philosophical Association* 47: 5–20.

Dawson, Hannah. 2007. *Locke, Language and Early-Modern Philosophy*. Cambridge University Press.

DeBernardi, Jean. 1997. Whorf in China. Paper presented at the Annual Meeting of the American Anthropological Society, Washington.

Demetracopoulou, Dorothy (= Dorothy D. Lee). 1935. Wintu Songs. *Anthropos* 30: 483–94.

Demonet, Marie-Luce. 1992. *Les Voix du signe. Nature et origine du langage à la Renaissance (1480–1580)*. Paris: Champion.

Derrida, Jacques. 1967 (1978). Structure, Sign, and Play in the Discourse of the Human Sciences. In *Writing and Difference*. Trans. Alan Bass, pp. 278–94. University of Chicago Press.

1973 (1980). *The Archeology of the Frivolous: Reading Condillac*. Trans. John P. Leavey, Jr. Pittsburgh, PA: Duquesne University Press.

Descartes, René. 1984. *The Philosophical Writings*. Trans. John Cottingham, Robert Stoothoff, and Dugald Murdoch. Cambridge University Press.

Deutscher, Guy. 2010. *Through the Language Glass: How Words Colour Your World*. London: Heinemann.

Diderot, Denis. 1916. *Early Philosophical Works*. Trans. Margaret Jourdain. Chicago, IL: Open Court.

Dinwoodie, David W. 2006. Time and the Individual. In Sergei A. Kan and Pauline Turner Strong, eds., *New Perspectives on Native North America*, pp. 327–48. Lincoln, NE: University of Nebraska Press.

Domergue, Urbain. 1785. Compte-rendu de Rivarol, *De l'universalité de la langue françoise. Journal de la Langue Françoise* 2: 886–7.

Dryhurst, James. 1971. Les premières activités de l'Académie française: Le *Discours sur le dessein de l'Académie et sur le différent génie des langues*, de Bourzeys. *Zeitschrift für französische Sprache und Literatur* 81: 225–42.

Dubois, Claude-Gilbert. 1970. *Mythe et langage au seizième siècle*. Bordeaux: Ducros.

Du Marsais, César Chesneau. 1730. *Des tropes, ou des différens sens dans lesquels on peut prendre un même mot dans une même langue*. Paris: Veuve Brocas.

Duranti, Alessandro. 2003. Language as Culture in U.S. Anthropology: Three Paradigms. *Current Anthropology* 44: 323–35.

Durkheim, Emile, and Marcel Mauss. 1902 (1963). *Primitive Classification*. Trans. Rodney Needham. London: Routledge and Kegan Paul.

Eco, Umberto. 1993 (1995). *The Search for the Perfect Language*. Trans. James Fentress. Oxford: Blackwell.

Eliot, John. 1666. *The Indian Grammar Begun; or, an Essay to Bring the Indian Language into Rules*. Cambridge, MA: Marmaduke Johnson.

Elliott, Ralph W. V. 1957. Isaac Newton's *Of an Universall Language. Modern Language Review* 52: 1–18.

Emmorey, Karen. 2002. *Language, Cognition, and the Brain: Insights from Sign Language Research*. Mahwah, NJ: Erlbaum.

Erickson, Jon, Marion Gymnich, and Ansgar Nünning. 1997. Wilhelm von Humboldt, Edward Sapir, and the Constructivist Framework. *Historiographia Linguistica* 24: 285–306.

Ervin, Susan. 1962. The Connotations of Gender. *Word* 18: 249–61.

Evans, Nicholas. 2003. Context, Culture, and Structuration in the Languages of Australia. *Annual Reviews in Anthropology* 32: 13–40.

Evans, Nicholas, and Stephen C. Levinson. 2009. The Myth of Language Universals: Language Diversity and Its Importance for Cognitive Science. *Behavioral and Brain Sciences* 32: 429–48.

Everett, Daniel L. 2005. Cultural Constraints on Grammar and Cognition in Pirahã: Another Look at the Design Features of Human Language. *Current Anthropology* 46: 621–34.

Fabian, Johannes. 1971. Language, History and Anthropology. *Philosophy of the Social Sciences* 1: 19–47.

Farrar, Frederick William. 1865. *Chapters on Language*. London: Longmans, Green.

Faust, Manfred. 1981. Schottelius' Concept of Word Formation. In Jürgen Trabant, ed., *Logos Semantikos*, I, pp. 359–70. Madrid: Gredos.

Fénelon, François de la Mothe. 1716. *Réflexions sur la grammaire, la rhétorique, la poétique et l'histoire*. Paris: Coignard.

Fernandez, James W., ed. 1991. *Beyond Metaphor: The Play of Tropes in Culture*. Stanford University Press.

2006. La tropología y la figuración del pensamiento y de la acción social. *Revista de Antropología Social* 15.

Feuer, Lewis S. 1953. Sociological Aspects of the Relation between Language and Philosophy. *Philosophy of Science* 20: 85–93.

Fichant, Michel. 1973. L'épistemologie en France. In François Chatelet, ed., *Histoire de la Philosophie*, VIII, pp. 135–78. Paris: Hachette.

Firth, J. R. 1937. *The Tongues of Men*. London: Watts.

Fodor, Jerry A. 1985. Précis of The Modularity of Mind. *Behavioral and Brain Sciences* 8(1–42): 1–5.

Foley, William A. 1997. *Anthropological Linguistics*. Oxford: Blackwell.

2005. Do Humans Have Innate Mental Structures? Some Arguments from Linguistics. In Susan McKinnon and Sydel Silverman, eds., *Complexities: Beyond Nature and Nurture*, pp. 43–63. University of Chicago Press.

Formigari, Lia. 2003. Herder entre universalisme et relativité. Trans. Mathilde Anquetil. *Revue germanique internationale* 20: 133–43.

Fornel, Michel de. 2002. Le destin d'un argument. Le relativisme linguistique de Sapir–Whorf. In Michel de Fornel and Jean-Claude Passeron, eds., *L'argumentation*, pp. 121–47. Paris: EHESS.

Forster, Michael N. 2002. Herder's Philosophy of Language, Interpretation, and Translation: Three Fundamental Principles. *Review of Metaphysics* 56: 323–56.

2007. Johann Gottfried von Herder. Revised version. In Edward N. Zalta, ed., *Stanford Encyclopedia of Philosophy*. http://plato.stanford.edu/ /entries/herder/.

Foucault, Michel. 1966 (1970). *The Order of Things: An Archaeology of the Human Sciences*. London: Tavistock.

1969. Introduction. In Antoine Arnauld and Claude Lancelot, *Grammaire générale et raisonnée*, pp. iii–xxvii. Paris: Republications Paulet.

Freud, Sigmund. 1895 (1953). Project for a Scientific Psychology. Trans. James Strachey. In *Complete Psychological Works*, I, pp. 281–391. London: Hogarth Press.

Friedrich, Paul. 1979. Poetic Language and the Imagination: A Reformulation of the Sapir Hypothesis. In *Language, Context, and the Imagination*, pp. 441–517. Stanford University Press.

1985. Review of Paul Hopper, ed., *Tense-Aspect: Between Semantics and Pragmatics*. *Language* 61: 182–7.

1986. *The Language Parallax: Linguistic Relativism and Poetic Indeterminacy*. Austin, TX: University of Texas Press.

1989. Language, Ideology, and Political Economy. *American Anthropologist* 91: 295–312.

1996. The Culture in Poetry and the Poetry in Culture. In E. Valentine Daniel and Jeffrey M. Peck, eds., *Culture/Contexture*, pp. 37–58. Berkeley, CA: University of California Press.

2006. Maximizing Ethnopoetics. In Christine Jourdan and Kevin Tuite, eds., *Language, Culture, and Society*, pp. 207–28. Cambridge University Press.

Gadet, Françoise. 1990. *Saussure. Une science de la langue*. Second edition. Paris: PUF.

Garat, Dominique-Joseph. 1785. Compte-rendu de Rivarol, *De l'universalité de la langue française. Mercure de France* 33(13): 10–34, 63–73.

Gelli, Giovan Battista. 1551 (1976). I caprici del Bottaio. In Delmo Maestri, ed., *Gelli, Opere*, third edition, pp. 125–288. Turin: Unione Tipografico-Editrice Torinese.

Gensini, Stefano. 1990. "Vulgaris opinio babelica." Sui fondamenti storico-teorico della pluralità delle lingue nel pensiero di Leibniz. In Tullio De Mauro and Lisa Formigari, eds., *Leibniz, Humboldt, and the Origins of Comparativism*, pp. 61–83. Amsterdam: Benjamins.

Gilbert, Aubrey L., Terry Regier, Paul Kay, and Richard B. Ivry. 2006. Whorf Hypothesis Is Supported in the Right Visual Field but Not the Left. *Proceedings of the National Academy of Sciences* 103: 489–94.

Gipper, Helmut. 1956. Muttersprachliches und wissenschaftliches Weltbild. *Sprachforum* 2: 1–10.

1963. *Bausteine zur Sprachinhaltforschung*. Düsseldorf: Schwann.

1972. *Gibt es ein sprachliches Relativitätsprinzip? Untersuchungen zur Sapir–Whorf-Hypothese*. Frankfurt am Main: Fischer.

1987. *Das Sprachapriori*. Strassburg: Frommann-Holzboog.

1994. Wie Humboldts Sprachauffassung Korrekturen an B.L. Whorfs provozierenden Aussagen über die Hopi-Sprache erleichtert hat. In Klaus Zimmermann, *et al.*, eds., *Wilhelm von Humboldt und die amerikanischen Sprachen*, pp. 281–93. Paderborn: Schöningh.

Gleason, H. A., Jr. 1961. *An Introduction to Descriptive Linguistics*. Revised edition. New York: Holt, Rinehart and Winston.

Gopnik, Alison. 2001. Theories of Language and Culture: Whorf without Wincing. In Melissa Bowerman and Stephen C. Levinson, eds., *Language Acquisition and Conceptual Development*, pp. 45–69. Cambridge University Press.

Gordon, Peter. 2004. Numerical Cognition without Words: Evidence from Amazonia. *Science* 306: 496–9.

Gould, Stephen Jay. 1990. *Time's Arrow, Time's Cycle*. Cambridge, MA: Harvard University Press.

Granet, Marcel. 1934. *La pensée chinoise*. Paris: Renaissance du Livre.

Griaule, Marcel. 1948 (1965). *Conversations with Ogotemmêli: An Introduction to Dogon Religious Ideas*. London: Oxford University Press.

Gruppe, Otto Friedrich. 1831 (1914). *Antäus: Ein Briefwechsel über speculative Philosophie in ihrem Conflict mit Wissenschaft und Sprache*. Fritz Mauthner, ed. Munich: Georg Müller.

1834. *Wendepunkt der Philosophie im neunzehnten Jahrhundert*. Berlin: Reimer.

1859. *Deutsche Übersetzerkunst*. Hanover: Rümpler.

Guiora, Alexander Z. 1983. Language and Concept Formation: A Cross-Lingual Analysis. *Behavior Science Research* 18: 228–54.

Gumperz, John J., and Stephen C. Levinson, eds. 1996. *Rethinking Linguistic Relativity*. Cambridge University Press.

Güntert, Hermann. 1938. Neue Zeit – neues Ziel. *Wörter und Sachen* n.s. 1: 1–11.

Hagège, Claude. 1986. *L'homme de paroles*. Second edition. Paris: Fayard.

Hale, Horatio. 1884. On Some Doubtful or Intermediate Articulations. An Experiment in Phonetics. *Journal of the Royal Anthropological Institute* 14: 233–43.

Hall, Alfred J. 1889. *A Grammar of the Kwagiutl Language*. Montreal: Dawson Bros.

Hamann, Johann Georg. 2007. *Writings on Philosophy and Language*. Ed. and trans. Kenneth Haynes. Cambridge University Press.

Hanks, William F. 1996. *Language and Communicative Practices*. Boulder, CO: Westview.

Hanzeli, Victor Egon. 1969. *Missionary Linguistics in New France*. The Hague: Mouton.

Haroche, Claudine, and Dominique Maingueneau. 1985. Du mythique au problématique: la "clarté" de la langue française. In Sylvain Auroux *et al.*, eds., *La linguistique fantastique*, pp. 347–57. Paris: Joseph Clims et Denoël.

Harris, James. 1751. *Hermes: or, A Philosophical Enquiry Concerning Language and Universal Grammar*. London: Woodfall.

Harris, Marvin. 1968. *The Rise of Anthropological Theory*. New York: Crowell.

Harvey, William. 1996. Linguistic Relativity in French, English, and German Philosophy. *Philosophy Today* 40: 273–88.

Haspelmath, Martin. 2001. The European Linguistic Area: Standard Average European. In Martin Haspelmath *et al.*, eds., *Language Typology and Language Universals*, pp. 1492–510. Berlin: de Gruyter.

    2007. Pre-Established Categories Don't Exist: Consequences for Language Description and Typology. *Linguistic Typology* 11: 119–32.

Haspelmath, Martin, Ekkehard König, Wulf Oesterreicher, and Wolfgang Raible, eds. 2001. *Language Typology and Language Universals: An International Handbook*. Berlin: de Gruyter.

Haugen, Einar. 1987. *Blessings of Babel*. Berlin: Mouton de Gruyter.

Haviland, John. 1998. Guugu Yimithirr Cardinal Directions. *Ethos* 26: 25–47.

Heider, Eleanor Rosch (= Eleanor Rosch). 1972. Universals in Color Naming and Memory. *Journal of Experimental Psychology* 93: 10–20.

Henderson, John. 2007. *The Medieval World of Isidore of Seville: Truth from Words*. Cambridge University Press.

Henson, Hilary. 1974. *British Social Anthropologists and Language: A History of Separate Development*. Oxford University Press.

Herder, Johann Gottfried. 1783 (1833). *On the Spirit of Hebrew Poetry*. Trans. James March. Burlington, VT: Edward Smith.

    1992. *Selected Early Works, 1764–1767*. Ernest A. Menze and Karl Menges, eds., trans. Ernest A. Menze and Michael Palma. Pennsylvania State University Press.

    2002. *Philosophical Writings*. Ed. and trans. Michael N. Forster. Cambridge University Press.

Hermann, Conrad. 1858. *Philosophische Grammatik*. Leipzig: Fleischer.

Heynick, Frank. 1983. From Einstein to Whorf: Space, Time, Matter, and Reference Frames in Physical and Linguistic Relativity. *Semiotica* 45(1–2): 35–64.

Hill, Jane H., and Bruce Mannheim. 1992. Language and World View. *Annual Review of Anthropology* 21: 381–406.

Hinton, Leanne, Johanna Nichols, and John J. Ohala, eds. 1994. *Sound Symbolism*. Cambridge University Press.

Hobson, Marion. 1976. La *Letter sur les sourds et muets* de Diderot: labyrinthe et langage. *Semiotica* 16: 291–327.

Hockett, Charles F. 1966. The Problem of Universals in Language. In Joseph H. Greenberg, ed., *Universals of Language*, pp. 1–29. Cambridge, MA: MIT Press.

Hoijer, Harry. 1954. The Sapir–Whorf Hypothesis. In Harry Hoijer, ed., *Language in Culture*, pp. 92–105. University of Chicago Press.

Holden, Constance. 2004. Life without Numbers in the Amazon. *Science* 305: 1093.

Horguelin, Paul. 1981. *Anthologie de la manière de traduire. Domaine français*. Montreal: Linguatech.

Horne Tooke, John. 1798. *Epea pteroenta, or, The Diversions of Purley*, Second Edition, Part I. London: J. Johnson.

House, Juliane. 2000. Linguistic Relativity and Translation. In Martin Pütz and Marjolijn H. Verspoor, eds., *Explorations in Linguistic Relativity*, pp. 69–88. Amsterdam: Benjamins.

Hüllen, Werner. 2001. Reflections on Language in the Renaissance. In Martin Haspelmath *et al.*, eds., *Language Typology and Language Universals*, pp. 210–21. Berlin: de Gruyter.

Humboldt, Wilhelm von. 1836 (1999). *On Language: The Diversity of Human Language-Structure and Its Influence on the Development of Mankind*. Trans. Peter Heath. Cambridge University Press.

1997. *Essays on Language*. Theo Harden and Dan Farrelly, eds., trans. John Wieczorek and Ian Roe. Frankfurt: Peter Lang.

2000. *Sur le caractère national des langues*. Ed. and trans. Denis Thouard. Paris: Seuil.

Hutton, Christopher M. 1999. *Linguistics and the Third Reich*. London: Routledge.

2005. *Race and the Third Reich*. Cambridge: Polity.

Hymes, Dell. 1961. On Typology of Cognitive Styles in Language. *Anthropological Linguistics* 3(1): 22–54.

1966. Two Types of Linguistic Relativity. In William Bright, ed., *Sociolinguistics*, pp. 131–56. The Hague: Mouton.

1974. *Foundations in Sociolinguistics*. University of Pennsylvania Press.

Hymes, Dell, and John Fought. 1981. *American Structuralism*. The Hague: Mouton.

Ildefonse, Frédérique, and Jean Lallot, eds. 2002. *Aristote. Catégories*. Paris: Seuil.

Isermann, Michael. 1996. John Wallis on Adjectives: The Discovery of Phrase Structure in the *Grammatica Linguae Anglicanae* (1653). *Historiographia Linguistica* 23: 47–72.

Isidore of Seville. 615 (1960). *Isidore de Séville: Traité de la nature*. Ed. and trans. Jacques Fontaine. Bordeaux: Féret.

636 (2006). *The Etymologies*. Ed. and trans. Stephen J. Barney *et al.* Cambridge University Press.

Jakobson, Roman. 1941 (1968). *Child Language, Aphasia, and Phonological Universals*. Trans. Allan R. Keiler. The Hague: Mouton.

1960. Linguistics and Poetics. In Thomas E. Sebeok, ed., *Style in Language*, pp. 350–77. Cambridge, MA: MIT Press.

1971. *Selected Writings*, II. The Hague: Mouton.

1985. *Selected Writings*, VII. Berlin: Mouton.

Jakobson, Roman, and Morris Halle. 1956. *Fundamentals of Language*. The Hague: Mouton.

Joos, Martin, ed. 1966. *Readings in Linguistics*, I. University of Chicago Press.

Joseph, John E. 1996. The Immediate Sources of the "Sapir–Whorf Hypothesis." *Historiographia Linguistica* 23: 365–404.

Kalmar, Ivan. 1987. The *Völkerpsychologie* of Lazarus and Steinthal and the Modern Concept of Culture. *Journal of the History of Ideas* 48: 671–90.

Kenneally, Christine. 2007. *The First Word: The Search for the Origins of Language*. New York: Penguin.

Knobloch, Clemens. 2000. Begriffspolitik und Wissenschaftsrhetorik bei Leo Weisgerber. In Klaus Dieter Dutz, ed., *Interpretation und Re-Interpretation*, pp. 145–74. Münster: Nodus.

Koerner, E. F. Konrad. 1976. 1876 as a Turning-Point in the History of Linguistics. *Journal of Indo-European Studies* 4: 333–53.

1977. The Humboldtian Trend in Linguistics. In Paul J. Hopper, ed., *Studies in Descriptive and Historical Linguistics*, pp. 145–58. Amsterdam: Benjamins.

Kohrt, Manfred. 1984. *Phonetik, Phonologie und die "Relativität der Verhältnisse."* Stuttgart: Franz Steiner.

Konishi, Toshi. 1993. The Semantics of Grammatical Gender: A Cross-Cultural Study. *Journal of Psycholinguistic Research* 22: 519–34.

Koyré, Alexandre. 1942. *Entretiens sur Descartes*. New York: Brentano's.

Krausz, Michael. 2009. Mapping Relativisms. Paper presented at A Transcultural Exploration of Ethics: A Dialogue between Western and Indian Traditions, Carleton University, Ottawa, June 2009.

Kroeber, Alfred. 1943. Franz Boas: The Man. In *Franz Boas, 1858–1942*, pp. 5–27. Menasha, WI: American Anthropological Association.

Kroskrity, Paul V., ed. 2000. *Regimes of Language: Ideologies, Polities, and Identities*. Santa Fe, NM: School of American Studies Press.

Krulwich, Robert. 2009. Shakespeare Had Roses All Wrong. Krulwich on Science, National Public Radio, 6 April 2009. www.npr.org/templates/story/story.php?storyId=102518565.

Ladborough, R. W. 1938. Translation from the Ancients in Seventeenth-Century France. *Journal of the Warburg Institute* 2(2): 85–104.

Lafitau, Joseph-François. 1724. *Mœurs des sauvages amériquains, comparées aux mœurs des premiers temps*. Paris: Saugrain et Hochereau.

Lakoff, George. 1987. *Women, Fire, and Dangerous Things: What Categories Reveal about the Mind*. University of Chicago Press.

Lakoff, George, and Mark Johnson. 1981. *Metaphors We Live By*. University of Chicago Press.

Lamy, Bernard. 1676. *De l'art de parler*. Paris: André Pralard.

1712. *La Rhétorique, ou L'art de parler*. Fifth edition. Amsterdam: Veuve Marret.

Lauzon, Matthew. 1996. Savage Eloquence in America and the Linguistic Construction of a British Identity in the 18th Century. *Historiographia Linguistica* 23: 123–58.

2008. Welsh Indians and Savage Scots: History, Antiquarianism, and Indian Languages in 18th-Century Britain. *History of European Ideas* 34: 250–69.

Leavitt, John. 1991a. The Shapes of Modernity: Philosophical Foundations of Anthropological Doctrines. *Culture* 11(1–2): 29–42.

1991b. Review of Wallace Chafe and Johanna Nichols, eds., *Evidentiality: The Linguistic Coding of Epistemology*. *Language* 67: 133–41.

1996. Meaning and Feeling in the Anthropology of Emotions. *American Ethnologist* 23: 514–39.

2001. Prophecy. In Alessandro Duranti, ed., *Key Terms in Language and Culture*, pp. 197–200. Oxford: Blackwell.

2006a. Linguistic Relativities. In Christine Jourdan and Kevin Tuite, eds., *Language, Culture, and Society*, pp. 47–81. Cambridge University Press.

2006b. Thick Translation: Three Soundings. In Catherine O'Neil, Mary Scoggin, and Kevin Tuite, eds., *Language, Culture, and the Individual*, pp. 79–108. Munich: LINCOM.

2010. L'ethnopoétique: histoire d'une frontière interdisciplinaire. In Claude Calame, Florence Dupont, et al., eds., *La voix actée. Pour une nouvelle ethnopoétique*, pp. 125–42. Paris: Kimé.

Lee, Dorothy D. (= Dorothy Demetracopoulou). 1938. Conceptual Implications of an Indian Language. *Philosophy of Science* 5: 89–102.

1944. Linguistic Reflection of Wintu Thought. *International Journal of American Linguistics* 10: 181–7.

Lee, Penny. 1991. Whorf's Hopi Tensors: Subtle Articulators in the Language/Thought Nexus? *Cognitive Linguistics* 2: 123–47.

1996. *The Whorf Theory Complex*. Amsterdam: Benjamins.

Lefevere, André, ed. 1992. *Translation/History/Culture: A Sourcebook*. London: Routledge.

Leibniz, Gottfried Wilhelm. 1677 (1951). Dialogue on the Connection between Things and Words. In Philip P. Wiener, ed., *Leibniz Selections*, pp. 5–11. New York: Scribner.

1695 (1989). Dialogue on Human Freedom and the Origin of Evil. In Leibniz, *Philosophical Works*, second edition, pp. 111–7. Indianapolis, IN: Hackett.

1705 (1996). *New Essays on Human Understanding*. Trans. Peter Remnant and Jonathan Bennett. Cambridge University Press.

1903. *Opuscules et fragments inédits*. Paris: Alcan.

1998. *Philosophical Texts*. Trans. Richard Francks and R. S. Woolhouse. Oxford University Press.

2000. *L'harmonie des langues*. Trans. Marc Crépon. Paris: Seuil.

Le Laboureur, Louis. 1669. *Avantages de la langue françoise sur la langue latine*. Paris: Guillaume de Luyne.

Lenneberg, Eric H. 1953. Cognition in Ethnolinguistics. *Language* 29: 463–71.

Levi, Anthony. 2000. Belles infidèles. In Olive Classe, ed., *Encyclopedia of Literary Translation into English*, I, pp. 126–7. London: Fitzroy Dearborn.

Levinson, Stephen C. 1996. Language and Space. *Annual Review of Anthropology* 25: 353–82.

2003. *Space in Language and Cognition: Explorations in Cognitive Diversity*. Cambridge University Press.

Levinson, Stephen C., Sotaro Kita, *et al.* 2002. Returning the Tables: Language Affects Spatial Reasoning. *Cognition* 84: 155–88.

Levinson, Stephen C., and David P. Wilkins. 2006. *Grammars of Space: Explorations in Cognitive Diversity*. Cambridge University Press.

Lévi-Strauss, Claude. 1949 (1969). *The Elementary Structures of Kinship*. Revised edition. Trans. James Harle Bell *et al.* London: Eyre and Spottiswoode.

1962. *La pensée sauvage*. Paris: Plon.

Lewis, Rhodri. 2007. *Language, Mind and Nature*. Cambridge University Press.

Li, Peggy, and Lila Gleitman. 2002. Turning the Tables: Language and Spatial Reasoning. *Cognition* 83: 265–94.

Liss, Julia E. 1996. German Culture and German Science in the *Bildung* of Franz Boas. In George W. Stocking, Jr., ed., *Volksgeist as Method and Ethic*, pp. 155–84. Madison, WI: University of Wisconsin Press.

Locke, John. 1700 (1975). *An Essay Concerning Human Understanding*. Fourth edition. Oxford University Press.

Lowell, Robert. 1961. *Imitations*. New York: Farrar, Straus and Cudahy.

Lucy, John A. 1992a. *Language Diversity and Thought: A Reformulation of the Linguistic Relativity Hypothesis*. Cambridge University Press.

　1992b. *Grammatical Categories and Cognition: A Case Study of the Linguistic Relativity Hypothesis*. Cambridge University Press.

　1997a. The Linguistics of "Color." In C. L. Hardin and Luissa Maffi, eds., *Color Categories in Thought and Language*, pp. 320–46. Cambridge University Press.

　1997b. Linguistic Relativity. *Annual Review of Anthropology* 26: 291–312.

　2003. Semantic Accent and Linguistic Relativity. Paper presented at the Conference on Cross-Linguistic Data and Theories of Meaning, Max Planck Institute, Nijmegen, the Netherlands.

Lyons, John. 1968. *Introduction to Theoretical Linguistics*. Cambridge University Press.

Mackert, Michael. 1993. The Roots of Franz Boas' View of Linguistic Categories as a Window to the Human Mind. *Historiographia Linguistica* 20: 331–51.

　1994. Franz Boas' Theory of Phonetics. *Historiographia Linguistica* 21: 351–86.

MacLaury, Robert E. 2001. Color Terms. In Martin Haspelmath et al., eds., *Language Typology and Linguistic Universals*, II, pp. 1227–51. Berlin: de Gruyter.

Maingueneau, Dominique. 1979. *Les livres d'école de la République 1870–194 (discours et idéologie)*. Paris: Le Sycomore.

Malkiel, Yakov. 1974. A Herder–Humboldt–Sapir–Whorf Hypothesis? *Romance Philology* 28: 199.

Malotki, Ekkehart. 1979. *Hopi-Raum*. Tübingen: Narr.

　1983. *Hopi Time: A Linguistic Analysis of the Temporal Concepts in the Hopi Language*. Berlin: Mouton.

Marrache-Gouraud, Myriam. 2003. *"Hors toute intimidation." Panurge ou la parole singulière*. Geneva: Droz.

Martin, Laura. 1986. Eskimo Words for Snow: A Case Study in the Genesis and Decay of an Anthropological Example. *American Anthropologist* 88: 418–23.

Marx, Karl. 1857 (1973). *The Grundrisse*. Trans. Martin Nicolaus. Harmondsworth: Penguin.

　1867 (1967). *Capital: A Critique of Political Economy*. Trans. I. Samuel Moore and Edward Aveling. New York: International Publishers.

Matthews, Washington. 1877. *Ethnography and Philology of the Hidatsa Indians*. Washington, DC: Government Printing Office.

McLelland, Nicola. 2001. Albertus (1573) and Ölinger (1574): Creating the First Grammars of German. *Historiographia Linguistica* 28: 2–38.

McNamara, John. 1970. Bilingualism and Thought. In James E. Alatis, ed., *Bilingualism and Language Contact*, pp. 25–40. Washington, DC: Georgetown University Press.

McRae, Robert. 1988. Locke and Leibniz on Linguistic Particles. *Synthese* 75: 155–61.

Meigret, Louis. 1550 (1880). *Tretté de la grammere françoèze*. Wendelin Foerster, ed. Heilbron: Henninger.

Mertz, Elizabeth, and Richard J. Parmentier, eds. 1985. *Semiotic Mediation*. New York: Academic Press.

Miller, Robert L. 1968. *The Linguistic Relativity Principle and Humboldtian Ethnolinguistics*. The Hague: Mouton.

Miner, Kenneth L. 1974. John Eliot of Massachusetts and the Beginnings of American Linguistics. *Historiographia Linguistica* 1: 169–83.

Montag, Warren. 1994. *The Unthinkable Swift: The Spontaneous Philosophy of a Church of England Man*. London: Verso.

2000. *Bodies, Masses, Power: Spinoza and His Contemporaries*. London: Verso.

Morgan, Lewis Henry. 1877. *Ancient Society*. Chicago, IL: C. H. Kerr.

Morton, Michael. 1989. *Herder and the Poetics of Thought*. Pennsylvania State University Press.

Müller, Friedrich Max. 1887a. *Three Introductory Lectures on the Science of Thought*. London: Kegan Paul.

1887b. *The Science of Thought*. London: Longmans, Green.

Newton, Isaac. 1687 (1934). *Philosophiae naturalis principia mathematica*. Trans. Andrew Motte. Berkeley, CA: University of California Press.

Niemeier, Susanne, and René Dirven, eds. 2000. *Evidence for Linguistic Relativity*. Amsterdam: Benjamins.

O'Brien, Flann. 1977. *The Hair of the Dogma*. London: Hart-Davis, McGibbon.

Obrist, Barbara. 1997. Wind Diagrams and Medieval Cosmology. *Speculum* 72: 33–84.

Öhman, Suzanne. 1953. Theories of the "Linguistic Field." *Word* 9: 123–34.

Olender, Maurice. 1989 (1992). *The Languages of Paradise*. Trans. Maurice Olender and Arthur Goldhammer. Cambridge, MA: Harvard University Press.

Olin, Dirk. 2003. Crash Course; Color Cognition. *New York Times Magazine*, 30 November 2003, Section 6, p. 55.

O'Neil, Catherine, Mary Scoggin, and Kevin Tuite, eds. 2006. *Language, Culture, and the Individual: A Tribute to Paul Friedrich*. Munich: LINCOM.

Padley, G. A. 1976. *Grammatical Theory in Western Europe, 1500–1700: The Latin Tradition*. Cambridge University Press.

Palmer, F.R. 1976. *Semantics: A New Outline*. Cambridge University Press.

Parmentier, Richard J. 1985. Semiotic Mediation: Ancestral Genealogy and Final Interpretant. In Elizabeth Mertz and Richard J. Parmentier, eds., *Semiotic Mediation*, pp. 359–85. New York: Academic Press.

Paxman, David B. 2003. *Voyage into Language: Space and the Linguistic Encounter, 1500–1800*. Aldershot: Ashgate.

Payne, Edward John. 1899. *History of the New World Called America*, II. Oxford University Press.

Penn, Julia M. 1972. *Linguistic Relativity versus Innate Ideas: The Origins of the Sapir–Whorf Hypothesis in German Thought*. The Hague: Mouton.

Penny, H. Glenn, and Matti Bunzl, eds. 2003. *Worldly Provincialism: German Anthropology in the Age of Empire*. Ann Arbor: University of Michigan Press.

Percival, W. Keith. 1975. The Grammatical Tradition and the Rise of the Vernaculars. In Thomas A. Sebeok, ed., *Current Trends in Linguistics*, XIII, pp. 231–75. The Hague: Mouton.

Pinker, Steven. 1990. Language Acquisition. In Daniel N. Osherson and Howard Lasnik, eds., *An Invitation to Cognitive Science*, I. Language, pp. 199–242. Cambridge, MA: MIT Press.

1994. *The Language Instinct*. New York: William Morrow.

1997. *How the Mind Works*. New York: Norton.

2007. *The Stuff of Thought: Language as a Window into Human Nature*. New York: Viking.

Porzig, Walter. 1923. Der Begriff der inneren Sprachform. *Indogermanische Forschungen* 41: 150–69.

Pound, Ezra. 1934. *ABC of Reading*. London: Routledge.

Powell, John Wesley. 1880. *Introduction to the Study of Indian Languages*. Second edition. Washington, DC: Government Printing Office.

Pullum, Geoffrey. 1989 (1991). The Great Eskimo Vocabulary Hoax. In *The Great Eskimo Vocabulary Hoax and Other Irreverent Essays on the Study of Language*, pp. 159–71. University of Chicago Press.

Rabelais, François. 2006. *Gargantua and Pantagruel*. Trans. M. A. Screech. London: Penguin.

Ramanujan, A. K. 1985. *Poems of Love and War*. New York: Columbia University Press.

1989. Is There an Indian Way of Thinking? *Contributions to Indian Sociology* 23: 41–58.

Ray, Verne F. Techniques and Problems in the Study of Human Color Perception. *Southwestern Journal of Anthropology* 8: 251–9.

Reines, Maria Francisca, and Jesse Prinz. 2009. Reviving Whorf: The Return of Linguistic Relativity. *Philosophy Compass* 4: 1022–32.

Ricken, Ulrich. 1978. *Grammaire et philosophie au siècle des Lumières*. Villeneuve d'Ascq: Université de Lille III.

1984 (1994). *Linguistics, Anthropology and Philosophy in the French Enlightenment*. Trans. Robert E. Norton. London: Routledge.

1990. Sprachtheoretische Positionen une Entwicklungen in der deutschen Aufklärung. In Ulrich Ricken *et al.*, *Sprachtheorie und Weltanschauung in der europäischen Aufklärung*, pp. 210–73. Berlin: Akademie-Verlag.

Ridington, Robin. 2006. *When You Sing It Now, Just Like New*. Lincoln, NE: University of Nebraska Press.

Rivarol, Antoine de. 1784. *De l'universalité de la langue française*. Berlin: Académie Royale.

Roberson, Debi, and J. Richard Hanley. 2009. Relatively Speaking: An Account of the Relationship between Language and Thought in the Color Domain. *Glimpse* 2(3): 68–77.

Römer, Ruth. 1985. *Sprachwissenschaft und Rassenideologie in Deutschland*. Munich: Wilhelm Fink.

Rosch, Eleanor (= Eleanor Rosch Heider). 1974. Linguistic Relativity. In Albert Silverstein, ed., *Human Communication: Theoretical Explorations*, pp. 96–121. Hillsdale, NJ: Erlbaum.

Rotenstreich, Nathan. 1972. Volksgeist. In Philip P. Wiener, ed., *Dictionary of the History of Ideas*, IV, pp. 490–6. New York: Scribner's.

Roth Pierpont, Claudia. 2004. The Measure of America: How a Rebel Anthropologist Waged War on Racism. *The New Yorker*, 8 March 2004, pp. 48–63.

Runze, Georg. 1889. *Sprache und Religion*. Berlin: R. Gaertner.

Sachs, Aaron. 2006. *The Humboldt Current*. New York: Viking.

Sahlins, Marshall. 1976. Colors and Cultures. *Semiotica* 16: 1–22.

1977. *Culture and Practical Reason*. University of Chicago Press.

Salus, Peter H. 1976. Universal Grammar 1000–1850. In Herman Parret, ed., *History of Linguistic Thought and Contemporary Linguistics*, pp. 85–101. Berlin: de Gruyter.

Sapir, Edward. 1907. Herder's *Ursprung der Sprache*. *Modern Philology* 5: 109–142.

1921. *Language: An Introduction to the Study of Speech*. New York: Harcourt, Brace & World.

1931 (1964). Conceptual Categories in Primitive Languages. In Dell Hymes, ed., *Language in Culture and Society*, p. 128. New York: Harper & Row.

1949. *Selected Writings in Language, Culture and Personality*. David G. Mandelbaum, ed. Berkeley, CA: University of California Press.

Saussure, Ferdinand de. 1916 (1972). *Cours de linguistique générale*. Charles Bally and Albert Sechehaye, eds. Paris: Payot.

Scaglione, Aldo D. 1972. *The Classical Theory of Composition, from Its Origins to the Present: A Historical Survey*. Chapel Hill, NC: University of North Carolina Press.

Schaff, Adam. 1964 (1973). *Language and Cognition*. Trans. Olgierd Wojtasiewicz. New York: McGraw-Hill.

Schieffellin, Bambi, Kathryn A. Woolard, and Paul V. Kroskrity, eds. 1998. *Language Ideologies: Practice and Theory*. New York: Oxford University Press.

Schlegel, August Wilhelm von. 1818. *Observations sur la langue et la littérature provençales*. Paris: Librairie Grecque-Latine-Allemande.

Schlegel, Friedrich von. 1808. *Über die Sprache und Weisheit der Indier*. Heidelberg: Mohr und Zimmer.

Schleiermacher, Friedrich. 1813 (1973). Über die verschiedenen Methoden des Übersetzens. In Hans Joachim Störig, ed., *Das Problem des Übersetzens*, pp. 38–70. Darmstadt: Wissenschaftliche Buchgesellschaft.

Schlesinger, I.M. 1991. The Wax and Wane of Whorfian Views. In Robert L. Cooper and Bernard Spolsky, eds., *The Influence of Language on Culture and Thought*, pp. 7–44. Berlin: Mouton de Gruyter.

Schlichter, Alice. 1986. The Origins and Deictic Nature of Wintu Evidentials. In Wallace Chafe and Johanna Nichols, eds., *Evidentiality: The Linguistic Coding of Epistemology*, pp. 46–59. Norwood, NJ: Ablex.

Schmidt-Rohr, Georg. 1932. *Die Sprache als Bildnerin der Völker. Eine Wesens- und Lebenskunde der Volkstümer*. Jena: Eugen Diederich.

1933. *Mutter Sprache: vom Amt der Sprachen bei der Volkwerdung*. Jena: Eugen Diederich.

Schottelius, Justus Georg. 1663. *Ausführliche Arbeit von der Teutschen Haubt Sprache*. Brunswick: Zilliger.

Schulenburg, Sigrid von der. 1973. *Leibniz als Sprachforscher*. Frankfurt: Vittorio Klostermann.

Schultz, Emily A. 1990. *Dialogue at the Margins: Whorf, Bakhtin, and Linguistic Relativity*. Madison, WI: University of Wisconsin Press.

Sdun, Winfried. 1967. *Probleme und Theorien des Übersetzens in Deutschland*. Munich: Hueber.

Seiffert, Leslie. 1968. Neo-Humboldtian Semantics in Perspective: "Sprache und Gemeinschaft." *Journal of Linguistics* 4: 93–108.

Sera, Maria D., Christian A.H. Berge, and Javier del Castillo Pintado. 1994. Grammatical and Conceptual Forces in the Attribution of Gender by English and Spanish Speakers. *Cognitive Development* 9: 261–92.

Sherzer, Joel. 1983. *Kuna Ways of Speaking*. Austin, TX: University of Texas Press.

Shetter, William Z. 1962. Review of Helmut Gipper, ed., *Sprache, Schlüssel zur Welt. Language* 38: 318–24.

Sikka, Sonia. 2007. On the Value of Happiness: Herder contra Kant. *Canadian Journal of Philosophy* 37: 515–46.

Silverstein, Michael. 1977. Cultural Prerequisites to Grammatical Analysis. In Muriel Saville-Troike, ed., *Anthropology and Linguistics*, pp. 139–51. Washington, DC: Georgetown University Press.

1979. Language Structure and Linguistic Ideology. In Paul Clyne *et al.*, eds., *The Elements*, pp. 193–247. Chicago Linguistic Society.

1981 (2001). The Limits of Awareness. In Alessandro Duranti, ed., *Linguistic Anthropology: A Reader*, pp. 382–401. Oxford: Blackwell.

2000. Whorfianism and the Linguistic Imagination of Nationality. In Paul V. Kroskrity, ed., *Regimes of Language*, pp. 85–138. Santa Fe, NM: School of American Research.

Slobin, Dan Isaac, ed. 1985–1997. *The Crosslinguistic Study of Language Acquisition*. 5 volumes. Mahwah, NJ: Erlbaum.

Spencer, Herbert. 1862. *First Principles*. London: Williams and Norgate.

Stankiewicz, Edward. 1981. The "Genius" of Language in Sixteenth-Century Linguistics. In Jürgen Trabant, ed., *Logos Semantikos*, I, pp. 177–89. Madrid: Gredos.

Starr, Frederick. 1901. *Some First Steps in Human Progress*. Cleveland, NY: Chautauqua.

Stegmann von Pritzwald, Kurt. 1936. Kräfte und Köpfe in der Geschichte der indogermanischen Sprachwissenschaft. In Helmut Arntz, ed., *Germanen und Indogermanen: Volkstum, Sprache, Heimat, Kultur*, pp. 1–24. Heidelberg: Carl Winter.

Steiner, George. 1975. *After Babel: Aspects of Language and Translation*. London: Oxford University Press.

Steinthal, Heymann. 1855. *Grammatik, Logik und Psychologie, ihre Principien und ihr Verhältniss zu einander*. Berlin: Dümmler.

1860. *Charakteristik der hauptsächlichsten Typen des Sprachbaues*. Berlin: Dümmler.

1867. *Die Mande-Neger-Sprachen psychologisch und phonetisch betrachtet*. Berlin: Dümmler.

1877. *Der Ursprung der Sprache im Zusammenhange mit den letzten Fragen alles Wissens*. Third edition. Berlin: Dümmler.

Stewart, Matthew. 2006. *The Courtier and the Heretic: Leibniz, Spinoza, and the Fate of God in the Modern World*. New York: Norton.

Stimson, Dorothy. 1932. Ballad of Gresham Colledge. *Isis* 18: 103–17.

Stocking, George W., Jr. 1968. *Race, Culture, and Evolution*. New York: Free Press.

1974. The Boas Plan for the Study of American Indian Languages. In Dell Hymes, ed., *Studies in the History of Linguistics*, pp. 454–84. Bloomington, IN: Indiana University Press.

Subbiondo, Joseph L., ed. 1992. *John Wilkins and 17th-Century British Linguistics*. Amsterdam: Benjamins.

Swiggers, Pierre. 1985. Catégories grammaticales et catégories culturelles dans la philosophie du langage de Humboldt: les implications de la "forme grammaticale." *Zeitschrift für Phonetik, Sprachwissenschaft und Kommunikationsforschung* 38: 729–36.

Terezakis, Katie. 2007. *The Immanent Word: The Turn to Language in German Philosophy, 1759–1801.* New York: Routledge.

Terray, Emmanuel. 1968 (1972). *Marxism and "Primitive" Societies.* Trans. Mary Klopper. New York: Monthly Review Press.

Thurber, James. 1950. *The Thirteen Clocks.* New York: Simon & Schuster.

Trabant, Jürgen. 1986. *Apeliotes oder Der Sinn der Sprache.* Munich: Wilhelm Fink.

1990a. *Traditionen Humboldts.* Frankfurt: Suhrkamp.

1990b. Humboldt et Leibniz: le concept intérieur de la linguistique. In Tullio De Mauro and Lisa Formigari, eds., *Leibniz, Humboldt, and the Origins of Comparativism,* pp. 135–56. Amsterdam: Benjamins.

2000a. Le courant humboldtien. In Sylvain Auroux, ed., *Histoire des idées linguistiques,* III, pp. 311–22. Brussels: Madarga.

2000b. How Relativistic Are Humboldt's "Weltansichten"? In Martin Pütz and Marjolijn H. Verspoor, eds., *Explorations in Linguistic Relativity,* pp. 25–44. Amsterdam: Benjamins.

Trautmann-Waller, Céline. 2004. La *Zeitschrift für Völkerpsychologie une Sprachwissenschaft* (1859–1890). In Céline Trautmann-Waller, ed., *Quand Berlin pensait les peuples,* pp. 105–20. Paris: CNRS.

2006. *Aux origines d'une science allemande de la culture.* Paris: CNRS.

Tuite, Kevin. 2006. Interpreting Language Variation and Change. In Christine Jourdan and Kevin Tuite, eds., *Language, Culture, and Society,* pp. 229–56. Cambridge University Press.

Tyler, Stephen, ed. 1969. *Cognitive Anthropology.* New York: Prentice-Hall.

Tylor, Edward Burnett. 1871. *Primitive Culture.* London: John Murray.

Ullmann, Stephen. 1962. *Semantics.* Oxford: Blackwell.

Varchi, Benedetto. 1570 (1995). *L'Hercolano.* Antonio Sorella, ed. Pescara: Libreria dell'Università.

Venuti, Lawrence. 1995. *The Translator's Invisibility.* New York: Routledge.

Venuti, Lawrence, ed. 2004. *The Translation Studies Reader.* 2nd edition. Abingdon, Oxon: Routledge.

Verdon, Michel. 2006. Boas and Holism: A Textual Analysis. *Philosophy of the Social Sciences* 36: 276–302.

Vickers, Brian, ed. 1987. *English Science: Bacon to Newton.* Cambridge University Press.

Vinciguerra, Lorenzo. 2005. *Spinoza et le signe: la genèse de l'imagination.* Paris: Vrin.

Voegelin, Carl F., Florence M. Voegelin, and LaVerne Masayesva Jeanne. 1979. Hopi Semantics. In Alfonso Ortiz, ed., *Handbook of North American Indians,* 9. Southwest, pp. 581–7. Washington, DC: Smithsonian.

Vonk, Frank. 1999. Gustav Gerber and "Kantian" Linguistics. In David Cram *et al.,* eds., *History of Linguistics 1996,* II, pp. 289–95. Amsterdam: Benjamins.

Vossler, Karl. 1910 (1923). Grammatik und Sprachgeschichte oder das Verhältnis von "richtig" und "wahr" in der Sprachwissenschaft. In Vossler, *Gesammelte Aufsätze der Sprachphilosophie,* pp. 1–19. Munich: Max Hueber.

1925 (1932). *The Spirit of Language in Civilization.* Trans. Oscar Oeser. London: Kegan Paul.

Wallerstein, Immanuel. 1974. *The Modern World-System.* New York: Academic Press.

Watterson, Bill. 1994. *Homicidal Psycho Jungle Cat: A Calvin and Hobbes Collection.* Kansas City: Andrews McMeel.

Weisgerber, Leo. 1926. Das Problem der inneren Sprachform und seine Bedeutung für die deutsche Sprache. *Germanisch-Romanische Monatsschrift* 14: 241–56.

1939. *Die volkhaften Kräfte der Muttersprache.* Frankfurt am Main: Diesterweg.

1950. *Vom Weltbild der deutschen Sprache.* Düsseldorf: Schwann. [Von den Kräften der deutschen Sprache, 2.]

1954. *Vom Weltbild der deutschen Sprache II. Die sprachliche Erschliessung der Welt.* Düsseldorf: Schwann. [Von den Kräften der deutschen Sprache, 2nd edn., 2.]

1962. *Die sprachliche Gestaltung der Welt.* Third edition. Düsseldorf: Schwann. [Von den Kräften der deutschen Sprache, 3rd edition, 2.]

1963. *Die vier Stufen in der Erforschung der Sprachen.* Düsseldorf: Schwann.

Whitfield, John. 2008. Across the Curious Parallel of Language and Species Evolution. *PLoS Biology* 6(7): e186

Whorf, Benjamin Lee. 1946. The Hopi Language, Toreva Dialect. In Harry Hoijer *et al.*, *Linguistic Structures of Native America*, pp. 158–83. New York: Viking Fund.

1956. *Language, Thought, and Reality.* John B. Carroll, ed. Cambridge, MA: MIT Press.

Wierzbicka, Anna. 1992. *Semantics, Culture, and Cognition.* New York: Oxford University Press.

Wilkins, John. 1668. *An Essay towards a Real Character and a Philosophical Language.* London: Gellibrand and the Royal Society.

Winteler, Jost. 1876. *Die Kerenzer Mundart des Kantons Glarus.* Leipzig: Winter.

Woodworth, R.S. 1910. The Puzzle of Color Vocabularies. *Psychological Bulletin* 7: 325–34.

Zammito, John H. 2002. *Kant, Herder, and the Birth of Anthropology.* University of Chicago Press.

Zimmerman, Andrew. 2001. *Anthropology and Antihumanism in Imperial Germany.* University of Chicago Press.

Zuber, Roger. 1968. *Les "belles infidèles" et la formation du goût classique.* Paris Armand Colin.

Index

Aarsleff, Hans, 61
Académie Française, 31, 40
accent, 167, 210
  semantic, 210
Agrippa, Cornelius, 21, 218
Albertus, Laurentius, 29
alternating sounds, 107, 119–20, 125, 173–4
Althusser, Louis, 7, 8, 97, 151, 152, 192
anthropology, 76, 87, 89, 96, 113, 114, 115,
    117, 120, 134, 146, 148, 165, 166,
    188, 203
  Berlin School, 104
  Boasian, 14, 123–4, 154, 188, 189, 190
  cognitive, *see* ethnosemantics
  evolutionist, 104–5, 109
  symbolic, 154, 192
Antisemitism, 112, 134
Aristotle, 3, 6, 58, 98, 191

Babel, Tower of, 5, 19, 21, 25, 41, 52, 77, 218
Bachelard, Gaston, 8, 9, 15, 42, 175, 187,
    192–7
Bacon, Francis, 7, 13, 30, 38–9, 42, 44, 88,
    106
Bacon, Roger, 19
Barthes, Roland, 137
Bastian, Adolf, 104, 112, 117
Batteux, Charles, 61, 62, 63
Beauzée, Nicolas, 62
Becker, A. L., 178, 187, 202
Bellay, Joachim du, 22, 24
belles infidèles, *see* translation
Benedict, Ruth, 114, 192
Benveniste, Emile, 191–2
Berlin Academy, 62, 74, 80, 89, 90, 91
Berlin, Brent, 170–1, 176
Bible, 100, 218
bilingualism, 10, 177, 209
Black, Max, 177
Bloom, Alfred, 171
Bloomfield, Leonard, 149, 165, 170, 172

Boas, Franz, 2, 9, 10, 14, 57, 81, 96, 102, 104,
    105, 108, 112, 113, 114–32, 133, 134,
    135, 137, 140, 141, 142, 151, 152, 153,
    155, 157, 164, 165, 169, 172, 173–4,
    176, 177, 179, 187, 190, 191, 192, 210
Bonald, Louis Gabriel de, 64
Bopp, Franz, 100, 106, 160
Borges, Jorge Luis, 41
Boroditsky, Lera, 10, 205, 206, 207, 213
Bouhours, Dominique de, 36, 52, 56, 74, 79
Bourzeys, Amable de, 31
Bowerman, Melissa, 3, 204
Brinton, Daniel Garrison, 110–11, 122
Brown, Penelope, 204–5
Buffier, Claude, 56–7, 61, 62, 81, 92, 102
Burnett, James, *see* Monboddo, Lord

Calame-Griaule, Geneviève, 198
calibration, 120, 130–2, 136, 144, 149, 157,
    178
Calvin and Hobbes, 27
Calvin, John, 21
Cambridge Platonists, 52, 65
Cardano, Girolamo, 22
Carroll, Lewis, *see* Dodgson, Charles
    Lutwidge
Cassirer, Ernst, 65, 154–5
categories
  conceptual, 18, 159
  grammatical, 1, 10, 101, 102, 114, 121,
      127–8, 129, 137, 140–1, 143–4, 160,
      163, 183, 184, 185, 190, 191, 199,
      200–1, 202, 203, 210, 213, 215
  deictics, 182, 200, 210
  evidentiality, 10, 128, 140, 185, 210
  gender, 10, 26, 56, 69, 107, 110, 127,
      137, 140, 162, 186, 204, 206, 213
  number, 26, 107, 127, 128, 137, 140,
      203, 204
  person, 26, 122, 127, 205
  shape, 199, 210

categories (*cont.*)
 tense, 10, 26, 68, 69, 84, 123, 127, 128,
  137, 140, 143–4, 179, 183–5, 187, 200,
  205, 210
 of knowledge, 83, 84, 98, 145, 172, 191
 of things, 40–1, 44, 67
Charbonneau, Dominic, 172
Charpentier, François, 36
Chateaubriand, François-René de, 88
child language acquisition, 3, 5, 9, 22, 35, 67,
  125, 166, 203, 204
Chomsky, Noam, 5, 7, 34, 168, 169
Classicism, 37
colonialism, 12, 20, 71, 91, 112, 154
colors, 80, 157, 160, 162, 170–1, 172–7, 198,
  203, 204, 206–7, 213
Comrie, Bernard, 181, 183, 185
Condillac, Etienne Bonnot de, 59–61, 62, 64,
  71, 73, 74, 102, 104, 109
Conklin, Harold, 175
context, 96, 103, 113, 130, 143, 149, 165, 184,
  185, 190, 199, 201–2, 210
Cooper, Anthony Ashley, *see* Shaftesbury,
  Third Earl of
Copernicus, Nicolaus, 83
Cordemoy, Géraud de, 35, 67

Dacier, Anne, 38
Darwin, Charles, 101, 109
Davidson, Donald, 178, 179
Descartes, René, 3, 7, 13, 24, 30, 31–4, 35, 40,
  42, 49, 50, 59, 60, 82, 88, 102, 196,
  205, 212
Diderot, Denis, 59, 61–2, 79, 80, 104, 202
Dinwoodie, David, 182
Dodgson, Charles Lutwidge, 45–6
Domergue, Urbain, 63, 64
Donatus, 19, 21
Du Marsais, César Chesneau, 58, 62

Einstein, Albert, 11, 116, 137, 148–50
Eliot, John, 39
empiricism, 7, 13, 30, 38, 40, 44, 45, 49, 51,
  52, 54, 57, 59, 64, 65, 69, 70, 71, 82,
  83, 110, 151
Erasmus, Desiderius, 22
essentialism, 2, 6–9, 11, 13, 14, 30, 47, 48, 84,
  87, 90, 96, 97, 98, 113, 114, 115, 116,
  129, 150, 151, 152, 154, 156, 158, 159,
  160, 164, 167, 170, 189, 192, 193, 211,
  212, 214, 216
ethnography of communication, 198
ethnopoetics, 198–9, 202
ethnosemantics, 175, 192, 198
Euclid, 145, 146, 197, 208

evolutionism, 14, 66, 81, 96, 104–11, 114,
  119, 124, 130, 134, 150, 151, 171, 176,
  190, 191, 214

Farrar, Frederick William, 109, 112
Fénelon, François de Salignac de la Mothe, 57
Feuer, Lewis, 177
figures of speech, 35, 58, 131, 133, 199
Fodor, Jerry, 166
Foucault, Michel, 20, 192
Freud, Sigmund, 113, 174, 221
Friedrich, Paul, 10, 198–9, 202
Fruchtbringende Gesellschaft, 47

Garat, Dominique-Joseph, 63, 64
Geertz, Clifford, 192
Gelli, Giovan Battista, 22
genius of languages and nations, 22, 25, 31,
  36, 52, 60, 61, 65, 66, 74, 75, 81, 84,
  92, 98, 135
geography, 13, 19, 87, 88, 104, 116, 117
Gerber, Gustav, 99
Gipper, Helmut, 162–4, 179–80, 181, 186,
  187, 193
Gleason, H. A., 170
Gobineau, Arthur de, 112
Goethe, Johann Wolfgang von, 75, 85, 135
Grant, Madison, 112
Greenberg, Joseph, 168
Grimm, Jakob, 13, 86–7, 100, 101
Grimm, Wilhelm, 13, 86–7
Gruppe, Otto Friedrich, 97–8, 191
Gumperz, John J., 204
Güntert, Hermann, 161, 162

Hagège, Claude, 5, 187
Hale, Horatio, 107
Hall, Alfred J., 121
Hamann, Johann Georg, 73–5, 79, 82, 83, 118
Harris, James, 65–6
Harsdörffer, Georg Philipp, 47
Hegel, G. W. F., 85, 96–7, 102, 103, 164
Heider, Eleanor Rosch, *see* Rosch, Eleanor
Herbart, Johann Friedrich, 85, 102, 119, 130
Herder, Johann Gottfried, 7, 8, 13, 75–82,
  83–4, 85, 87, 89, 90, 91, 92, 94, 96, 97,
  98, 100, 114, 128, 129, 131, 133–4,
  135, 136, 138, 145, 152, 154, 159, 205,
  212, 214
Hermann, Conrad, 98, 100
Herschel, John, 109
Hobbes, Thomas, 34
Hoijer, Harry, 165, 169
Horne Tooke, John, 69–70
Humboldt, Alexander von, 13, 85, 87, 88, 117

Humboldt, Wilhelm von, 13, 57, 61, 85, 86, 87, 88–95, 96, 98, 100, 101, 102, 103, 104, 105, 110, 114, 116, 117, 122, 128, 131, 133, 135, 145, 151, 154, 155, 156, 157, 159, 162, 163, 164, 189, 202
Hume, David, 76, 82
Husserl, Edmund, 113
Hymes, Dell, 198

incommensurability, 136–8, 177
inflection, 26, 63, 68, 86, 93, 105, 106, 110, 116, 127, 171
  languages, 133
Isidore of Seville, 16–19, 20, 21, 22, 58, 70, 105, 196

Jakobson, Roman, 128, 149, 150, 190, 191, 202, 213
Joos, Martin, 168
Jung, Carl Gustav, 137, 174

Kant, Immanuel, 73, 75, 82–5, 89, 92, 98, 99, 102, 145, 154, 163, 179, 180, 186, 191, 194, 197, 205
Kay, Paul, 170–1, 176
Koerner, E. F. Konrad, 150

La Bruyère, Jean de, 57
Lafitau, Joseph-François, 58–9, 66
Lakoff, George, 200, 217
Lamy, Bernard, 54–6, 61, 62, 102
language universals, 3–5, 168–9, 170, 171, 191, 201, 204, 207, 209
languages
  Abenaki, 68–9
  Albinaquois, see languages: Abenaki
  Algonquian, 39, 68
  Arabic, 80, 135
  Australian, 202, 205
  Aztec, see languages: Nahuatl
  Bantu, 133
  Basque, 25, 88, 89, 94
  Carib, 80
  Chinese, 86, 89, 94, 105, 106, 109, 135, 171–2
  Chinook, 121, 123, 151, 191
  English, 10, 26, 27–8, 30, 34, 36, 38, 39, 48, 56, 63, 70, 71, 106, 110, 111, 115, 120, 126, 127, 128, 131, 135, 136, 142, 166, 170, 171, 173, 181, 185, 199, 203, 205, 207, 209, 210, 214
  Eskimo, see languages: Inuktitut
  French, 24, 26–7, 30, 34–6, 48, 54–8, 59, 60, 61, 63–4, 74, 79, 80, 87, 110, 111, 155, 206, 214

German, 19, 24, 25, 26, 27, 28–9, 30, 36, 47–8, 51–2, 56, 73, 74–5, 77, 79–80, 87, 100, 110, 123, 131, 142, 149, 155, 157, 158, 159, 162, 163, 202, 206, 213
Greek, 19, 22, 25, 26, 27, 34, 36, 56, 63, 66, 68, 69, 77, 98, 100, 184, 191
Guugu Yimithirr, 205, 209
Haida, 120, 124
Hanunóo, 175
Hebrew, 19, 21, 22, 151
Hidatsa, 107
Hopi, 131, 142, 143–4, 167, 178, 179–85, 195
Hottentot, 77, 112, 135
Huron, 58, 59, 66, 67, 68, 80
Indo-European, 26, 86, 87, 93, 99, 100, 101, 102, 112, 116, 124, 127, 128, 131, 137, 147, 156, 160, 161, 162
Indonesian, 205
Inuktitut, 116, 119, 120, 135
  words for snow, 126, 177
Iroquoian, 58, 59
Italian, 19, 22, 25, 36, 56, 63, 108
Japanese, 92, 162
Jaqi, 201
Kawi, 89
Kwak'wala, 10, 121–3, 128, 140, 151
Kwakiutl, see languages: Kwak'wala
Latin, 18, 19, 22, 25, 26, 27, 28, 29, 34, 35–6, 39, 56, 57, 58, 60, 61, 63, 64, 73, 79, 92, 100, 122, 135, 187, 209
Mandarin, see languages: Chinese
Mande, 102, 123
Mayan, 203
Nahuatl, 116
Natick, see languages: Wampanoag
New Guinea, 171
Nootka, 136
Orenock, 81
Paiute, Southern, 136
Pirahã, 206
Ponca, 110
Russian, 10, 79, 106, 135
sign, 62
Sioux, 123, 135
Soso, 103
Spanish, 25, 206, 213
Standard Average European, 143, 144, 183, 199, 220
Tarascan, 10, 199
Turkish, 86, 135
universal, 33, 40–2, 45, 50, 77, 163
Ute, 142
Wampanoag, 39

languages (*cont.*)
  Wintu, 10, 140–1, 201
  Yiddish, 112
  Yucatec, *see* languages: Mayan
Lazarus, Moritz, 103, 104
Lee, Dorothy Demetracopoulou, 14, 133,
    140–1, 165, 172
Lee, Penny, 182, 200
Leibniz, Gottfried Wilhelm, 3, 7, 13, 30,
    48–52, 60, 72, 73, 74, 76, 82, 83, 87,
    89, 90, 97, 98, 102, 127, 138, 158, 159,
    189, 205, 212
Le Laboureur, Louis, 58, 62, 187, 208
Lenneberg, Eric H., 169, 170, 206
Leroy, Louis, 21
Levinson, Stephen C., 204
Lévi-Strauss, Claude, 108, 191
linguistic relativity, principle of, 2, 141, 148,
    158, 177, 208, 216
linguistics, historical, 51, 70, 86, 87, 100–1,
    116, 155, 160, 199
literature, 21, 22, 36, 45, 79, 85, 87, 96, 102,
    123, 133, 140, 197
Locke, John, 3, 7, 13, 30, 43–5, 46, 51, 54,
    57, 59, 60, 65, 69, 82, 84, 106, 127,
    129, 149
Lucy, John A., 146, 168, 175, 180, 200, 203,
    210
Lyell, Charles, 101, 104, 109

Macpherson, James, 72, 80
Maistre, Joseph de, 64
Malinowski, Bronislaw, 123, 221
Malotki, Ekkehart, 181–7
Marx, Karl, 20, 97, 103, 118, 151–2
Matthews, Washington, 107
McNamara, John, 177
Meigret, Louis, 27
Ménage, Gilles, 37
Meyerson, Emile, 193
Middle Ages, 16–19, 20, 27
Miller, George, 3
Miller, Robert L., 179
Monboddo, Lord, 65, 66–9, 71, 83
Morgan, Lewis Henry, 108
Mulcaster, Richard, 28
Müller, Friedrich Max, 99

National Socialism, 160–2
Neogrammarians, 101, 149, 151, 157, 190
Neohumboldtians, 14, 15, 128, 156–64, 174,
    179–81, 212, 215
Newton, Isaac, 7, 42–3, 50, 54, 57, 83, 84,
    88, 145, 148, 179, 180, 187, 193, 194,
    197, 205
Noiré, Ludwig, 99

numbers, 17, 21, 81, 108, 124–5, 176, 206

O'Brien, Flann, 28
Ogotemmêli, 3, 197
Ossian, *see* Macpherson, James
Otfrid of Weissenburg, 19

Payne, Edward John, 108
Perrault, Charles, 87
Perrin, Pierre, 37
Perrot d'Ablancourt, Nicolas, 37
phonology, 121, 136, 173, 190, 202,
    206, 210
Pike, Kenneth L., 198
Pinker, Steven, 3, 5, 166, 171, 172, 176, 182,
    188, 195
poetry, 10, 22, 31, 61, 63, 80, 83, 85, 134, 139,
    140, 202, 203, 209
Port-Royal, 34–5, 39, 44, 54, 151
Porzig, Walter, 156, 159, 160, 162
Pott, August Friedrich, 112
Powell, John Wesley, 109–10, 111
Priscian, 19, 21, 23
psychology
  cognitive, 4, 165, 166, 169–70, 203–7
  folk, 103
  Gestalt, 141, 142, 145, 146, 173, 180, 191,
    195, 205
psychophysics, 116, 119, 130

Rabelais, François, 23–5, 94
racism, 11, 94, 111–12, 113, 150, 156, 160,
    161
rationalism, 7, 13, 27, 30, 31–6, 38, 44, 49, 50,
    51, 52, 54, 58, 59, 62, 63, 64, 66, 69,
    72, 73, 83, 85, 151, 169, 187
relativity, principle of, 11, 148, 149, 178, 216
Renaissance, 7, 20–3, 36, 38, 54, 74, 133,
    212
Rivarol, Antoine de, 63–4
Romantics, 7, 13, 48, 52, 61, 85–7, 96, 97,
    114, 136, 157, 159, 192, 203, 212, 214
Rosch, Eleanor, 167, 171, 207
Roubaud, Pierre-Joseph-Antoine, 68, 219
Royal Society, 39–40, 41, 42, 43, 45
Runze, Georg, 99

Sagard, Gabriel, 66
Sahlins, Marshall, 192
Sapir, Edward, 2, 11, 14, 15, 116, 120, 130,
    131, 133–40, 141, 142, 146, 148, 149,
    155, 157, 164, 165, 169, 170, 172, 187,
    190, 191, 192, 193, 195, 197, 198, 199,
    200, 202, 203, 209, 211
Sapir–Whorf hypothesis, 2, 163, 164, 167,
    169, 172

Saussure, Ferdinand de, 113, 157, 190, 191, 192
Schlegel, August Wilhelm von, 13, 85, 86, 91
Schlegel, Friedrich von, 13, 86, 91, 127
Schleicher, August, 101
Schleiermacher, Friedrich, 85, 98
Schmidt-Rohr, Georg, 159, 160
Schneider, David, 192
Schottelius, Justus Georg, 47–8
Schultz, Emily, 195
semantic fields, 73, 157, 158, 202
Shaftesbury, Third Earl of, 65
Shakespeare,William, 218
Silverstein, Michael, 199–200, 201, 202
Slobin, Dan, 203
space, 16, 17, 18, 33, 42, 43, 50, 67, 83, 84, 105, 141, 145, 146, 148, 179, 180, 181, 182, 186, 194, 196, 204, 207
Spencer, Herbert, 104, 105, 106
Speroni, Sperone, 22
Spinoza, Benedictus de, 151
Sprat, Thomas, 39
stage theories, 60, 61, 62, 66, 67–8, 71, 94, 97, 104, 105, 107, 111, 114, 150, 163, 214
Starr, Frederick, 105, 108
Stegmann von Pritzwald, Kurt, 160, 162
Steiner, George, 5, 6, 158, 189
Steinthal, Heymann, 101–4, 109, 111, 112, 115, 116, 117, 119, 123, 130, 131, 135, 151
structuralism, 15, 189–92, 193
Swift, Jonathan, 45
syntax, 28, 31, 41, 60, 63, 67, 68, 75, 158, 162, 168, 202

time, 4, 16, 17, 18, 20, 33, 42, 43, 50, 70, 83, 84, 101, 104, 105, 123, 141, 143, 144, 145, 146, 149, 160, 179, 180, 181–7, 194, 204, 205, 207
Trabant, Jürgen, 52

translation, 10, 11, 22, 23, 37–8, 44, 51, 73, 77, 80, 85, 93, 98, 161, 162, 167, 174, 177, 178, 179, 180, 181, 184, 190, 201, 203, 209, 212, 213, 214, 215
Trier, Jost, 157, 158–9, 160, 162, 179
Tylor, Edward Burnett, 104, 106, 108, 130
typology, 92, 123, 135, 168, 169, 198, 200–1

universalism, 2, 5, 6–9, 11, 13, 14, 30, 50, 73, 83, 84, 90, 92, 99, 100, 104, 114, 115, 116, 129, 131, 151, 152, 164, 166, 168–9, 175, 179, 187, 189, 192, 197, 198, 201, 203, 204, 205, 207, 211, 212, 213, 214

Valla, Lorenzo, 21
Varchi, Benedetto, 22
Virchow, Rudolf, 104
Voegelin, Carl, 184
Voegelin, Florence, 184
Voltaire, 38, 72
Vossler, Karl, 155–6

Wallis, John, 39
Weisgerber, Leo, 157, 158, 159, 160, 161, 162, 170, 174, 178, 202
Whorf, Benjamin Lee, 2, 11, 14, 15, 96, 116, 120, 126, 131, 133, 134, 137, 138, 140, 141–9, 152, 154, 155, 157, 163, 164, 165, 166, 167, 169, 170, 172, 173, 178, 179, 188, 189, 190, 191, 192–7, 198, 200, 203, 204, 205, 206, 208, 210
Winteler, Jost, 149–50, 210
Wolff, Christian, 60, 72–3, 100
word order, 4, 13, 26–7, 28, 34, 36, 40, 41, 48, 54–8, 59–64, 68, 71, 74–5, 79, 87, 110, 162, 202
world view, 93, 105, 145, 146, 157, 160, 161, 162, 163, 165, 167, 178, 199
Wundt, Wilhelm, 104
Wüst, Walther, 162

Lightning Source UK Ltd.
Milton Keynes UK
UKHW010643121218
333861UK00021B/531/P

9 781107 558632